Eagles over the Alps

Suvorov in Italy and Switzerland, 1799

Christopher Duffy

Original Artwork by Bill Younghusband

The Emperor's Press
Chicago, Illinois

Original edition; Published in 1999

ISBN 1-883476-18-6

Printed and bound in the United States of America
by Print Systems, Grand Rapids, Michigan

Book Layout by Bitter Books

Original Artwork by Bill Younghusband

The Emperor's Press
5744 West Irving Park Road
Chicago, Illinois 60634 U.S.A.
(773) 777 7307

TABLE OF CONTENTS

	Preface	5
Chapter 1	The Revolutionary Challenge	7
Chapter 2	Suvorov. The Man and his Armies	14
Chapter 3	To the South	39
Chapter 4	First Strike - against Schérer and Moreau	58
Chapter 5	Against Macdonald	87
Chapter 6	The Sieges	118
Chapter 7	Against Joubert	129
Chapter 8	Frustration	150
Chapter 9	The Assault on the Alpine Ramparts	155
Chapter 10	The Débâcle	212
Chapter 11	Combat, Evasion and Termination	222
	Bibliography	272
	Index	275

Suvorov

PREFACE

'Such is my account. It is unadorned by fertile conceits, and devoid of those florid expressions that are calculated to excite the fancies of the reader and enrapture his soul. Providence has failed to endow me with that eloquence which enkindles the imagination of others, and persuades them to feel what I feel within my innermost self. But this I can say, that my relation is authentic as I can make it' (Captain Gryazev).

This work was prompted by an interest which has extended over many years, and more immediately by the approach of the bicentenary of one of the more unlikely of historical events —when an army of Russians progressed triumphantly through Italy, and then, to general astonishment, battled its way over some of the highest passes of the Swiss Alps in the teeth of a fast-approaching winter, and was locked in combat with Soult, Massena, Molitor and other members of the future Napoleonic pantheon.

The story has been related often enough in such terms, but seldom free of contamination (not too strong a word) through ideology, ultra-nationalism and the cult of personality. I shall address each of these infections in turn.

In 1918 the Bolsheviks incorporated the precepts of Suvorov's *How to Win* (1795) in the first *Red Army Text Book.* Over its life of seventy-odd years Soviet historiography and military doctrine proceeded to devote fulsome praise to Suvorov the 'progressive' leader and strategist, while dismissing his regard for religion and hereditary authority as the regrettable traits of a man of his time. The distinction was unfortunate, for Suvorov put his contest against the Revolution on a ideological as well as a military plane, and the principle of legitimacy was the mainspring of his actions. Russian historical writing of the twenty-first century

will in all probability present the man in his entirety.

It will take a good deal more effort on the part of the Russians to overcome the nationalist traditions which long pre-date the revolution of 1917. Just as Russian historians have always painted dramatic contrasts between the 'German' Barclay de Tolly and the Russian patriot Kutuzov in 1812, so they have established a total polarity for 1799 between the Austrians —pedantic, cautious, reactionary—and the fast-moving Russians under their forceful chief Suvorov. The present book is not an exercise in revisionism for its own sake, but it will try to show forth the campaigns of that year in the perspective in which Suvorov himself viewed them, namely as a joint Russo-Austrian operation in which each party had much of worth to give the other.

As for the cult of personality, generations of historians (and not just in Russia) have been content to accept the Suvorovian myth-making at face value, to the extent of assuming that Austrian interests ought necessarily to have been subordinate to the Russian, and that the first objective of both the Austrian and Russian sovereigns ought to have to promote the personal glory of Suvorov. It is time to set the record straight.

There is a further dimension. In Western historiography, the campaigns of 1799 on the European continent have been set in a convincing context by historians of the calibre of Tim Blanning, Paddy Griffith, Kenneth Mackesy, John Lynn and Paul Schroeder. What is still lacking is an old-fashioned narrative-based operational and tactical history, and the reason is that Napoleon Bonaparte was absent from the scene (he had betaken himself to the Orient). In this case the hero-worship has reached altogether unhealthy proportions. Whereas the students of Napoleon's campaigns and great battles have inherited the work of generations, as presented in literally thousands of books, the same does not hold true of Suvorov's activities in 1799.

For that reason there is scarcely a paragraph of the narrative passages of the present book which has not had to be worked out from the beginning from some pretty intractable material, or with reference to the ground - and especially in Switzerland, where I have walked every pass and every key location at least once. Every time I have revisited the sources and the terrain I have had to make substantial changes to my manuscript, and I have no doubt that the process would have continued indefinitely if the publisher had not reminded me of his deadlines. When a battle as heavily-researched as Waterloo can still generate controversy, it would be stupid as well as arrogant to claim that my present text is in any way definitive. I will be more than content if you regard it as your well-intentioned companion on one of the great adventure stories of history.

I owe a great deal to the help I received from the staff of the Vienna Kriegsarchiv, and especially Hofrat Dr. P. Broucek and Dr. R. Egger. Among many agreeable days in Switzerland one of the most profitable was spent in a visit to Herr Walter Gähler's *Surowow Museum* in Glarus (Landesgemeindeplatz 8750 Glarus, tel. 055 640 62 33), a testimony to what may be achieved by the enthusiasm and expertise of an individual. I did not encounter a Swiss on the scene of Suvorov's operations who did not have an active interest in the events of 1799, and I would like to render particular thanks to the family Tresch of the Hotel Stern und Post at Amsteg, Herr Van Spungen of the Hotel Rhodannenberg on the Klöntaler See, and Claude and Ueli of the Restaurant Teufelsbrücke. I am also grateful to my friend and former colleague Nigel de Lee for furnishing a fresh pair of eyes on my final visit to Switzerland. The experience of Italy was more frustrating. When I was fortunate enough to encounter patches of battlefield that were not fenced off, or obliterated by autostrade or gravel workings, the local people had a way of hurrying their children indoors, summoning the Carabinieri and setting loose their dogs.

The maps show as far as possible the shapes of lakes and the courses of rivers as they existed in 1799. For place names in Switzerland I have adopted the modern un-Germanified Swiss spellings; the 'ch' now often substituted for 'k' should sound like the beginning of a long and satisfactory expectoration.

Dates are rendered in the Western European New Style, which in 1799 ran eleven days ahead of the Russian calendar.

The heights on the maps appear in meters.

1
THE REVOLUTIONARY CHALLENGE

13 April 1799: The crowd applauded the young man who was heaving himself up one of the great figures which supported the balcony. For days now the citizens of Vienna had been affronted by the sight of Jean-Baptiste Bernadotte and the staff of the new embassy of the French Republic, as they swaggered through the streets, sporting Caps of Liberty instead of the hats of polite society. The large tricolour suspended from the balcony of the Palais Caprara had been the last affront. The young man reached the balcony, tugged the flag free and threw it to the people, who tore it in two, set one of the parts on fire, and bore off the other to present to the Emperor at the Hofburg. The accounts differ as to what happened next, but by eleven at night troops had arrived in force and the excitement was over. Bernadotte was satisfied at having goaded the placid Viennese beyond endurance, and he left the city two days later, fuming with assumed outrage.

The incident in the Wallnergasse was typical of what was happening throughout the German and Italian lands, complete with the French provocations, the counter-violence of the people, and the embarrassed and tardy response of the authorities.

Ten years had passed since the earliest days of the French Revolution, nearly seven since the first of the Revolutionary Wars had broken out, and just over six since the Jacobins had beheaded Louis XVI and Marie Antoinette. All the same, observers in monarchical Europe had not necessarily been averse to everything that had happened in France since 1789. The prospect of constitutional reform had been welcome to open-minded commentators, while harder-headed statesmen were not displeased at the prospect of a France preoccupied by a long period of internal adjustment.

Europe might have remained at peace if the French had been left to their own devices, if Marie Antoinette had not been the sister of the Austrian emperor Leopold II, and if Leopold had not heard unexpectedly encouraging noises from Prussia. In the course of 1791 Leopold took an increasingly overt and intrusive interest in the affairs of France, moving from a position of concern for the welfare of the royal family to that of support for the trouble-making émigrés in Germany, and from vague talk of a league of monarchs to a threat (in December) of military intervention. Leopold dispatched a further provocative note on 17 February 1792. He died a matter of days later, leaving his son and successor Francis II to confront the war which the French Legislative Assembly declared in April. A year later France was a republic, and in a state or actual or impending war not just with Austria and Prussia, but against Piedmont-Sardinia, Britain and the United Provinces (Holland), Spain and the loose association of states which made up the German Empire.

The anti-French 'First Coalition' expired in a series of betrayals and fallings-away. Prussia, having contributed to hostilities in the first place, abandoned the allies in April 1795. By that time the French had accomplished the *de facto* annexation of the Austrian Netherlands (the rough equivalent of present-day Belgium), converted the United Provinces to a satellite under the name of the 'Batavian Republic', and occupied almost all of Germany up to the Rhine.

Until now Catherine the Great of Russia had stood aside from the quarrel. She had been content to let the process of French reform run its course in its early days, and from May 1792 until the end of 1795 she was concerned with the business of winning, absorbing and ultimately subjugating Russia's share of the disintegrating Polish state. At last, in August 1796, Catherine committed herself to sending 60,000 Russian troops under General Suvorov to revive the flagging war against the French. Suvorov responded to his commission enthusiastically, and his men were already on the march westwards through Poland when Catherine died on 17 November. Catherine's successor Emperor Paul at once recalled the troops, for he believed that Russia and its army needed to be rested and consolidated, and that it would be realistic to recognise the French Republic and some of its territorial gains.

The British were still in the fight, but, now that Prussia and Russia were out of the reckoning, Austria was left as the only belligerent of consequence on the mainland of Europe. In 1794 the Austrian forces had been compelled to retreat from the Netherlands. In the subsequent campaigns an equilibrium of sorts was established on the German theatre, but in the south the French achieved a decisive breakthrough under the leadership of Napoleon Bonaparte. In April 1796 he evicted the Piedmontese from their positions in the Ligurian mountains, and forced them out of the war. Turning against the Austrians, he bundled them from the river lines of the north Italian plain and laid siege to the fortress-town of Mantua, which was the last Austrian strongpoint south of the Alps. Between August 1796 and January 1797 Bonaparte defeated four successive attempts by the Austrians to bring relief to Mantua, and after that place fell on 2 February he was free to turn against the historic provinces of Austria. He penetrated the Carnic Alps, pushed through Carinthia into Styria, and advanced his forward units to the Semmering Pass, within three or four marches of Vienna. On 18 April Bonaparte and the Austrians concluded preliminary terms of peace at Leoben, and the conditions hardened into a formal settlement at Campo Formio on 17 October.

At Campo Formio the Austrians were given the Italian lands of the Venetian Republic, which passed into extinction, and the French consented to their annexation of the archbishopric of Salzburg. These gains were bought at a heavy price, for in return the Austrians had to link themselves with the brutal way the French were re-ordering ancient borders and institutions. In Italy the richest part of Austrian Lombardy, with the city of Milan, was ceded to the new Cisalpine Republic, and the Austrian borders recoiled to the Adige. Still more damaging was the way the Austrians sacrificed their historic constitutional and moral authority in Germany by consigning the settlement of the borders to a congress at Rastatt. The Austrians were already in the process of deserting the German prince-bishops, who had hitherto been their most steadfast allies in the Empire.

The Austrian chancellor (foreign minister) Baron Johann Amadeus Franz Thugut (1734-1818) remained a bitter opponent of the Revolution, but he was unwilling to put the Austrian armies and finances at risk for anything but the most certain gains, since he believed that any further setbacks would leave Austria at a disadvantage not only with respect to the new France, but to old dynastic rivals like Sardinia-Piedmont and Prussia. For Thugut, Europe remained a field of play for conventional politics, however much the familiar patterns might have been jumbled up by the Revolution. Thus, depending on one's perspective, Thugut was either extremely short-sighted in his contest with the Revolution, or extremely far-seeing with regard to Austria's position two or three generations hence, when a hostile Italy was forming around Piedmont, and the German states were coalescing around Prussia.

Thugut was therefore alarmed by any outbursts of counter-revolutionary enthusiasm which threatened to lead Austria down unknown paths.[1] The Neapolitan episode was a case in point. The Austrian lieutenant-general Baron Karl von Mack von Leiberich (the 'unfortunate Mack' of 1805) had gone to command the forces of the Kingdom of the Two Sicilies in virtue of an Austro-Neapolitan treaty of 18 May 1798. The agreement was a purely defensive one. When he was in Naples, however, Mack was caught up in the collective disordering of wits which affected King Ferdinand IV, Queen Maria Carolina, the British ambassador Sir William Hamiliton and his wife the celebrated Lady Emma, and the concussed hero Horatio Nelson, whose victory of the Nile (1 August) sealed up Bonaparte and a French army of

45,000 troops in the Levant.

The Neapolitan army opened an offensive against the puppet Roman Republic on 23 November 1798. The French commander Championnet fell back from Rome, but only to organise a counteroffensive which regained the city on 12 December, and chased the regular Neapolitan forces from the mainland in January 1799 ('Dress them in red or green coats', so the saying went, 'they'll run away just the same').

Thugut declined to engage in the conflict, which he suspected was a British plot to draw Austria back into the war. Relations between the two parties were already poisoned by a complicated and rather ridiculous dispute concerning the repayment of a British loan. Thugut offered to give the money back to the British, though without the paying of interest at the normal London rate of 6.18 per cent (outrageously high by Austrian standards). The British in their turn considered the Austrians doubly in default, for having deserted the alliance in the first place, and then reneging on their debt.

In this, and all his dealings with foreign powers, Thugut was hindered by frustrated ambitions, and an unappealing language and style. The British would have recognised the character given to him by one of the Russian diplomats:

> He has an unfortunate inclination towards a profession which he has never practised, that of war. There are a number of curious stories which could be told in that regard… it is a foible which complements his urge to rule and direct everything in person. Once he became minister of war he took over the management of the Hofkriegsrath [Court Council of War], and in order to conduct it according to his wishes he drove away Field-Marshal Lacy [the President] by making his position intolerable, and he left this department under the direction of the counsellors Türkheim [Baron Karl Ludwig Türkheim] and Tige [General Count Ferdinand Tige] who are totally under his thumb. If there happens to be one of the Austrian armies where the commander is not his blind devotee, he forms a party of people who keep him comprehensively informed, and, because they know his tastes, seek to please him by fomenting intrigue, finding fault with everything, and creating factions.
>
> This reduces Archduke Charles to despair. He loathes Thugut, and the feeling is mutual. Thugut does everything he can to frustrate him, and that is the reason why he sent Count Dietrichstein, one of his creatures [Major-General Franz Joseph Dietrichstein] to the archduke's headquarters.[2]

When we take everything into account — the way the First Coalition fell apart, the run of Austrian defeats, and the bad blood between Austria and Britain — it is evident that the French could have had their peace, if they had been so inclined. Indeed Thugut had concluded that Bonaparte was a man with whom it was possible to do business, and he was disappointed to learn that the general (who was already travelling to Toulon to embark for Egypt) had failed to appear in person at the talks at Rastatt, where the Austrians were hoping to reconcile differences concerning the new boundaries in Germany. The French substitute, Nicolas Francois de Neufchâteau, was willing to talk only about the notorious incident of the Vienna flag.

Nothing short of a series of the most crass aggrandisement on the part of the Republic could have succeeded in bringing together a new league to fight the French.

The Revolution's style of conquest was made possible, and ultimately essential, by its style of making war. While a proper examination of the French military machine falls well beyond the scope of the present study, a few points are still worth making. By the seventh year of hostilities the Revolutionary forces had put the worst of their institutional traumas behind them, and were carrying forward a military revolution which had been in progress long before 1792. They had supplanted the 'regimental' system of military organisation (which allowed for no permanent groupings between the individual two-battalion regiments on the one hand, and the army command on the other), by bringing together forces at useful levels in stable and coherent ways. On the large-unit plane the battalions were associated by trios into powerful demi-brigades. One to three such demi-brigades made a full brigade, and two brigades, or half a dozen demi-brigades, formed the main component of the all-arms division of 15,000 or so troops, which also comprised one or two regiments of cavalry and two companies of artillery. These large-unit and formation groupings greatly simplified the conduct of war at the operational level. Indeed, one of the greatest services of Suvorov's Austrian chief of staff, Major-General Chasteler, was to reorganise the Austro-Russian army in Italy into comparable divisions in 1799.

When it came to tactics—the detailed business of fighting—the new French methods usually worked most effectively when the situation was confused, or the terrain more broken, for then the hammering action of the French battalion-sized attacks, or 'impulses', had the best chance of breaking through. The tactical details were left to the discretion of the commander of the battalion or demi-brigade, who employed clouds of skirmishers, battalion columns or lines as best fitted the circumstances. The same resilience and determination were evident when the French happened to be thrown on the defensive. A Russian captain conceded that 'when we come to talk of their purely military qualities, we have to allow that the French showed themselves to be firm and clever—splendid troops. As for their chiefs, they were daring, they acted in concert, their schemes sensible and cleverly thought out…' [3] The French were capable of being matched only by soldiers who could show equal flexibility, like the Russians of Suvorov and Austrians of Melas in 1799.

Living off the country, the French enjoyed a degree of logistic freedom which was denied to the Austrians, who were bound more closely to magazines and fixed lines of supply. In the French campaigns war truly lived on war, to the extent that the French military machine itself generated conflict by pushing its armies forward into territories that would yield untapped sources of cash, provisions, fodder and recruits. Every new conquest gave the French troops fresh opportunity for robberies and vandalism, while their chiefs could indulge their growing appetite for life in the vice-regal style.

In southern Italy the French not only chased the Bourbon forces from the Italian mainland, after Mack's débâcle, but set up another of their puppet republics (the Parthenopean) on Neapolitan territory. Up in the north the defeated kingdom of Sardinia-Piedmont was hemmed in by a further four of the republics—and not just by that of the French, but the new Genoese, Cisalpine and Helvetic (Swiss). Piedmont was now militarily indefensible. *Général de division* Barthelemy Joubert advanced from Milan to depose King Charles IV on 5 December 1798, and he placed Piedmont under an administration which put the excellent Piedmontese fortresses, arsenals and troops at the disposal of France. As a sign of domination the French requisitioned the hilltop basilica of Superga above Turin and decreed that 'the vaults will be cleansed of the remains of the kings and princes which have been deposited there… The Superga will be renamed "The Temple of Gratitude", and receive the ashes of those Piedmontese patriots who died in the cause of liberty, and of other great men who are deemed worthy of being accommodated there.' [4]

Such conquests were of a different order from the old-fashioned exchanges of sovereignty between one prince and another, which had left the lives of the people essentially untouched. The new aggressions amounted to

> a thorough change in every respect of their political and civil existence. Their property, religion, manners and prejudices had been the objects of the avidity, contempt and insults of their new masters… It was natural, therefore, that although three years of a revolutionary regimen had in some degree bent the spirit of the Italians to it, the majority of them, with whom ancient customs retain their force the longest, should be inclined to resume those customs, and to seize the first opportunity of emancipating themselves with all the warmth inherent in their national character. [5]

French rule was welcomed by quisling opportunists, and 'Enlightened' and frenchified bourgeois and aristocrats, but resented bitterly by peasants, street toughs and the clergy. A popular uprising broke out in Naples in January 1799, and by the summer the revolts in the Papal

States, former Austrian Lombardy and the hill country of Piedmont threatened the authority of the French and their local appointees.

The events in Switzerland are particularly relevant to our story. This loose association of neutral cantons presented an annoying barrier between France and its new client states in Italy, and it was in order to seize the Alpine passes (and especially the Great St. Bernard and the St. Gotthard) and to acquire fresh sources of booty that the French sought to reduce Switzerland to the status of a satellite. In the early weeks of 1798 a first invasion carried the French into the western cantons, and permitted Rapinat and their other agents to raise plunder and cash from the occupied territories. Swiss society now divided on roughly the same lines as in Italy, though with some very pronounced local and family variations. The French enjoyed a measure of support in Geneva and in the relatively low-lying northern Mittelland, and especially in the little villages along the shores of Lake Zürich, 'where the principles of the Revolution had taken deeper root and made a greater progress than in any other part of Switzerland.'[6] However many of the Swiss alike owned proud records of generations of service to the old French monarchy, and a tradition of sturdy patriotism flourished in the conservative and Catholic Little (or 'Forest') Cantons of east-central Switzerland

In April 1798 French pressure prevailed on ten of the cantons to proclaim an Helvetic Republic, which left Geneva to be annexed by France, Lausanne and the region of the upper Rhone isolated in the west as the Republic Rhodianne, and the Little Cantons re-designated the Republic of Tellgovie or Tellgau.

This cynical and presumptuous appropriation of the name of the patriot-hero Tell was just one insult among many to the spirit of the mountain men, who were breaking out in open revolt. At the beginning of May the French responded with a full-scale military conquest which precipitated actions at Rapperschwyl, Küsnacht and Schindellegi, and the sacking of the great church at Einsiedeln, which was the centre of Swiss Catholicism.

The survivors of the rebellion scattered into the mountains, and effective opposition to the French might have been at an end but for a curious association which linked the British foreign minister Lord William Grenville with Switzerland through his friend William Wickham, an academic lawyer who had married a Swiss girl (the daughter of a Geneva professor). In June 1798 Grenville informed Vienna that the British would fund a new Swiss rebellion if the Austrians were willing to lend their support. Thugut closed with the offer, for Switzerland fronted directly onto the western Austrian provinces of the Tyrol and Vorarlberg, and the Austrians had an interest in maintaining the independence of the remote south-eastern canton of Grisons (Graubünden) as a buffer between themselves and the French.

Thus Britain and Austria began to find their way to a new working relationship. The British were willing to commit £500,000 to help to form a corps of 15-20,000 Swiss auxiliaries, and in the spring of 1799 Colonel Robert Craufurd arrived to take over the work of organising the Swiss troops. By July the Little Cantons were once more aflame, and only with difficulty could Austrian officers restrain the peasants from rushing once more into suicidal attacks, and torturing and killing their prisoners. In the canton of Schwyz, so reported Wickham,

> they not only desire to be commanded by foreigners, being determined not to serve under any Swiss gentleman, considering the whole body as dishonoured... 'our gentlemen, by treating with the French, and accepting places under them, have dishonoured themselves and us, and brought the name of a Swiss into lasting disgrace.' They seemed particularly anxious that their principles of democracy should not be confounded with those of the French, and boasted that there was not a peasant in the canton that had not in his cottage some testimonial of the fidelity of himself or his family to some one of the different sovereigns of Europe.

The people were furious that the Austrians had appointed Lieutenant-General Johann Konrad Hotze to command the Austrian force in nearby Vorarlberg and Grisons. He was Swiss-born, but he hailed from Richterswyl, which was one of the villages on Lake Zürich, which was a disqualification in itself, and he had supplanted the authority of the local hero Paul Steiger, a warlike Capuchin monk:

> This man, who is quite adored by the people, entered Schwyz the day it was evacuated by the French, followed by an immense crowd of the inhabitants, rode into the great church dressed in the uniform of the Swiss Legion, with a banner in his hand, and harangued the people *from his horse*, saying that all those were traitors to the country, and worse than Frenchmen, who, in times like those, wore shoes and stockings, instead of boots and spurs, alluding in such direct and pointed terms to the gentlemen of that country, that a general massacre of that class might have been the consequence, if the Austrian officers had not protected them.[7]

In Germany, meanwhile, it had proved impossible to apply the terms of the treaty of Treaty of Campo Formio in the sense in which the Austrians had accepted them in their talks with Bonaparte, for the French were pressing amongst other things for an apology for the incident of the Vienna Flag, and the last talks at Selz ended without agreement on 6 July 1798.

News of the breakdown at Selz reached Emperor Paul I of Russia at the same time as tidings came that a great French expedition under Bonaparte had seized Malta and expelled the Knights of St. John. Sentiment and idealism formed incongruous elements in Paul's otherwise brutal makeup. After his first reservations he had been willing to allow the French Republic a place in the civilised world. In recent years, however, he had given a home to émigrés at St. Petersburg, accommodated the Prince de Condé's corps of royalist troops in the Russian provinces, and allowed Louis XVIII to install himself at Mitau. He now refused to expel those symbols of legitimacy at the demand of the Republic.

Again, as a conservative romantic Paul had long been a devotee of the Maltese Knights of St. John. He had been glad to admit the Polish Grand Priory to Russia, and he was now deeply moved by his appointment as the Knights' Grand Master. Nothing, therefore, could have been calculated to outrage him more certainly than Bonaparte's action in evicting the Knights from their Maltese island home and confiscating their treasury.

Commercial and political interests were also at stake. The French were already installed in the former Venetian Ionian Islands in virtue of the Treaty of Campo Formio, and they were busy making contacts among the Orthodox Christians under Ottoman rule, who up to now had looked solely to Russia for protection. Bonaparte's expedition had sailed on from Malta to invade Egypt, a possession of the unoffending Turks—a move which endangered Russia's growing trade in the eastern Mediterranean, and seemed to offer a military threat to the Crimea itself. The Russians and Turks, although historic enemies, now came together. With Ottoman permission the fleet of Admiral Ushakov made the passage from the Black Sea through the Bosphorus and Dardanelles to the Mediterranean in September 1798, and in the following month the Russians and Turks opened joint operations in the Ionian Islands, which were to culminate when they captured Corfu in March 1799.

By that time a sequence of alliances and agreements had bound Russia and other powers in a league which became known as the 'Second Coalition.' The Russians reached a working agreement with the Turks by a treaty of 3 January 1799, and negotiated an alliance with British through the agency of the anglophile Russian ambassador Count Semen Romanovich Vorontsov, who was virtually a member of the British Cabinet. There was no need of a fresh treaty with Austria, since relations between the two states were governed by a defensive alliance of 1792, as renewed in 1795: if one of the partners came under attack, the other would render support through troops or subsidies; in the event of Russian troops entering Austrian territory for that purpose, these forces were to be regarded as auxiliaries at the free disposal of the Austrians, while the Austrians would take on the responsibility of supply.

In late July 1799 Emperor Paul told Thugut's personal representative, Count Dietrichstein, that he was prepared to send both the auxiliary corps in virtue of the treaties, and an additional force of 60-70,000 troops. Ultimately Paul set in motion four corps or armies, in addition to Ushakov's amphibious command:

— an initial force of 20,000 troops (Rosenberg, later Suvorov) originally destined for the Rhine, but diverted to Italy,
— 10,000 (Hermann, later Rehbinder) originally assigned for operations in Naples,
— 27,000 (Numsen, later Rimsky-Korsakov), followed by Condé's 6-7,000 French royalists, marching for the lower Rhine,
— 12,000 who sailed to join the British in an expedition to North Holland.

Such a commitment of Russian forces to Western Europe was not to be matched until 1813-14, and the result in both case was to shake French armies, and carry the war to within a potentially decisive distance of the French borders.

NOTES TO CHAPTER 1

[1] See also the Austrian reactions to the disorders in Cremona (KA CA 1799 IV 3, Melas to Francis, Valeggio, 18 April) and in the Grand Duchy of Tuscany (KA CA 1799 VIII ad 27, Major-General Klenau to Melas, Borchetto, 19 August.

[2] Kolychev to Vorontsov, Vienna, 31 August 1799, 'Dropmore Papers,' 1892-1915, V,402-3.

[3] Gryazev, 1898, 166.
[4] Gachot, 1903, 165.
[5] Anon., 1801-3, IV,47-8.
[6] Wickham to Grenville, Zürich, 5 July 1799, Wickham, 1870, II,120
[7] Wickham to Grenville, Schwyz, 29 July 1799, Ibid., II,136-8,138-9.

2
SUVOROV
THE MAN AND HIS ARMIES

A LIFE OF ACTION

Emperor Paul was aware that his troops would be on display in front of Europe, and like the sovereigns Anna and Elizabeth before him, he was determined to put forth the best that the realm could provide. The issue of command therefore became of central importance.

The Imperial summons came to Aleksandr Vasilevich Suvorov in February 1799, when the old general was in his sixty-ninth year. He had spent fifty-seven of those years campaigning against the Prussians, Poles, Turks and Tartars on theatres which extended from the Oder to the Danube, and from the Baltic to the Black Sea and the Caspian. He had sustained a multiplicity of wounds, three of them in the right leg alone.

Aleksandr Vasilevich was born on 24 November 1730 to a middle-ranking family of Swedish origin which had settled in the province of Orel. His grandfather Ivan had been an associate of Peter the Great in the work of reforming the Russian army, and his father Vasily Ivanovich was the author of the first Russian translation (1724) of the works of Vauban. As a member of his class young Suvorov was admitted to the regiment of the Semenovsky Guards, where his duties as private soldier then NCO consisted in little more than allowing his name to remain on the books. Vasily Ivanovich allowed his son no further privileges, and in fact probably the most valuable thing he did for him was to allow him the freedom of the paternal library and encourage the youth's bent for study: 'One may assert that no other man has reflected more on the campaigns of the great captains, and none has devoted more study to the art of war, whether of the ancient or modern periods.'[1]

When so many descriptions of the Suvorov of 1799 might leave us with the impression of the man as a demented *muzhik,* it is worth bearing in mind that his reading extended well beyond military affairs to political philosophy and the sciences, and that he had an excellent spoken and written command of French, German, Polish and Italian. He picked up Turkish too in the course of his wars, and in 1799 he sought to open a conversation in that language with the Austrian major-general Karaiczay, with whom he had campaigned along the Danube. The Austrian could make only a halting reply, and he had to admit that had forgotten most of his Turkish over the intervening years.[2]

Suvorov's talents fitted him to be a scholar of European renown, but he was content to remain a soldier of remarkable intellectual attainments: 'More given to reflection than are most warriors, he feels that man is more than purely and simply a machine; if the body, which is one of a man's components, is indeed subject to physical laws, his more noble faculty, the one which directs and governs the feelings, obeys laws which are peculiar to the individual.'[3]

Real soldiering for Suvorov began in the Seven Years War. He was made lieutenant-colonel of the Kazan infantry regiment in 1758, served on General Fermor's staff in 1759, and on 25 July of that year received his baptism of fire in action against the Prussians at Crossen. He survived the bloody Russo-Austrian victory at Kunersdorf on 12 August, and in October 1760 shared in another celebrated feat of arms when he accompanied the Russian raiding corps to Berlin. In July 1761 Suvorov was appointed chief of staff to the corps of Berg in Pomerania, and he proceeded to command a flying column of Cossacks and hussars in a series of spectacularly successful operations against the Prussian hussars. At that period the leadership of light troops was reckoned to be the best possible training for higher command, for it fostered initiative, and developed an understanding of the relationships between forces, terrain, distance and speed.

On 6 September 1762 Suvorov was promoted to colonel, and simultaneously made commander of the Astrakhan infantry regiment, and so gained an opportunity to form a body of troops according to his philosophies:

> He was keen to show the regiment how it ought to execute a storm. On the march they came across a monastery, and Suvorov's fertile imagination at once conjured up a plan of assault. At his signal the regiment threw itself at the walls, according to the accepted rules for storming a fortress, and the victory was crowned by the capture of the monastery. Catherine expressed a desire to see the madman who was responsible for this deed, and their first meeting, as Suvorov says, opened for him the path to glory.[4]

Suvorov transferred to the Suzdal infantry regiment on 17 April 1763, and in the course of the next two years he worked out his *Suzdal Regimental Code*, which anticipated his celebrated *How to Win*. Motivation was as important to Suvorov as tactical detail, and he enjoined his soldiers amongst other things to love their Sovereign Mother Catherine, as their first ruler on earth after God.

Suvorov was made commander of a brigade of three battalions on 26 May 1769, and from then until the spring of 1772 he was engaged in campaigning against the dissident Confederation of Bar, which tried to withstand Russian power in nominally independent Poland. It was an experience not different in kind from the scamperings of the light horse in Pomerania in 1761, it though punctuated by serious little actions like Suvorov's victory at Stalowicz (23 September 1771) and it ended when he laid siege to the Castle of Cracow, which finally surrendered on terms (26 April 1772). He was rewarded with a crop of distinctions—promotion to major-general and the award of the St. Anna in 1770, and the St. George Third Class in 1771.

Suvorov was beginning to make a name for himself through his improvised escalades of fortress walls, his dashing raids, and the ingenious ways he contrived to train the troops under his command. However the true Suvorovian style was first displayed to the full in the course of his campaigns in the army of Field-Marshal Petr Aleksandrovich Rumyantsev against the Turks in 1773 and 1774. As a newly-promoted lieutenant-general and the commander of a division of 8,000 troops Suvorov defeated an army of no less than 40,000 Turks at Kozludji on 21 June 1774. The action began as little more than a reconnaissance in force, and it developed in some disarray, but Suvorov's succeeded in driving it to a triumphant conclusion. This victory did more than anything else to force the Turks to the conference table, and it brought Suvorov's name before the entire army.

Suvorov was promoted to full general in 1784, and in the third year (1789) of a new Turkish war we find Suvorov as commander of an elite Third or 'Suvorov' Division, and designated to co-operate with the Austrian army of Field-Marshal Josias of Saxe-Coburg. Coburg himself was mild and slow, but Suvorov found a fellow spirit in one of his Austrian colonels, Baron Andreas Karaiczay von Vályeszáka, and they worked together to defeat the Turks at Fokshani (2 July). The subsequent battle of Rymnik (22 September) was a joint set-piece attack, which ended with the Turks driven from their position and routed, leaving 5,000 dead on the field. Catherine awarded Suvorov the cross and the black and gold riband of the St. George First Class, and bestowed on him the title of count with the suffix 'Rymniksky.' Suvorov had already worked with the Austrians when their respective sovereigns had helped themselves to large areas of Poland in 1772, and he had now acquired useful experience of their ways in war. Karaiczay became a close friend, to the extent of naming his son 'Alexander,' and as a major-general he was to renew Suvorov's acquaintance in 1799.

It was unfortunate for Suvorov's wider reputation that his name was now linked with two of the bloodiest episodes of the century.

Late in 1790 Catherine was eager to bring her Turkish war to an end, and a Russian army of 31,000 troops accordingly closed in on the major Turkish fortress of Izmail in the Danube delta. On 13 December Suvorov arrived to take immediate command of the operation. He did not have time to besiege Izmail in the same leisurely way he had attacked Cracow, and after putting his troops through a brief but intensive series of rehearsals he took the place by open storm on 22 December. About one in every three of the Russians was a casualty, but the survivors revenged themselves in a frightful way, by killing some 26,000 Turkish soldiers and civilians. Prince Repnin proceeded to defeat the Turks at Machin, and the subsequent Peace of Jassy gave the Russians full possession of the northern shores of the Black Sea, along with the Crimea.

In 1793 the second of the discreditable treaties of partition reduced Poland to a patch of territory standing under the 'protection' of Russia and Prussia. The efforts of the Confederation of Bar between 1768 and 1772 had been little more than an aristocratic *fronde* compared with the mass uprising which now broke out under the leadership of Tadeusz Kosciuszko on 24 March 1794. The Poles defeated a Russian army at Radowice on 4 April, and were beaten in their turn by the Russians and Prussians in May, but they held on so grimly at Warsaw that their oppressors had to give up the siege. The Prussians were gone for good, but the Russians returned to the charge in a counteroffensive. While the Russian general Fersen confronted the main force of the Poles, and defeated it in the open field at Maciejowice on 9 October, Suvorov brought up a little army from the Ukraine by forced marches, beat a number of smaller Polish formations, and finally joined Fersen in front of Warsaw.

Suvorov had only some 16,000 footsore troops under his command, but on 4 November he threw them into the storm of Praga, Warsaw's bridgehead on the right bank of the Vistula. The Russians finished off the defenders and townspeople alike in the same style as at Izmail, putting 13,000 Poles to the sword and bayonet, making 14,500 prisoners, and leaving 2,000 fugitives to drown when they tried to swim the river: 'You would have had to have been present on the spot to imagine the horrors of the storm towards its conclusion. Every conceivable form of violent death had been perpetuated on every yard of ground as far as the Vistula, while the river bank itself was piled with heaps of the dead and dying—warriors, townspeople, Jews, monks, women and lads.'[5]

Suvorov's enemies laid these atrocities to his personal account: 'He is a man in whom an inborn savagery takes the place of courage… When Suvorov embraced the people of Warsaw, and accorded mercy on the bodies of 20,000 citizens—of every age, and male and female alike—he resembled nothing so much as a satiated tiger, toying with his prey amid the bones littering his den.'[6] In his subsequent instructions Suvorov almost invariably emphasised the duty of sparing a beaten enemy, which would suggest an element of regret, and yet, when the massacre at Praga came up in conversation with his Austrian chief of staff in 1799, Suvorov described the deed as a calculated act, which spared blood over the long term by shocking the rest of the Poles into laying down their arms.

This time Suvorov was rewarded with a fine new uniform, the rank of field-marshal (30 November 1794) and an estate of 6,922 male serfs at Kobrin in White Russia. More precious still was the commission he received from his monarch to assemble an army of 60,000 picked troops to lead against the Revolutionary French. Suvorov looked on his task as a holy vocation, and he took care to inculcate his distinctive philosophy of war in every regiment.

Suvorov had been working up his ideas in orders and instructions since the middle 1760s, and he now put them together in his celebrated *How to Win. A Talk to Soldiers in their own Language* (1795).[7] This talk took the form of a recommended address by a senior regimental officer to his troops. After a few comments on posture and standing in the ranks, Suvorov went to the heart of the matter. 'Fire sparingly, but fire accurately. Thrust home forcefully with the bayonet. A bullet can go astray, but the bayonet doesn't; the bullet is a crazy bitch, but the bayonet is a good lad! Jab once, and then throw the Turk off your bayonet—be careful, he may seem to be dead on your bayonet, but he could still be alive enough to scratch you in the neck with his sword. A real warrior will skewer half a dozen, and even more—as I have witnessed myself [probably a reference to the feat of Stepan Novikov at Kinburn in 1787]. Keep a bullet up the spout. Suppose three enemy are running at you—you bayonet the first, shoot the second, and use your bayonet again on the third. This doesn't happen very often, but remember that you won't have time to re-load. And don't hang about on the attack.'

Suvorov went on to suggest that the same tactics of rush and stab would work just as well against a battery which was about to open fire with canister, though he rather spoilt his case by adding that the soldier must 'die for the Virgin Mary, for our mother the Empress, and for the Imperial House!'[8]

An attack against a weak flank of an enemy position could be effective, as long as marshy woods or rivers did not stand in the way. An attack against the enemy centre was inadvisable. An attack against the rear was the most advantageous of all, through it was practicable only for smaller bodies. As for the battle formations, the line was to be used against conventional Western European troops, and squares against the Turks. 'Now we turn to the Godless, frivolous and crazy French… They go out in columns to hit the Germans and other people. Well, if we find ourselves pitted against them, we will have to defeat them in columns too.' Columns were also employed to beat through the defences of towns. Once the troops had stormed into the town, the Russian commander had to satisfy himself that his conquest was secured. 'Have we occupied the ramparts?' he must ask himself. 'Yes! Well, let's get on with the plunder!'[9]

There were three fundamental military principles:

— *Coup d'oeil* (*glazomer*), by which Suvorov meant an eye for situation and ground,
— speed (*bystrota*),
— impetus (*natisk*).

Now followed some words on hospitals (to be avoided), German medicines (likewise) and the proper diet for a soldier. But more deadly than hospital were 'those bloody know-nothings! — those people who talk in riddles, the liars, the crafty ones, the flatterers, the prayer-skimpers, the two-faced, the obsequious, the incoherent. The know-nothings (*Nichtswisser*) are pure trouble!'[10]

'Training is light; the lack of training is darkness… the trained soldier is worth three soldiers who are untrained. No! It's more than that—say six still not enough—ten is more like it! There you are, my friends! That's military training for you!'

The harangue was to end with a litany:

'Subordination — obedience,
Drill — instruction,
Discipline,
Military order — military regularity,
Neatness,
Good health,
Tidiness,
Cheerfulness,
Daring,
Courage,
Victory,
Glory!
Glory!
Glory!'[11]

Many of Suvorov's soldiers knew the phrases by heart, and he was to recall them to their minds repeatedly in Italy and Switzerland in 1799.

Suvorov's beloved Catherine died on 17 November 1796, and her successor, the former Grand Prince Paul, pulled back the troops to their garrisons. Paul and Suvorov had been on passably good terms, and a few weeks later Paul invited the field-marshal to Moscow for the coronation: 'Accept my best wishes, and do not forget your old friend!'[12]

Within a short time everything had changed, almost certainly on account of some remarks which Suvorov had ventured on the subject of the new Prussian-style dress regulations. Paul wrote to him that he had been surprised to discover 'that you of all people, whom We had every reason to expect to be the first to comply with Our wishes, should have turned out to be the last of all. Bear in mind that the authority of

17

the service must be upheld at all times, and We trust that you will never again allow yourself such comments.'[13]

Suvorov requested permission to take one year's leave, and then, when that was refused, he asked to be allowed to retire. Before this second letter arrived the Emperor placed Suvorov in a state of suspended animation by retaining him in the service without any functions. Suvorov's flow of comments continued unabated, for he was an amusing conversationalist and letter-writer, and in March 1797 he learned that Paul had consigned him to exile in the countryside. He betook himself to his new estate at Kobrin, along with a number of officers of his staff. He had scarcely arrived before he was hauled off under escort to the paternal estate of Konchansk in the government of Novgorod.

Suvorov knew how to make himself valued. Sensing, perhaps, that the mercurial Paul would sooner or later change his mind, he immured himself in a little hut on the estate and disappeared from human view.

> The year 1798 arrived [wrote a soldier concerning life in a remote garrison] and we had already begun to forget about our campaign against the demented French, for which we had been prepared by Aleksandr Vasilevich Suvorov, the father of the Russian warriors. We did not know where he lived, or whether he was alive at all, or in what state of health. But every evening, when we gathered in the hut designated for the issue of orders, we used to call him to mind, and offer prayers to Our Lord God on his behalf.[14]

Resentment against Paul and his Prussianising reforms was now growing fast among the aristocracy and the officer corps, and Suvorov chose this time to write to the Emperor for leave to spend the rest of his days in a monastery. Paul was now the one to feel in need of company and reassurance, but he had to send two messages before Suvorov finally consented to see him at St. Petersburg. Suvorov arrived on horseback on 9 or 10 March 1798, in a state of real or feigned ill-health. On the next day he accompanied Paul to the watch parade, where the Emperor had arranged for a number of

Suvorovian bayonet attacks to vary the Prussian-style drill. Suvorov refused to be impressed, and on the plea of indisposition he asked to be excused before the end of the show. He was unwilling to return to the service on the terms set out by Paul, and he lingered only a short time at St. Petersburg before he returned to the bosky seclusion of Konchansk.

A few months later the deteriorating state of affairs in Europe impelled Paul to send Major-General Prévost de Lumian to discover Suvorov's way of thinking on a possible war with France. Suvorov dictated his reply on 16 September. He passed the commitments and resources of the European states under rapid review, and advocated a massive joint push by 100,000 Austrians and another 100,000 Russians across the middle Rhine. The target was Paris, so as to sever the Medusa's heads with one blow, after which the French power in the rest of Europe would collapse. Coburg was to command the Austrian army, and Suvorov the Russians, and they would act together like Eugene and Marlborough.[15]

The advice was ignored, for Paul preferred to engage his forces on a multiplicity of fronts. There was no indication of any further employment for Suvorov until Paul wrote him a terse note on 15 February 1799, to inform him that it was the urgent wish of the Austrians that he should take command of the forces which were already on the march to Italy, and that he, Paul, considered that it was Suvorov's duty to comply.[16] Suvorov later explained to an Englishman that he would have been content to live out the rest of his days in retirement, secure in his fortune and honours, and that when he then chose to obey the Emperor he had been 'influenced alone by an anxious wish for the emancipation of Europe, and the deliverance of an extensive empire from a savage and ambitious government, pretending to the name of a republic, but being in fact the tyranny of usurpation of the meanest birth and basest minds.'[17]

The invitation had come in a roundabout way, for the man first destined for the command of the Austro-Russian forces in Italy, the young Prince Frederick of Orange, had died on 6

January 1799, which left the Austrians casting about for a successor. The British ambassador in Vienna, Sir Morton Eden, suggested to his Russian counterpart that Suvorov would do very well in his place. Chancellor Thugut closed with the idea, because he hoped that Suvorov would be able to breathe life into the operations.

When Thugut, largely through his own fault, is represented in the histories as the enemy of Suvorov, it is perhaps worth remembering how far he was willing to enforce the field-marshal's authority among the Austrians in the joint army which went to war in the spring. He wrote to one of his diplomats:

> The eccentricities of Suvorov have been known for a considerable time, but in case anyone in our army takes the liberty of laughing about him, this will be regarded as further proof of the indiscipline and insubordination which are endemic there, and which will surely lead to the ruin of the monarchy. We cannot know for certain whether Suvorov will succeed, but we may state that, taken collectively, the officers who wear His [Austrian] Majesty's uniform will never have to their credit half the glorious deeds and prosperous enterprises which have distinguished the career of this old field-marshal.[18]

The Russian emperor had still not undergone a complete change of heart on the subject of Suvorov, whom he considered to be dangerously unpredictable. That sound man, the Saxon-born General Johann Hermann, a master of Prussian tactics, was already on the way with the second instalment of troops. Paul told him of Suvorov's nomination, and instructed him to 'keep a close eye on his conduct of operations, which could otherwise turn out to the detriment of the men and the common cause if he gets carried away by his peculiar notions, which preoccupy him to the exclusion of everything else.'[19] It would have been an impossible combination, for the two were personal enemies, and Hermann had once challenged Suvorov to a duel. Paul reconsidered the matter, and transferred Hermann to the command of the troops who ultimately found themselves disembarked to fight alongside the British in their abortive expedition to North Holland.

Meanwhile Paul had summoned Suvorov to St. Petersburg, and on 23 February 1799 he greeted him with seemingly unaffected joy. He invested him with the Grand Cross of the Order of St. John of Jerusalem, and commissioned him to carry out his new and holy task: 'We pray to Our Lord God to bless our army, and grant us victory over the enemies of the Christian Faith and the order which has been instituted by Him. May the warriors of Russia show themselves in thought, word and deed to be loyal sons to Us and to the Fatherland!'[20]

Appearance, Ways and Principles

The Suvorov who went to war in 1799 was sixty-eight years old. He stood scarcely five feet high, which was below medium height even by the standards of the time. His shoulders and arms were heavy, but he walked as if he were about to break into a dance—and indeed he had a way of surprising the most solemn companies by doing just that. 'His head wanders so much that it is with the greatest difficulty he collects himself through two sentences, and in order to accomplish this he is always clasping his hand before his eyes, and applying to his nephew [Prince Aleksei Ivanovich Gorchakov] for a word, and for the subject he is speaking on[21]… Almost at the same moment you could see him grinding his teeth like a madman, smile and grimace like a monkey, and weep pathetically like an old woman.'[22]

Suvorov's features were of a Scandinavian rather than Muscovite cast. His face was long, and characterised by a high forehead, lively eyes, and the deep furrows down the cheeks which betrayed years of campaigning and a constantly mobile expression. He retained all his teeth, but his hair was grey and scanty, and gathered at the nape of the neck.

Suvorov's ways of dress tended to extremes. Nobody could look more splendid than when he wished to put on a display, and when he attended a religious ceremony or reception after one of his victories, for then he would appear in his green full dress uniform, sporting the decorations and diamonds he selected from the box of treasures which accompanied him on campaign. Otherwise his appearance was casual and unmilitary to the point of scandal. Heat and cold seemed to mean nothing to him, for his habitual garb winter and summer comprised a round hat, an open shirt, stout cotton trousers, and comfortable boots—or no footgear at all.

For mobility in the field in 1799 Suvorov depended on small carriage, and on the riding horse with which he was presented by Emperor Francis of Austria. On his longer journeys he settled into his famous *kibitka*, a primitive but spacious covered peasant wagon. Suvorov's immediate entourage consisted of his Cossack servants and cooks, led by his valet Proshka, of whom (all authority being relative) he was in awe. Suvorov often chose the worst of the accommodation that was on offer to him. Once the selection had been made, the first of his people to enter were the Cossacks bearing his treasure chest and his portable thunder-box, which would serve as a seat from where to do business.

> The officer entrusted with preparing his lodging took great care to remove anything that he might find shocking or offensive, like books, engravings, ornaments and especially mirrors. If, by mischance, one of the mirrors had been forgotten, Suvorov would smash it into a thousand pieces. He often also had the windows taken out, saying that he was not cold, and the doors as well, because he was not afraid. He then lay down on the fresh straw which was spread out for him on the bed.[23]

Suvorov usually rose at four or earlier in the morning, and he refreshed himself by jumping into a trough of cold water, or having the liquid dashed over him by the bucketful. All serious affairs had to be conducted between the field-marshal's levée, and the notorious breakfast-cum-lunch, which began at nine in the morning at the latest and was prolonged for hours on end. The ordeal opened when Suvorov invited his companions to down a glass of spirits, and an appetiser of chopped-up radishes in vinegar. With their digestive tracts aflame from one end to the other the guests sat down to a meal of six,

seven or eight courses, prepared to the highest Cossack standards, and served on badly-plated copper dishes in lieu of silver.

Suvorov led the conversation in his raucous voice, slipping from one language to the next, and varying his expression and emphasis according to the nature of the company. At one of the meals Lord Minto noted that before he sat down Suvorov had already consumed a tumblerful of powerful spirits which left even that old warrior gasping—'it is the sort of thing that people drink thimblefuls of.' As the lunch wore on 'he drank a variety of strong things, among others a cupful of champagne which went round the table; and as the bottle was going round, he held out his beer tumbler and had it filled again with champagne. The bottle was set down by him at last. Afterwards a servant filled him with a large tumblerful of something which I did not know, but I presume it was not water.'[24]

The company finally dispersed with splitting heads, and 'the field-marshal at once lies down to sleep, an example followed by most of his suite. No matter how urgent the situation, which could be ignored only at the risk of extreme danger and damage, no more orders are sent, and everything is put off until the field-marshal comes to himself, which is never before six in the evening. He then goes to have himself sluiced down again, and gets down to business only at seven, and often later still.'[25]

The distinctive ways were not confined to mealtimes. 'At the head of his army or on parade Suvorov could stand for half an hour at a time, shouting or singing. In a salon, in the midst of a most numerous company, he was likely to jump on a table or chair, or throw himself flat on the floor. On one occasion he gave vent to lamentations on the death of a pet turkey, which had been decapitated by a soldier. He kissed the defunct fowl, and tried to set the head back on the neck.'[26]

Suvorov had a way of bringing up his hearers short by tasking with seemingly unanswerable questions: 'How many fish are there in the Caspian? How far is it to the sky? How many stars are there in the heavens?' When the questions were patent nonsense of this kind he was not looking for scientific answers, but the ability to confront something unexpected, and come back with a speedy and witty response — qualities which corresponded closely with the *coup d'oeil* he sought to cultivate in his officers.

Suvorov was not satisfied with a happy conceit if his question touched on military matters. In the course of his Italian campaign he verified that 3,500 Piedmontese troops had joined the allied army, but when he put his officers to the test by asking for their estimates he found that the answers varied from 200 men to 20,000. He was not pleased, and he reminded his people that 'Rumyantsev knew not only the size of his army, but the names of the soldiers. Ten years after the battle of Kagul he learned of a gatekeeper in the town of Orel, who had served on that glorious day as a private soldier. He stopped him, called him by name and kissed him.'[27]

As soon as he arrived in Italy, Suvorov laid down that the correspondence among commanders must be brief and to the point, and devoid of honorifics. He refused to tolerate the kind of report which spoke in a vague way of the enemy advancing with 'several' battalions or a 'large force' of cavalry, or of losses being 'considerable.' People who failed these challenges were filed by Suvorov as *Nichtswisser*. These 'know-nothings' in their turn were likely to dismiss Suvorov as the 'mad mountebank' encountered by Lord Minto.

The list of Suvorov's devotees and converts was probably just as long as that of his detractors, and it comprised the Austrian staff officers Chasteler, MacDermott, Weyrother and Zach, the British military representatives Clinton and Mulgrave, and the Swiss colonel Ferdinand Roverea who maintained that 'no man in my acquaintance was more level-headed, more amiable, more upright or more generous. His sensibilities were finely attuned, and he had an uncanny awareness of what was happening, or about to happen, around him.'[28] William Wickham met Suvorov for the first time on 14 October 1799, after the Russians had emerged from the Swiss mountains, and he noted that 'through the whole of his discourse he gave the most evident proofs of a strong and vigorous mind and of a clear and sound understanding as

little impaired as it could have been in the prime of life.'[29]

It was not by chance that on his way to the war Suvorov stopped at Mitau to receive the blessing of the exiled Louis XVIII. This was more than a social call, for it was at one with the instinct that urged Suvorov to fall to his knees in thanksgiving at any good news on campaign, or halt at every wayside shrine. Such demonstrations of 'enthusiasm' had long been unfashionable in polite society in the West, and Lord Minto might have been speaking for the Scottish Enlightenment when he observed the field-marshal's behaviour at the Orthodox Christmas in Prague on 5 January 1800: 'We all got yesterday at six in the morning to attend Suvorov at mass... We saw him crawl on all fours to kiss the ground, and hold his head on the ground for almost a quarter of an hour, with various other antics. The vocal music, however, was good and entertained us.'[30]

In fact Suvorov was only being true to himself, and to his attachment to religion and royal legitimacy: 'The soggy (*vlazhnyi*) principles of Liberty and Equality cannot long withstand the weighty (*vazhnyi*) ones of Religion and Sovereignty.'[31] These notions were at once instinctive and carefully thought-out.

Suvorov explained to Clinton that 'he had been taken from the plough like Cincinnatus to take a principal share in a war the object of which was nearest to his heart, and prepared to conduct it on principles both military and political which he entirely approved.'[32] In Suvorov's way of thinking the authority of kings, the clergy and the old order in general was the earthly expression of the sovereignty of the Almighty. He inculcated these beliefs among his men in ways that suited their temperament. 'He drilled his troops in person in three kinds of bayonet attack. When he commanded "Get at the Poles!" the soldiers dug in their bayonets once. "Get at the Prussians!" meant that the soldiers dug in their bayonets twice. "Get at the filthy French!" signified that the soldier thrust twice, then a third time into the ground, burying his bayonet and giving it a twist.'[33]

Suvorov the well-read intellectual was also willing to confront the Revolution on ideological grounds. His ancestors had encountered religious fanaticism among the Moslems, but 'it has been left to us to witness another phenomenon, just as frightful, namely political fanaticism.'[34] Words like *gagner* or *républicaniser* had become cloaks for plunder, as perpetrated by Berthier in Rome. 'Can you show me,' he once asked, 'a single Frenchman who has been made a whit happier by the Revolution?'[35]

Although he was a was an arch ripper-up of tricolours and cutter-down of Trees of Liberty, Suvorov as a man of ideals harboured a respect for simple republicanism, and he once showed Fuchs a chart which he had drawn up for his convenience:

The Directory
The Den of Brigands

Its Bloodsuckers (Just bloodsuckers)	Its Proconsuls (Honourable but unfortunate Republicans)
Bonaparte	Moreau
Massena	Macdonald
Suchet	Joubert
Lemoine	Championnet
Montrichard	Sérurier
Brune	
Reille	
Rusca	

'It is not enough to know', he explained, 'just the military talents of the enemy. We must also be acquainted with their characters.'[36] It is strange not to find Macdonald ranked among the 'bloodsuckers,' but otherwise Suvorov's judgement was sound enough on this occasion.

THE AUSTRIANS

'The question of the motivation of the old régime armies is almost wholly unresearched, partly because evidence is so spare and partly because it is tempting to assume that soldiers only signed up because of the bounty on offer, because they were pressed or because they were on the run and sought to desert at the earliest opportunity. In other words, the conventional picture corresponds to Revolutionary rhetoric, which contrasted an army of citizen-soldiers with an army of mercenaries. Yet examination of the battles shows that the latter were capable of feats of heroism, both individual

and collective, which cannot be explained simply in terms of iron discipline making the soldiers fear their officers more than the enemy.' (T.C.W. Blanning, *The French Revolutionary Wars 1787-1802*, London 1996, 119).

'I found the Austrian army in Italy victorious, and it made me too into a victor.' (Suvorov's proclamation on leaving Italy).

Suvorov's resentments against his Austrian allies were manifold. He objected to being turned aside from his victorious counter-revolutionary crusade in Italy by the desire of Emperor Francis and his advisers to secure Austrian Lombardy by reducing the fortresses still held by the French, and by their ambition to treat 'liberated' Piedmont as a conquered province. When Suvorov was diverted north into Switzerland it seemed to him (or so he claimed afterwards) that the Austrians were leading him into a trap. Nobody on the Austrian side took enough trouble to remind Suvorov that the allies were executing a grand strategic combination which had been conceived by the British Cabinet. Moreover evidence was mounting for the Austrians that the Russians had political designs on Italy which were at least as dangerous as those of the French.

Failures of language and manners were evident throughout the campaign. That clarity and warmth of expression, so evident in the communications of Vienna in the time of Maria Theresa, seemed to have fallen into abeyance. In the letters of Francis to Suvorov, the few heavy-handed compliments were more than counterbalanced by reproaches and sentiments of offended superiority. Archduke Charles, on the far side of the Alps, was grumpy and withdrawn. The memoranda of the foreign minister Thugut and his military associate General Tige were turgid to the point of frequent incomprehensibility, and objectionable in the passages which were capable of being puzzled out.

Suvorov on his side had a way of dismissing his Austrian generals or staff officers on occasion as *Mietlinge* (hirelings), or as *Bestimmtsager* or *Unbestimmtsager* (sayers respectively or 'assuredly' or 'can't be certain'), when they were only trying to draw his attention to practical details of terrain, weather and logistics—all of which Suvorov was inclined to dismiss as tedious and irrelevant *Unterkunft* (supply). Moreover the position of Tige as acting head of the Hofkriegsrath misled Suvorov into targeting that body as his great enemy, as if it had been some kind of war cabinet, instead being concerned just with military administration. Again many of the misunderstandings could have been averted if more of the Austrians had taken the opportunity to explain, and if Suvorov had been more willing to listen.

As commander of the Austrian contingent in Italy, General of Cavalry Michael Friedrich Melas (1729-1806) was caught unhappily between the Russians and his distant superiors in Vienna. He had been chosen for his post as 'an old soldier, very much esteemed in the army.'[40] He was greatly traduced by the Russian diplomat Kolychev as being unable to string more than four lines together, whereas he wrote eloquently and forcefully in his dispatches to Vienna, and never more so than in praise of his private soldiers. He confided his griefs to his friend Lieutenant-General Camillo Lambertie:

> You would not believe, my dear marquis, how much it pains me to see what the people of Lombardy, who received us with open arms, have had to endure [from the Russians], and how much it hurts me to consider that I must be disgraced in the eyes of our August Sovereign [Francis]. His Majesty promised me the proprietorship of a regiment, and I made the blunder of wearing its uniform, and so I look entirely ridiculous while I still wait for the confirmation to come through; His Majesty also promised that I would be dispensed from the appropriate fees, but the Hofkriegsrath demands them anyway—which is beyond my resources, since everything I receive from His Majesty I spend on his service.[41]

A few days' acquaintance enabled Melas to take the measure of Suvorov and his Russians, and on 26 April he submitted a number of appropriate remarks to Vienna. The answer came from Emperor Francis in person, who was outraged that Melas, through 'exaggerations and thoughtless public gossip' had sought to undermine the army's trust in the generalissimo

whom he had appointed. [42]

Relations between Russians and Austrians in Italy had come closer to a breach than either Melas or Francis knew. On 21 April Melas had drawn the attention of Suvorov to the sufferings of the Austrian columns as they ploughed through the rain-filled tracks between the Mincio and the Adda. Suvorov summoned his Austrian chief of staff Chasteler and dictated a reply:

> It comes to my attention that certain people complain that the infantry have got their feet wet. That is what happens in wet weather, and we all march in the service of the Almighty Emperor. Only women, dandies and slugabeds want to keep their feet dry.
>
> In future any loudmouth who complains against the imperial service will be dismissed from his command as a big-head. We must drive forward our operations before the enemy can come to their senses.
>
> If anybody feels ill, he can stay behind.
>
> Italy must be freed from the yoke of the godless French, and every upright officer must be prepared to sacrifice himself to that end.
>
> There is no place in the army for barrack-room lawyers.
>
> *Coup d'oeil*, speed and impetus—that's all we need to know for now.[43]

Chasteler had to summon up all his powers of persuasion to convince Suvorov that he could not possibly send such a message.

Only by June did the weight of evidence persuade Francis and his advisers that the complaints of Melas were only too well founded. They now wrote much more sympathetically, and expressed the hope that Melas would be able to employ 'quite exceptional composure and shrewdness' to overcome 'any awkward situations which might arise.'[44]

Grand Prince Constantine, Colonel Lavrov and other members of Suvorov's suite delighted in aggravating any causes of friction, and they added fresh irritations on their own account. People on the Austrian side were ready to reply in kind:

> In his relations he [Suvorov] proclaims his Russians and himself to be the men who recovered the whole of Italy, and forgets that he not only turned up too late for this

reconquest, but made not the slightest contribution to the planning behind it... He seems to have forgotten his own words, when he said in public that the Russians can only measure themselves against the enemy when they are alongside the Austrians, and never without them. The facts speak for themselves. On the two occasions the Russians attacked in isolation, on the Adda and in the battle of Novi, they were beaten both times.[45]

When all the resentments and conflicts of interest have been laid aside, Suvorov's campaigns in Italy and Switzerland remain as remarkable testimony to what could be achieved in a joint enterprise. Austria's contribution to the war as a whole was on an impressive scale. In terms of combatant manpower the most complete figures available relate to the end of June 1799:

Army in Italy:	91,917
Corps in Dalmatia:	8,547
Army in Germany:	91,945
Total:	192,409

There had been many comings and goings. By the end of June the Austrians had lost 77,099 men killed, wounded, captured or missing, while in compensation 14,151 had arrived as recruits, 30,000 as exchanged prisoners and 7,800 as men who had recovered from their wounds. The Austrian reverses in the Grisons in March had alerted the Hofkriegsrath of the need to raise and forward recruits and replacements, 'and from that time on a whole series of initiatives was taken to maintain the army at such a strength in men and horses as to be able to conduct the operations with the force and energy that the Emperor commanded.'[46]

Although the British loan had ended, the Austrians were managing well enough financially in the short term, for the income from revenue, other loans and paper money enabled their army to be paid entirely in cash until the end of May at least.[47]

On 4 February 1798 Emperor Francis had appointed General Joseph Allvintzi to preside over a commission of military reform. The group made few specific changes to the official tactics or to the equipment, apart from establishing a M1798 pattern musket, which was of smaller calibre (17.6 mm v. 18.3 mm), and at 4,35 kg about 1 kg lighter than the Theresian *Commissflinte* of 1754—which nevertheless equipped most of the regiments during the war. Otherwise the work of the commission was concerned with the administrative complications of converting or raising units, while the authorities in Vienna were content to let the field armies adapt the existing tactical codes of 1769 as they saw fit. Essentially, therefore, the weaknesses and strengths of the Austrian army remained what they had been over recent decades.

Eighteenth-century Austrians were rarely downcast overlong after defeats, and William Wickham was struck by how much morale had recovered after the run of misfortunes in 1796 and 1797:

In the few corps [regiments] I have seen I can observe a manifest difference in the whole appearance and countenance of the officers, as well as of the men; instead of the discontented and dejected appearance which was but too visible among them during the campaign of 1796, they now appear cheerful and animated, and look as if they were conscious of their own strength... It is impossible for those who had seen the Austrians at the former period not to observe and be struck with the difference.[48]

When he compared the Austrians with the Russians, the Swiss colonel Ferdinand Roverea found that 'taken as a body, the Austrian generals and officers were professionally better formed, and more adapted to the present style of war... No army in Europe was better organised, trained, maintained or recruited—the product of a regular and stable system. Down to the last detail of the service it was able to reconcile discipline with morale, and an exact subordination with that consistent mildness that can alone accustom a man to arduous duties.'[49] It was unfortunate, added Roverea, that the Austrians had to measure themselves not only alongside their Russian allies but against the French—to cope with dangerous enemies like that the Austrians in later wars had to cast aside something of what had made them so admirable.

The Austrian commissaries let Suvorov down badly when they failed to deliver the promised train of mules at Taverne, at the outset of the Swiss campaign. With this one exception the Austrian staff work and logistics were excellent, and made up for what the Russians lacked in those respects. On 19 April 1799 Suvorov's chief of staff Chasteler organised the new joint army on the most modern lines, transforming it from a collection of individual regiments into permanent multi-regimental all-arms divisions. He attached Austrian staff officers to every division of Russians,

> and the Austrian army too was arranged into divisions, which were to be permanent. Each division was assigned one major, two captains and one first lieutenant from the headquarters staff; the major was to function as the divisional chief of staff, the first lieutenant as his adjutant, and the captains as column guides for the two component brigades of the division… The artillery was similarly allotted to the divisions, so that each division was given a half battery of horse artillery of two 6-pounders and one howitzer, and a whole positional battery of four 12-pounders and one howitzer. These batteries carried along with them the reserve ammunition for their own use and that of the battalion pieces, and also the ammunition for the infantry.
>
> At army level there were a number of further mounted, positional and battalion pieces, and reserves of artillery ammunition… Since according to the field-marshal's principles, everything in military operations comes down to speed, impetus and making use of time, such a reorganisation of the combined army was a matter of absolute necessity. Our aim was to make each division ready for immediate action by a single order and march route, without having to lose an inordinate amount of time beforehand by having to put the division together and assigning its advance guard. Another advantage was that the troops got accustomed to their commanding general, and thus to working together.[50]

Suvorov was particularly glad to have those Austrian staff officers with his divisions 'since neither the Russian staff officers nor the Russian

troops were accustomed to fighting over terrain so intersected by ditches as in Italy.[51] Among the middle-ranking staff officers whom Melas singled out for praise were the majors Brusch, Sulkowsky and Torres, and above all Lieutenant-Colonel Joseph Radetzky (the future field-marshal). Melas kept Radetzky with him as general adjutant (to the annoyance of Francis, who complained that only a commander-in-chief was entitled to such a functionary), and he commended him warmly for his work at the Trebbia, Novi and other actions.

Suvorov received devoted service from his successive Austrian chiefs of staff Chasteler, Zach and Weyrother. The style of this relationship was set by Major-General Jacques Gabriel Marquis de Chasteler (1763-1825), who represented the last generation of the talented and lively southern Netherlanders in the Austrian army. He was brave as well as expert, but also bespectacled and short-sighted—an unfortunate combination of characteristics which brought him into the path of many a missile in the course of his career. Suvorov did not take Chasteler's protest about the 'wet feet' order amiss, and a few days later he wrote to Francis that he deserved to be promoted to lieutenant-general.

Chasteler was one of the few people in recorded history to have got on good terms with Constantine, the foul-tempered second son of Emperor Paul, and he invited him to the opening of the siege of the citadel of Turin in May. 'Grand Prince Constantine attended this operation for some time during the night, showing himself both courageous and thirsty for knowledge. In justice to this prince I must also say that he often spent whole hours on end in my office at the staff headquarters, where he made himself familiar with the terrain from the map under my guidance, read reports and memoranda, and studied the war in Italy [the Austrian Succession] from that fascinating work by Maillebois.'[52]

It was at a further siege, that of the citadel of Alessandria, that Chasteler was rendered *hors de combat* by a canister shot on the night of 16/17 July. Chasteler would in any case have been removed from his post in a matter of days, for his Austrian masters had decided that he was by now thoroughly russified, and must be dismissed on a charge that was being trumped up by Melas and the creatures of Thugut in Vienna.[53] The Russian ambassador in Vienna provides the full explanation:

> Marquis Chasteler is known to be a man of great ability. Suvorov took a liking to him, and their companionship has endured, in spite of a number of tiffs. Chasteler thereby forfeited the friendship of Thugut, and aroused the jealousy of Melas and still more of Bellegarde. Chasteler was unwise enough to write to his friends here by the ordinary post to tell them how much he admired Suvorov, his opinion of his plans, and what he thinks of his detractors. His letters have been intercepted, and ever since then Chasteler's enemies have been cogitating how to make things difficult for him.[54]

When Chasteler had thereby come close to sacrificing his career for the sake of Suvorov, we find the field-marshal writing of his fate in the following terms: 'he made himself really useful here, but all the same he was a spy of Dietrichstein.'[55] Major-General Franz Joseph Dietrichstein was the confidant and personal envoy of Thugut, and there were no grounds whatsoever for Suvorov's accusation. Chasteler is the only person to emerge with credit from this shaming episode.

Chasteler's immediate replacement was Major-General Anton Zach (1747-1826), whom Suvorov described to the Russian ambassador in Vienna as 'sound, discreet and professional, but a great deviser of *Unterkunft* (logistics) just when I want to burst into flaming action.'[56] These lines came to Zach's knowledge when the letter was intercepted by the Austrians, but he was amused rather than offended.

Lieutenant-Colonel Franz Weyrother (1754-1806) was a protégé of the Field-Marshal Franz Moritz Lacy who had founded the Austrian General Staff, and he commended himself so well to the Russians during the campaigns in Italy that Suvorov gained permission from Emperor Francis to keep him with him for the new operations in Switzerland. From the story of Chasteler we will be aware that Weyrother was now in a singularly vulnerable position. Lacy had been driven from the Hofkriegsrath by the machinations of Thugut, and Melas wrote to his effective successor Tige that Weyrother had 'contrived to gain the unconditional trust of the commanding field-marshal, and on the strength of his advice alone the army has made a number of pointless marches which have done more harm than good... I trust that Your Excellency, with your usual insight, will fall in with my suggestion to post the said lieutenant-colonel somewhere well away from the army.'[57]

Yet again it was left to a foreign representative, in this case Sir William Wickham, to uncover the truth, namely that there was 'an intrigue in the Austrian army to take Colonel Vinerode [Weyrother] away from Marshal Suvorov. From all that I can learn Colonel Vinerode is the man of all others who ought, at any price, to be kept where he is.'[58]

Suvorov retained his regard for Weyrother throughout the harrowing campaign in Switzerland. When the danger was over Suvorov's Gorchakov nephews managed to have Weyrother excluded from the great man's office, but after the elapse of ten days Suvorov restored Weyrother to favour and assured him of his eternal friendship. The immediate reason was that the Russian staff arrangements had collapsed in the meantime.

Regardless of changes in regime, a consistent tradition in Russian historiography traduces the relationship of Suvorov and the Austrian army of 1799. Suvorov chafed at the restrictions imposed on him from Vienna, and the pedantry of some of the Austrian procedures, but as an astute leader he was willing to identify himself with the traditions of the Austrian army. His passwords for the morning of the second day of the battle of the Trebbia on 18 June were 'Theresia' and 'Kolin,' names which called to mind the anniversary of a celebrated victory of the Austrians over Frederick the Great in 1757. He declared himself to Archduke Charles as an old Austrian soldier in his own right, 'who has borne arms for sixty years... a soldier who led the armies of Joseph II and Francis II to victory, and brought Galicia under the authority of the illustrious Austrian crown.'[59] Suvorov probably spoke better German than did many of the Austrians (which was admittedly not difficult), and he made a point of renewing his friendships with Major-General Karaiczay and Major Thielen, whom he had come to know on campaign against the Turks.

A Russian Grenadier

It would be curious to rate the Austrian army in 1799 any less highly than did Suvorov himself. As long as the two armies were together in Italy, Suvorov never consulted the Russian generals,

making no scruple of saying to them openly before the Austrians… that they were too ignorant to be consulted upon anything… He spoke in the warmest terms of the troops and of the formation and internal economy of the [Austrian] army, said many handsome things of the generals and officers, with whose conduct on almost every occasion he said he had the highest reason to be satisfied, adding that when the troops were well commanded they had all the good points of the Russians without their faults, and were it not for the folly and wickedness of the Austrian Cabinet their army before this would have conquered the world.[60]

THE RUSSIANS

In 1799 the Russian army was just a few months short of one hundred years old, if we date its foundation from November 1699, when Peter the Great announced that he was expanding his regular forces beyond his household troops—the Guard regiments of Preobrazhensky and Semenovsky. The Russians proceeded to campaign with success against the Swedes and Prussians, but by the end of the eighteenth century the reality of war against first-rate Western armies was being overlain by the brutalising experience of operations against Turks, Tartars and Poles. The Russian troops had become accustomed to living off the country on campaign, and at free quarters in occupied lands in peacetime, and in the last years of Catherine examples of theft and corruption were being set at the highest levels of command.

The proper ordering of military affairs was a matter of obsessive concern to the new emperor Paul I (1754-1801), who may be regarded as another victim of the simplifying procedures of Russian historiography. No man who was totally incapable could have sent squadrons to operate in the Aegean, the Mediterranean and the English Channel, or have launched some 100,000 troops to Italy, the Ionian Islands, Germany and North Holland. The strategy was flawed, but the achievement is worthy of attention. The necessary recruits were raised in virtue of an order of September 1798, which summoned three males out of every five hundred for military service. The potential soldiers were rejected if they fell short of physical perfection, and so 'the men enlisted were the finest of the population.'[61]

Paul was determined that the troops should be treated well. He increased the pay of the ordinary musketeers, and he laid down that the soldier must be regarded as a human being, and motivated by trust and good treatment rather than fear. Much of the hostility which Paul encountered from his senior officers came in fact from his ambition to curb their drunkenness, their gambling, their absenteeism and the frauds they perpetrated at the expense of the private soldiers. He dismissed 340 generals and 2,261 officers in the course of his reign, and another 3,500 officers resigned of their own accord.

Paul's intentions were undermined by his capriciousness, and by a number of oversights and blunders. Lieutenant-General Friedrich Wilhelm Bauer had set up an excellent General Staff for Catherine in 1770, but he was hated as a pushy German by the native Russian commanders, and forced into effective retirement in 1774. Paul failed to revive the staff, and substituted a personal 'Suite' of officers who were sent forth to represent him on military or diplomatic missions, report on the generals, or arrange his journeys—everything in fact except the vital staff functions of making maps, investigating terrain and resources, and planning movements. In all of these respects the Russians in Italy and Switzerland had to look to the Austrians for help.

Frederick of Prussia had made a clear distinction in his own mind between smart turnout and mechanical drills on the one hand (useful for impressing tourists, and keeping soldiers out of trouble in peacetime), and what was really practicable in combat. Paul failed to grasp the difference, and he insisted on an absolute and permanent perfection of appearance and practice. The Infantry Codes of 1796 and 1798 reverted to the letter of the old Prussian regulations, what with the open column of platoons for the approach marches, the two-line order of battle, the three-rank tactical formation of the infantry, and the rolling fire by platoon volleys. Suvorov dismissed the Code of 1796 as a rat-chewed package found in a castle,

and one of his sayings on the subject was taken up as a chant in the army:

> *'You can't explode hair powder! You can't use buckles as bullets! A pigtail is no good as a bayonet!'*

Suvorov made no attempt to enforce the Code among his troops when he was out of Imperial sight in 1799, and an Austrian colonel noted 'they are very handy at drill. Their dressing is good, when they advance in line, and their manoeuvres are simple and rapid.'[62] It was a different story with the troops whom Rimsky-Korsakov accompanied to north Switzerland, and those with Hermann in North Holland who 'waddled slowly forward to the tap-tap of their monotonous drums, and if they were beaten they waddled slowly back again, without appearing in either case to feel a sense of danger, or of the need of taking ultra tap-taps to better their condition.'[63]

In 1786 Field-Marshal Grigory Aleksandrovich Potemkin had re-clothed the Russian infantry in a short jacket (*kurtka*), red trousers edged with leather at the bottom, light boots of soft but hard-wearing leather, and peaked caps. The hair was no longer dressed into a pigtail, but trimmed into an unpowdered basin cut. The ensemble was not particularly elegant, but it was very serviceable.

In 1797 Paul ordered the Potemkin outfit to be replaced by one in the Prussian style, and a captain described the dress in which his troops began the long march from Russia the next year:

> A heavy dark green coat with lapels, turned-down collar and cuffs of brick red with white buttons. Also a long waistcoat and short breeches of a uniform yellow colour. Our hair was cut close in front and covered with stinking grease… A pigtail twenty-eight inches long was tied down as far as the nape of the neck and powdered with flour. We had a hat with wide bands of silver lace, a large buttonhole of the same material and a black cockade—this headgear was of amazing form and gave our heads little cover. A flannel stock was pulled as tightly as possible around the neck. Our feet were pushed into snub-nosed black shoes, and the leg as far as the knee was encased in black cloth gaiters which

were done up along the whole length with red buttons.[64]

The uniform was not that of the Prussian army of the Seven Years War, with its glorious if alien associations, but that of a pattern which was introduced in 1786 and was disliked by the Prussians themselves. Equally offensive in its way was a decree of 31 October 1798, whereby the historic provincial names of the regiments were changed to those of the *Chefs*, or colonel proprietors—as often as not 'some German or other' who remained unknown to the soldiers.

Suvorov's forces in Italy and Switzerland comprised units of musketeers, grenadiers, Jäger, Cossacks and artillery.

The musketeer regiment of a nominal 1,700 troops (in practice considerably less) formed the backbone of the army, and was made up of two battalions of five companies each. For purposes of combat every company was divided into two platoons, or half-companies, which formed the basic units of fire.

Two companies of grenadiers stood on the regimental establishment, but were detached in wartime to make up battalions of combined grenadiers. Four such grenadier battalions did excellent service with Suvorov in 1799, and they were brigaded with two of his small regiments of Jäger to serve as the advance guard of the army. The Russian army also had on its establishment thirteen permanent regiments of grenadiers, but only one of these (Rosenberg) went with Suvorov to Italy in 1799.

The term 'grenadiers' signified an elite infantry and a style of uniform rather than any specialised function; these people sported distinctive brass-fronted caps, but they had long ceased to throw grenades. The Jäger were specialised light infantrymen, and originally supposed to be the only troops capable of fighting in open order; they wore plain and practical coats of green, and were armed with the M1798 rifle, which, like all of its kind, was more accurate than the standard smooth-bore musket, but took longer to load.

In reality all of Suvorov's infantry in 1799 were capable of doing any task which might be allotted to them. Four men in every corporal's command of musketeers were designated as marksmen, and given the freedom to run out ahead of the line of the battle and skirmish with the enemy. Moreover musketeers were detached or combined for light infantry work by the company, the battalion or even the whole regiment as a matter of course. On the second day of Rosenberg's battle in the Muotatal (1 October) the only Russian infantry visible to sharp-eyed Swiss peasants from the hillsides were the men of the regiment of Mansurov, and even they were deployed in dispersed order and difficult to see.

The infantry as a whole did good service with Suvorov in Italy and Switzerland, and their strength (uniquely in Europe) came from their men rather than their officers, for 'the common soldiers... seem to make up for everything by courage and hardiness and obedience in the field.'[65]

> In general the Russian infantry are made up of men who are tall, strong and fine-looking. They are well-disciplined, and blindly obedient towards their superiors, whose orders they sometimes fulfil with a fanatical zeal. They are gloomy and taciturn—the result of harsh treatment—and so when they are on the march they are ordered to sing, in order to raise their spirits. When they are on the offensive they are fortified by copious distributions of alcohol, and they attack with a courage which verges on a frenzy, and would rather get killed than fall back. The only way to make them desist is to kill a great number of their officers, for then the fear of being wiped out in detail induces them to seek safety in flight. The Russian soldiers withstand fire fearlessly, but their own fire is badly directed... they are machines which are actuated only by the orders of their officers.[66]

These words come from the Polish revolutionary leader Thadeusz Kosciuszko, who did not entirely do the Russians justice. The Russian infantrymen were picked conscripts, who had survived the privations of Russian rural life; once they had been enlisted they were counted as dead by their families, but they made new lives for themselves in the service of their tent comrades, and their religion sustained their loyalties to death and beyond. Comparing the discipline of the Austrians and the French with that of the Russians, Captain Gryazev of the Rosenberg Grenadiers judged that the Western style was actually more oppressive, for the officers were dealing with soldiers recruited from free men, who needed to be kept under strict watch and the threat of punishment by formal proceedings; the Russian soldier on the other hand was a serf, who responded best to 'patience and mildness.'[67]

When he looked back from the 1840s one of these soldiers concluded: 'Our lives? Our lives were a secondary consideration, and the soldiers of the Tsar gave them hardly a thought. It's quite true—things were exactly like that at the time, and nowadays it is scarcely possible to imagine what thorough-going Christians were the warriors of the Tsar.'[68]

In any other period but this the artillery would have been counted as the mainstay of the Russian army. However the able Director Petr Ivanovich Melissino had been forced to resign through ill health in 1797, and the campaigns of 1799 found this arm 'in a most pitiable state; the horses were poor to start with, and they were badly fed and badly tended. They were rarely strong enough to haul the pieces even up low hills, and so the men had to help them.'[69]

The Russian regimental artillery was assigned to the units on the scale of four or five pieces per regiment, and was made up of conventional 3- and 6-pounder cannon, and 8- and 12-pounder unicorns (the unicorn was a long-barrelled howitzer peculiar to the Russians). The pieces of the Field Artillery were kept together in batteries, and were composed of 6- and 12-pounder cannon and 24-pounder unicorns.

The Austrians in Italy noted that the Russian artillerymen fired with gusto, but little co-ordination or accuracy, and they ran quickly through the reserves of ammunition in their little caissons, which held less than half the number of rounds of the Austrian counterparts. From Italy the Russian pieces were diverted by way of the Tyrol, being too heavy for service in the mountains, and they did not meet up again with Suvorov until after the Swiss campaign was over. Meanwhile the Russian gunners had to made do with the little Piedmontese 2-pounder mountain pieces, and most of these vanished over precipices.

Suvorov had no regular Russian cavalry with him in 1799, and he was grateful to his old Austrian comrade Major-General Andreas Karaiczay, who split up the six squadrons of his regiment of dragoons among the Russian divisions in Italy. All the work of cavalry therefore fell to Suvorov's eight small regiments of Don Cossacks (Denisov, Grekov, Kurnakov, Molchanov, Posdeev (two regiments), Semernikov and Sychov). The Cossacks faced some exceedingly difficult physical and institutional problems in adapting themselves to the conditions of warfare in Italy, which was heavily cultivated and settled, and in the mountains of Switzerland. The lines of sight were very constricted, compared with those of the limitless steppes, while the unshod hooves of the Cossack horses—perfectly suited to the soft, uniform and grass-grown plains—were unequal to Italian roads and the rocky Alpine tracks.[70]

The nominal responsibility of making the most of the Cossacks fell to the Don Cossack Hetman (chief), namely Colonel (and from 1 July major-general) Adrian Karpovich Denisov (1763-1841), an artless and quarrelsome individual whose authority was tribal rather than military, and who seldom had more than three regiments under his tactical command at any given time. Denisov got on badly with the commander of the Russian advance guard, Prince Bagration, who was only just senior to him in the military hierarchy, and after the forcing of the Adda he found the generals so uninterested in making use of his services that he forged ahead on his own authority, and so became the first of the allied commanders to break into Bergamo and Milan. When the generals called him to mind in the course of the Italian campaign it was usually to order him to execute a task that was totally unsuited to the Cossacks, like attacking a defended position head-on.

The allied chief of staff Major-General Chasteler was the single person who was willing to take proper account of the Cossacks' limitations and potentials. Denisov had to explain to him that the Cossack officers were unable to read maps, and that most of them were too poor to own watches. Denisov and Chasteler therefore divided the Cossacks into four or five mobile detachments, and sent them out to discover fords, bring back prisoners, and make detailed observations of the places they had seen, even if the names meant nothing to them. Chasteler had native Italians on his staff, and these officers were able to make sense of the Cossack descriptions, and put together an accurate picture of the enemy positions and forces.[71]

In Switzerland many of the Cossack horses had to do service as pack animals, and some of their riders as light infantry, and there was an unpleasant incident in the old style when Denisov held back from a further attack, and General Rosenberg threatened to rip the five decorations from his chest, unless he could show that he deserved to wear them.[72] Denisov and his Cossacks were able to redeem themselves in their three days of action in the Muotatal, where they finally showed their traditional virtues of speed and agility to the best advantage.

SUVOROV'S ART OF WAR

Suvorov set down his notions for war against the Revolution at the operational level when he dictated his note to Prévost de Lumian on 16 September 1798:

> Act solely on the offensive
> Speedy marches, impetus in the attack, cold steel
> Banish formalism—instead, *coup d'oeil*
> Unfettered authority for the commander in chief
> Attack and beat the enemy in the open field
> Don't lose time on sieges, except perhaps that of Mainz, which we need as a depot. We might detach a few corps of observation to keep up blockades, but it is better to take fortresses by outright assault—you lose fewer men in the long run
> Never split your forces to guard a variety of points. If the enemy by-passes them— all to the good— he comes up and we beat him.[73]

His maxims as given here related immediately to his plan for the campaign in Germany, which was never taken up, but they formed the basis for his war in north Italy. The seventh principle touched on the concentration of force, and it applied equally well in the attack as on the offensive. Fuchs relates that

> One day Prince Bagration and Marquis Chasteler went with me to the field-marshal. We found him deep in thought. In front of him lay a plan of Kray's action at Verona, with the accompanying relation and map. He suddenly broke his silence, and, looking at the map, he began to talk:
> 'Schérer is a schoolboy, judging by the position he chose to take up. It is an object lesson in how a mediocre and cowardly commander can reduce things to confusion, while one who is dangerous and experienced can display his talents to the full. If a commander happens to be weaker than an enemy, then he must never reveal that inferiority; if he is stronger, he must exploit that strength to outflank and encircle the enemy, and bar all their lines of retreat. To bring that off you need to be well informed of the ground, together with every little path, every hill, every passage and so on. You can't lay down any rules—it just comes down to taking advantage of opportunity and every fleeting minute—and that is the product of talent as informed by experience. I can detect none of this in Schérer. Just look at the plan and the map—on that ground he ought to have been able to concentrate up to 18,000 men. Look again and congratulate my friend Kray on his victory. Like the hero he is he manoeuvred his forces, threw them on the left flank of the enemy, broke through, reduced the French to panic, and kept them in a state of fright by chasing after them with cannon shot and cavalry. But then an evil spirit whispered in his ear; *Unterkunft!* And the pursuit came to an end.[74]

At first sight statements like these accord strangely with the criticism which Melas made of Suvorov's general conduct of the campaign in Italy, namely that he split the allied forces and thereby made them vulnerable. In fact Suvorov had no alternative but to divide his troops, for this was the only way he could sustain the impetus of the offensive, while obeying orders from Vienna to keep Mantua and other places under blockade or siege. In such a state of affairs Suvorov grasped that the important thing was the facility to concentrate his forces, rather than a permanent physical massing; he kept times and distances under constant review, so that he retained to ability to bring his troops together to decisive effect.

One of the most intractable problems in military history is to discover how actions were actually fought in detail—to establish how far the 'unofficial' practice corresponded with precept. In the present case there appears to be no lack of information from observers and the word or pen of Suvorov himself.

The French in Italy were informed of the general nature of Russian tactics by Tadeusz Kosciuszko. He had been released from prison by Paul in 1796, and he had kept to the letter of his pledge never to take up arms against the Tsar; at the request of the French Directory he nevertheless compiled a *Notice sur les Russes* which formed the basis of an instruction which was circulated in Macdonald's army on 2 June 1799. Kosciuszko mentioned amongst other things that:

> Their most frequent manoeuvres are to form a dead-straight line, to march by battalions and divisions, and to change front and form square—which they unfailingly do when they are under pressure. Their main principle of war is to get in their attack first, which they often perform in several columns. They advance confidently enough, but when they are attacked in their turn their only recourse is to form square, in which formation they hold out until the bitter end.[75]

This corresponds reasonably well with the tactical ideas which Suvorov inculcated in *How to Win* in 1795, and the *Regulations* he compiled for the army he had formed at Catherine's command for employment against the Revolution in northern Europe. When he arrived in Italy in 1799 he repeated the fundamental maxims to his generals in a torrent of words, as if to remind them that the principles still held good in this new theatre of war.[76]

This time, however, the Russians were not fighting Turks or Poles, but a disciplined and resourceful enemy, and we find that once Suvorov had set a certain mood of aggression, his tactical prescriptions for the allied army in Italy were of a more conventional nature. In detail he postulated a battle formation of two lines of infantry, with the cavalry held in squadrons or half-squadron divisions behind the second line or on the flanks. A separate body of six battalions, six squadrons, six pieces and two regiments of Cossacks was to be detached as a kind of flying corps.

The lines in question were to be deployed from platoon column at a distance of one thousand paces (at two feet to the pace) from the enemy, and then advance with sounding music to within three hundred paces, whereupon the infantry opened fire with six or eight sequences of platoon volleys, and the artillery kept up a fire of canister:

> The drums then beat 'Cease fire!' When the men are ready the order is then given: 'Attention! The whole line will advance! Shoulder arms!' Upon this the troops shoulder their muskets and dress by their right.
> 'March!' The troops then advance at an accelerated pace with sounding music and flying colours.
> At two hundred paces from the enemy we command: 'March! March!' The troops double forward, and at one hundred paces and another 'March! March!' they level their muskets and throw themselves at the enemy to the shout of 'Hurrah!'
> The bayonet is to be thrust straight into the chest of your enemy, and in the event of the bayonet not penetrating you must beat him down with the butt... The second line follows two hundred paces behind the first with shouldered muskets, leaving intervals of three hundred paces between the battalions.
> As circumstances dictate the cavalry is formed up as a third line, or on the flanks of the second line, though always by squadrons or divisions. While the attack is in progress it throws itself against the enemy from the flank or rear... The Cossacks remain in column behind the [regular] cavalry. Their speed is their great asset—it rounds off the victory, and makes sure that none of the enemy escape after they have been overthrown.

Speed and impetus—they are the essential ingredients of the kind of war I command you to put into effect. When the enemy are on the run, pursuit is the only way to finish them off. But, humanity is to the credit of the victor. If the enemy are fleeing before you, and ask for mercy—you should give it to them. You eliminate them just as effectively by taking them prisoner as by killing them.[77]

It is clear that the battle formation that Suvorov had in mind for 1799 was one by lines rather than columns, which establishes a first divergence from classic 'Suvorovian' tactics. More striking still was the extent to which Suvorov was willing to see tight formations of any kind broken up in favour of mass skirmishing by battalions or regiments, and an entire corps dispersed in penny packets (see previous page).

As for the talk of the bayonet, the evidence surviving from 1799 does not establish whether Suvorov was confident that his men would actually close to bayonet point, or whether he was exhorting his men to keep up their attack across the zone of enemy fire and to such short range that their own fire would be truly decisive, or the sight of their levelled bayonets would persuade the enemy to turn and run.

The Russians certainly did not trust to cold steel alone, and the bayonet attack was not the peculiar preserve of their troops, as the guardians of some kind of primitive virtue. The Russians were prodigal in their expenditure of ammunition on the Adda on 27 and 28 April. Again, one of the turning points of the Swiss campaign occurred between 2 and 4 October, when Suvorov renounced the idea of joining the Austrian corps of Jellachich on the Walensee. The reason that Suvorov gave to Archduke Charles was the series of actions on 1 October 'which have consumed all our ammunition and compelled us to renounce any further combat.'[78]

Just before the campaign in Italy opened Suvorov made the mistake of sending Russian officers to the Austrian contingent to instruct the whitecoats how to employ the bayonet:

These orders were all the more astonishing to the Austrian soldiers because they learned nothing new, and certainly nothing better than what they had already put into successful practice. They were also taken aback by the presumption of people who had come hundreds of miles to teach the Austrians to fight against an enemy who they [the Russians] knew only by name[79]... The army felt itself humiliated, offended. Trust in the leadership disappeared. The consequence was an extraordinary division in the allied forces—a division which extended all the way up to headquarters.[80]

The Russians were accustomed to Suvorov's ways, for he was a man skilled

above all in the art of conducting and employing the troops of his nation according to their particular genius. It is only by considering him in the latter point of view, that his true rank can best be estimated. He was a general formed by nature for the Russians.

The Russian officers and men alike were forbidden to mention the word 'retreat,' just as they were under orders never to fall sick. Only a few astute observers came to suspect

that the eccentricities of the character and manners of Suvorov may have been as much the result of design as of the constitution of his mind. He may have reflected that a people still in many respects half barbarians, credulous, acquainted with no other political sentiment but that of a devoted obedience would be likely, and even must be impressed by rude and ancient manners, by striking practises of external worship, and by the example of an unlimited devotedness to sovereign authority.[81]

By 1799 the pretence, if it was one, had been absorbed completely in the man's character.

Only a commander of unusual experience and perception could have had so many tricks of management at his disposal. Suvorov was aware some crimes in an officer, like stealing from his soldiers, were so reprehensible that they would cause wider damage if they ever came to light; he would therefore take due note at the time, say nothing, and wait until a mistake at drill or such like would give him an excuse to dismiss the man on the spot. Thus justice was done, scandal was averted, and Suvorov augmented his reputation for unpredictable behaviour. Frederick of Prussia had used the same ploy to equal effect. When Suvorov had to reprimand an otherwise deserving officer he liked to leaven his strictures with a hint of praise, so that the recipient, while taking the lesson to heart, would go away with a positive encouragement to do better.[82]

Suvorov considered himself duty-bound to keep his troops entertained on the march. One of his devices was to have a dozen common French words written out on placards in Russian characters, for the soldiers to learn by heart; when the officers noted that the columns were becoming strung out through straggling, they got the NCOs to call out to the troops to repeat the chant, whereupon the men crowded forward and forgot how tired they might have been.

In 1799 the Austrians would probably have been more willing to take lessons from Suvorov if the Russians had shown themselves more proficient at the business (scorned by Suvorov) of moving, supplying and directing the army in an organised way. This was the one failing of the Suvorovian style of leadership.

Apart from the Cossack servants, the people most frequently in Suvorov's presence were the two Councillors of State, Leontin Fedorovich Trefort and Egor Borisovich Fuchs (who were effectively political commissars acting on part of Paul), and Colonel Nikolai Ivanovich Lavrov, who was mainly concerned to protect the interests of the Russians vis-à-vis the Austrians. 'In the lodgings of neither the field-marshal nor the other Russian generals could be found anything which resembled an office. Instead, even the most urgent and important matters were transmitted verbally by Cossacks, or written down almost illegibly on a scrap of paper and frequently sent off unsealed… In the room you would see a single light, and on the table a coffee cup containing some ink, along with a few sheets of paper and a pen—these are the only tools whereby all business is conducted.' Couriers attending Suvorov with pressing news were frequently forced to wait half a day, and 'his battle relations were invariably composed only ten days or more after the event, so that everyone—even those who had not been present—had an opportunity to make their mark with the counsellors Fuchs and Trefort.'[83]

An element of continuity and expertise was provided by Suvorov's permanent *général du jour* (senior duty officer) Lieutenant-General Yakov Ivanovich Povalo-Schveikovsky (1750-1807), a reasonably able man who had learned something of Switzerland from a visit in 1785. Schevikovsky was removed from office as soon as the active campaign in Switzerland was over, and all power was now assumed by the members of Suvorov's large military suite—where the leading members were the Colonel Lavrov already mentioned, Colonel Sergei Sergeevich Kushnikov, and especially Suvorov's two Gorchakov nephews—the princes Lieutenant-General Aleksei Ivanovich (1769-1817) and Major-General Andrei Ivanovich (1779-1855).[84]

While the army was still in Italy the ultra-nationalists at headquarters were reinforced by the arrival of Grand Prince Constantine (Konstantin Pavlovich, 1779-1831), a brutal lout who had none of the amiability or accessibility of his elder brother Alexander, the future emperor. As a child he had beaten and bitten his tutors, and he was said to have abandoned his bride on his wedding night to drill the soldiers of his guard and belabour them with his stick. Paul had considered that it would be good for Constantine to see some campaigning under Suvorov, and dispatched him to the Italian theatre of war in the company of General Derfelden as his military mentor. Constantine stopped for two weeks in Vienna, where he was regaled by court and society, and he reached the army when the campaign was already under way. Suvorov hastened to meet him and fell to his knees with the words: 'Good God! The son of my Emperor!' Suvorov retained a moral ascendancy over Constantine for the rest of the Italian campaign, but the later disappointments and privations sapped the field-marshal's authority, and by the time the army withdrew into Germany the reign of Constantine and his Gorchakov allies was complete.

Suvorov's army in 1799 therefore had no native staff worthy of the name, and it also happened to be very short of good regimental officers. To a limited degree the shortcomings were made up by some useful men at the higher level of command. General Andrei Grigorevich Rosenberg (1739-1813) represented the military traditions of the German Baltic nobility, and was a veteran of campaigns against the Prussians, Turks and Poles. He commanded the 20,000 troops who made up the first contingent to march to Italy, and on the way he lived up to the reputation of being one of the few truly professional officers in the Russian service. In Habsburg territory he earned the respect of the Austrians for the firm and reasoned way he stood up for the rights of his troops in the matter of supply and facilities, and for the strict order he maintained when the Russians overwintered along the Danube.

When Suvorov caught up with the corps in Italy he presented the Russian generals formally to the Austrians. He affected to be displeased with what Rosenberg had to say on this occasion, and he strode up and down muttering to himself: 'Just little men, who fumble and guess... I can't abide gossips, empty promises and know-nothings.'[85] All the same Suvorov proceeded to put Rosenberg in charge of the second Russian contingent to reach the army; this in turn became the rearguard during the campaign in Switzerland, and Rosenberg repaid the trust by his expert handling of the actions in the Muotatal on 30 September and 1 October.

Suvorov's ambiguity concerning Rosenberg was shared in the army. Gryazev was a captain in Rosenberg's regiment of grenadiers, and remembered him as a commander who was considerate and a master of his trade. Conversely a veteran of the regiment of Rehbinder claims Rosenberg was a remote figure, incapable of inspiring love, trust or respect in his new corps: 'he was a good man, admittedly, but the Lord God failed to endow him with the gift of outstanding leadership.'[86]

Suvorov knew and admired General Vilim Khristoforovich Derfelden (1735-1819) from the times they had campaigned together on the Danube and in Poland. Derfelden came to Italy as Constantine's military chaperone, as we have seen, and Suvorov retained him with the army to lead Rosenberg's 'old' corps, and thus from the middle of July the Russian forces comprised two major formations—the corps of Derfelden (formerly Rosenberg), and the 'new' corps of Rosenberg (the newly-arrived second contingent).

Both Rosenberg and Derfelden lost much of their influence in Suvorov's counsels after the close of the Swiss campaign, and William Wickham reported that Derfelden had chosen to retire from the service 'after writing a letter to the marshal full of the most cruel reproaches, which he concludes by saying that the honour of a soldier is contaminated by living with such a band of robbers as the marshal commands. The marshal's nephews have taken care to suppress the letter.'[87]

When the Russian ultra-nationalists looked around for people more to their tastes they found them in the rising major-general Mikhail Andreevich Miloradovich (1771-1825), and more spectacularly in the charismatic Georgian prince Petr Ivanovich Bagration (1765-1812), who had won the esteem of Suvorov in the Caucasus, fought under his orders at Ochakov and Praga, and now in 1799 commanded the Russian advance guard. It is nevertheless striking that Bagration is depicted in a consistently hostile light by two or our most helpful Russian informants. The Bagration in the memoirs of Denisov is self-seeking and vindictive, while Gryazev describes his conduct in early October as totally irresponsible.

What the Russians lacked most notably was the ability to work together in an effective way against an unfamiliar enemy in an unfamiliar setting. The want of coherence derived from Paul's blunder when he abolished the Russian general staff, from Suvorov's absence of interest in logistics and staff work, and from the habits acquired by the army from years of campaigning in Asia and Poland. The Russian private soldiers were fine physical specimens, and accustomed to extremes of heat and cold, but 'unequal to the expertise demanded in a mountainous country, where individuals of all ranks must show skill and intelligence if they are to do any good.'[88] Melas found that the Russian generals were 'quick enough to recognise the profound difference between the steppes of Arabia (sic) and the broken terrain to be found here, but they are unable to adapt themselves so readily to the different style of making war which is required. None of them dares to register the slightest protest with the field-marshal, and I can understand their difficulty, since I myself am left unheard, and hardly ever manage to see him.'[89]

One of the reasons why the Russian advance guard under Bagration experienced such exciting times was that Suvorov, although putting great emphasis on the knowledge of the ground, did not believe in sounding the way ahead by stealth: 'What—reconnaissances? Not for me! Only timorous people believe in reconnaissance, and the only result is to warn the enemy. You can always find the enemy if you really want to. Columns, bayonets, cold steel, attacking and hacking into the enemy—those are my reconnaissances!'[90] Suvorov gave equally short shrift to diversions, for he claimed that they never amounted to anything and only weakened the main effort (an opinion shared by Clausewitz).

Such intelligence as reached the Russian commanders was presented in a rudimentary form, at Suvorov's request. Every plan was to be accompanied by a sketch map, which indicated only the larger towns and villages, and gave a simplified representation of higher ground. It was all in keeping with his direct philosophy of war.

Suvorov spent the greater part of most days asleep, and was 'unaware of what is going on in his own army, apart from that which his suite wishes him to know.'[91] Suvorov in his waking hours rarely consulted his generals, but dictated his thoughts to his Austrian chiefs of staff—Chasteler, Zach or Weyrother—who had to work them up into intelligible orders as best they could.

In the previous wars the armies of Suvorov had been famously fast-marching, and in the present one his troops could still perform some *tours de force*, like the rush to catch up with the Austrians at the beginning of the campaign, the race from Alessandria to the Tidone (eighty kilometres in thirty-six hours), and the forced marches from Tortona to Taverne (though on that occasion he could have spared himself the trouble).

Suvorov described his ideal march to the Austrian lieutenant-general Bellegarde. The troops set off at three in the morning, marched for a German *Meile* (nearly eight km) and rested for an hour; after a march of a second *Meile* they arrived at the next rest stop, where the cooks (who had been sent in advance) had their stew ready for them in the cooking pots. The men ate, sang their songs, and remained at their ease until the worst of the heat of the day was over. The soldiers got on the road again, marched for a *Meile*, halted for an hour, and marched a final *Meile* to reach their camp site at nine in the evening. They found their tents (again sent in advance) pitched for them, and all they had to do was wait until the cycle resumed on the next morning.[92]

The reality was different, at least in the early stages of the Italian campaign, for neither Suvorov nor his Russian officers were capable of drawing up a coherent plan of march. It was left for the Austrian staff officers to elicit some mutterings from Suvorov and set them down on paper in the way just described. Until the Russians got used to the new ways their columns set off after three in the afternoon, rather than three in the morning, and the delays and collisions on the march could be such that many troops were still trailing into their destination well into the following day, when the leading elements were setting out without bothering to wait for them. The scandalised Melas relates how on 22 April the advance guard ended up behind the columns of the main army, which strode forward regardless, 'and, since no attempt was made to discover the enemy positions—because they give credence only to such reports as correspond with their own ideas—the officers entrusted with staking out the camp found themselves at first light up with the enemy outposts.'[93]

Chaos reigned in the rear of the Russian regiments and columns. On 19 April Chasteler organised the joint army into divisions, but the Russians rejected his proposal to attach an Austrian commissary to their new formations, so as to supply them on Western lines. The Russians were not to be weaned from their

Asiatic ways, whereby they had subsisted for months at a time off their great transport trains and whatever the troops could plunder from the countryside. Thus in 1799 the Russians stole carts from the Italian peasants, while their own transport train (at a lavish fifty carts and 250 horses to the battalion) went about empty; they drove their convoys straight through the marching columns, and with a fine impartiality they plundered French prisoners, the local population, the officials of the Austrian field post, and the Austrian field depots, leaving their allies without bread for days at a time.[94] The Russian soldiers were dissatisfied in the extreme with the rations they received from the Austrians by right, and complained that the wine and spirits were thin, that the beef came from ancient cattle, and that the biscuit was sour, coarsely-ground, stale and tasteless.[95]

NOTES TO CHAPTER 2

[1]   Vorontsov to Grenville, London 1 July 1799, 'Dropmore Papers,' 1892-1915, V,110

[2]   Fuchs, 1827, 166

[3]   Vorontsov to Grenville, London 1 July 1799, 'Dropmore Papers,' 1892-1915, V, 110

[4]   Fuchs, 1827, 115

[5]   Engelhardt,. 1868, 177

[6]   Masson, 1859, 150

[7]   I have used the text as reproduced in Lopatin, 1986, 397-400. The language is highly idiomatic, to the extent that a number of the expressions would probably have been incomprehensible to an educated Russian of Suvorov's time. In the present translation I have as far as possible taken as my guide the meaning of the words as used by Suvorov in other contexts, and rendered the title as *How to Win*, which is truer to the sense of the original (*Nauk Pobezhdat'*) than the conventional *Art of Victory*.

[8]   Lopatin, 1986, 397

[9]   Ibid., 397-8

[10]   Ibid., 399

[11]   Ibid., 400

[12]   Milyutin, 1856-8, I,111

[13]   Ibid., I,112

[14]   'Ratnik,' 1844, No. 1, 125

[15]   Suvorov to Prévost de Lumian, Konchansk, 16 September 1799, Lopatinm, 1986, 325

[16]   Meshcheryakov, 1949-53, IV,3

[17]   PRO FO 74/27, Major-General Mulgrave, 12 September 1799

[18]   Thugut to Count Ludwig Cobenzl, 10 March 1799, Thugut, 1872, II,153

[19]   Milyutin, 1856-8, I,113-4

[20]   Paul to Suvorov, 12 March 1799, Meshcheryakov, 1949-53, IV,5

[21]   Lord Minto to Lady Minto, Prague, 3 January 1800, Minto, 1874, III,108-9

[22]   Masson, 1859, 152

[23]   Ibid., 371

[24]   Lord Minto to Lady Minto, Prague, 3 January 1800, Minto, 1874, III,111

[25]   KA FA Italien 1799 XIII 43, Anon. 'Bemerkungen über die Beschaffenheit der russischen Armeen'

[26]   Langeron, 1895, LXXXVIII,156

[27]   Fuchs, 1827, 7

[28]   Roverea, 1848, II,302

[29]   Wickham to Grenville, Wangen, 17 October 1799, Wickham, 1870, II,274

[30]   Lord Minto to Lady Minto, Prague, 6 January 1800, Minto, 1874, III,110

[31]   Suvorov to Razumovsky, 7 June 1799, Lopatin, 1986, 339

[32]   As reported to Lieutenant-Colonel Clinton, in Wickham to Grenville, Schaffhausen, 12 September 1799, Wickham, 1870, II,207

[33]   Masson, 1859, 152

[34]   Fuchs, 1827, 36

[35]   Ibid., 160

[36]   Ibid., 181-2

[37]   Milyutin, 1856-8, II,20-1

[38]   Suvorov to Nelson, Alessandria, 30 June 1799, 'Dropmore Papers,' 1892-1915, V,109

[39]   Suvorov to Nelson, Prague, 12 January 1800, Lopatin, 1986, 377

[40]   Stutterheim, 1812, I,iii,19

[41]   KA FA Italien 1799 V 289, Melas to Lambertie, Casal Pusterlengo, 4 May

[42]   KA HKRA Deutschland und Italien 1799 IV 32 D, marginal comments by Francis on Tige's 'Allerunterthänigste Note' of 3 May

[43]   KA FA Italien 1799 XIII 1, Chasteler's Journal

[44]   Tige to Melas, 6 June 1799, Hüffer. 1900-1, I,207

[45]   KA FA Italien 1799 XIII 43, 'Bemerkungen über die Beschaffenheit der russischen Armeen'

[46]   KA FA Deutschland und Schweiz 1799 XIII 15, S. Settele, 'Darstellung des gegenwärtigen Feldzugs vom Jahr 1799, vorzüglich auf den Standen von denen Armeen'

[47]   KA HKRA Deutschland und Italien 1799 IV 32 D, Tige 'Allerunterthänigste Note,' 3 May

[48]   Wickham to Grenville, Schaffhausen, 29 June 1799, Wickham, 1870, II,117-8

[49]   Roverea, 1848, II,313,315

[50]   KA FA Italien 1799 XIII 1, Chasteler's Journal

[51]   Ibid.

52 Ibid.

53 Melas to Tige, Tortona, 11 May 1799, Hüffer, 1900-1, I,201; KA HkrA Deutschland und Italien 1799 IX 3, Tige to Melas, 24 June

54 Kolychev to Vorontsov, Vienna, 31 August 1799, 'Dropmore Papers,' 1892-1914, V,203; see also Chasteler's pathetic note to Thugut of 1 June, KA FA Italien 1799 XIII 1, Chasteler's Journal

55 Suvorov to Razumovsky, Asti, 3 September 1799, Lopatin, 1986, 354

56 Suvorov to Razumovsky, Bosco Marengo, 7 August 1799, Ibid., 348-9

57 Melas to Tige, Novi, 10 August 1799, Hüffer, 1900-1, I,263-4

58 Wickham to Grenville, Schaffhausen, 6 September 1799, 'Dropmore Papers,' 1892-1915, V,367

59 KA FA Italien 1799 VIII 301, Suvorov to Archduke Charles, Lindau, 29 October

60 Wickham to Grenville, Wangen, 17 October 1799, Wickham, 1870, II,283,274

61 Masson, 1859, 449

62 KA FA Italien 1799 XIII 44, MacDermott, 'Militärisches Dage Buch'

63 Bunbury, 1927, 145

64 Gryazev, 1898, 27

65 Lord Minto to Lady Minto, Prague, 3 January 1800, Minto, 1874, III,110

66 Kosciuszko, 'Notice sur les Russes,' Hüffer, 1900-1, I,143-4

67 Gryazev, 1898, 161

68 'Ratnik,' 1844, No. 7, 34

69 Levenshtern, 1900, CIII, No. 3, 490

70 Stutterheim, 1812, II,v,14; Masson, 1859, 316

71 Denisov, 1874-5, XI,618-9

72 KA FA Italien 1799 XIII 43, 'Bemerkungen über die Beschaffenheit der russischen Armeen'

73 To Prévost de Lumian, Konchansk, 16 September 1798, Lopatin, 1986, 325

74 Fuchs, 1827, 174-5

75 Kosciuszko's 'Notice sur les Russes,' Hüffer, 1900-1, I,144

76 Milyutin, 1856-8, I,209

77 Ibid., I,559,651

78 Suvorov to Archduke Charles, Panix, 7 October 1799, Hüffer, 1900-1, I,413; see also Linken to Petrasch, Chur, 8 October 1799, Ibid., I,413-4. The Russian troops also used every opportunity to replenish their cartridge pouches on their own account, see 'Ratnik,' 1844, No. 6, 262; Gryazev, 1898, 111

79 Stutterheim, 1812, II,v,6

80 Radetzky, quoted in Regele, 1957, 58

81 Anon., 1801-3, IV,250,253. See also Soult, 1854, III,129; Masson, 1859, 331,371

82 Roverea, 1848, II,305-6

83 KA FA Italien 1799 XIII 43, 'Bemerkungen über die Beschaffenheit der russischen Armeen'

84 Lord Minto to Lady Minto, Prague, 3 January 1800, Minto, 1874, III,108. See also Wickham to Grenville, Augsburg, 13 December 1799, Wickham, 1870, II,360-1

85 Milyutin, 1856-8, I,209

86 'Ratnik', 1844, No. 6, 266

87 Wickham to Grenville, Augsburg, 13 December 1799, Wickham, 1870, II,362

88 Roverea, 1848, II,222

89 KA FA Italien 1799 IV 127, Melas to Archduke Charles, Chiari, 23 April

90 Suvorov to Chasteler, undated, Milyutin, 1856-8, I,219-20

91 KA FA Italien 1799 XIII 43, 'Bermerkungen über die Beschaffenheit der russischen Armeen'

92 Suvorov to Bellegarde, Turin, 31 May 1799, Milyutin, 1856-8, II,495-6

93 KA FA Italien 1799 IV 127, Melas to Archduke Charles, Chiari, 23 April

94 KA FA Italien 1799 IV 127, Melas to Archduke Charles, Chiari, 23 April; KA FA Italien 1799 V 289, Melas to Lambertie, Casal Pusterlengo, 4 May

95 'Ratnik,' 1844, No. 7, 41

3

TO THE SOUTH

THE TASK

Suvorov left St.Petersburg to take up his new command on 28 February 1799. He stopped at Mitau to pay his respects to the exiled Louis XVIII, crossed into the Austrian territory of Galicia on 20 March, and reached Vienna on the evening of the 25th. On the next day Suvorov made the short passage from his quarters in the palace of the ambassador Razumovsky to the Imperial Hofburg Palace. The streets were thronged with citizens who called out: 'Hurrah Paul! Hurrah Suvorov!' Suvorov was deeply moved, and to every wave of acclamations he replied with a: 'Hurrah Kaiser Franz!' He spoke with the Emperor for an hour, but he had little to say about it afterwards, except to mention that Francis was impatient with the slow progress of the Russian corps of Numsen (below). On the 31st Suvorov was appointed an Austrian field-marshal with full pay and emoluments.

Suvorov refused to be drawn on what he might have in mind for the campaign, explaining that he must wait until he had taken stock of the ground and the troops under his command. He likewise observed the Orthodox Lent in all its rigour, and declined every invitation of a social nature. At the farewell audience on 3 April Francis invested him with full local authority over all the Austrian forces in Italy, and furnished him with a few general directions:

It is My intention that the first offensive operations of My army should be conducted in such a way that the advance covers My own states, and renders the danger of enemy invasion progressively more remote. Our efforts should therefore be concentrated in the direction of Lombardy and the territories on the left [i.e. north] bank of the Po—it is there and in Piedmont that the enemy have the seat

and true centre of their forces, and it is from there that they threaten and dominate the rest of Italy.

This first operation would cover the Tyrol, and set free 15-20,000 Austrian troops to guard the Alpine flank of Suvorov's further advance,

Moreover, if it pleases God to bless My arms in their operations in Lombardy and towards Piedmont, the French will soon be forced to abandon southern Italy, or at least weaken their forces in that part of the world so considerably that the people, goaded by the tyrannical rule of the French, will probably be strong enough to rise up and crush them.

As his first specific objective Suvorov should seize the Mincio with the key fortress of Peschiera,

after which it is left to your discretion whether circumstances are such that you should lay siege to Mantua, or just keep it under blockade while you continue your thrust towards the Oglio and the Adda.

Finally Suvorov was to keep the Emperor briefed on the progress of his operations and what he intended to do next.[1]

It is time to outline the deployment of the forces of the French and the allies on the strategic scale:

STRATEGIC OVERVIEW

The Batavian Republic (Holland):
The French held this satellite with up to 12,000 of their own troops and 12,000 more of their Dutch auxiliaries.

Germany: Hostilities had opened here on 1 March. On the left or northern flank of the French General Bernadotte had concentrated 8,000 troops to besiege Mainz, while Jourdan with 37-40,000 troops of the Army of the Danube had moved from Alsace across the Rhine and the Black Forest. Archduke Charles held his 80,000 Austrians on the Lech in Bavaria, with another 15,000 in deep reserve in Bohemia.

Switzerland, Vorarlberg and the Tyrol:

Massena had taken the offensive at the outbreak of the war, and caught the Austrians badly off their guard in the Grisons (Graubünden), the south-easternmost of the Swiss cantons. Massena now held Switzerland with the main force of the *Armée d'Hélvetie*, consisting of 30,000 French troops and 10,000 Swiss auxiliaries, while 10,000 additional troops under Lecourbe were detached to the area of the St. Gotthard Pass, the main avenue towards Italy.

The Austrians were still coming to terms with the entry of Switzerland into the strategic system of Europe, and they had considerable if ill-articulated forces on the threatened western approaches to their Hereditary Lands—on their right Lieutenant-General Hotze in Vorarlberg at the eastern end of Lake Constance with 26,000 men, and on the left Major-General Auffenberg with up to 10,000 troops in the Grisons, and in their rear Lieutenant-General Bellegarde with 47-50,000 spanning the Tyrolean Alps between the Inn and Lake Garda.

Italy:

All told the French had about 117,000 troops in Italy, a number which weighted the balance of their forces on the European continent heavily towards the southern theatre. However the concentration of active operations at the two extremities of Italy—on the northern plain and in Naples—was pulling their troops in opposite directions, and this, together with the desire of the French to hold down and plunder the peninsula, had brought about a considerable dispersal.

Up in the north the Schérer had about 83,000 men under his command in the Army of Italy, but of these only 58,000 were available for active operations in the field, the remaining 25,000 being scattered in garrisons. The 25,000 Piedmontese were of doubtful loyalty. The Austrians had 86,000 troops in Venetia, Illyria and Istria, and 50,700 of them stood at the disposal of the hard-fighting Lieutenant-General Kray behind the Adige.

In central Italy and Naples the 34,000 troops of the French Army of Naples were debauched by plunder, easy living and slack discipline, and would require time to coalesce into an effective field force. The French still occupied the Papal States and the cities of Rome and Naples, but the people of the Neapolitan provinces of Calabria, Basilicata, Taranto and Puglia were in full rebellion.

THE RUSSIAN REINFORCEMENTS

The French had taken the initiative at the outbreak of hostilities, but they had now run out of momentum, and were therefore vulnerable to Austrian counter-offensives on both sides of the Alps—in northern Switzerland and in the plain of Lombardy. The Austrian efforts might be given decisive weight by the Russian forces which Paul released in successive waves (see also above page 13):

1   Rosenberg's corps of some 20,000 troops set out from Russia from the end of September. Originally destined for the upper Rhine, this force was now diverted towards Italy and formed the first element of Suvorov's new command. We shall trace its fortunes shortly.

2   Hermann's corps of 10,000 troops marched from the Dniester on 4 April 1799. On the way its destination was changed from Naples to northern Italy, and Lieutenant-General Rehbinder assumed the acting command. This force reached Suvorov in the middle of July 1799, when it came under the orders of General Derfelden as the second of the two Russian formations on the Italian theatre. Hermann himself later took charge of a Russian contingent of 12,000 men which joined the British expeditionary force in North Holland.

3   Finally a large and elite body of 27,000 troops had been earmarked to co-operate with the Prussians on the lower Rhine. Since the Prussians chose to stay out of the war, these troops were reassigned to the northern flank of the Alps to reinforce the efforts of Archduke Charles. The command was

typically changed in the course of the march, in this case from that of General Numsen to Lieutenant-General Rimsky-Korsakov. The path of the Numsen/Korsakov corps was followed by the 6-7,000 French royalist troops of the Prince de Condé, who had found refuge and support in Russia.

The Russians on the March

We take up the story of Rosenberg's command, which was the first of the Russian forces to arrive on the Italian theatre.

In the course of July and August 1798 the component troops from the interior of Russia began to assemble along the Dniester. The advance guard set off on 29 September, and it was followed by the main force which marched in two columns under the orders of the lieutenant-generals Lvov and Schveikovsky. The troops coalesced at Brest just short of the border with Austrian Poland, where wrangling between Rosenberg and the Austrian supply officers imposed a considerable delay.

According to a provisional agreement the Austrians agreed to furnish the Russians with ammunition in return for payment, and 'even before formal discussions opened the [Austrian] Director General of Artillery began to manufacture ammunition on the Russian calibres.'[2] However the further negotiations stuck fast when Rosenberg demanded that the Russian troops must be provided with the rations of bread to the full three pounds they enjoyed in Russia. Rosenberg appealed to Emperor Francis, who wrote to St. Petersburg that it would be mean-spirited of the Austrians to haggle on this point when Peter far exceeded the letter of his treaty obligations. Agreement was reached on a formula suggested by Francis, according to which the Russians would receive their three pounds in flour rather than bread, so that the Austrian troops would not notice the difference. (Once active campaigning was under way we nevertheless find the Russians being fed with biscuit).

The leading Russian troops crossed the Bug into Austrian territory on 25 October 1798. 'I bade farewell to the beloved country of my birth,' records Captain Gryazev, 'where I left everything that was dear to me. The demands of war were taking us to far distant lands… we all felt the same way, and we all swore vengeance on those French who were responsible for disturbing the public peace.'[3]

On the far side of the river Rosenberg met the Austrian major-general Prince Ferdinand of Württemberg (brother of the Russian Empress Maria Fedorovna) who asked him to hasten the march of his corps across Galicia, Moravia and Lower Austria to the Danube. The march proceeded by well-regulated stages, and Grayzev (no lover of Germans) conceded that the Austrians delivered the provisions with teutonic accuracy. An early and severe winter descended when the troops were on the march through Cracow in November. There was as yet little snow, but many vehicles and gun carriages came to grief on the icy roads.

After a taxing haul over the Moravian Gate, Rosenberg prolonged his march across the open plains of Moravia, and reached the city of Brünn on 16 December, having had only fifty-nine men fall out on the march from the Bug. He asked, and received permission from Emperor Francis to allow the troops to spend two weeks in the neighbourhood of Brünn to assemble and recuperate. Rosenberg had kept fine discipline on the march, and Russians and Austrians were confident that they would get on well together. In Brünn the Don Cossack colonel Denisov made the acquaintance of an Italian lady of considerable means, who had left her country when it was occupied by the French.

> From curiosity she came out to view our army. Seeing this, I rode up to her carriage and offered to be of whatever service I could, which she said she would be pleased to accept. She was full of small questions concerning our army. I made the due explanations, after which she asked me in a most affecting way whether I would give her the opportunity to get to know me better.

On the following day Denisov paid his respects at her house, and thus entered the social life of the city.[4]

Emperor Francis in person came to Brünn on 26 December, which occasioned four days of

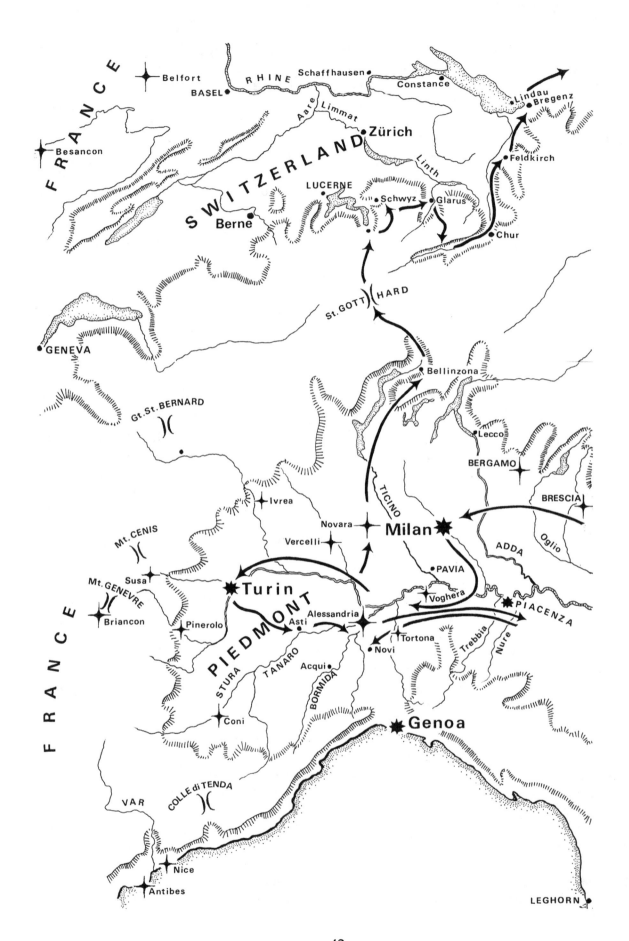

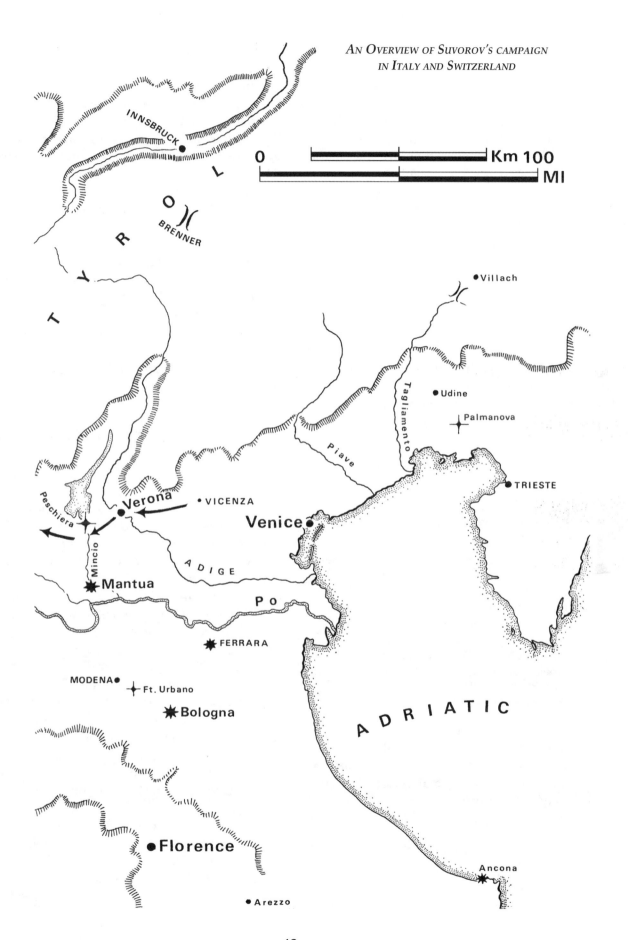

INNSBRUCK

T Y R O L

BRENNER

Km 100

MI

0

Villach

Tagliamento

Udine

Palmanova

Piave

TRIESTE

Verona

VICENZA

Venice

Peschiera

Mincio

A D I G E

Mantua

P o

FERRARA

MODENA Ft. Urbano

Bologna

ADRIATIC

Florence

Ancona

Arezzo

43

parades, presentations, receptions and mock battles. Denisov put his three available regiments of Cossacks through their paces over the snow-covered ground, and Francis was much taken by a manoeuvre whereby the horsemen approached in a solid mass in which it was impossible to discover their numbers, then fanned out to the full extent for the attack. Denisov noted that the Hungarian officers were observing with particular attention. Francis left on 30 December, and wrote to Paul that he was carrying away some excellent impressions. Paul replied: 'Only lead My troops against the enemy, and you will see that they know how to fight. My soldiers love war.'[5]

Rosenberg's troops set out from Brünn by instalments between 1 and 9 January 1799, and marched through Lower Austria to reach their winter quarters in the prosperous villages and little towns along the Danube upstream from Vienna. The artillery lieutenant Tararicsky wrote to his brother on the way to Krems:

> As you are aware, we had been persuaded to form a frightful vision of the people here, as beasts in human form and one-eyed monsters. Well, you can rest assured—these same folk have received us with a friendliness and warmth that leaves nothing to be desired, though it's true that we pay for everything we take. We will go forth to fight with courage. Oh, you atheists who have forsaken God! Open your ears!—they will be assailed soon enough by the tramp of our marching feet. Nobody can reasonably doubt that we will smash everything that comes in the way of our blows—everything which smacks of atheism, everything which has employed violence to overthrow the sacred order of things and Heaven itself![6]

Warmed, fed and rested, Rosenberg's troops resumed their march when winter drew to a close. Their destination had meanwhile been changed from Germany to Italy, and their route now lay to the south.

From 15 March 1799 the echelons of the first column set out at intervals from St. Pölten, Tulln and Langenrohr (proceeding by way of Perschling, Sieghartskirchen, Purkersdorf, Perchtoldsdorf, Neunkirchen, Schottwein, Mürzzuschlag, Kindberg, Bruck, Leoben, Knittelfeld, Judenburg, Unzmarkt, Neumark, Friesach, St. Veit and Feldkirchen). The second column left Herzogenburg between 23 and 25 March. The snow was already retreating up the Styrian and Carinthian mountains, and the first half of the march was accomplished under the direction of Rosenberg in the usual, disciplined style.

Suvorov was coming up fast behind. His *kibitka* rattled over the Semmering Pass, began to pass the marching columns at Friesach on 8 April, and deposited him briefly at Villach in Carinthia, from where he reported to Paul on the 9th that his force amounted to one combined grenadier battalion (1,491 troops), seven regiments of musketeers (10,584), two regiments of Jäger (1,487), four combined grenadier battalions (2,451), six regiments of Cossacks (2.930) and 1,304 gunners, or a total of 20,247 men.

The Hofkriegsrath had allowed a comfortable twenty-nine days for the Russians to march the 320 odd kilometres from the Danube to Villach. Suvorov, however, was impatient to bring his Russians onto the scene of action in Italy, where great things were being accomplished without him. About 350 kilometres still separated many of the Russians from the Austrian base area at Verona, and the early stages lay across the Carnic Alps—authentic mountains still deep in snow. Suvorov now reorganised the corps into a tighter formation in eight echelons, staged in such a way that the last was never more than twelve days behind the first. He likewise ordered a doubling of the rate of march once the Russians had left the mountain wall behind them and reached Udine in the plain. On some of the days the troops were ordered to march a distance of up to sixty kilometres, with the result that only about one hundred men in a regiment might reach the designated stopping place in a formed body, leaving the rest strung out behind. The pace in itself was less destructive than the lack of rest days. The troops carried awls and waxed thread, but now they were given no opportunity to repair their Prussian-style snub-nosed shoes, which were disintegrating fast.

The good order inculcated by Rosenberg

had not yet entirely vanished, and the Italians' first impressions of the newcomers were favourable:

> The Russians have a considerable quantity of baggage and a fine train of artillery. The soldiers are tireless, agile and proud, but at the same time disciplined and reverent. They are consumed with a hatred of the French nation, and never stop asking whether they have far to go before they reach France. Before eating they cross themselves, then get down to devouring everything that is set before them— but especially salt fish, vermicelli, polenta and mushrooms… The appearance of the infantry is pretty good—but not so that of the Cossacks, whose horses are small, skinny and ugly, though strong and fast.[7]

KRAY AND THE OPENING OF HOSTILITIES

Suvorov was not the only man in a hurry. In his earlier career the French *général de division* Barthélémy Louis Schérer (1747-1804) hovered between cultures and allegiances. He was born in Alsace, and served successively in the

SCHÉRER

Austrian, French and Dutch armies before he committed himself finally to the cause of Revolutionary France in 1792. He went on to acquire considerable experience of filed command, leading the Army of the North in 1794, and the Army of the Pyrenees and (twice over) the Army of Italy in the course of 1795. This second Italian command was distinguished by his victory at Loano. Much of his credit was lost in his spell as Minister of War (July 1797 - February 1799), when the name of this round and comfortable man was associated by the fighting troops with corruption. Upon the outbreak of hostilities in 1799 Schérer was assigned to take command of the Army of Italy (i.e. northern Italy) under less than happy circumstances. The French troops in northern Italy were not those who had conquered with Bonaparte in 1796 and 1797 (these were now stranded in Egypt), but mainly veterans of the Army of the Rhine and Moselle who owed their allegiance to their old chief *général de division* Jean Victor Moreau (1763-1813), now serving under Schérer as second in command. Schérer had arrived in Milan only on 21 March, and found his army indisciplined and disgruntled, the people on the verge of revolt, and the Russians on the march to Italy.

Schérer decided to resolve his problem by taking the offensive from the Mincio and driving the Austrians from the line of the Adige, which formed the last coherent position of any strength in the north-east Italian plain. To the rear, the Brenta, Piave and Tagliamento rivers were easy to ford, and distant Palmanova was the only fortress worthy of the name.

The Austrian chief was Lieutenant-General Paul Kray von Krajova und Topolya (1735-1804). He too was eager for a fight, as befitted his character. According to a British commentator

> General Kray was born in Hungary, and has served since his infancy in the Imperial army. He has always shown himself possessed to an eminent degree of that qualification which distinguishes Hungarian officers, viz., a perfect knowledge of the kind of war to be carried out with light troops and on the advanced posts… General Kray is now about sixty years of age, but he is active, robust, and

is likely to be long able to exert his talents for the defence of his country and of his Sovereign.[8]

Kray had no 'interest' with the circle of Thugut in Vienna. He was about to be replaced as immediate commander of the Austrian forces by Melas, and Suvorov as the commander-in-chief would soon debouch onto the theatre with his Russians, leaving Kray altogether in the shadows. Kray's impatience was sharpened by Major-General Chasteler, who arrived as the new chief of staff on 21 March, and was bubbling with enthusiastic talk about Suvorov's military talents and charisma.

Hostilities in north Italy opened on 26 March 1799, when Schérer's troops advanced east from the Mincio and Mantua on a wide frontage. Upon the Director's orders Schérer had been forced to dispatch Gauthier's division of 6,400 troops towards Tuscany, which reduced his main body to about 46,000 French and auxiliaries. Schérer nevertheless managed to achieve an effective concentration of force on his left or northern wing, where three divisions commanded by Moreau evicted 5,000 Austrians from the camp of Pastrengo on the southern prolongation of the celebrated plateau of Rivoli—thus barring the upper Adige route from the Tyrol. Schérer in person advanced with two divisions as far as the immediate approaches to Verona, with the intention of pinning down the Austrian forces in that part of the world, while the division of Montrichard out to the far right executed to a diversionary attack against Legnano to fix the Austrian left (divisions Frelich and Mercantin) on the middle Adige.

Kray took the bait, and at first turned all his attention to his southern wing, where the 8,500 defenders of Legnano held out long enough to enable him to bring up 19,000 troops (the main force of his left wing) from the rearward position of Bevilacqua. Kray's counterattack drove the French back towards Mantua:

> The Polish legion of Dabrowski composed almost entirely of Austrian deserters having been at this affair, the Austrian soldiers, to whom their officers called out 'Parce ferro!' ['spare the sword!'] in vain as Hannibal called

to his at Trasimene, would give no quarter, and exterminated with their bayonets and with the butt ends of their muskets all the men of that legion which fell into their hands.[9]

The continuing battle to the north (it went on at Verona for eighteen hours) now convinced Kray that the real danger was to his right wing, where 23,000 Austrians (divisions Kaim and Hohenzollern) were facing some 30,000 French, Italians and Swiss. Leaving 8,000 troops on the middle Adige, Kray executed a speedy march up the left bank overnight and into 27 March. Moving by way of Arcole he was able to concentrate 35,000 men to stabilise the situation around Verona, while Schérer failed to exploit his breakthrough further north at Pastrengo. These two days of fighting cost the Austrians 4,320 in dead and wounded and 2,631 men captured, while the French lost 4,600 casualties and 900 prisoners. A truce was proclaimed on 29 March to enable to dead to be buried.

On 30 March Schérer made a tardy attempt to capitalise on his breakthrough on the upper Adige. Sérurier with 6,000 enthusiastic troops crossed the river by a bridge and moved down on Verona from the north, whereupon 15,000 Austrians irrupted from the camp of Parona and advanced to meet the French with equal brio. Sérurier recoiled and fell back across the Adige, leaving 1,000 men as prisoners when two battalions of Austrian grenadiers advanced along the river bank and cut off their retreat. French losses amounted to 600 casualties and 1,177 captured, as against the 390 Austrian casualties and prisoners, which left the balance in the campaign so far approximately equal.

On 5 April the two armies met head-on in a battle which decided the opening campaign. The forces of Kray and Schérer advanced at ten in the morning and the action opened on a wide frontage south of Verona. Reinforcements had brought Kray's army to a strength of 44,000 troops, and this preponderance of numbers helped to resolve the outcome on the central axis, even though Schérer and Moreau brought up the reserve to second the efforts of the divisions of Montrichard and Hatry. By five in the afternoon Kaim was being driven back on Verona, but the Austrian reserve under Lusignan still held three uncommitted grenadier battalions, and Kaim and Lusignan were able to withstand the French attack, and finally drive it back in confusion. The division of Victor on the right had run into Kray's main force behind San Giovanni Lupatoto and had been wrecked. The lively Sérurier on the French left captured Villafranca and had been making good progress, but the general rout of the French army compelled him to fall back.

This battle of Magnano (called after the French camp) cost the Austrians some 5,500 men. Kray counted eleven cannon and 2,400 prisoners among his trophies, and he put the French casualties accurately enough at 6,000. More significant than the figures was the collapse of confidence among Schérer's generals and the disintegration of the soldiers' morale. Schérer himself wrote to the Directory on 7 April:

> more than half of the regiments of this army are from the old Army of the Rhine, and they repose their entire trust in General Moreau, who has always led them to victory. They do not know me, and they have no confidence in me at all. Soldiers identify themselves with successful generals, and Moreau is one of those… Citizen Directors, with the fate of the army in mind I beg you to find some excuse to recall me or send me wherever you like—as long as it is not to command an army—and that you give the command to General Moreau.[10]

For the time being Schérer's army was saved from destruction by the natural and artificial strength of the line of the Mincio, on the stretch between the little fortress town of Peschiera (where the river left Lake Garda) and the lake fortress of Mantua. However Schérer's nerve broke completely when he learned that considerable forces were on the march from the Austrian Army of the Tyrol (Bellegarde), and were threatening him with deep envelopment on his left rear. The formations in question amounted to 12,000 men, and comprised:

> A column under Colonel Strauch, marching down the Oglio valley,

> The column of Colonel Brodanovich who was making for the western shore of Lake Como,

> Major-General Vukassovich with the main body of 7,000 troops marching for Lake Idro and its choke point at Fort Anfo.*

On 12 April Schérer abandoned the Mincio without a shot, leaving 12,000 troops to hold Mantua, and another 1,600 in Peschiera. Schérer had detached no less than 7,500 men from his field forces to bring the existing garrisons up to these strengths, which reduced his army to a disintegrating body of 25,000 men. The work of destruction was completed by a hasty retreat through the constant and heavy rain. The faithful French troops were reduced to a state of sodden, ragged exhaustion, while many of the Italian and Swiss auxiliaries took advantage of the chaos to desert. Melas reached Verona on 9 April and took over the command of the Austrians from Kray. The leading Russian troops were at Vicenza on the 14th, and on the next day Suvorov established himself at Valeggio as commander-in-chief.

The Bible has something to say about people who sow that others may reap, and the phrase applies very well to Kray. His achievement must stand in its own right. He had received the unexpected blow of the French offensive, and although he possessed only the authority of an interim commander, he had broken the cohesion of the enemy army and thrown it back with losses which amounted to 10,000 men by the end of the first week of the campaign; 'It is… in war, the same as in commerce; the first battle is like the first guinea, the most difficult to gain; and he who opens a career of victory, renders a very different service, and has a much better title to renown, than he who has only to pursue the course.'[11] News of the belated promotion to full general reached Kray on 1 May, and he was right to suspect that Thugut and his friends had been forced to give him some recognition against their will.

---

*Long after the war Napoleon took care to bar this route by re-fortifying the position as the defensive complex of Rocca d'Anfo, crowned by a drum-like fort perched on the top of the dominating crag.

As the designated chief of staff of the combined army, Major-General Chasteler left Verona to meet Suvorov on 14 April, and found him just behind Montebello at eight in the morning. Suvorov was watching his troops as they waded the sheet of floodwater which extended for the full three thousand paces from the Gua stream to the Chiampo. 'The field-marshal received me in the most friendly way you could imagine. I knew Count Suvorov from the time of the Turkish War, when I served in the army under the command of Field-Marshal the Prince of Coburg. At that time I saw him at the battles of Fokshani and Martineshti [Rymnik] in Wallachia, and I was often sent on missions to him as the Russian commander.' Suvorov took Chasteler by the arm, led him into an inn, and they shared a soldierly Russian dish of greasy mutton and cold boiled maize. At the end of the meal Chasteler deployed a map and detailed the positions and strengths of the Austrian and French forces as far as they were known to him. He recorded his words verbatim, since they formed the basis of the subsequent operations:

> The Austrian army in Italy consists of 42,683 combatants, with the advance guard on the Chiese, and the main army behind the Mincio.
> The French army stood at an original 47,000 troops, but between 26 March and 5 April they have lost 15,000, and at least another 14,000 have been detached to garrison Peschiera and Mantua, so leaving scarcely 18,000. There are an additional 19,800 in Piedmont, but they are still several marches away… and on the approach of a victorious army they will be hardly sufficient to garrison the fortresses.
> Macdonald is in Naples with 25,000 troops, but these are scattered all over Italy.
> The field-marshal replied: 'I am bringing 20,000 Russians. With the 42,000 Austrians and the corps of Vukassovich this makes a total of 71,000, and with that I shall smash those 18,000 Frenchmen.[12]

Suvorov invited Chasteler into his carriage for the journey to Verona, but the commander-in-chief was too excited to be drawn into matters of detail, and gave vent to warlike noises:

'Bayonets! Bayonets! We must attack!' and so on. At noon the carriage entered the renaissance ramparts of Verona by the Porta Vescovo. Here Suvorov was greeted by General Melas. The Austrian knew something of what to expect from a briefing by the Hofkriegsrath:

> Count Suvorov is a man whose mind and entire military career have been taken up by enterprises against the enemy. He is not open to representations concerning supply, or any of the other matters (however important) which have to do with the maintenance of the army. Since he devotes himself solely to active operations, he looks to others to furnish him with the necessary information. He likes such answers to be prompt, short, devoid of compliments—but reliable. This means we must place at his side someone who knows his business, and has style, discretion and intelligence. Such a man must be able to preserve his composure in situations which will frequently try his patience, and retain his dignity and calm under provocations that would goad anybody else to say or do something over-hasty.[13]

This describes Chasteler's experience exactly.

Melas moved forward to embrace Suvorov, but the commander-in-chief merely extended his hand, and turned his attention back to Chasteler. The crowds converged on Suvorov's route shouting *'Eviva nostro liberatore!'* and the carriage made its way over the Adige by the Ponte Navi, across the Arena square and then to the Castelvecchio. Here the people unhitched the little carriage horses, and pulled the vehicle for the last stretch along the Via Santa Eufemia to Suvorov's destination at the Casa Emilia (where Bonaparte had lodged in June 1796).

Suvorov ascended to his chambers, ordered all the mirrors to be covered with curtains, and arrayed himself in a dress uniform ablaze with decorations. He emerged in the audience room, and, after singling out the archbishop among the throng of civilian and military he advanced to seek his blessing. Suvorov listened to the addresses from the clergy and citizens with dignified attention, and replied that he had been sent by the emperors of Austria and Russia to expel the godless French, restore peace among peoples, and protect thrones and the Christian religion. He closed by reminding the city fathers of their duty to serve their masters with loyal zeal, then turned and almost bolted through the door.

Only the Russian generals and a few of the Austrians remained when Suvorov returned to the anteroom a little later. He screwed up his eyes and asked Rosenberg to introduce the gentlemen to him. Unfamiliar names elicited little more than a bow and the spoken formula; 'Good God! You are a stranger. But we will get to know one another soon!'[14] He came alive when Bagration, Miloradovich and others of his acquaintance were brought before him, and he reminded them in a cheerful way of times when they had fought alongside.

Bagration had reached the neighbourhood of Verona with a small advance guard consisting of his own Jäger regiment, the combined grenadier battalion of Lomonosov and the Cossack regiment of Posdeev. Suvorov ordered the rest of the troops to make directly for the assembly area south-west of Verona at Valeggio, just short of the Mincio. The columns arrived by forced marches and without notification, and the first Russian 'victories' were attained by Cossacks over such French fugitives as had escaped the Austrian cavalry. All the same 'this start to operations bolstered the confidence of the Russians, while it induced terror among the beaten and fleeing French—a terror which grew in the telling. Thus the Austrians had to escort their prisoners through the outposts and lines of their savage allies, to save the French from being cut down without mercy.'[15]

The momentary pause in operations enabled all parties to take stock of unfamiliar surroundings and comrades. Like every northerner of education and sensibility, Suvorov was struck by the transition from one side of the great European watershed to the other, and the contrast was never more acute than at this season, when the black forests, crags, snows and blanched meadows of the Alps gave way to the springtime verdure of Italy. Suvorov knew the land in one dimension from his books, and now his physical senses could populate his mind with what was still lacking. He could set the armies of Carthage and Rome trooping across the landscapes he saw before him, and he listened entranced at the peasant songs that reached him across the fields, and which reminded him of the music of the country people in Russia.

To the Russian soldiers it seemed that they were marching through a landscape of parks, gardens, orchards and architectural set-pieces. The people they encountered were 'of medium stature, with swarthy complexions, big noses, dark cropped hair, and brown eyes in which it was impossible to read any benevolence.'[16] Every now and then could be seen the handiwork of the French. Beyond Treviso there was a villa which had once been the residence of a Neapolitan envoy, and was adorned with frescoes, mosaics and marble floors,

> But now everything had been mutilated. They had built fires on the floors, and so all the rooms were blackened with soot. The walls had been gouged all over with bayonets. Likewise the effigies of great men, set in bas relief on the walls, had been smashed. Everything had been destroyed, down to the frames of the mirrors, and now pieces of mirror glass and shards of precious vases were scattered over the floors… going into the garden, we saw that pedestals had once been set out all over the wide spaces between the woodlands, and supported statues of gods, goddesses and heroes, fashioned most excellently from marble and plaster. These now littered the ground in profusion—some without arms, some without legs, some without heads. But most of all we were struck by the marble cupids, the work of great artists, who now lay with their wings, quivers and bows smashed, and their faces disfigured by bayonets. The assiduous way the French cannibals had gone to work indicated wicked satisfaction, and not just playful vandalism.[17]

While Chasteler had been correct to put the Austrian troops in Italy at a total of 42,683, we have to bear in mind that Klenau and other commanders had taken off in pursuit of the French, while Vukassovich, Brodanovich and Strauch were arriving with reinforcements from Bellegarde's army in the Tyrol. Altogether about 29,000 troops stood at Suvorov's immediate disposal. On 14 April Chasteler's calculation of

Schérer's mobile effectives (18,000) was an under-estimate, but the total sank to something that approached that number when major operations resumed.

The French information on the allied numbers and deployment was altogether defective. One French appreciation states that 'despite all the promises, and all the money I laid out, it never proved possible for me to obtain reliable and intelligent informants. The enemy, on the other hand, had the entire country on their side, and knew my position as soon as I took it up.'[18]

MAIN FIELD FORCES AT THE OPENING OF THE NORTH ITALIAN CAMPAIGN

It is impossible to set out comprehensive orders of battle for all parties for any one date at this stage of operations, since units were transferred frequently from one formation to another, and whole formations were coming and going between garrisons and field armies. The Russian numbers presented here are those of 9 April, the Austrian forces and numbers of 14 April, and the French forces and numbers of 30 March.

ALLIED FIELD ARMY, FIELD-MARSHAL SUVOROV
RUSSIAN FORCES

Grenadier regiment Rosenberg:	1,491
Musketeer regiments:	
Jung-Baden (later Veletsky)	1,424
Schveikovsky	1,510
Förster	1,503
Tyrtov	1,527
Dalheim (later Kamensky)	1,514
Miloradovich	1,516
Baranovsky	1,590
Jäger regiments:	
Chubarov (later Miller)	750
Bagration	737
Combined grenadier battalions:	
Dendrygin	623
Lomonosov	606
Sanaev	608
Kalemin	614
Cossack regiments:	
Denisov	490
Sychov	498
Grekov	494
Semernikov	484

Posdeev	470
Molchanov	494
Field artillery:	632
Regimental artillery:	672

Russian Totals:
16,013 infantry, 2,930 Cossacks, 1,304 gunners
Russian Grand Total: *20,247*

AUSTRIAN FORCES, GENERAL OF CAVALRY MELAS

Division Lt-Gen Kaim	
Infantry regiments:	
Frelich	2,376
Preiss	1,393
Total:	*3,769*
Division Lt-Gen Zopf	
Infantry regiments:	
Mittrowsky (later in garrison)	1,909
Anton Esterhazy	528
Allvintzi	1,476
Grenadier battalions:	
Stentsch	613
Persch	600
Total:	*5,126*
Division Lt-Gen Frelich	
Grenadier battalions:	
Mercantin	623
Ficquelmont	577
Weber	347
Paar	477
Total:	*2,047*
Division Maj-Gen Lattermann	
Infantry regiments:	
Thurn	1,948
Reisky	1,611
Nádasdy	2,629
Total:	*6,188*
Div Lt-Gen Ott	
6th Banal Croats	888
d'Aspre Jäger (6 coys)	860
Total:	*1,748*
Cavalry:	
Dragoon regiments:	
Karaiczay (on attachment	
with Russians)	935
Levenehr	816
Lobkowitz	827
Kaiser	1,015
Hussar regiments:	
Erzherzog Joseph	1,430
5th	260
7th	1,002
Cavalry Total:	*6,285*

Austrian Totals:
29 bn, 9 coys, 42 sq; 18,855 infantry, 6,285 cavalry
Austrian Grand Total: *28,128,*
with unknown number of gunners in addition

Detachment under Maj-Gen Hohenzollern
  Infantry regiments:
    Gyulai   1,304
    Fürstenberg   1,624
  6th Hussar regiment: 782
    Total: *3,710*

Allied Totals:
37,796 infantry, 9,997 cavalry, 1,304 Russian gunners
Allied Grand Total: *49,097*
with an unknown number of Austrian gunners and technicians to be added. Austrian reinforcements amounting to 12,000 men were on the march from the Army of the Tyrol.

FRENCH ARMY
UNDER *GÉNÉRAL DE DIVISION* SCHÉRER

Division Richard, brigades Vignes and Gardanne
  Line demi-brigades:

5th	1,940
14th	1,950
3rd	1,000
45th	1,800
Polish volunteers:	780
Cavalry:	1,900
Artillery:	120
Total:	*9,490*

Division Victor, brigades Pigeon and Chamberlac
  Line demi-brigades

56th	1,900
92nd	1,870
99th	1,800
1st Helvetic Legion:	800
1st Polish Legion;	700
Cavalry:	1,000
Artillery:	120
Total:	*8,190*

Division Hatry, brigade Fresia
  Line demi-brigades

21st	900
33rd	1,900
63rd	1,700
3rd Piedmontese	900
Cavalry:	800
Artillery:	60
Total:	*6,260*

Division Delmas, brigades Grandjean and Dalesme
  Line demi-brigades:

26th	1,600
31st	1,736
93rd	1,850
Grenadiers:	600
Cavalry:	1,800
Artillery;	120
Total:	*7,706*

Division Sérurier, brigade Meyer
  Light demi-brigades

18th	1,967
29th	1,450
30th	1,950
1st	940
Grenadiers:	180
Cavalry:	850
Artillery:	60
Total:	*7,397*

Division Grenier, brigades Quesnel and Kister
  Light demi-brigades:

17th	1,483
24th	1,800
106th	1,920
2nd Helvetic Legion;	800
2nd Polish Legion:	800
Cavalry:	450
Artillery:	120
Total:	*7,373*

French Totals:
38,966 infantry, 6,809 cavalry, 600 gunners
French Grand Total: *46,466*

Suvorov had finally to take account of the terrain of the theatre of war, where a variety of natural and artificial features turned to the advantage of the defensive. With the exception of the Adige, all the watercourses on the scene of operations were tributaries of the Po. That river flowed north from the Maritime Alps Maritimes, then trended east across the north Italian plain to reach the Adriatic south of Venice. The lowest permanent bridge spanning the Po stood well upstream at Turin, and down river the water could be crossed only by ferries or whatever bridges of boats were built in the course of the campaign.

The river lines combined with fortresses to heap up obstacles around the allies. The French had abandoned the open banks of the Mincio, but they still held Peschiera at its exit from Lake

Garda and Mantua downstream. Out on the allies' left rear the French held garrisons south of the Po at Ferrara and Fort Urbano, which compelled the Austrians to detach a corps of observation to Rovigo in the lower Polesine.

The fortresses clustered still more thickly where the great plain narrowed to the west between the Alps and the Apennines. The citadels of Brescia and Bergamo stood guard under the Alps on the northern flank of the avenue to Milan. The long winding Adda with the fortress of Pizzighettone offered the French a continuous defensive line in front of the city, and Milan itself was guarded by a bastioned rampart and a bastioned citadel. Any kind of outflanking movement attempted up the right (south) bank of the Po would entail masking of seizing the fortified town of Piacenza, and gaining the narrows at Stradella, where the Apennines advanced almost to the Po.

Behind Milan again the fortresses of Piedmont—Alessandria, Turin, Tortona, Ceva and others were all strong and in good repair, and in the hands of the French.

Details of the terrain naturally influenced the conduct of the war at the tactical level, and in ways that were unfamiliar to the Russians. The Taro, Nure, Trebbia, Tanaro, Bormida, Sesia and other south-bank tributaries of the Po were essentially torrents, fed by the waters falling on the nearby Apennines, and the wide, pebble-strewn beds of their lower reaches were liable to flash flooding after heavy downpours upstream. 'In such a state they are certainly wild and dangerous, but it seldom lasts long. They dry out considerably in high summer or in a fine autumn, when you can ride and drive across them almost everywhere.'[19]

On the left (north) bank of the Po, the Oglio, the Adda and the Lambro were meandering lake-fed rivers of more predictable behaviour, though like all the rivers of the north Italian plain they were bordered by high artificial dykes, and flanked by systems of canals.

Almost all of the towns of northern Italy had defensive value, for the fortified and open places alike were surrounded by a sprawl of houses, villas, gardens and vineyards, and the properties were divided by hedges, ditches or walls, 'so that you can travel the whole distance from Gorizia to Turin without having a field of view which extends for as much as a quarter of an hour's journey, and is often limited to one hundred paces. From any distance it is impossible to see a marching column or a body of troops in camp, unless you climb towers or rooftops.'[20]

Deeper into the country the massively-built farmhouse complexes (cassines) required only to be loopholed and barricaded to become fortresses in their own right. The low ground in northern Italy was more heavily wooded than it is now, and the only open plains of any extent were to be found at Marengo, Castiglione della Stiviera and Campo Aviano (the future air base). Cavalry and artillery could therefore act only at short range and in penny packets on the level ground, and they experienced greater difficulties still on the heights:

> As outcrops of the Alps and Apennines, whose summits are covered in perpetual snow, their slopes are short but very steep. You encounter very few of the broad, wave-like hills you see in Germany; instead they seemed to have chopped-off ends with sharp edges, and along their saw-toothed summits the highest peaks are either bare rock, or have a thin covering of earth which supports a poor vegetation of trees, bushes or moss; the lower slopes are planted with vines, olives and fruit trees, but here too the gradient is very steep. It follows that the paths over the top are extremely difficult… and that the water is shed so easily and rapidly that the hills are very arid, and thus a force placed on the top is likely to go thirsty. A further corollary is that infantry are the only sort of troops you can employ in operations in these mountains.[21]

Bonaparte had assessed all of this accurately in 1796, and he had at his disposal infantry who had been schooled in fighting in the Alps and in the close-set country of the Vendée:

> In this connection [comments Stutterheim] I must mention that in those earlier campaigns hard experience taught our [Austrian] infantry to fight as small groups and in open and mutually-supporting ranks, and that many officers of the army acquired… a complete understanding of the kleine Krieg—both of

them prerequisites for fighting in Italy. Conversely very many of the troops of the old French army had embarked with Bonaparte for Egypt, and the newcomers from Germany could not at once get their bearings in Italy. I mention this circumstance because it told very much to the advantage of the Austrian army, and contributed greatly to the successful outcome of its operations in Italy.[22]

On 15 April Suvorov assumed command of the joint army at headquarters in Valeggio, and the next day the Austrian generals were presented to him formally. He now received Kray and 'Papa' Melas in a particularly warm way. The nearby Austrian troops then marched for an hour. His eyes never left them once, and he was moved to exclaim: 'They keep magnificent step! Victory! On to victory!'

The last of the green-coated Russian columns entered the Valeggio camp on 19 April, and on the same day Suvorov opened his campaign.

NOTES TO CHAPTER 3

1   Francis to Suvorov, 3 April 1799, Milyutin, 1856-8, I,544-5

2   KA FA Italien 1799 IV 21, 'Extract von einem Schreiben aus Theresopol,, 15 September 1798

3   Gryazev, 1898, 25

4   Denisov, 1874-5, XI,614

5   Milyutin, 1856-8, I,90

6   Intercepted letter in Gachot, 1903, 16-17

7   Giralamo Cavazzocca, in Fasanari, 1952, 27-8

8   Anon., 1801-3, IV,26

9   Ibid., IV,17

10   Gachot, 1903, 91

11   Anon., 1801-3, IV,346-7

12   KA FA Italien 1799 XIII 1, Chasteler's Journal

13   Hüffer, 1900-1, I,176

14   Milyutin, 1856-8, I,208

15   Masson, 1859, 335

16   'Ratnik,' 1844, No. 7, 42

17   Ibid.., No. 7, 44

18   Gachot, 1903, 32

19   Stutterheim, 1812, I,iii),15

20   Ibid., I,iii),15

21   Ibid., I,iii),17

22   Ibid., I,iii)18

Field Conference between Chasteler, Suvorov, and Melas

Austrian fusilier and Russian musketeers on the attack

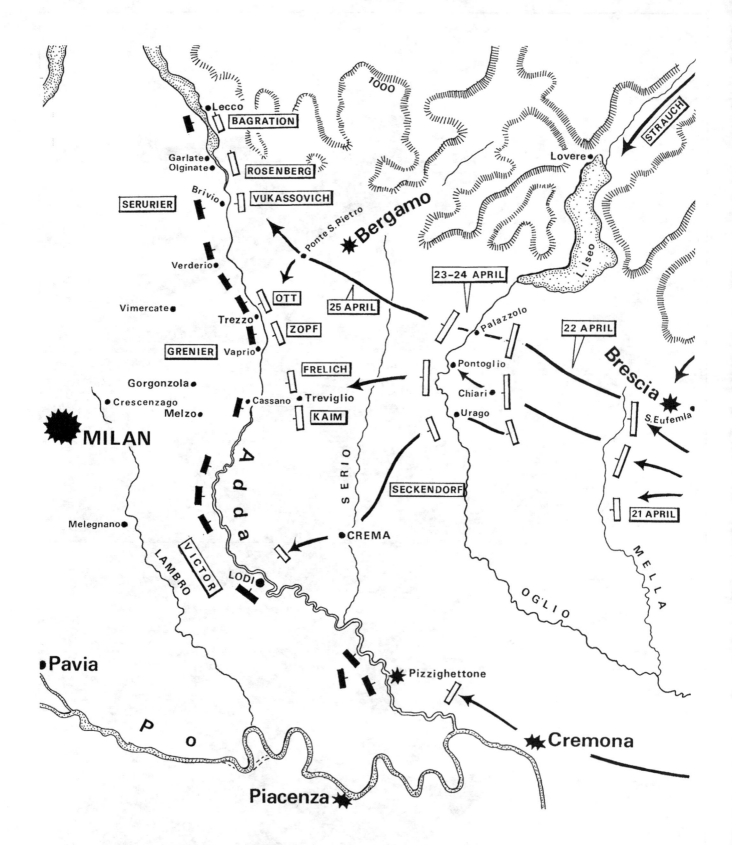

FROM THE MINCIO

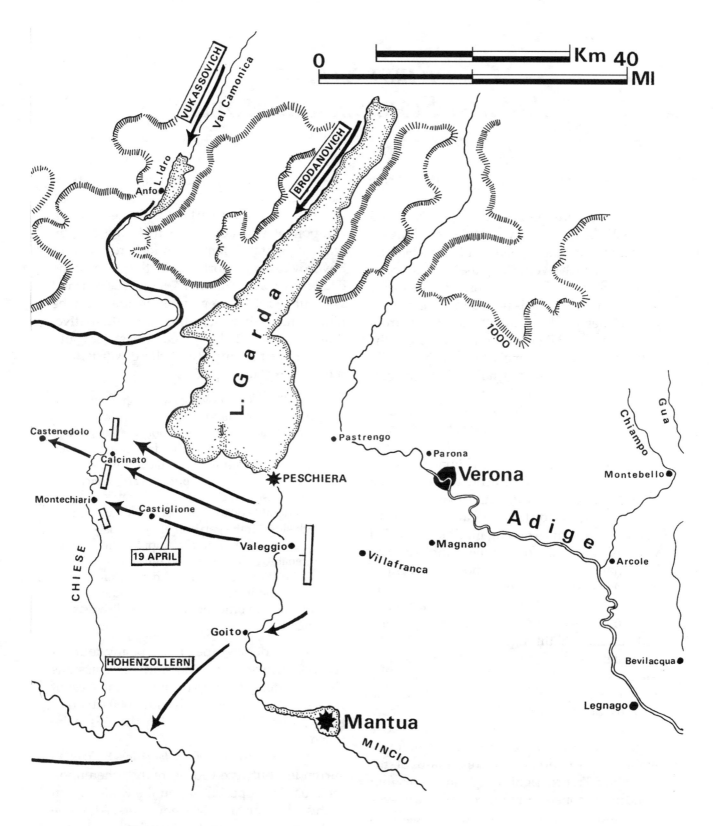

VUKASSOVICH

Val Camonica

BRODANOVICH

L. Idro

Anfo

L. Garda

1000

Km 40

0

MI

Castenedolo

Calcinato

PESCHIERA

Pastrengo

Parona

Verona

Montechiari

Castiglione

19 APRIL

Magnano

Villafranca

Valeggio

Chiampo

Gua

Montebello

A d i g e

Arcole

CHIESE

Goito

HOHENZOLLERN

Bevilacqua

Legnago

Mantua

MINCIO

TO THE ADDA

4

FIRST STRIKE
AGAINST SCHÉRER AND MOREAU

BRESCIA, PALAZZOLO AND BERGAMO, 19-25 APRIL

When Schérer put his trust in dispersal and static obstacles, Suvorov staked everything on concentration and speed, and launched an offensive which swept along the northern edge of the plain under the Alps. His vigorous advance along this axis forced the rivers along their upper reaches, cut off the French from Switzerland and their strongholds, and met the requirement from Francis to keep in contact with the Austrian forces in the Tyrol and Grisons.

On 19 April the Austro-Russian forces made their first general advance. Kray combined Bagration's Russians and the Austrian division of Ott into a joint advance guard, and strode ahead to Castenedolo, just ten kilometres short of Brescia. The rest of the army was echeloned away to the left, in the direction of Montichiari.

The army was on the move again on the 21st. There was an embarrassing muddle on the left wing of the main force, where the Austrian lieutenant-general Kaim and the recently-arrived Lieutenant-General Schveikovsky were making for the bridges over the Mella stream. The Austrians were disgruntled at the long and difficult march through the rain, while the Russians lost their way completely. General Melas blamed Suvorov for subjecting the Austrians to this ordeal, and the field-marshal had to be restrained by Chasteler from responding in unacceptable terms (see above page 23). In spite of everything the joint forces managed to overhaul the rearguard of the retreating French right wing, and took four hundred prisoners: 'Strange consequence of the Revolution! That the inhabitants of the banks of the Seine and the Volga should meet for purposes of mutual destruction on those of the Po.'[1]

On the same day Kray's Austro-Russian advance guard of 11,000 troops was enveloping the town of Brescia, which sprawled up from the plain towards the Alpine foothills. Lieutenant-General Karl Ott with the Austrian component was advancing from the east by way of Santa Eufemia, under orders from Suvorov to make short work of the place: 'If the citadel rejects the summons, it must be stormed without delay and everyone inside must be killed with the bayonet—there is no alternative, if more lives are to be spared.' Chasteler could not conceal his surprise at these words, and Suvorov explained that

> according to your own description the walls of Brescia are feeble, and the citadel is in a very bad state and poorly provisioned. Now, if the enemy put up a defence, and we consent to an honourable capitulation, it means that the enemy will try to hold out in every wretched blockhouse, which will not only cause considerable delay, but cost a lot of men on both sides. If the garrison of Brescia is massacred, they won't attempt to defend those untenable little places, and time and blood will be saved. That's what I did at Praga [1794], and it resulted in the surrender of Warsaw and brought the whole Polish war to an end.[2]

So as to deprive the French of any route of escape, Prince Bagration and his Russians simultaneously took up position to the west of Brescia, while Vukassovich with 7,000 Austrian troops from the Tyrol arrived on the hills to the north.

Ott summoned *chef de bataillon* Bouzet to surrender, but received no reply, whereupon the Austrians opened fire on the walled town with six cannon and eight howitzers. After one and a half hours of fire the Austrian battalion of Nádasdy advanced towards the eastern gate, a move which persuaded the French to retreat towards the lofty citadel. The townspeople let down the bridge at Ott's appeal, whereupon the Austrians entered the gate with flying colours and sounding music, and moved through the town to join Bagration's Russians, who had been admitted on the far side. The sound of chopping indicated that the citizens were cutting down the Trees of Liberty, while crashing and tumult showed where the houses of the French supporters were being ransacked.

Bouzet made a show of defiance by cannonading the town from the citadel, then tried to bargain for a free evacuation for the French. Kray was present in person, 'and showed them the ladders he had ready for his brave Hungarians to storm the citadel, in the case of a refusal. This induced the commandant and… his troops in the citadel to give up.'[3] That was at four in the afternoon. The allies took the 1,128 as prisoners of war, and inside the citadel they found forty cannon, eighteen mortars and 480 hundredweight of gunpowder.

The news of the capture of Brescia reached Paul at Pavlovsk on 16 May. It was a small enough episode, in all conscience, but it was the first victory in which the Russians had had a part, and Paul at once held a service of thanksgiving in the court chapel:

> The son of the field-marshal, Count Arkady Aleksandrovich Suvorov, was also present at this service, and when he heard the name of his father he was so moved that he threw himself to his knees in front of the Emperor, and kissed his hand. His tears and feelings prevented him from uttering a word. The Emperor was so touched at this display of childish emotion on the part of the young Suvorov that he called him to his study after the service, and told him: 'I applaud your attachment to your father. Go to him, and form yourself into a warrior under his guidance. He is the best of models and I could not commit you to more reliable hands.'[4]

Congratulations, decorations, bounties and promotions were showered on the Russian advance guard, and Bagration was awarded with the Order of St. Anna First Class and advanced to major-general out of turn (much to the disgruntlement of Colonel Denisov).

Meanwhile events in Italy had been unfolding at a furious rate. Kray records that moments after the French surrendered at Brescia 'Major-General Chasteler… wrote me a letter in which he said that the field-marshal was ordering me to set off with all the troops I could collect, and find and attack the enemy—not the kind of order to be expected from a great commander. If you are to seek out the enemy you must first send out fighting patrols and make due plans.'[5] Suvorov quickly changed his mind, and instead assigned Kray with 23,000 of the Austrians to blockade the Mincio fortresses of Peschiera and Mantua—it was a large but inevitable diversion of force, since the two places were now well to the rear of the allied army, and Suvorov could not risk leaving their garrisons uncontained.

For the main army the task in hand for 22 April was to catch and destroy the French before they could escape across the Oglio. The allies' total frontage amounted to seventy-five kilometres, if we take in the detachments of Major-General Seckendorf and Lieutenant-General Hohenzollern advancing out to the left on Crema and Pizzighettone respectively, and the command of Colonel Strauch in the far north, which had descended from the Tyrol down the Val Camonica to the head of Lake Iseo at Lovere, thus threatening the French left flank with a deep envelopment.

All the rest of the army was concentrated in Suvorovian style against a twelve-kilometre stretch of the upper Oglio—the Austrian divisions of Frelich and Kaim on the left against Pontoglio, and the divisions of Ott and Zopf, the brigade of Vukassovich and the combined Russians on the right against Palazzolo on the main road to Bergamo.

Suvorov explained his intentions in a few rushed phrases. Even after Kray had been detached Suvorov still had 30,000 Austrians and 20,000 Russians at his disposal, and he was thinking beyond the forcing of the Oglio to that of the Adda, and so to the capture of Milan, the passing of the Ticino and the entry to Piedmont. 'We must get used to marching just as energetically through the night as in daytime— to God all hours are the same. If my carriage can drive over the worst paths and in pitch darkness, it means that the whole of the artillery can do likewise.'[6]

This was all very fine, but Schérer was already slipping across the Oglio, and the Russians had a way of going to pieces when they were in a hurry.[7] As commander of the advance guard of the right-hand force Bagration was over-eager to perform a dashing feat of arms, and he threw his troops against the rearguard of the division of Sérurier, which was still holding the bridge at Palazzolo.

Advancing in dense masses, the Russian infantry were shot up by the French concealed in the houses and gardens on the near bank of the Oglio, and taken under fire by French guns emplaced on high ground on the far side. The Austrian artillery major Friedrich Schimpf brought up a number of Austrian and Russian batteries and drove the enemy gunners away, but the Russian lieutenant-general Schveikovsky halted his division at the reports of the combat, and just came up in person to discover what was going on. The action ended with the French scampering over the half-demolished bridge, blowing up what was left, and making good their escape. The Russians had lost 227 men killed or wounded, and Suvorov turned on Schveikovsky: 'You should have been duty bound, Jakov Ivanovich, to continue with the whole column and go straight into action. Instead, you brought the column to a halt, and appeared with just a penny packet of your troops on the scene of the fighting.'[8]

In the course of 23 April the allies repaired the bridges over the Oglio, and began to march across the sodden plain towards the Adda, arriving in dribs and drabs within two kilometres of that river on the 25th. The only action of note was staged on the 24th, when a body of Cossacks burst into Bergamo simultaneously with the French rearguard, and seized the citadel and town almost without opposition.

This was the doing of Colonel Adrian Karpovich Denisov and one thousand of his Don Cossacks. The Austrian general Ott had refused to admit him into his corps, because Denisov could show him no written order to this effect, and so the Cossacks ranged ahead on their own authority. Denisov espied a column of French infantry, with 150 cavalry and six pieces (the French rearguard) marching along the excellent road which led along the foot of the mountains, and he sent out Colonel Grekov with his regiment to lunge against the line of retreat, with the hope of panicking the French into breaking formation. Both the enemy and Grekov disappeared from Denisov's view behind a wood of tall old trees, where the road described a sharp bend, but Cossack war cries and the sound of heavy firing soon carried to his ears:

> I hastened up with my regiment, and saw that just beyond the wood there was a walled town [Bergamo] where the last regiment of French was engaged with the Grekov regiment— hence the shooting and the cries. I was at first taken aback by this unexpected encounter, but I ordered my regiment to divide in two, and gallop around the town yelling, so as to alarm the enemy still further. I myself hastened to the town, where I found the [Grekov] regiment rushing at the enemy like lions and skewering them with their lances as they crowded into the streets. The most useful thing I could do was to join the heroic Grekov, and encourage the Cossacks by crying out: 'Keep on, dear comrades, keep on!' It seemed that for every Cossack in pursuit there were one hundred French who were being hunted down, for only one of my regiments was in action. The French did not even think of turning about, but instead fled through the town from one end to the other, and erupted from the far side. [9]

The prizes amounted to 130 prisoners and nineteen pieces of artillery. Suvorov arrived at night on horseback, soaked and covered with mud, and congratulated Denisov and Colonel Grekov on their brilliant coup de main.

THE FORCING OF THE ADDA, 26-28 APRIL

Schérer had just 27-28,000 troops at his disposal, and he chose to string them along the Adda on a frontage of 115 kilometres. His three corps each comprised ten battalions and three regiments of horse, and Schérer deployed:

Sérurier's corps on the left flank on the upper Adda, from Lecco downstream,

Grenier's corps in the centre in the neighbourhood of Trezzo and Vaprio, and Victor's corps in an extended series of posts on the right flank downstream from Cassano.

The arrangement made little sense in tactical terms, but Schérer was just hoping to hold off the allies long enough for reinforcements to arrive from Switzerland, Tuscany and Naples, and to allay the tumult in Milan in his rear, where the nobles, priests and leading citizens were fomenting unrest against the Cisalpine Republic.

All of this demanded time, and Suvorov was not the person to allow his opponents the

THE REPULSE AT LECCO, 26 APRIL

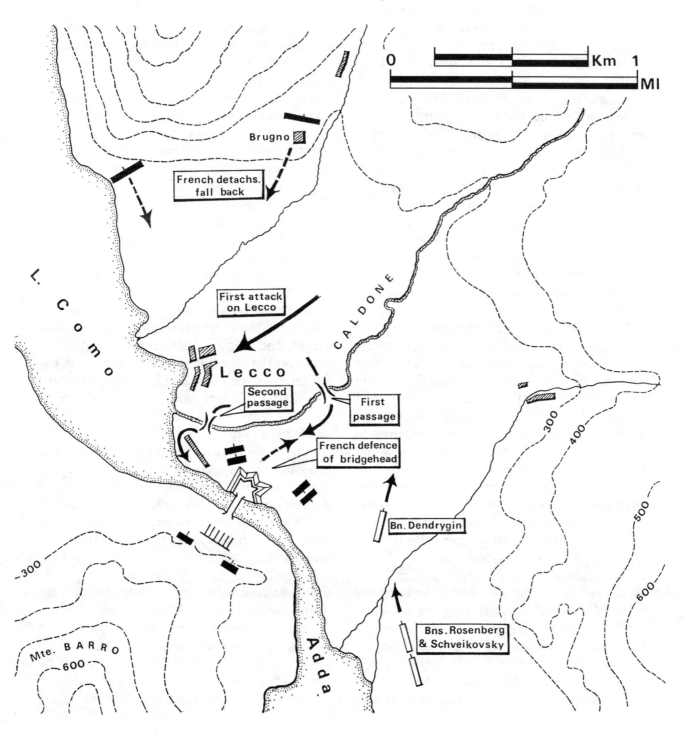

necessary respite. True to his practice of concentrating his forces against the French mountain flank, he intended to throw the Russian contingent against the extreme left or northern flank of the French positions in the neighbourhood of Lecco, where the long south-eastern branch of Lake Como narrowed into the channel of the Adda in a zone of lakes and swamps.

Bagration took the lead with the Russian advance guard (Jäger regiment Bagration, grenadier battalion Lomonosov, Cossack regiments Denisov, Grekov, Molchanov—about 3,000 troops in all). He climbed along the slopes of the mountains which overlooked the Adige valley, crossed the Caldone torrent upstream, and at eight in the morning of 26 April descended the hillside paths towards the densely-packed little town of Lecco. It is curious that he did not stop short of the Caldone and turn at once against the only objective of military worth— the French bridgehead on the Adda, which lay to the south of Lecco—but perhaps he hoped to take the French by surprised by cutting in against the fortification from the north.

The Lecco position was held by *chef de brigade* Soyez with his 108th demi-brigade. The French pulled in their outlying detachments with speed, and skirmished against the advancing Russians among the rocks, gardens and vineyards in front of Lecco, then put up another fight inside the town itself, and finally made a determined stand behind the Caldone. The Russians forced a first passage upstream by a bridge opposite the Villa Manzone, but they were checked before they made much progress towards the bridgehead. They had more luck when they stormed a bridge over the Caldone some nine hundred metres downstream, and advanced up the left bank of the Adige against the flank of the bridgehead fortification. However Soyez consolidated his companies around the threatened work, and the move of the Russians brought them within easy range of a French gunboat, and of a battery of six pieces which was sited on the far side of the Adda on the lower slopes of Monte Barro. Bagration had dismounted some of his Cossacks to thicken up his firing lines, but he had ventured too far, and

he was thrown back behind the Caldone by a general French counterattack which was given added impetus by a troop of horse which crossed the Adige bridge and pursued the Russians for some distance on the far side of the stream. Bagration had to call on Rosenberg for help.

The main Russian force was meanwhile moving up in columns from behind Ponte San Pietro. Major-General Miloradovich (perhaps mindful of the rebuke to Schveikovsky for having failed Bagration at Palazzolo) piled the grenadier battalion of Dendrygin onto peasant carts, and arrived on the scene at four in the afternoon. The fighting was still in full progress, and since Colonel Bagration was still in effective control Miloradovich sensibly left him in tactical command: 'Now is not the time to argue about rank!' (Bagration's promotion to major-general had not yet come through).

The Russians finally retook Lecco town with the help of two battalions of the regiments of Rosenberg and Baranovsky, which came up as a second batch of reinforcements under Schveikovsky, but the action ended at nine in the evening with the French still in possession of the Adige crossing. The Russians had lost 385 men, and taken no more than one hundred French prisoners. The town was of no account in itself, and no immediate reinforcements could be expected, for the other battalion of the Baranovsky regiment had be halted to guard the Russian artillery, which had stuck at Sala, while Rosenberg's main force was strung out still further behind.

On orders from Suvorov (below) the Russians disengaged from Lecco during the night, and Schveikovsky told Denisov to cover the retreat with his Cossacks. Denisov replied that Cossacks were unsuited to defensive fighting in broken country, and that if they broke under pressure they would endanger the whole force. 'To this he rejoined most pompously that he had not asked for my advice, but only for me to obey his orders.'[10] In the event Denisov dismounted between sixty and eighty of his best men to hold the position on foot. Bagration knew that he had failed in his mission, and he approached Denisov to make sure that their would be no incriminating discrepancies in their reports to Suvorov.

Meanwhile local concentrations and enterprising leaders were winning bridgeheads for the allies on the far side of the Adda further downstream. To Bagration's left the Austrian major-general Vukassovich had found a weak sector in the enemy cordon at Brivio. The accounts of what happened next differ in many details, but it is evident that he used local boats or a partially-demolished French bridge to make his first passage, then fed a force of 3,500 infantry and 150 hussars to the far bank, and sent out parties which encountered the French only at Olginate and Garlate. Here was a bridgehead worth exploiting. The news reached Chasteler and a delighted Suvorov in the evening. They sent pontoons in that direction to make a respectable crossing, and ordered the Russians at Lecco to leave a screen to contain the French in that part of the world, and march with the rest of their forces to Brivio.

On the same dark and windy evening Suvorov built up his main concentration of force on the central axis at San Gervasio, where the division of Ott was screened by 8,000 of Rosenberg's Russians and the Austrian division of Zopf. At ten at night Ott's leading troops and two regiments of Cossacks arrived to support the Austrian colonel d'Aspre and his six companies of Jäger, who were holding San Gervasio, above the valley of the Adda. Major-General Chasteler consulted d'Aspre about the best place to throw a bridge, and the two of them made their way stealthily across the valley to the suggested location opposite Trezzo, where the 59-metre wide river, now high with melt water, raced between rocky banks, and where the French were present in strength on the far side.

The expected convoy of pontoons arrived at eleven at night, 'and since the officer in charge said that the bends in the road were too acute to allow the pontoons to be driven as far as the bank, I [Chasteler] replied that we would have to manhandle them the rest of the way, and that there was no shortage of labour in the army.' Three hundred of the Jäger and one battalion of Banater Croats were ordered to pile their muskets and get to work, and Chasteler

'remarked to Colonel d'Aspre and the commanding major Paulich that it would encourage the men no end if the three of us—a general and two senior regimental officers—lent a hand, instead of just standing by to give orders and watch. Without further ado we threw our swords aside, seized hold of the nearest pontoon, and managed to manoeuvre it on its cart to the water's edge. The rest were brought down in the same way, and we then set about casting the bridge across the river.' [11]

The work on the bridge was screened by a first party of fifty volunteers from the Jäger and another fifty from the infantry, who passed the river on the pontoons and a small craft which Chasteler had discovered in San Gervasio. Chasteler reinforced the bridgehead successively by the rest of the Jäger, and planted three batteries of 24-pounders in support on the near bank on the heights of San Gervasio. The French in Trezzo showed no signs of life, which was just as well, because the pontoon anchors refused to bite on the rocky river bed, and it proved difficult to tether the pontoons securely to the only available fastening points—the trees on the near bank and the rocks on the far side. The allies knew moments of near-despair, but the water level began to subside, and at four in the morning the bridge was complete.

D'Aspre's Jäger and one battalion of the regiment of Nádasdy swarmed up the far bank, seized Trezzo from the sleepy and unsuspecting French outpost, and opened the way for the rest of Ott's advance guard to progress in brilliant sunshine down the right bank towards Vaprio.

By the morning of 27 April, therefore, the allies had broken across the Adda at two points—upriver to the north at Brivio near Lecco, and towards the centre at Trezzo. For the French the task of throwing the Austrians and Russians back fell not upon the broken Schérer, but on his former second in command, Jean-Victor Moreau (1763-1813). Whereas Schérer was something of a soldier of fortune, rumoured to be over-fond of the bottle, Moreau was an ardent republican, who was reserved in his manner, but decisive in action and respected by his troops. When news of the change in command reached Suvorov he remarked: 'Here too I can see the hand of

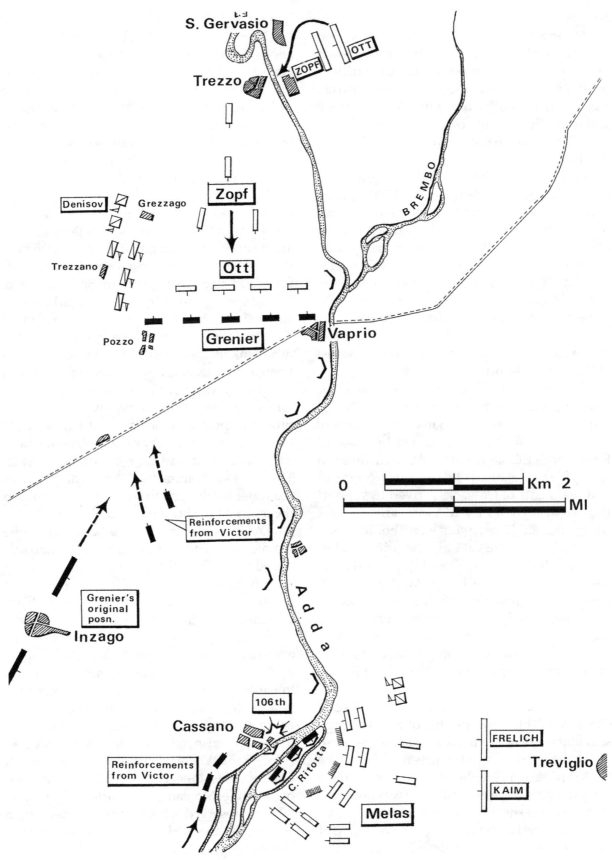

ACTIONS AT VAPRIO AND CASSANO, 27 APRIL

Providence. There would have been no great glory in fighting it out with a charlatan. But to beat Moreau—that would be something worth doing.'[12]

At nine in the morning Moreau ordered his unengaged divisions to move against the crossing at Trezzo—Grenier from Inzago, and Victor from the lower Adda, while Sérurier stood his ground as best he could. The leading Austrian forces were emerging from the Adda hollow—d'Aspre and his six companies of Jäger, a number of sotnias of Cossacks, the main body of Ott's division (making the passage of the pontoon bridge battalion by battalion)—and the Cossack regiments of Denisov, Molchanov and Grekov, which had moved down at speed from Lecco.

The advantage of concentration now lay with the French, for the allies were inevitably strung out, whereas Grenier was able to unite with Sérurier's troops falling back from Trezzo, and so a bitterly-fought encounter battle now developed on the fields between Trezzo, Vaprio and Pozzo. This ground on the immediate approaches to Milan had been the scene of battles by Frederick Barbarossa in 1158 and

between the Austrians and French in 1705, and now Sérurier and Grenier were holding excellent defensive terrain: 'the village [Vaprio] itself was very advantageous for the enemy infantry. The neighbourhood was close country and mostly planted with vines, while the highway from Milan had on either side high banks built up with stones collected from the fields, like a natural parapet. The enemy posted themselves behind it, and took a heavy toll of our brave infantry as they advanced.'[13]

On the allied side the rearward Austrian division of Zopf was now making its passage of the river, and Chasteler extracted two grenadier battalions and the regiment of Mittrowsky to help the leading division (Ott's), which was now under heavy pressure, while Moreau brought up his own rearward brigades of Quesnel and Kister respectively to the right and left of Grenier's leading troops. A new allied push was turned back late in the morning, and with the balance of reinforcements turning in favour of the French, the Chasseurs were able to annihilate the Austrian grenadier battalion of Stentsch, and Moreau deployed fresh troops from Victor to turn the Austrian right flank.

A number of French battalions were already wheeling to deliver the coup de grace when they in turn were taken in flank by Lieutenant-Colonel Hertelendy and Major Dobay with four squadrons of the Erzherzog Joseph Hussars. The intervening ground was littered with garden walls and heaps of stones, but the hussars were determined to seize the opportunity: 'The enemy maintained their composure, and delivered a volley which toppled many of our brave Hungarians from the saddle. But our hussars were among them before they could fire a second time, and a bloody massacre ensued.'[14] This intervention proved to be decisive. Driven from Pozzo, Moreau tried to get his troops to make a stand at Vaprio in the hope of receiving support from the main body of Victor, but he was overcome by the tide of fleeing humanity.

Colonel Denisov and his Cossacks had been the only Russian troops present on this central sector, and they had been working around the French left flank. 'The Austrians were fighting bravely, and the French every bit as bravely.

Moreau

65

Neither army could be seen, on account of the dense woods, but they must have been engaged close by, since every now and then the bullets carried to us.'[15] Having arrived in the French rear, the Cossacks had taken four hundred prisoners before Suvorov arrived virtually unescorted, and ordered them to carry on with the pursuit. 'He added that he would join in, but I absolutely refused, despite his repeated representations. I told him that he would be in immediate and extreme danger, and my argument was emphasised by the fact that two or three balls from the battling infantry flew over his head.' [16]

By this time the French were also being pressed by Austrian reinforcements debouching from the second allied crossing in the central sector, which was ten kilometres downstream from Trezzo at Cassano. The odds here were overwhelmingly against the French, even after the 106th demi-brigade was reinforced from the corps of Victor, for they confronted Melas and the two Austrian divisions of Kaim and Frelich. However the 106th had an outer defence in the form of a bridgehead fortification on the left (eastern) bank of the Adda, and this in turn was covered by the outlying Canale Ritorto.

For most of the day Melas had contented himself with cannonading the French works until, under pressure from Suvorov, his pioneers braved heavy fire to make a trestle bridge across the canal. Once the passage was complete, the regiment of Reisky doubled across with such speed that the French at once abandoned the bridgehead along with three pieces, and did not have the time to set fire to the combustible materials which they had heaped upon on the Adda bridge behind. The main Austrian force now crossed the intact bridge, and encountered little more than a token resistance on the far side, for Ott, Zopf and the Russians had already broken through further to the north in the way already described.

Suvorov rode from one victorious unit to the next, urging the men on to final efforts. Discovering the second battalion of the Austrian regiment of Esterhazy resting at a halt, he called out: 'Bayonets! On with the advance!' Colonel d'Aspre protested that the men had been on the march for fifty hours, and were totally spent, at which Suvorov answered: 'Well, I still have my Russians—I know that *they* will be after the enemy!' The action ended at about six in the evening of 27 April, by when the French were breaking apart. Moreau and the division of Grenier—what we might call the 'central' force—found that the allies had both severed the communication with Sérurier to the north at Vaprio, and barred the direct path of retreat to Milan by way of Gorgonzola. Moreau therefore made a roundabout march south and west via Melzo and Lambriote, marched through Milan, and out again by the Vercelli Gate, having left a garrison of about 2,500 troops in the citadel. The retreat went on without a halt through the 28th, and it ended only when Moreau crossed the Ticino to the west of Milan and encamped on the far side.

It was high time for the outlying French forces to make their escape. On the lower Adda a detachment under Laboissière destroyed the bridge at Lodi, then joined the main force of Victor's division to reach the temporary refuge of the Ticino by way of Melegnano and Pavia. Up in the north Soyez blew up twenty-one arches of the bridge at Lecco, requisitioned a number of boats, and made his way to the far side of Lake Como at Menaggio.

Sérurier had been left in the lurch when all the rest of the French retreated from the Adda, but in accordance with the last orders received from Moreau he was still standing between Trezzo and Brivio. While waiting (in vain) for further instructions he entrenched himself overnight on 27/28 April in an extremely strong position. His right wing extended to the steep and flooded Adige valley east of Paderno, while the left rested on Verderio, which stood where the ground began to rise from the north Italian plain, and which he now fortified by earthworks for all-round defence. He commanded 2,600 men by his own account, but more than 3,700 according to Vukassovich, and well over 4,000 according to the Russians.

Jean Mathieu Philibert Sérurier (1742-1819) was a formidable object in his own right. He was a professional officer of the old school, born to the minor country nobility and owning a record

66

of service which went back to the Seven Years War. He is usually depicted behatted and standing ramrod-straight.

We left the Austrian major-general Vukassovich on the upper Adda at Brivio, where the French cordon had first broken. He set off for Milan according to orders early on 28 April, probably expecting to take part in an unresisted pursuit, but in the course of his march he was surprised to learn that the division of Sérurier was barring his way in an entrenched position. Thereafter the accounts vary considerably in detail, but according to the original relation of Vukassovich he divided his brigade into three columns—that of Colonel Charles Rohan with one battalion, one squadron of hussars and two hundred Posdeev Cossacks advancing by way of Paderno against the French right flank on the Adige inundation; Colonel Brodanovich marching with two battalions by way of Osnago

SÉRURIER

against the French left; Vukassovich in person with the rest of the brigade executing a wide right-flanking move to Vimercate in the path of any French retreat.

The Austrian columns converged against the French position at 4.30 in the afternoon of the 28th, and the action soon became general and uncommonly fierce. While Vukassovich fed the infantry of both wings into the fighting on his left, or eastern, flank near Paderno, the superior French cavalry inflicted heavy losses on the unsupported Austrian hussars in the centre. Vukassovich relates that

> both sides were fighting with desperate determination. I began to think that I would have to abandon my mission, since my steadfast and brave troops were exhausted and being thinned out by casualties. I was about to apply to the Russian general Rosenberg for help when the enemy divisional commander sent a staff officer to me with proposals for a negotiated surrender. I at first declared that the enemy must yield unconditionally, but the continuing pleas of the Frenchman and the exhaustion of my own troops induced me to give way. I was asked to show particular regard for the enemy general Sérurier, because he had extended the same to old Field-Marshal Count Wurmser [after the capitulation of Mantua in 1797]. I replied that the word of an Imperial general would have to satisfy him, and that he would be in good hands… hostages were duly exchanged, and a capitulation… was drawn up.[17]

We should add that darkness was falling, the French were out of ammunition, and the Austrian assault by separate columns (a favourite tactic since 1758) had convinced Sérurier that the odds were against him.

When Vukassovich enumerated his prisoners he found that they amounted to two divisional generals (Sérurier and his cavalry commander Fresia), 241 other officers, 3,487 NCOs and men and 151 non-combatants, along with five cannon. The Austrians agreed to allow Sérurier and his officers to return to France under parole: 'This latter condition was a mark of respect shown to the bravery of old General Sérurier, and to the probity of his conduct. It is known that preserving under the Republican standard that sense of honour which had raised him to the rank of lieutenant-colonel under the old government, he kept himself so pure in the midst of the extortions committed by the other generals, that he was called the "Virgin of the Army."'[18]

Shortly afterwards Suvorov invited Sérurier to dinner, but found that his guest was not to be drawn on the subject of the French plans. The field-marshal expressed his surprise that a man of such worth should be serving the Republic, to which Sérurier replied that 'my father, in giving me my sword, expressly ordered me to use it only to defend my country.'[19]

The French had been broken into so many fragments during the fighting on the Adda that no consensus emerges as to their losses between 26 and 28 April. Moreau's figure of 2,542 is probably too low, even if we assume that it excludes the command of Sérurier, which had been captured whole. Chasteler estimated that the French had lost 2,000 men prisoner and 3,000 casualties. The staff officer MacDermott postulates 5,000 prisoners and more than 3,000 casualties, which is the highest of the Austrian calculations, but corresponds closely with a French list found later in the citadel of Alessandria which pitched the French losses at about 6,900, including the prisoners at Verderio.[20]

According to Chasteler the Austrians and Russians had 761 men killed, 2,913 wounded, and 1,212 taken prisoner. About 2,750 of these losses, or well over half, were sustained in the battle of Vukassovich against Sérurier.

The victory on the Adda broke the French forces in northern Italy, doomed their puppet Cisalpine Republic and opened the way to the liberation of Piedmont. As regards the management of the battle on the French side, it is difficult to dissent from the judgement of Moreau in his report to the Directory, in which he pointed out that Schérer had teased out the army along an immense length, and that he himself had taken command 'without knowing how the army was placed, and at a time when the line was already broken—a fact which was not known at headquarters.'[21]

Suvorov had effected a decisive

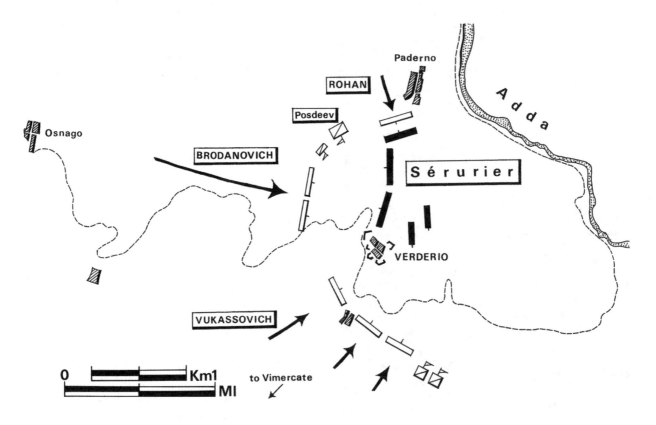

ACTION AT VERDERIO, 28 APRIL

68

concentration of force on the upper Adda, He had been up with the foremost troops to urge them on, and, having learned that Bagration had failed at Lecco, he had the mental agility to recall the forces which had been committed in that direction and feed them across the Adda further downstream, where the allies were having more luck. On the far side of the river much of the tactical detail was managed by Chasteler, whose example 'may encourage military men who are short-sighted not to despair of being useful and of advancing in their military career. Few people labour under this disadvantage to a greater degree than himself; but making greater use of glasses and spectacles which he always wears in battle, he has ever found himself capable of seeing everything as well as doing everything.' [22]

The Russians might criticise Melas for being so slow in front of Cassano, just as the Austrians could point to the fact that the Russians, despite all of Suvorov's talk of the bayonet, shot off vast quantities of cartridges without resorting to cold steel,[23] but the action as a whole stood as a joint victory of a model kind. Suvorov was typically generous in his report to Vienna, and recommended Melas, Vukassovich, d'Aspre and Chasteler for decorations or promotions. The delighted Emperor Francis awarded Chasteler the Commander's Cross of the Military Order of Maria Theresa, and made Vukassovich colonel proprietor of a regiment of infantry.

Major Rumyantsev carried the news of the victory to St. Petersburg. In reply Paul sent Suvorov a diamond ring bearing the Imperial likeness in a tiny portrait: 'take it as a sign of your great deeds—wear it on your hand, the same hand that has laid low the enemy of all that is to the good of society.'[24]

THE LIBERATION OF MILAN, 29 APRIL

Milan was the capital of Austrian Lombardy, about to return to its lawful sovereign, and for the Austrians the first priority was to arrive there before the marauding Russians arrived in strength. Colonel Denisov, by his own account, learned that one of his patrols had arrived in front of the city and encountered a friendly reception from the people on the ramparts. Denisov brought up the rest of his Cossacks, who even now seemed totally inadequate to take over the place, which was now thronged with people celebrating the end of Lent, 'but I called to mind that Russian glory had not been attained without great deeds, and I had a further incentive because I knew that the Austrian army was very close.'[25]

Denisov negotiated with a person he describes as 'the president of the city,' and once they had reached an agreement he sent two of his regiments around the outside of Milan to invest the citadel, whither 2,500-odd of the French had repaired. Denisov entered the city with the remainder of his force, and shut one of the far gates in the face of a dense French column which was advancing from the citadel. Denisov was aware that he would be unable to hold his prize without support, and now that he had established his claim to fame he sent word to Melas to ask him to make haste with his army. Denisov also dispatched a message to Suvorov, and he claims that it was only on learning that the Russian field-marshal was on the way that Melas bestirred himself to get the Austrians on the march.

Melas naturally tells a different story. He reported to Vienna how he

brought up the two divisions of Frelich and Kaim with the greatest possible speed (which I ventured against the express order of Field-Marshal Count Suvorov), and owing to this the city of Milan was saved from being totally plundered by the Russian Cossacks. Only an insignificant body of those people were able to hasten ahead of my column. Few though the Cossacks were, their behaviour was so unbridled that when the people came out towards us with outstretched arms on the open road they despoiled them of their clothing, watches and money, and stripped naked everyone they encountered inside the city... they plundered, tore up and threw away the post packets on the highways, and by stealing all the horses from the post stations they made the transmission of correspondence and orders not just difficult, but downright impossible. [26]

That was on 29 April, when the early start of

Melas and the two Austrian divisions enabled them to gain a decisive lead over the main force of the Russians. At Crescenzago the Austrians were greeted by Archbishop Visconti and the leaders of the municipality, who had retrieved the keys from the Cossacks and now presented them to Melas with well-honed eloquence. The head of the Austrian column entered by way of the Porta Orientale, and 'the Imperial troops were received in that populous capital with the same demonstrations of joy they had lavished on the French three years before. The tricoloured flag did not receive more homage than was paid that day to the Imperial eagle. Such is the nature of men whenever their imaginations are struck by any striking change—such especially is that of the people of Italy.' [27]

Almost as an afterthought Melas sent an adjutant back with the keys to Suvorov. The field-marshal was furious to learn that the Austrians had got to Milan before him. He mounted a light horse, and galloped from Vaprio with a pulk of Cossacks, shadowed by several squadrons of Austrian cavalry, which were under orders from Melas to curb the Russian depredations. It was a warm day, and the first of the Easter holiday, and hundreds of prosperous citizens had left Milan in their carriages to join the archbishop, the city fathers and the nobility who were waiting for Suvorov in front of Crescenzago. Suvorov dismounted, walked up to the archbishop and declared that he had been 'sent to restore the ancient throne of the Papacy, and bring back the people to their obedience towards their monarchs. Help me to complete this holy work!' [28] Visconti in his turn compared Suvorov with St. Michael, and told him of the contents of the appropriate pastoral letter that was about to be read in the churches.

Suvorov galloped the rest of the way to the Porta Orientale where, according to Chasteler, he arrived at ten in the morning,

> and found the Austrian troops drawn up in the principal streets and squares. When the coming of the commander in chief was reported to Melas, the Austrian general hastened towards him with lowered sword to report the various measures he had taken. Suvorov did not listen to him, but moved by

spontaneous joy he cuffed him in the head and threw his arms about him. Melas's horse bucked, and because Suvorov held his comrade so fast, Melas could neither control his horse nor keep himself in the saddle. Sliding to the ground he fortunately managed to land on his feet, which drew a general *Eviva!* from the people watching from the windows. Suvorov, with Melas and his suite behind him, hurried along a number of streets until he espied a church with an open door; he sprang from his horse, pressed through the crowd, ran to the high altar and stretched himself in front of it full-length on the floor. After he lay there a few minutes he jumped up, gave a sign of blessing to his suite, ran out of church, remounted, and rode on in the direction of his quarters. He retained his whip in his right hand, while he never ceased extending gestures of benediction left and right to the folk on the streets or looking on from the windows. You must imagine Field-Marshal Suvorov riding a Cossack horse, on which was set a worn-out German riding school saddle with a green shabraque with silken fringes. He wore little boots, with his stockings hanging over them from the knee. His trousers were short, and of a white striped material, fastened loosely under the knee with straps, but left unbuttoned. His shirt was devoid of frills, and puffed up by the air which entered by the open neck; over this he wore an open white house coat with short cuffs. His headgear was a helmet of black leather with a crest of black and gold silk.[29]

For the final stage of the progress to his quarters, in the Palazzo Belgiojoso, Suvorov reined back with Chasteler and two adjutants, secreted himself at the tail of the procession of clergy, and told his cabinet secretary Fuchs to station himself in his splendid diplomatic uniform at the head of the staff at the front of the column. At the sight of the 'field-marshal' the spectators cried out *Eviva Suvorov! Eviva l'imperatore Paulo!* Fuchs played his part to perfection, saluting to either side, and at the palace entrance Suvorov caught up with him and declared: 'Hearty thanks, Egor Borisovich— magnificent, I can't compliment you enough— again, hearty thanks!' [30]

The Austrians and Russians were meanwhile making themselves busy in various ways. From his headquarters in the Palazzo Castiglione, Melas organised a new police and national guard and dismantled the apparatus of the defunct Cisalpine Republic. He was seconded in a disorganised fashion by the people, who broke the windows of the Serbelloni and Bovara palaces, which were associated with French sympathisers. The citizens were astonished to see Russian soldiers hugging and kissing one another in honour of Easter, and alarmed when they themselves were taken in a bear-like embrace. In spite of every precaution parties of Cossacks roamed the streets, plundering churches, demanding wine, snatching jewels from the necks of eminent ladies and raping girls. The main forces of the allies were encamped outside the city, and here the Russian depredations continued almost unchecked.

Suvorov had at first intended to launch the army into a storm of the citadel, and he commissioned Colonel Denisov to draw up an appropriate plan and then put it into execution. On 30 April Denisov and Chasteler ascended to a tall church tower which gave them a good view of the fortifications, and Chasteler concluded that the citadel was so strongly held that the cost of an assault would be altogether prohibitive. Denisov reported as much to Suvorov, and suggested that the field-marshal's glory would be compromised by a failure. 'Hearing this, Suvorov suddenly fastened me with a look, embraced me in a gracious way and said; "Thank you Karpovich," for so he always called me, "you and your Cossacks go with God."' [31]

Suvorov still had to complete the unavoidable round of ceremonies, and on the same day he decked himself out in the white, scarlet and gold of his Austrian field-marshal's uniform, and drove in a gala coach between two lines of troops to the Duomo for the singing of the Te Deum. The archbishop came out to greet him at the entrance to the cathedral, and Suvorov replied 'Pray God to help me in the work of restoring thrones and altars!' Suvorov bowed when he entered the great church, in which there was scarcely room to stand, and proceeded down the nave through the forest of pillars,

though he declined to take the place of honour which had been prepared for him beneath a red and gold baldachino.

Back in his quarters Suvorov invited the Austrian generals to dine with him, together with the captured enemy commanders Sérurier and Fresia, to whom he pronounced the salutation of the Orthodox Easter: 'Indeed, He is arisen!' Sérurier made bold to ask for the release of all the men who had been captured with him at Verderio. Suvorov replied that this was beyond his powers, for men in the grip of the Revolution were like wild beasts who must be held in chains. He assured Sérurier that the prisoners would be treated well, and repeated in Russian some half-remembered lines from Lomonosov's *Tamira Selim*:

> The lion is a big-hearted creature who is content to beat his enemy down.
> The predatory wolf tears at his prey when the enemy lies defenceless on the ground.

Some of the Russian officers translated the words for the benefit of Sérurier, and Suvorov added: 'I used the same expression to the Polish deputation after the storm of Praga.' When he finally left the room Sérurier exclaimed: 'What a man!'[32] —a statement that will always remain ambiguous.

In Milan as earlier in Verona, concerts and theatrical shows were laid on in honour of Suvorov, 'but nobody in Italy can claim to have had the honour of receiving a present from him—and Italian actors, and virtuosi in particular, are avid for presents.'[33] In truth Suvorov was impatient to be on the move: 'Dear God! I fear if I stay any longer I shall suffocate in incense. It is time to get back to work!'[34]

INTO PIEDMONT, 1-11 MAY

After the Austrians had detached the necessary forces to contain or besiege the French-held fortresses to the rear, the two main allied contingents stood at an equal strength of approximately 18,000 Austrians and 18,000 Russians (excluding the Cossacks). For the immediate future Suvorov decided to follow Chasteler's advice to march the main force of the field army from Milan and across the Po to Piacenza, as 'the nodal point of our operations in Italy,'[35] where they could take stock of the threats and opportunities.

There was little to fear for the moment from the 20,000 survivors of Moreau's beaten army, but the second grouping of French forces in Italy—Macdonald's Army of Naples—was now disengaging its field forces from the plundered lands in the south, and Suvorov and Chasteler believed that it might seek to contest the allied gains in northern Italy, in which case the Russians and Austrians would advance against Macdonald and knock him out of the reckoning before he could join the French troops who had recoiled to Piedmont.

With this in mind Suvorov marched his forces south-east from Milan on 1 May. Three days later, when the troops were still on the way to the Po, Suvorov and Chasteler decided to resume the original westerly direction of the offensive. They had come to the conclusion that there was no imminent danger from Macdonald's Army of Naples, which was still somewhere well down the Italian peninsula, and believed to number scarcely 10,000 effectives. Timely warning of any trouble from that direction would in any case be given by two Austrian formations which were detached towards central Italy—a mobile force of 6,200 troops under the able Major-General Klenau, and the division of Lieutenant-General Ott, who was given the special responsibility of watching the eastern exits of the Apennines.

Suvorov and Chasteler were just as ignorant about the location of Moreau, after he had fallen back west from Milan, but Suvorov's attention was drawn towards Piedmont and Genoa by a mistaken report that the French had abandoned Tortona, which was situated where the routes from Genoa over the Ligurian Apennines debouched into the northern plain. 'Our objective is Piedmont,' declared Suvorov. 'Artillery must be brought together to attack the fortresses, if necessary from the captured ordnance.' [36] Suvorov and Chasteler in fact intended to use the Revolutionary system of war against the Revolution, by employing captured lands as springboards for further

conquest. Chasteler wrote to Thugut on 4 May to suggest inviting the captive Piedmontese officers and soldiers to swear allegiance to their old king, and fight alongside the allies against the French, while the remaining Piedmontese troops should be incited to desert the French colours. He was confident that 20,000 Piedmontese troops could be assembled at short notice and a total of 40,000 over the long term, and distributed among the Austrian divisions, 'the intention of this letter being to continue the war in Italy from the region's own resources, and conduct it with more vigour and energy.' Chasteler's ambitions did not stop there, for he made bold to propose a whole plan of war to a staff officer who had been sent by Archduke Charles. Chasteler afterwards lost his copy from his files, 'but I remember very well that the essential point was an attack by united forces on Switzerland, as the point of union of our armies and the key to Germany and Italy.'[37] This was to be accomplished by concerted operations on the part of the Austrian armies of Archduke Charles and Lieutenant-General Hotze from the north of the Alps, the Austrian army of Lieutenant-General Bellegarde from the Tyrol, and the Russo-Austrian Army of Italy and the reconstituted forces of liberated Piedmont. Chasteler was not privy to the schemes of the British Cabinet, but his plan bore some remarkable resemblances to the strategy now being evolved by Pitt and Grenville. (See below page 152).

By 7 May the allies in Italy had completed the rearrangement of their forces, and with the exception of the commands of Klenau and Ott (marching towards central Italy) everyone was moving west:

On the right (south) bank of the Po the main Austrian force (13,865 troops) had completed the crossing of the Po by pontoon bridges, and had reached Castel San Giovanni west of Piacenza, as the first stage of its march up the right bank. Prince Bagration with the Russian advance guard (5,862) had crossed further upstream by ferry, and was out ahead at Voghera.

Suvorov had decided the retain the greater part of his forces on the left (northern) bank of the Po. Rosenberg with the main body (10,571) had crossed the Ticino and was at Dorno, and his advance guard (3,075) under Major-General Chubarov had marched to Lomello. The Austrian division of Major-General Vukassovich (5,100) was deep into Piedmont and already sounding the way to Turin.

There was no sign of the French, apart from the troops in Tortona, which proved to be garrisoned after all, 'from all of which it is clear that the enemy are seeking refuge in the Piedmontese fortresses, and awaiting their fate under the protection of these strongholds.'[38] Moreau had in fact deployed his 20,000 available troops between Valenza (division Grenier) and Alessandria (division Victor) in a position at the meeting of the rivers Po, Tanaro and Bormida— a kind of delta in reverse— which covered the plain of south-western Piedmont and the most direct approaches to the city of Turin, which was the capital of the old kingdom of Sardinia-Piedmont and now the most important French base in Italy.

Bagration's Cossacks were now scouting up the Scrivia, while the main Austrian army had pushed by way of Voghera to Pontecurone just nine kilometres short of Tortona. Chasteler was close under the walls of Tortona itself, escorted by the Austrian advance guard proper, and he could see that the ramparts were in a bad state and unprotected by a palisade. He sent word to Suvorov, who authorised him to take the town by assault. In the afternoon of 9 May Chasteler deployed his troops under the cover of houses and hedges five hundred paces from the town walls, and at four he learned that the French commandant had refused the summons to surrender:

> Shortly afterwards, when I was drawing up plans to storm the place, a townsman got through to me with the news that the people were engaged in hand-to-hand fighting with the French. Without a moment's though I ran towards the gate in the company of just one [French royalist] Bussy Chasseur and twenty-three Cossacks. The townspeople opened the gate, and I stationed as many of them as were armed in the houses to right and left to delay the French until our infantry came up. I had

> the drawbridge thrown down, and brought up the two battalions of the regiment of Allvintzi with all possible speed. They arrived at the double to sounding music, under a violent fire of canister from the citadel. The first two companies were at once placed in the houses nearest the gate, while the others marched through the town to occupy the far gate and the avenues leading to the citadel. And so we became masters of that town with trifling loss.[39]

Suvorov was now forming a picture of how the French were deployed behind the confluence of the Piedmontese rivers. He had at first hoped to turn the French left or northern flank by sending Rosenberg across the upper Po, where the French were reported to have evacuated the south-bank fortress of Valenza. On 10 May, however, Constantine, Miloradovich and three adjutants rode on a reconnaissance along the north bank opposite. The grand prince had reached the army only three days before, and he was anxious to prove his mettle. He dismounted opposite a French picket, and remained within musket range until his companions prevailed on him to remove himself from the scene. He then rode along the bank to a point facing Valenza, which was clearly occupied by the French, and after a further delay he returned to his quarters in Frascarolo, his appetite for action still dangerously unsatisfied.

BASSIGNANA, 12 MAY

True to his principle of concentration, Suvorov decided to regroup all the available forces on the right (south) bank of the Po at Torre di Garofoli, west of Tortona. The Austrians, Bagration and the Russian division of Förster were all now south of the Po, and only had to wade the Scrivia to arrive at the assembly area, but Rosenberg was still on the north side of the Po, and Suvorov therefore dispatched an order to him to move with all possible speed to Cambio, cross the river by ferry, and join the rest of the combined army.

Cambio lay downstream of the meeting of the Po and the Tanaro, and if Rosenberg had crossed there he would have been safely clear of

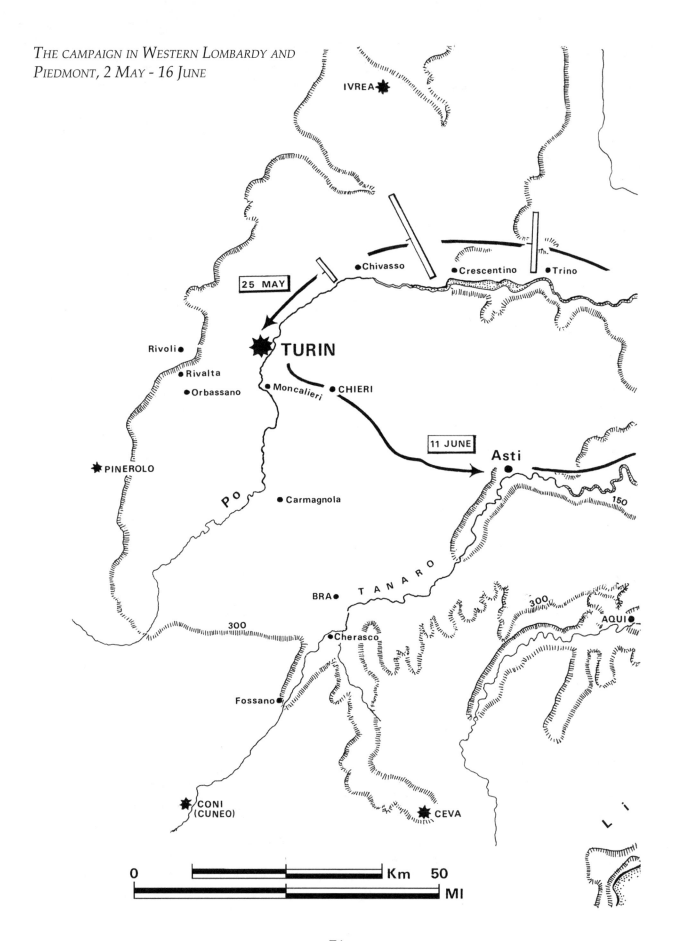

IVREA

25 MAY

Chivasso   Crescentino   Trino

Rivoli

Rivalta

TURIN

Orbassano

Moncalieri   CHIERI

11 JUNE   Asti

PINEROLO

Carmagnola

PO

150

TANARO

BRA

300

AQUI

300

Cherasco

Fossano

CONI
(CUNEO)   CEVA

L i

0   Km   50

MI

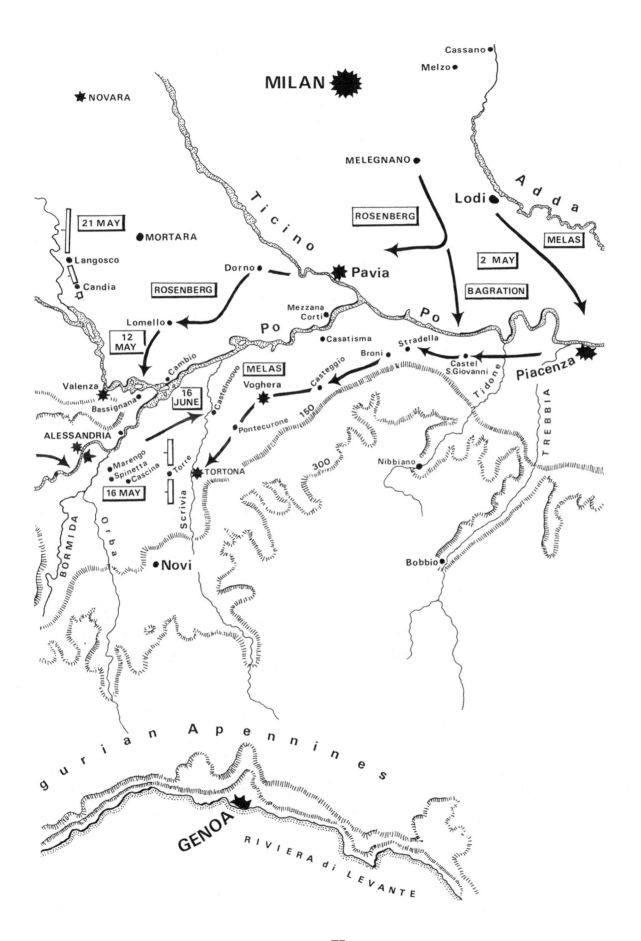

the French. Instead —and almost certainly at the insistence of Constantine—Rosenberg fed his forces across the Po a crucial five kilometres further upstream, where they would be decanted onto the south bank just above the confluence with the Tanaro, and thus directly into the left flank of the French concentration.

Along this stretch of the Po the river broadened into a number of islands. One of the islands, thickly grown with willows, had already been explored by Major-General Chubarov, the commander of Rosenberg's advance guard, and it offered the Russians a stepping stone to the right bank between Mugarone and Bassignana, from where it was separated only by a narrow channel. Chubarov accordingly began work to establish a flying bridge—a large ferry running along a cable which was secured at one end to the northern bank of the Po, and at the other to the island.

The preparations were so blatant that Moreau concluded that all this activity amounted to no more than a clumsy attempt at a feint. He instructed Paul Grenier to leave small detachments on observation at Valenza and Bassignana, and move the rest of his division to Alessandria to join Victor and confront Suvorov.

On the night of 11/12 May Rosenberg concentrated an initial force of about 4,000 troops—three companies of Jäger, three grenadier battalions and the Semernikov Cossacks—which passed by means of the ferry in relays—and two battalions of infantry under Major-General Dalheim which crossed on boats which had been collected at Borgoforte. The French outposts were close by on the south bank, and the Russian infantry waited patiently on the island in the cold and silence, while the Cossacks calmed their horses to prevent any

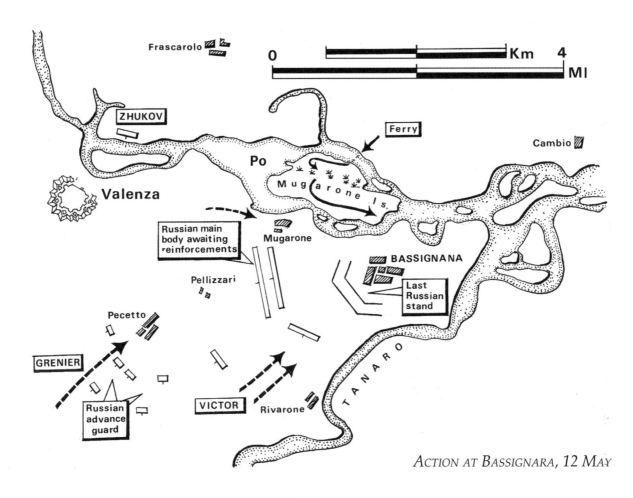

Action at Bassignara, 12 May

76

sound of neighing from carrying across the water.

Peasants had shown the Russians two fords which led from the island to the 'enemy' bank, and on the morning of 12 May the infantry of the advance guard waded the channel, which even now reached to their shoulders, and the Semernikov Cossacks swam alongside their horses. Grand Prince Constantine was present in person, and 'consumed with warlike courage and zeal'[40] he opened the action on the far bank. Rosenberg's main force had meanwhile arrived on the north bank of the river, and was beginning to cross to the island.

On the south bank 'the deceitful people of Bassignana received our troops with every show of joy, and of their own accord they hacked down the Tree of Liberty which had been set up by the French.'[41] Grenier's outposts had recoiled from the bank, and the Russians marched south-west in the direction of Alessandria without incident, until the screen of Cossacks encountered a more substantial force beyond Pellizzari. The French were holding the vine-covered slopes which extended over the spur of Pecetto to the hillock of Brico di San Antonio over to their left, and they turned the Cossacks back by a withering fire. The Russian infantry arrived on the scene early in the afternoon, and by about 4.15 they had forced the French from their positions, and gained enough ground to deploy the artillery.

By now Moreau's attention had been caught by this totally unexpected threat to his left flank. Far from being a feint, it appeared to him to be a genuine attack by Suvorov's whole army.[42] He ordered the main force of Grenier's division, which had been on the way to Alessandria, to execute an about turn, and he brought the reserve under Gardanne back north to execute a frontal attack against the impudent Russians. Moreau simultaneously ordered his other division, that of Victor, to move up on his right or eastern flank, and cut in on the Russian left flank and rear.

Advancing at the *pas de charge*, Grenier's troops dispersed the Cossacks, and pushed the Russian infantry from Pecetto and down towards the river. Chubarov rallied his troops among the farmsteads, vineyards and sunken roads, and stood his ground in the hope of receiving support from Rosenberg's main force. At this juncture an adjutant arrived with a repetition of Suvorov's previous order, which had gone astray:

> The count [Suvorov] has commanded you to dispatch a courier to inform him whether you are really crossing to join us. We have completely abandoned the project of taking Valenza. You can bring down boats from Borgoforte to effect the crossing and the junction, and there are also craft ready at Cervesina. Move as fast as possible and don't hang about any longer. Bring as many troops as you can and join us here, and just leave pickets and observation posts opposite Valenza. [43]

The brilliant young adjutant added that he had taken it on himself to halt the passage of any further troops, and commanded those already on the right bank to return. Constantine hastened back to the crossing point and used his princely authority to order up one battalion of the regiment of Miloradovich, two companies of the regiment of Tyrtov, and one battalion each of the regiments of Schveikovsky and Rosenberg. The Tyrtov companies and the Semernikov Cossacks repulsed the French cavalry which had been in the process of turning the Russian right flank, but it is evident that no further support was coming from the island to the south bank, and the Russians would have been bundled up altogether if the division of Victor had not come to a halt from exhaustion and hunger. As it was, the Russians on the right bank were heaped up in Bassignana and the triangle of land between the Tanaro and the Po.

The Austrian colonel MacDermott declared that 'what saved the Russians from total destruction on this occasion was their extraordinary steadfastness and innate courage. They gave ground only step by step.'[44] Captain Gryazev of the Rosenberg Grenadiers was caught up more immediately in the fighting, and believed that the Russians were behaving so badly that they almost deserved to be destroyed, and owed their salvation to the fact that the French cavalry were so weak, for by then neither authority nor force was capable of restoring our battalions to order, or preventing them from turning their backs in scandalous flight. I was an unfortunate witness of these happenings, and it makes me shudder whenever I think about them. Major Filosov and I believed that we could count on the loyalty of our men, and time and time again we tried to stop them from running. We appealed to their love of honour, we told them how disgraceful if was to abandon their duty, we threatened them with death, we pleaded with them—nothing worked. Not only did we suffer from the enemy canister, which snatched away troops from the fleeing mob, but when we were moving through the village of Borgofranco [he means Bassignana] the inhabitants, those treacherous Italians, opened fire on us and inflicted considerable casualties.[45]

In the evening the Russians forded the small branch of the Po and crowded together on the island, which was being scourged by the French canister. Escape across the main channel to the north bank was for the moment impossible, 'for when we tried to haul the ferry back from the far bank to receive the wounded, the peasants emerged from the huts and cut the cable along which the ferry passed. The water was running high and the ferry was carried downstream.'[46]

Priority was given to the passage of the wounded, once the ferry was retrieved by the Cossacks and the cable repaired, and so for several hours more the other troops remained packed together around the crossing point and still within range of the French artillery. Rosenberg sought to relieve the pressure by demonstrating against the French posts upstream: he directed Colonel Mikhail Semenovich Zhukov against Valenza, while the Austrian division of Vukassovich lunged against Casale, but in both locations only a few troops reached the far bank successfully, and they were all driven off or cut down.

Back on the island Constantine's horse shied at the clamour and bolted into the river; one of the Cossacks thereupon plunged into the water, took hold of the horse and brought it back to the bank. The sodden grand prince finally embarked on a little boat at two in the morning, and his aide-de-camp navigated the craft to the left bank, using his spontoon as an oar.

In the days following the action the reassembled corps marched to a new crossing points further down the Po at Mezzana Corti and Cambio, and made its way by way of Voghera to join the rest of the army.

The French had sustained 617 casualties in the action at Bassignana. Some 7,000 Russians had been caught up in the fighting, and the estimates of their losses vary from 992 (Suvorov), about 1,200 (Milyutin) and 1,500 (Chasteler) to nearly 2,000 (MacDermott).

'This expedition was undertaken without the knowledge of Field-Marshal Suvorov. He was furious, and laid most of the blame on General Rosenberg.' [47] The actual sequence of events was probably as follows:

1. The original scheme of crossing the Po upstream of the confluence with the Tanaro had been hatched on the basis of an incorrect report of 8 May, to the effect that the French had abandoned Valenza.

2. The reconnaissance of 10 May indicated the contrary, but Constantine (vile-tempered and the second son of the Emperor) insisted that the crossing must go ahead as planned. Rosenberg could not say as much in the defence he made to Suvorov:

> As a subordinate I accept my guilt without any excuses. But if Your Excellency will take the trouble to investigate my conduct of the expedition against Valenza more closely, you will find that I received the order to join the army when I was already engaged with the enemy, and I am therefore convinced that I will emerge fully vindicated.[48]

On 14 May Suvorov issued a long and curious order of the day to the combined army. He had accepted Rosenberg's version at least in part, for he began by explaining that the counter-order had arrived after some of the troops had already crossed to the island; the passage had continued regardless, and five battalions and two hundred Cossacks plunged on without any hope of immediate support. Reinforcements arrived eventually, and now the action took a new turn, for the enemy began to fall back, while the Russians pressed after them boldly and cut many of them down. Victory was almost ours, but suddenly the troops heard someone behind them beating the signal to fall back and dress their ranks—the same useless command you sometimes hear on the parade ground. Upon this signal our heroes fell back and arrayed themselves in order, pursued by the greatly superior enemy. Firing broke out again, and now the troops on the far bank also took part, and many men found their death amid the waves.

Suvorov finally drew attention to the failure of the feint of Vukassovich against Casale: 'Demonstrations are the kind of fooling-about which is typical of people inexperienced in war. Most of these feints are totally fruitless—they exhaust the troops and can cause them physical damage.'[49]

By now Suvorov had a better idea as to who was responsible for the little disaster. As soon as Constantine reached headquarters Suvorov took him aside into his office and shut the door. The grand prince emerged thirty minutes later with tears coursing down his woebegone face. Suvorov escorted him out of the room bowing deeply, then turned to Constantine's aide de camp: 'As for you, thoughtless young man! You will be responsible to me for the welfare of His Highness. If you allow him to do again, what he has already done, I will send you straight back to the Emperor.'[50]

FIRST MARENGO, 16 MAY

Moreau glimpsed an opportunity. He knew from the attack at Bassignana, and the subsequent retreat of the enemy to the far side of the Po, that the allies must be split in two, with large numbers of Russians still north of the Po, and separated from the main force of the Austrians, now standing beyond the Bormida to the east of Alessandria. On the night of 15/16 May the French constructed a flying bridge over the Bormida, which opened the way for Victor's infantry to pass over the river, while the cavalry forded a short distance upstream. The total force amounted to about 7,500 troops.

Colonel Denisov had been observing this stretch of the Bormida with two regiments of his Cossacks and a small contingent of Austrians—two companies of infantry, two pieces of artillery and four squadrons of horse. For a number of days he had suspected that something was afoot, from the fighting patrols the French had sent across the water. The massing of the French forces on the present occasion had been concealed by woods, but Denisov attacked the first French column to emerge from the marshes which bordered the river, and he learned from a captured French officer that he was facing a substantial body of troops under a general. The 74th demi-brigade chased the Austrian outposts from Marengo, Spinetta and Cascina Grossa, and the French advanced across the plain to the east, bothered rather than impeded by the Cossacks under Denisov, who sent repeated requests to Bagration to come to his support with the Russian advance guard.

The French might have advanced with unchecked momentum into the heart of the Austrian camp towards Torre di Garofoli, if Major-General Franz Joseph Lusignan, the interim commander of the division of Frelich, had not come out to meet them with the troops most immediately at hand—seven battalions of infantry, and six squadrons of the Lobkowitz Dragoons (if some of them were not already among the Austrian cavalry with Denisov). Bagration then arrived with his Russians, which enabled the allies to deploy seventeen battalions, twelve squadrons of Austrian cavalry and the two regiments of Cossacks, which formed up in two lines one thousand paces to the west of San Giuliano. The two forces advanced to contact, the French singing the *Marseillaise*, while the Cossacks answered with harsh cries and the Austrians struck up with their military bands.

According to Denisov the weight of the fighting fell on the Austrian infantry, for Bagration held his forces back in a wood, while neither the Austrian cavalry nor his own Cossacks were willing to close with the French infantry, who were keeping up a rolling fire by platoons. For a time the unsupported Austrian infantry were pushed back, but the odds turned in their favour when the division of Kaim came up on their left. Moreau knew that he had run into the main force of the Austrians, and at four in the afternoon he ordered the retreat, which was conducted in a controlled fashion, and covered by an obstinate defence of the manor house at Marengo and from behind the wet ditches of the neighbourhood. By Denisov's account Bagration was content to send a few volunteers and Jäger in pursuit, while the Austrians too failed to press home their attack at bayonet point.

> I had no occasion to do anything particularly fine with my Cossacks, for we remained virtual spectators—or rather we were frustrated by Bagration's diabolical intrigues and spite. Field-Marshal Suvorov and His Highness Grand Prince Constantine arrived on the scene when the French were already covered by the marshes and most of their army in the process of crossing the river, where we could do nothing against them. The field-marshal was affable enough when I presented myself to him, but several times he burst out: 'The enemy are getting away scot-free!' It was evident that he was displeased with someone.[51]

Such was the first 'battle' of Marengo (as distinct from the second engagement on 20 June 1799, and Bonaparte's hard-fought victory over Melas on 14 June 1800). The estimates of the losses are as diverse as usual, ranging from 480 to 710 among the allies, and between 500 and 1,500 among the French. In the evening Suvorov dined off a dish of fried onions with a few pieces of cured sturgeon (it was a fast day), and he once again had to meditate on a less than completely satisfactory outcome of an action. Denisov relates that

> on the next day, when I reported to Suvorov, he drew me to one side and asked if our battle had gone well. To this I replied that it had indeed gone well. He went on to ask: 'How bravely did Bagration attack?' This put me in considerable embarrassment. I knew that many people considered that I was in the habit of slandering others out of spite—which is something abhorrent to me, and which I have always avoided. Moreover I have always been loyal to my commanders, even those I

did not like, and I have never sought to deceive them. I therefore made no answer. I believe the field-marshal understood the reason for my silence. He put the question another way: 'Did Bagration close to bayonet point?' To this I had to reply: 'No.' The field-marshal turned and left me.[52]

THE LIBERATION OF TURIN, 25-26 MAY

The effects of the action at Marengo were felt on the operational rather than the tactical scale. More than any other consideration it induced Moreau to abandon the contest for the northern plain for the foreseeable future, and thereby closed the chapter which had opened when the French had precipitated hostilities on this theatre in March.

Moreau at first intended to reassemble his forces on the Genoese Riviera, and with this in view he divided his troops into two columns. The 7,200 men of the division of Victor had already received a mauling, and they now had to fight their way up the difficult Bormida valley against the swarming rebels of the Piedmontese *armata cristiana*. The French smashed their way into Dego after a hard contest, and they left it in smoking ruins behind them when they continued their march over the mountains on 19 May to establish contact with the division of Pérignon, holding the French Mediterranean bridgehead of the Ligurian (Genoese) Republic. Moreau had hoped to break through to Genoa with the other column—the division of Grenier and the artillery and cavalry of the old army—but he was instead forced to make his way south-west by way of Asti, Cherasco and Fossano to the fortress of Coni (Cuneo), isolated in an Alpine valley.

Turin was awaiting its liberator, and there were no French forces in the field to bar the way. The prospect was enough in itself to fire Suvorov's imagination. Moreover a number of officers of the Piedmontese artillery had come over to the allies and reported that the Arsenal in Turin town held over three hundred pieces of artillery and great quantities of ammunition, which would prove uncommonly useful for besieging the isolated strongpoints which were still held by the French—Mantua, and the citadels of Milan, Tortona and Alessandria.

> In addition [commented Chasteler], once we held the capital it would be all the easier for us to organise the Piedmontese army—which had invariably distinguished itself in all the previous wars in Italy—and employ it to work with us in our operations, as well as having all the resources of Piedmont at our disposal to conduct the war energetically and just as we liked. These were the main considerations which determined Suvorov to derive the greatest possible advantage from the present rout of the French, and liberate the whole of Piedmont at one stroke.[53]

Suvorov and Chasteler did not know how very far their vaulting ambitions surpassed anything that was borne in mind by Francis and Thugut. The Emperor and his foreign minister were bent on securing immediate and exclusive advantages for the Austrians in Italy, and they were taken aback to hear from Suvorov and Chasteler that they intended to restore Sardinia-Piedmont to King Charles Emanuel IV, and with this land as an active ally, proceed to clear Switzerland and invade France in co-operation with the army of Archduke Charles north of the Alps. Between 13 and 17 May couriers therefore hastened from Vienna to tell Suvorov that operations of this nature were out of the question. Suvorov was to purge the Jacobins from Piedmont, but hand over all the administrative and political affairs to an Austrian commissioner, who would rule Piedmont as a defeated enemy belligerent. Suvorov was therefore to confine himself to military operations, and give prime consideration to reducing the citadel of Milan (which in fact fell on 23 May) and the fortress of Mantua.

Still in happy ignorance, Suvorov and Chasteler planned a roundabout anti-clockwise route that would carry the army across the Po well clear of disturbance from the garrison of Alessandria, then up the left (north) bank of the Po to arrive at Turin from the north-east. The Austrians and the Russian division of Förster marched north to the Po at Casatisma, crossed by a bridge of boats, and on 21 May united with all the rest of the Russians in a camp on the left bank in a camp between Candia and Langosco. From here the combined force of 30,000 troops executed a succession of forced marches by way of Trino, Crescentino and Chivasso to arrive in the neighbourhood of Turin on 25 May. The seemingly endless rains had by now given way to a steady and oppressive heat, which was just as exhausting in its way, but Suvorov was determined to reach the city before the French garrison could come to its senses.

On that day Suvorov and two or three members of his suite packed themselves into a little two-horse cart and set off down the road, with their 'empty' horses being brought up behind. On the way Suvorov invited Denisov into the vehicle, which was now more cramped than ever, and drew curious glances from the Austrian columns. To general relief Suvorov decided to abandon the cart, mount horse and get ahead of the troops, who were now marching slowly through the dust and heat. Suvorov led the way by setting spurs to his horse and jumping the roadside ditch. Denisov tells how the field-marshal's companions called out in alarm to ask him whether the ditch was deep, but Suvorov just turned about with a challenging stare. 'Seeing the way Suvorov was looking at us, I conceived that it was up to me, as a Cossack, to follow his example. With this in mind I gave my horse a touch of the whip, set it at the ditch and gave the beast its head. My horse was fairly light, and by no means feeble, but it fell short by one of its rear legs and stumbled to one side, luckily without falling.'[54]

Darkness overtook the party when it was well ahead of the army but still short of Turin, which lay somewhere ahead. There were no local guides, and Denisov begged Suvorov to stop for the night, but the field-marshal merely drew attention to the flitting green sparks of the glow worms, and insisted that he must catch up with Chasteler, who was in front of them. They found Chasteler in a suburb just short of Turin with a party of Austrian cavalry and six 6-pounder cannon, with which he opened fire against the city ramparts. For some time the enemy failed to respond, but then 'the French pieces roared out like thunder, and their heavy-calibre shot, striking the masonry buildings and falling on the road… made a clatter which was just as frightening in its way.' Chasteler and his party made off at speed, but Suvorov refused to move. 'I told the field-marshal "It's a hot spot here!" He listened, but replied "No, Karpovich, I like it very much." He pointed to the tall poplars and commented "It's a fine place for growing trees!" I went up to Suvorov, grasped him by the hand, and succeeded in leading him to one side. "Damnation!" he called out, "what do you think you are doing?"' Suvorov grabbed Denisov by the hair and in the confusion the two of them tumbled into a ditch. It lay under a large wall, which would have collapsed on top of them if it had been hit by a cannon shot. They extricated themselves and remounted, and this time Denisov was able to persuade Suvorov to spend the rest of the night in a little house, where he went to sleep on a pile of grain.[55]

Suvorov awoke on 26 May to find that the Austrian division of Major-General Vukassovich had got into Turin before him. This formation had been acting as an unofficial advance guard, and Vukassovich had established contact with Major Lucioni and his Piedmontese militia, who furnished him with a plan of the fortifications. On the night of 25/26 May Vukassovich concerted measures for a coup de main with the sympathetic chief of the urban national guard. Speed and surprise were essential to the success of the enterprise, for the garrison (3,400 troops under the republican Piedmontese general Fiorella) had it in their power to hold the city ramparts long enough to wreck the ordnance in the great Arsenal, then fall back in good order to the powerful pentagonal citadel in the west of the city.

Early on 26 May Vukassovich grouped his forces outside the Porta Po, and at seven his howitzers opened a lively fire from the right bank of the Po against the neighbouring houses. This was the signal for a band of armed citizens to overpower the French guards, let down the drawbridge, and break open the internal barricade facing the town. Fiorella tried to take Vukassovich in the rear by dispatching a column from the town and in again by the Porta Nova, but the Austrians and townspeople counterattacked ferociously and chased the French to the citadel. The other gates were now being opened to the allies, and Chasteler moved at once to secure the Arsenal. He marched the regiment of Fürstenberg through the Porta Stura, and with the help of several companies of the National Guard and a number of officers of the Piedmontese regular army he gained the Piazza San Carlo; leaving one of the Fürstenberg battalions there, he set off with the other and reached the Arsenal unscathed, despite a constant fire from the citadel. 'When I entered the Arsenal gate old Colonel Rocato proffered his sword, but I gave it back to him with the words: "Wield it alongside us in the work of restoring religion and royalty!" Tears welled in the man's eyes. He then introduced the Arsenal Director Lieutenant-Colonel Ruffin and several officers, to whom I spoke in the same terms.'[56]

Meanwhile the main force of the allied army crossed the Dora above Turin, and established itself in a blocking position to the west at Rivoli, Rivalta and Orbassano, so cutting off the citadel from the open country. Fiorella refused a demand to surrender, but Chasteler used the parley as an opportunity to reconnoitre the fortifications in the company of Grand Prince Constantine. They had ridden along the highway to within half cannon-shot of the ramparts by the time the officer who had carried the summons came back with the commandant's refusal. Chasteler impressed on Constantine how dangerous it was to stay any longer, but the grand prince replied 'Wherever you are going I can go too!' At that instant the French fired two charges of canister from the citadel, which emphasised what Chasteler was saying, and the party withdrew behind the nearest house. Chasteler entered this incident in his journal to 'show that I can testify personally as to the prince's courage.'[57]

The frustrated Suvorov betook himself to Turin city and installed himself on the ground floor of the Palazzo Carignan. Denisov records that

the rest of the day passed without anything of note, and we retired peacefully enough. But all of a sudden at about midnight I heard a great noise and commotion; I jumped up, ran down the stairs (because I was on the third floor) and saw pandemonium in the courtyard, where lay two or three soldiers who had had arms or legs carried away by shot, along with some dead horses. I realised that the field-marshal could be in some danger, though he was in his chamber. I rushed to seek him out, and found him lying quietly on some kind of bed or couch. His room was sited on the side of the palace which was being hit by the flying shot and bombs; moreover the little window gave onto the street and its shutters were open. I was so shocked that I called out pretty rudely: 'For God's sake, Your Highness, get up and leave the room!' He awoke—if indeed he had ever been asleep—raised himself a little and asked: 'Is that you, Karpovich?' I told him the French were keeping up a heavy fire from the citadel against the town, and shooting with particular accuracy at this palace, where there were already a large number of dead and wounded men and horses. He looked at me a little, and replied: 'Leave me, I wish to sleep.' He turned his face to the wall and settled down, whereupon I left.[58]

Suvorov bestirred himself after Denisov had departed. The fire from the citadel was pointless from the military point of view, and Suvorov accordingly sent Prince Andrei Ivanovich Gorchakov to Fiorella to threaten to array the French prisoners, not excluding the wounded, in the line of fire on the citadel esplanade. The commandant now agreed to end his cannonade, on condition the allies did not attack the citadel on the side facing the town.

On 28 May Suvorov staged a series of festivities to honour the people of Turin and celebrate the news that the French had surrendered the citadel of Milan. In the morning he attended an Orthodox service at his quarters, then drove in his full uniform to the cathedral. After dining with generals and prominent citizens back in the palace, he betook himself to a formal reception in the Theatre. The gathering broke into a storm of applause when he made his entry, and the curtain rose to reveal a Temple of Glory, of which the centrepiece was a bust of Suvorov, surrounded with emblems of his triumphs. These were considerable by any reckoning, for the Russians and Austrians had carried the war from the Adige to the Maritime Alps, and from the Swiss Alps to the Romagna and the Adriatic.

RE-ORIENTATIONS, LATE MAY AND EARLY JUNE

Chasteler had been taking stock of the good things in the Arsenal. He was at first told that the pieces would be of no use to him, because the French had bored out all the touch holes, but Lieutenant-Colonel Ruffin informed him confidentially that he had the tool to screw in new vents, and that there was additional medium and heavy artillery in the depots at Valenza, Casale, Ivrea and Cherasco. Colonel Franz Bögner, the Director of Artillery of the Austrian forces in Italy, arrived on the 28th to prepare the artillery for the siege of the citadel, and declared portentously that he could not think of making a start until he had made an inventory, which would take twelve or fourteen days. Chasteler sent him away with a flea in his ear, and got to work to assemble a siege train (which was ready at Turin ten days later).

Chasteler wrote at the same time to Vienna to propose taking all the Piedmontese artillerymen into Austrian pay, 'for their officers are experienced, and the gunners brave and very well trained.' If he were given the money to obtain mules he could also mobilise the sixty-one pieces of mountain artillery he had found in the Arsenal. 'In addition I asked for a better provision of items of military apparel, and especially shoes, which are absolutely essential for those continuous and speedy marches which are the *sine qua non* for success in war.'[59] The influence of Suvorov is clear.

Chasteler, as a political innocent, likewise outlined to Thugut his schemes for further operations, writing from Turin on 1 June that they were formulated 'in the spirit of the system of war adopted by the field-marshal.'[60] Chasteler and Suvorov calculated that Moreau had at the most 17-18,000 disposable troops scattered over Piedmont and the Genoese territories, while Macdonald's Army of Naples could emerge from southern Italy with only another 17-18,000 men, after leaving the necessary garrisons in Naples city, Castel d'Oro, Capua, Gaeta and Civitavecchia.

We know now that Moreau's total stood at about 25,000 troops—a number which comprised not just the forces of Laboissière in the neighbourhood of Genoa city, and the division of Grenier (occupying the passes leading across the Genoese mountains to the Riviera di Ponente), but the companion division of Victor (which left Alessandria on 18 May) on the Riviera di Levante to the south-east of Genoa, and the divisions of Gauthier at Florence and Montrichard at Bologna.

The forces of Victor, Gauthier and Montrichard passed to the command of Macdonald during the latter's progress north, which brought his total to 36,728 troops. Suvorov and Chasteler were therefore not astray when they estimated the total French forces in Italy, but they were unaware of the shift away from Moreau to Macdonald.

In early June the allied forces were deployed as follows:

The main Austro-Russian army under the immediate command of the generals Melas and Rosenberg in the neighbourhood of Turin (29,000 infantry, 4,687 Austrian cavalry, 2,500 Cossacks = 47,087). A separate advance guard under Major-General Vukassovich stood at Moncaliere and Orbassano with outposts thrown out along a wide arc at Pinerolo, Carmagnola, and along the Tanaro from Bra to Asti.

The Austrian corps of Lieutenant-General Hadik deployed from the northern end of Lake Maggiore towards the Simplon pass, and towards the St. Gotthard Pass which he seized on 29 May (9,000 infantry, 900 cavalry = 9,900).

Suvorov had used his authority to call down the Austrian lieutenant-general Bellegarde to his help with the Army of the Tyrol. This force reached Milan on 5 June, and thus became an operational part of Suvorov's command (17,258 infantry, 2,200 cavalry = 19,458). This number includes the approximately 5,000 troops of Lieutenant-General Ott, which never actually joined Bellegarde's main force, but were sent south-east from Parma to support Klenau (below).

General Kray's siege army around Mantua (18,200 infantry, 1,564 cavalry = 19,760).

A separate advance guard under Major-General Klenau had occupied Ferrara, and will be relevant to our story as the first of the Austrian forces to encounter Macdonald on his march north (5,012 infantry, 1,110 cavalry = 6,122).

Suvorov and Chasteler counted on being able to combine the groupings of field forces in ways that would give decisive concentrations in whatever direction might prove necessary, to wit:

The main army, Hadik and Bellegarde variously at Turin, at Alessandria (to meet an advance from Genoa), or by Lake Maggiore (to counter an irruption from Switzerland)

Against Macdonald an initial concentration by Kray, Klenau and Ott within six days, and Suvorov and Hadik in another four, so assembling a total force of 58,000.

Chasteler explained to Thugut that 'speed and impetus endow the field-marshal's system of war with its magical strength. He invariably arrives with the greater part of his army at the decisive point, and leaves the others only lightly held, because the enemy cannot be equally strong everywhere.'[61]

In the second week of June the real or perceived progress by the French made it urgent for the allies to concentrate their forces in one direction of the other—whether south towards the Genoese mountains to confront Moreau afresh, or east against Macdonald to counter his move up through central Italy. On 9 June a courier reached headquarters at Turin from Lieutenant-General Ott with the news that Macdonald had been reinforced by the divisions of Victor and Montrichard from Moreau's army, and that he had driven an Austrian post from Pontremoli in the Apennines and forced the Austrians to raise their investment of Fort Urbano.

In order to meet the immediate emergency Suvorov therefore sent a courier to order Ott to keep out of trouble and fall back by way of Parma and Borgo San Donino to Piacenza on the middle Po, 'and if necessary retire to the vital point of Stradella, disputing the passages of the rivers Taro, Nure and Trebbia on the way—without exposing yourself to unnecessary risk—and throw a garrison and provisions into the citadel of Piacenza. But the Stradella position is to be defended to the utmost, and you can rely on the army coming to support you.'[62] This instruction of 9 June may be seen as the genesis of the Trebbia campaign.

Kray was likewise to leave Mantua under blockade, and rally on Piacenza with all his disposable forces. Suvorov harboured the greatest respect for the 'hero' Kray, and this last order was couched in the terms of an invitation: 'Your good fortune in war is famous, and the experience and energy you showed at Verona lead me to hope that you may take part in the coming battle, which will perhaps decide the fate of Italy... With God's help I hope to beat the enemy, and it would be agreeable to me to be able to owe half the victory to my brave friend.'[63]

It was now clear that the present concentration of the main Austro-Russian army at Turin lay altogether too far to the west, and Suvorov therefore ordered all his forces (except the Austrian division of Kaim) to make ready to march for Alessandria. He chose the most direct road (ninety-five kilometres) instead of following the arc of the Po to the north; this new route was picturesque but hilly, and the army had to brave an overnight march through heavy rain in order to be able to reach Asti by eight in the morning of 11 June. The troops set off again through the murk and damp at ten in the morning.

For a time it seemed that Suvorov would have a battle on his hands. On 2 June a powerful French squadron had reached Genoa and landed reinforcements of unknown strength. Intercepted dispatches likewise indicated (misleadingly) that Macdonald and the division of Montrichard—an estimated 17,000 troops in all—would turn aside to the western coast, and complete the rest of their journey to Genoa by sea.

All of this, together with rumours put into circulation by the French, and some lively attacks on the Austrian outposts, indicated that Moreau, instead of being beaten and scattered beyond recovery, was about to emerge from the Genoese mountains into the plain of Piedmont. Melas wrote to Thugut that Suvorov had laid himself open to this blow by dispersing his forces. Thugut believed that the allies would still be able to reassemble in time, but he feared that if they were defeated the consequences would be disastrous, for they had the swollen rivers Scirivia, Orba and Tanaro in their rear, and the crossings at Alessandria and Tortona were commanded by the French. The survivors could make a stand nowhere short of the Adda—a retreat that would endanger the Turin citadel siege corps and the detachments which had been sent out towards Switzerland.[64]

On 13 June Suvorov's army crossed the Tanaro, and encamped by the Bormida in the neighbourhood of Alessandria. In the evening he learned that, far from making for the western coast, Macdonald had emerged from the eastern flank of the Apennines into the great northern plain. Suvorov's recent marches from Turin had stood him in good stead, for he was now positioned at the junction of the routes which led south to Genoa, and east along the foothills of the Apennines. Not only had Suvorov restored his operational balance, but he grasped that bold measures were needed to frustrate the patent ambition of the French to unite in the northern plain. He does not appear to have considered for a moment the cautious, sensible—and ultimately fatal—option of staying where he was, and allowing Macdonald and Moreau to converge against him. Instead he would draw down Bellegarde's Army of the Tyrol to contain Moreau and the garrison of Alessandria citadel, and march east with the rest of his available forces to bring Macdonald to battle at the greatest possible distance from Moreau. This was one of the last great resolutions ever taken by Suvorov, and it stands comparison with any in his wars against the Prussians, Poles or Turks.

1 Anon., 1801-3, IV,42
2 KA FA Italien 1799 XIII 1, Chasteler's Journal
3 KA FA Italien 1799 XIII 44, Colonel MacDermott, 'Militärisches Dage Buch'
4 Milyutin, 1856-8, I,227. Suvorov was in fact more attached to his Gorchakov nephews. He refused to recognise this 'son' as his own, and broke with his wife Varva four months before Arkady was born, on 15 August 1784. The blameless Arkady lost his life in 1811, trying to save a man from drowning.
5 KA CA 1799 IV ad 4, Kray to Melas, Brescia, 21 April
6 Suvorov, 'Suworow. Beiträge', 1884, 352-3
7 KA FA Italien 1799 IV 127, Melas to Archduke Charles, Chiari, 23 April
8 Milyutin, 1856-8, I,230
9 Denisov, 1874-5, XI,621
10 Ibid., 624
11 KA FA Italien 1799 XIII 44, Chasteler's Journal
12 Milyutin, 1856-8, I,239
13 KA FA Italien 1799 XIII 44, Chasteler's Journal
14 Ibid.,
15 Denisov, 1874-5, XI,624
16 Ibid., XI,625
17 Report of Vukassovich, Hüffer, 1900-1, I,197
18 Anon., 1801-3, IV,62
19 Phipps, 1926-39, V,264
20 Milyutin, 1856-8, I,582. Suvorov's account is to be found in his report to Paul on 1 May, Meshcheryakov, 1949-53, IV,41-7
21 Phipps, 1926-39, V,264
22 Anon., 1801-3, IV,66
23 KA FA Italien 1799, 'Bemerkungen über die Beschaffenheit der russischen Armeen'
24 Milyutin, 1856-8, I,246
25 Denisov, 1874-5, XI,627
26 KA HKRA Deutschland und Italien 1799 V ad 12, Melas to Tige, Milan, 30 April
27 Anon., 1801-3, IV,59-60
28 Milyutin, 1856-8, I,249
29 KA FA Italien 1799 XIII 1, Chasteler's Journal
30 Milyutin, 1856-8, I,250
31 Denisov, 1974-5, I,629

32 Milyutin, 1856-8, I,251-2
33 KA FA Italien 1799 XIII 43, 'Bemerkungen über die Beschaffenheit der russischen Armeen'
34 Milyutin, 1856-8, I,253
35 KA FA Italien 1799 XIII 1, Chasteler's Journal
36 Milyutin, 1856-8, I,369
37 KA FA Italien 1799 XIII 1, Chasteler's Journal
38 KA FA Italien 1799 XIII 44, MacDermott, 'Militärisches Dage Buch'
39 KA FA Italien 1799 XIII 1, Chasteler's Journal
40 KA FA Italien 1799 XIII 44, MacDermott, 'Militärisches Dage Buch'
41 Komorovsky, quoted in Milyutin, 1856-8, II,42
42 Eggerking, 1914, 72
43 Colonel Lavrov to Rosenberg, Tortona, 12 May 1799, Fuchs, 1826, II,103
44 KA FA Italien 1799 XIII 44, MacDermott, 'Militärisches Dage Buch'
45 Gryazev, 1898, 42-3
46 Komorovsky, quoted in Milyutin, 1856-8, II,50
47 KA FA Italien 1799 XIII 44, MacDermott, 'Militärisches Dage Buch'
48 Rosenberg to Suvorov, 13 May 1799, Lopatin, 1986, 709
49 Meshcheryakov, 1949-53, IV,69-70
50 Milyutin, 1856-8, II,54
51 Denisov, 1874-5, XI,634
52 Ibid., XI,635
53 KA FA Italien, 1799 XIII 1, Chasteler's Journal
54 Denisov, 1874-5, XI,636
55 Ibid., XI,638-9
56 KA FA Italien 1799 XIII 1, Chasteler's Journal
57 Ibid.,
58 Denisov, 1874-5, XI,640-1
59 KA FA Italien 1799 XIII 1, Chasteler's Journal
60 Ibid.,
61 Ibid.,
62 Ibid.,
63 Suvorov to Kray, 10 June 1799, Milyutin, 1856-8, II,188-9
64 KA CA 1799 VI 14, Melas to Tige, Asti, 11 June

5

AGAINST MACDONALD

ADVANCE TO CONTACT

It is time to review the doings of *général de division* Jacques-Etienne Macdonald. There was something disreputable about the man and his forces from the beginning. He was an arch-plunderer in a society of plunderers, and Suvorov was at fault in failing to list him among the Revolutionary 'blood-suckers.' Among his ill-assorted subordinates the young and ardent François Watrin was an idealist, worthy of employment elsewhere, while Jean-Baptiste Olivier was brave but limited, and Jan-Baptiste Dominique Rusca a near-criminal in the same league as Macdonald himself; Jan Dabrowski and his Polish Legion were going to have a consistently unfortunate career in the coming campaign, while the divisions of Victor and Montrichard, which were picked up on the way, hailed from the old northern Army of Italy and never integrated fully with the rest of the command.

On 14 April Macdonald had received the Directory's order to join Moreau, and so he 'left all power in the land to the patriots, not however as in other countries of patriots of the lower classes, but of nobles and dignitaries of the Church, which at the time of the conquest, had thrown themselves in the arms of the French, and who having long before engaged in conspiracies against their sovereign, offered more certain assurances of Republican fidelity, than were found among those who commonly compose the forlorn hopes of Democracy.'[1]

Macdonald reached Rome on 16 May. He set out again on the 20th, and marched by way of Viterbo, Bolsena, Radicofani, Buoncontenta and Siena to arrive at Florence on the 26th. Even now Macdonald had a choice of avenues by which he could reach Moreau. By far the safest option would have been the western coast, for it was separated by the Apennines from the main allied land forces, and there was little danger of interference from the British fleet, which was spread very thinly. Macdonald however believed that the winding track of the corniche could be disputed by the Austrian detachments, and that it was totally impassable to his artillery, which would have to be dumped at Lerici for lack of boats to transport it to Genoa across the Ligurian Sea.

Moreau in his turn was supposed to facilitate the junction by marching some distance towards the approaching Army of Naples. The logical route was from the Riviera di Levante (the riviera east of Genoa) across the Apennine crests and so down the valleys of the Trebbia or Taro to reach the northern plain free of disturbance. Instead Macdonald called on Moreau to advance north from Genoa and then veer east by way of Tortona and Voghera to join him in the neighbourhood of Piacenza—a path that was certain to deposit him among considerable allied forces.

Macdonald was interested not only in joining Moreau, but in staging a dramatic entry to the north Italian plain on his own account, and deliberately bludgeoning his way through to Piacenza by main force. His targets were the Austrian corps and detachments which were deployed to the east of the main allied force, and he accordingly arranged his forces in four main columns:

Far right: Divisions of Rusca and Montrichard along the highway from Florence to Bologna,

Centre: Macdonald in person with the divisions of Olivier and Watrin, advancing from Pistoia on Modena by way of San Marcello, Pievepelago and Pavullo,

Left Centre: The Polish division of Dabrowski, descending the axis of the Secchia valley and arriving in the northern plain in the area of

Reggio,

Far Left: The division of Victor pushing from Borgo Val di Taro in the Apennines down the Taro valley by way of Fornovo on Parma.

Simply because it made so little sense in the context of joining Moreau, Macdonald's irruption in such force from the side of the

Apennines furthest from Genoa caught the Austrian detachments when they were still in three isolated groups, namely (and again from east to west):

Major-General Klenau's depleted detachment (3,500) from the original army of Melas; it had seized Ferrara on 29 May, and now stood at San

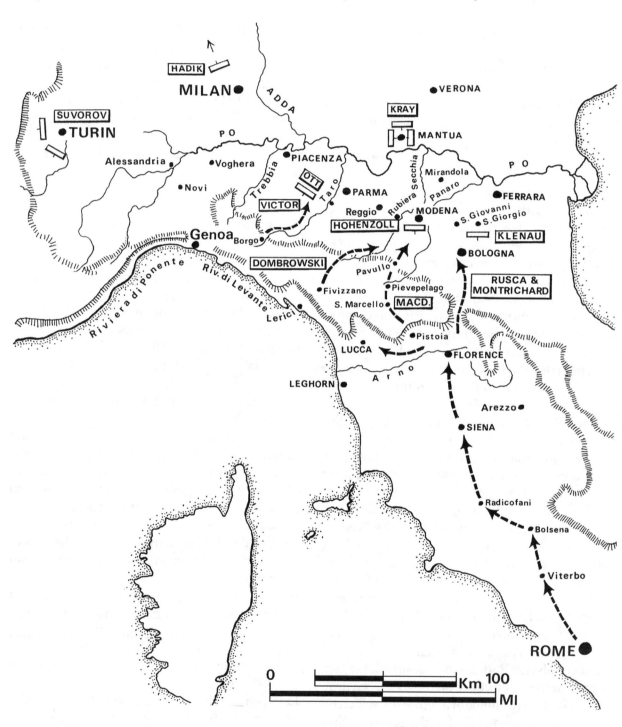

MACDONALD'S MARCH

Giorgio about thirty kilometres to the south west,

Major-General Hohenzollerns' detachment of 4,000 infantry from Kray's Mantua siege corps, together with the Chasseurs de Bussy (an 800-strong regiment of French royalist light horse), now deployed in front of Modena,

Lieutenant-General Ott's division (6,000) of Bellegarde's army, which had originally been positioned at the exit of the Taro valley at Fornovo, but was now extended far along the Strada Romana to the west.

Macdonald aimed first to destroy Hohenzollern's command in its entirety, by attacking him frontally at Modena by the division of Victor, while Dabrowski's Poles closed in from the west by way of Rubiera, and Rusca executed a deep outflanking movement to the east from Bologna by way of San Giovanni, so as to cut Hohenzollern's retreat to Mirandola.

The French struck on 12 June. Macdonald lost contact with the detachments of Dabrowski and Rusca, but he had the divisions of Oliver and Watrin under his immediate command, and he attacked the Austrians at Modena at ten in the morning. Hohenzollern stood his ground outside the town, evidently in the hope of being reinforced, but after putting up a brave fight his infantry were driven back with heavy losses to the southern ramparts, where they held out until four in the afternoon. Hohenzollern's command would have been lost altogether if Klenau had not divined the French plan and fallen back with his command north-east to the Panaro and defended that river line against Rusca—a move which preserved Hohenzollern's line of retreat.

Meanwhile at Modena the French gave themselves up to plundering the town. Macdonald feared that the impetus was weakening, and in the hope of getting the troops on the move again he led one hundred cavalry in a reconnaissance into the country on the far side of the town. About half way to Mirandola he unwittingly across the path of retreat of a group of the Bussy Chasseurs. The royalist light horse were commanded by a Lieutenant Lefevre, who called on his men to break through at any cost. Macdonald saw a great cloud of dust approaching along a road which ran perpendicularly to the highway. He believed himself in no great danger, for a battalion of his grenadiers had arrived nearby. He called on the enemy to surrender, but they spurred against him, and at that critical moment he got so caught up in his gear that he could neither draw his sword nor get his horse to move, and so found himself stranded between the fanatical royalists and his own grenadiers. 'The valiant Lefevre cried out to his men to hack into the enemy. "You are the commander-in-chief," he called out to Macdonald, "all the better for us!"—and dealt him two cuts, one in the head and the other in the arm. An instant afterwards Lefevre and all the chasseurs with him were hewn down, only one NCO and one trooper escaping across the ditches.' [2]

This nasty action cost Hohenzollern about 2,000 troops, or well over one-third of his command, and the authorities in Vienna took the opportunity to lay the blame on Chasteler, for having failed to inform Hohenzollern that Ott was too far away to lend him any support.[3]

Having emerged from the Apennines so far to the east, Macdonald seemed to be well placed

MACDONALD

to advance straight to the relief of Mantua. The Austrians therefore took urgent measures to bar his way. Kray raised the Po bridges and took up position on the north bank with several thousand armed peasants and all the troops who could be spared from his siege army, while Klenau stayed to the south of the river in a flanking position in the neighbourhood of Ferrara. Lieutenant-General Ott's division therefore remained as the only intermediate formation between Kray's command and the main allied army away to the west at Alessandria; Ott now hastened his march in that direction up the south bank of the Po, and he was followed by Hohenzollern with the survivors of the action at Modena.

The news of Hohenzollern's defeat reached Suvorov outside Alessandria on the evening of 13 June, and his insight and his powers of decision never revealed themselves more convincingly (above, page 87). It was clear enough that Macdonald had abandoned any intention of joining Moreau by way of the western coast, and Suvorov at once made up his mind to hasten east with his Russians and Austrians by forced marches, join the command of Ott (nine battalions and eighteen squadrons) and fight Macdonald before the French could make any significant progress towards Genoa. Bellegarde had meanwhile arrived with 14,500 fresh troops from his Army of the Tyrol, and Suvorov gave him the responsibility of containing Moreau and keeping Alessandria citadel under siege. Suvorov wrote to Rosenberg as commander of the Russian contingent: 'Your Excellency Andrei Grigorevich! Some news for you! The French are swarming like bees and are closing in on Mantua from almost all sides... We will set off soon. The enemy are present in force. God be with you!'[4]

That was on 13 June, when we left Suvorov encamped on the western side of the barrier of the Bormida river, which he had to pass before he could take up the highway which led to the

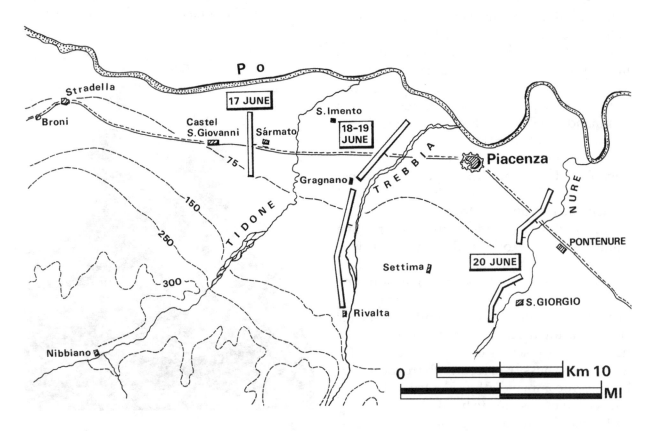

THE CAMPAIGN OF THE TREBBIA, 17-20 JUNE

east and thus to the army of Macdonald. The enemy garrison in Alessandria citadel commanded the permanent crossing, and compelled Suvorov to make his passage somewhere upstream. The necessary pontoons now had to be transported down the Po from Valenza, then up the Tanaro to Montecastello, dragged from there through heavy rain overland out of range of the French guns, and finally refloated on the Bormida above the citadel. Work on the bridges finally began at ten in the morning of 15 June, and was complete by five in the afternoon. The army marched across the bridges and into the night, and the wind dried the mud sufficiently to permit the Austrians on the left and the Russian column on the right to unite at Castelnuovo-di-Scrivia on the morning of 16 June.

Suvorov allowed the troops just three hours' rest, then continued the march in a single column to a new camp between Casteggio and Casatisma. The regiments had covered fifty-six kilometres in twenty-four hours, which testifies to Suvorov's ability to drive his men. His caution and his sense of operational 'balance' were just as much in evidence. The spurs of the Apennines were now closing in very hard on his right flank, and Suvorov therefore detached the Russian major-general Mikhail Mikhailovich Veletsky with one battalion of the Russian regiment of Jung-Baden, fifty Cossacks and eighty of the Austrian Karaiczay Dragoons over the mountains to Bobbio on the upper Trebbia to cover his army against any disturbance from that direction.

Chasteler later had occasion to talk with Moreau about what happened next, and he learned that Moreau had in fact detached General Jean Lapoype with 1,500 French troops and 2,000 Genoese of the Ligurian Legion over the Apennines and down the Trebbia. Suvorov's precautions were therefore fully justified.

Veletsky's force marched by way of Nibbiano, and on 18 June his leading troops descended on Bobbio in the valley of the upper Trebbia, taking Lapoype's command so completely by surprise that it disintegrated and fled back over the mountains towards Genoa. Lapoype might otherwise have intervened to decisive effect in the fighting down the Trebbia on the 19th. Chasteler noted how 'this fortunate turn of events secured the right flank of the army, and was due to the decisiveness of the Russian general Veletsky who led the column, and the good planning of Captain Quosdanovich of the [Austrian] General Staff. As I already mentioned I discussed this episode with the enemy general Moreau, and he could scarcely believe that our column which advanced against Bobbio numbered only eight hundred regular troops, while I for my part had always assumed that the enemy column consisted solely of Genoese.'[5]

Suvorov never allowed the word 'defeat' to pass his lips, but he knew that any reverse would leave the allies jammed against the Po. To guard against this eventuality he made a new bridge of boats which extended to the far side of the river at Mezzana Corti, and protected it on the near bank by a bridgehead fortification, while he ordered a further bridge to be constructed for Bellegarde on the upper Po at Valenza. Everyone therefore had a secure path of retreat. At six in the morning of 16 June Suvorov received a report by courier from Lieutenant-General Ott that he had clashed with the troops of Macdonald, who were advancing from the east, and that he had fallen back behind the Tidone.

Ott had been lucky to be spared from the general rout of the Austrian detachments when the French broke out of the mountains on 12 June (above). Over the following days he had fallen back west as far as Voghera, with the intention of rejoining the army at Alessandria. Suvorov had other ideas for him, since Ott's command was the only force capable of imposing any delay on Macdonald before the allied army could get to grips. Suvorov therefore commanded Ott to march back up the highway, and reinforced his previous order, namely to hold out as long as he could in front of Piacenza, and then, in the face of irresistible pressure, to execute a staged retreat from river line to river line, and finally to hold at all costs the choke point of Stradella, where the northernmost spur of the Apennines advanced to almost within cannon shot of the Po.

By 16 June the French had arrived to the east of Piacenza, and they opened their attack against Ott at ten in the morning. It was soon evident that Macdonald was advancing with the greater part of his army up the axis of the highway, with the division of Victor in the lead, and that of Rusca veering out to the south to extend the left flank. A lieutenant-colonel of the Austrian engineers, Albert Johann de Best, had been at work now for eight days setting up palisades at the citadel of Piacenza and putting it in a generally good state of defence, but it was vital to win extra hours to plant the artillery and enable Lieutenant-Colonel Rheinwald with two or three companies of the regiment of Frelich to arrive from the Trebbia and provide the garrison. De Best was aided by three squadrons of the Erzherzog Joseph Hussars which had fallen back from the Taro, and he found a good site for a holding action in front of Piacenza:

> Ott's division comprised scarcely 5,000 combatants, and the enemy general Macdonald advanced at speed in columnar formation to drive it from its position. I hastened against the enemy column with two pieces of horse artillery and an escort of cavalry, and shot up the head of the column so effectively that it had to halt and deploy, which gave Ott's division time to fall back in the presence of the enemy and without loss to the far side of the Tidone. He left his rearguard along the Tidone and encamped his divisional reserve at Castel San Giovanni. Ott's division remained in this position, even though it was under orders to fall back to Stradella.[6]

In reality Ott suspected that the French were inclining towards the Apennines to turn his right flank, and he doubted whether he would be able to hold firm on the Tidone when, as would surely happen, he came under full attack on 17 June.

On receiving Ott's report. Chasteler persuaded Suvorov that troops must be rushed from the main army to the Stradella position. Every minute counted, and the Russian advance guard under Bagration was standing inconveniently to the north of the highway at Casatisma. Chasteler therefore took command

of the forces most immediately at hand on the highway itself—these were components of the Austrian division of Frelich, and consisted of the grenadier battalion of Wouwermanns, the three battalions of the regiment of Frelich (minus the companies under Rheinwald), the dragoon regiment of Karaiczay and two batteries of horse artillery. He extracted one hundred of the Karaiczay Dragoons and the best-mounted half battery of the horse artillery, and set off for Stradella at ten at night, after ordering the rest of this little force to hasten up behind at their best possible speed.

THE BATTLE OF THE TIDONE, 17 JUNE

The rivers of the northernmost Apennines course between the verdant spurs of the foothills, then on reaching the plain of the Po they wind towards that river through shifting beds of white pebbles. The Trebbia just to the west of Piacenza was known to Suvorov and other students of Classical history as the scene of the victory of Hannibal over the Consul Sempronius in 218 B.C. Now in the middle of June 1799 the thoughts of Suvorov were focused more narrowly on the smaller river Tidone, between five and eight kilometres to the west, where the Austrian division of Ott stood in the way of Macdonald's army. The longer Ott stood his ground, the more time the allies would have to secure the Stradella passage, and reach the neighbourhood of Castel San Giovanni, where the plain first widened sufficiently to enable them to deploy their army. If Ott's troops broke, then the fugitives would be pressed back on the army when it was still in column of march, opening the prospect of the entire allied force being jammed between the Po and the foothills and being destroyed.

As far as it can be retrieved from the surviving evidence, Macdonald's first objective was to secure the line of the Tidone, which at a width of one hundred metres was much narrower than the Trebbia, but passed between steep banks two or three metres high, which gave it a greater defensive value. Here or in the neighbourhood he would await the coming of Moreau's troops from Genoa. The margins of

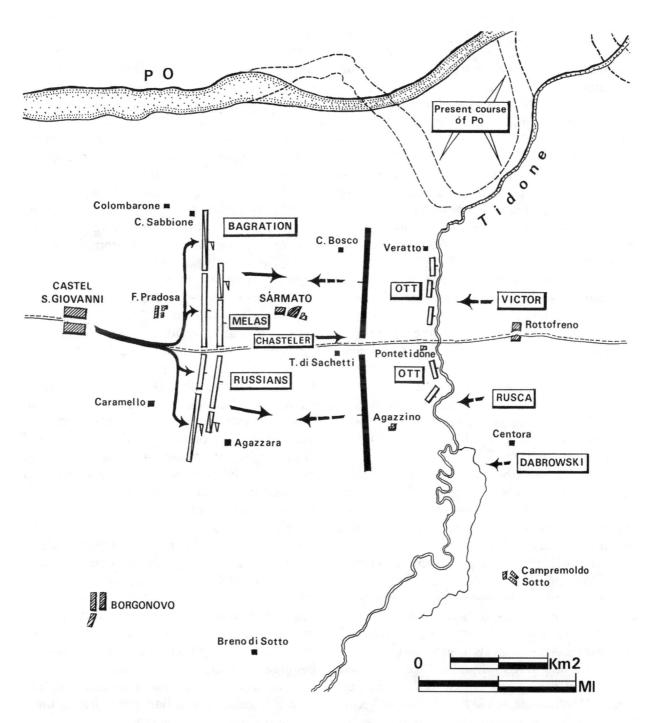

The Battle of the Tidone, 17 June

space, time and numbers were as tight for Macdonald as they were for the allies, which is why he decided to throw his first available 18,700 troops (divisions of Victor, Rusca and Dabrowski, advance guard under Salme) into the attack, and order up the rest of the army by forced marches. Even the troops at hand made an impressive array, drawn up from the Po to the foothills, with Victor as before on the right towards the Po and along the highway, Rusca in the centre, and the Poles on the left at Campremoldo.

Macdonald could not direct the arrangements in person, for his wounds (those relics of his encounter with the Bussy Chasseurs) had been aggravated by the jolting of his carriage, and he was unable to move from his lodging just to the west of Piacenza in Borgo San Antonio. He was not easy to find even in that little place. Captain Kolewsky came searching for him with a message from Dabrowski, and was rightly directed towards a modest building whose only remarkable feature was a mural of Our Lady, crowned with a circlet of stars and crushing the serpent underfoot. As a supporter of the godless Revolution he should have taken note of this sinister omen, but he exclaimed that it was 'inconceivable for a Republican to have taken up his lodging in this nest of Jesuits.'[7]

The command therefore devolved on Victor who, unknown to Macdonald, declined to stir from Piacenza town: 'thenceforward all co-ordination ceased, and that was the main reason for the disorder which ensued.'[8]

At eight in the morning of 17 June the French and Poles began to splash across the shallow waters of the Tidone, then pressed home their attacks against Colonel d'Aspre's Austrian Jäger 'with quite extraordinary determination,'[9] driving the Austrian posts from Veratto di Sopra, Pontetidone and Agazzino. The Poles exploited in an outflanking movement to the south by way of Mottaziana, while the division of Victor developed a powerful attack in the centre towards Sarmato, and was held at bay only by an Austrian battery which swept the highway with canister, and by two battalions of the regiment of Nádasdy in close support in the village of Sármato behind.

Chasteler had meanwhile rushed his improvised advance guard towards the ridge at Stradella. He had stretched out ahead with the leading troops, and soon after midnight he had climbed to the summit of this commanding feature, and emplaced there one of the 6-pounder cannon and fifty of the Karaiczay Dragoons, whom he deployed to fight on foot. He sent an officer to tell Ott that the main army would be up to support him at San Giovanni. The messenger had hardly set off downhill into the darkness when the rest of the advance guard arrived on the scene. Chasteler hastened on alone to the Tidone and reached Ott just before the French attack developed. He renewed his plea to Ott to delay the enemy as long as possible, and on turning back west he found that his reinforcements were already half-way on the highway from Stradella.

The fresh troops came into action from one in the afternoon of 17 June—first the Wouwermanns grenadier battalion at Monte dei Gabbi, then one of the Frelich battalions at Torre di Sachetti (on the site of the present sugar factory), and the other two along the Aversa stream on either side of the highway. In spite of this accession of force the odds were still overwhelmingly on the side of the enemy, and at three in the afternoon the village of Sármato and the outlying battery, both of which had changed hands several times, were seemingly lost once and for all.

However the outcome of the battle and the campaign as a whole hung on the possession of San Giovanni five kilometres to the west, and Ott and 3,000 survivors were still holding the vital ground in front of the little town when Melas arrived with three battalions of Austrian infantry, and the remaining squadrons of the Erzherzog Joseph Hussars. These troops belonged not to the main army, but to Ott's reserve, and Melas had cast aside all his dignity as a full general and had been urging them forward like a colonel or major.

Suvorov accompanied the Russian advance guard under Prince Bagration when the main army set itself in motion in the early hours of the 17th. He was escorted by a lone Cossack, which permitted him to conceal himself in ambush behind trees or houses along the route, then dash out in front of the startled and delighted troops and take the lead. The main body followed in six columns, with the artillery and baggage assigned to the highway in the centre. Strict march discipline was nevertheless applied whenever inspiration flagged in the heat. Stragglers who complained were beaten with ramrods, while the Cossacks who policed the rear of the columns were delighted to torment the suffering Austrians of the division of Frelich.

Suvorov and the main force of the Cossacks now hastened out ahead of the infantry of the Russian advance guard, and when the field-marshal arrived near the scene of the action he detached Major-General Andrei Ivanovich Gorchakov with the Molchanov and Semernikov Cossacks to the left against the French. The Grekov and Posdeev Cossacks, supported by Chasteler's command (the Karaiczay Dragoons, the grenadier battalion Wouwermanns and the three battalions of the regiment of Frelich) simultaneously veered to the right or south to attack the Poles. The Cossacks cried out 'Praga! Praga!' to remind the Poles of the massacre of 1794, 'and so these wandering remnants of a once famous nation... found themselves, by an extraordinary sequence of events, face-to-face with the despoilers of their native land.'[10]

Although the odds were turning against them, the French made such strenuous efforts to aid the Poles that they nearly succeeded in snatching back the initiative. Colonel Joseph Nimptsch of the Karaiczay Dragoons talks of a counterattack in the southern sector which repulsed the Cossacks and for a time threatened the flank and rear of the allied infantry.[11] Further accounts mention French pushes along the highway, and between there and the Po against Mezzana and Colombarone, however 'the speed of their movements, the superiority of their fire, the agility with which they side-stepped the enemy lunges, the personal courage of every leader—none of this proved of any avail against the Russian impassivity, that sheep-liked obstinacy against which the Prussian discipline and the tactics of Frederick the Great had likewise failed in their time.'[12]

The allies secured themselves in the direction of the Po by deploying the Jäger regiment of Bagration at Fontana Pradosa, while the four combined Russian grenadier battalions and the two battalions of the Austrian regiment of Mittrowsky gave close support, and succeeded in meeting and turning back the thrust along the highway. This was an encounter battle, and it would be misleading to attempt to fit such episodes into a coherent sequence. The contemporary maps are a more useful guide, and they emphasise how the successive forces of the allies pressed through Castel San Giovanni and along the highway in a dense column, then deployed in two lines of battle along a total frontage of some five kilometres, with the left (northern) wing extending to just in front of Ca' Sabbione, the centre athwart the highway on the swell of ground between Fontana Pradosa and Sármato, and the far right sited behind the cassines of Agazzara and Berlasco. A full-scale battle was now in progress, and 'several French officers here experienced their first encounter with Russian courage. They exclaimed: "Those Russians fight well! They throw themselves into the attack with cold steel, and come on singing. They are quite different people from the Neapolitans!'[13]

The allies recovered Sármato and the abandoned Austrian battery, and by the late afternoon the enemy were falling back towards the Tidone. The French still had plenty of fight in them, and they took advantage of the close-set country of hedges and ditches to inflict heavy losses on the combined Austrian cavalry, which launched a number of unsupported attacks. The final retreat of the main forces of the French across the little river was covered by the advance guard under Salme, who formed a battalion square at Ca' del Bosco. By nine in the evening the fighting was over.

The French had engaged more than 18,000 troops in the action, most of them from the outset, which for a time gave them a clear advantage over Ott's Austrians (reducing to 3,000 battered survivors). Ott had held on with the help of Chasteler, and then the arrival of Melas, Suvorov and Bagration in very rapid succession built up the allies to a decisively superior 30,656 men in regular troops alone.

The losses are not fully distinguishable from those incurred over the following three days of fighting, but Stutterheim (a good authority) records that the French left about 1,000 casualties and 1,200 prisoners on the field. [14]

Most immediately the action was probably lost by the French through the lack of effective higher command, and won for the allies by the speed with which Suvorov moved up to the Tidone. 'We are justified in seeing the action on the 17th as the preliminary to the main battle. We got to the Trebbia [Tidone] before the enemy, and delivered the first blow to their morale. They found themselves in combat with a new and unfamiliar foe.' [15]

In a wider context Macdonald recalled long afterwards how he had lain stricken near Piacenza, hearing the fire, and still without any news of Moreau, who should have arrived from Genoa and fallen on the allied flank and rear, 'and even now, nearly twenty-five years after those events, I am convinced that success would have been ours if it had not been for hesitation on the part of Moreau.' The divisions of Montrichard and Olivier were hurrying up from Macdonald's rear,

> but where was the Army of Italy ? [i.e. Moreau] What direction was it taking? I knew nothing. As long as we remained separated the most prudent course would have been to retreat, and thus avoid the risk of giving battle when the odds were so much against us. But if I made off, and the Army of Italy subsequently arrived over the mountains in the expectation of meeting the Army of Naples, then the Army of Italy would have been the one that was unsupported and certain to be beaten. I would have been unable to offer any kind of excuse if I had not put up a fight, and in that case you can be sure that I would have been accused of treason. Instead, they claimed in the Army of Italy that personal animosity impelled me to give battle before we could join them... I spent a miserable night in the fear of being attacked next morning before I had all my forces together, and before the disorder of the previous evening had been remedied. [16]

FORCES ON THE TREBBIA

ALLIED ARMY, FIELD-MARSHAL SUVOROV

General Rosenberg commanded the first two (mainly Russian) columns and was present with the second column; General Melas commanded the third (mainly Austrian) column.

First (left-hand Column)

Advance Guard, Maj-Gen Bagration	
Jäger regiment Bagration	2 bn
Combined grenadier battalions:	
Dendrygin	
Lomonosov	
Sanaev	
Kalemin	4 bn
Austrian Dragoon Regt Karaiczay:	6 sq
Cossack regiments:	
Grekov	
Posdeev	
Division Lt-Gen Schveikovsky	
Grenadier Regt Rosenberg:	2 bn
Musketeer regiments:	
Schveikovsky	1 bn
Dalheim	1 bn
Austrian Dragoon Regt Lobkowitz:	6 sq

Second (central) Column, Lt-Gen Förster

(General Rosenberg also present, and in tactical command of right-hand units)

Division Förster	
Musketeer regiments:	
Förster	1 bn
Baranovsky	1 bn
Tyrtov	2 bn
Miloradovich	2 bn
Jung-Baden	1 bn
Austrian Dragoon Regt Levenehr:	6 sq
Cossack Regt Molchanov	

Third (left-hand) Column, General Melas

Division Ott	
Infantry regiments:	
Nádasdy	4 bn
Mittrowsky	2 bn
Mihanovich (Serbian free bn)	1 bn
6th Banater Croats:	small bn
D'Aspre Jäger	6 coys
Hussar Regt Erzherzog Joseph	6 sq
Cossack Regt Semernikov	
Reserve Division Lt-Gen Frelich	6 bn
Combined grenadier battalions:	
Pertusi	

Paar
Weber
Morzin
Wouwermanns
Schiaffinatti

N.B: These is no record of allied unit strengths. The trustworthy Stutterheim puts the overall numbers at 9,851 Austrian infantry and 4586 cavalry, and 16,219 Russian infantry and 2,000 cossacks, or a grand total of 32,656, with an unknown number of gunners in addition.

FRENCH ARMY, GENERAL MACDONALD
(strengths as of the end of May)

Advance Guard Brigade Salme

15th Light demi-brigade:	1,390
11th Line demi-brigade:	1,440
25th Chasseur Regt (detachment)	94
Artillery and sappers:	53
Total:	*2,997*

Division Watrin

62nd Line demi-brigade	2,426
78th Line demi-brigade	2,137
25th Chasseur Regt:	284
Artillery and sappers:	33
Total:	*4,880*

Division Olivier

12th Line demi-brigade	1,374
30th Line demi-brigade	1,480
73rd Line demi-brigade	1,980
7th Chasseur regt	327
19th Chasseur regt	361
Artillery and sappers:	304
Total:	*5,826*

Division Montrichard

5th Light demi-brigade	1,900
2nd Line demi-brigade	730
21st Line demi-brigade	1,000
68th Line demi-brigade	900
1st Cavalry Regt	263
12th Dragoon Regt	200
11th Hussar Regt	250
Cisalpine Dragoon Regt	100
Cisalpine Hussar Regt	308
Artillery and sappers:	122
Total:	*5,773*

Division Victor

5th Line demi-brigade	1,300
39th Line demi-brigade	1,225
92nd Line demi-brigade	1,240
93rd Line demi-brigade	1,265
99th Line demi-brigade	1,320

15th Chasseur Regt:	400
Total:	*6,750*

Division Rusca

17th Light demi-brigade	1,883
55th Line demi-brigade	880
97th Line demi-brigade	1,755
16th Dragoon regt	490
19th Dragoon regt	339
Artillery and sappers:	50
Total:	*5,397*

Division Dabrowski

8th Line demi-brigade:	555
1st Polish Legion:	2,800
Polish cavalry:	200
Total:	*3,555*

Artillery Park	526

Army Total: 30,980 infantry, 3,616 cavalry, 1,088 gunners and sappers

Grand Total: *35,684.*

N.B: From these we must deduct the unknown losses sustained at Modena and on 17 June, which could bring the grand total down to about 33,500.

In terms of numbers, therefore the armies were probably evenly matched.

THE FIRST DAY ON THE TREBBIA, 18 JUNE

The events of the 17th told Macdonald that the main force of the allies had extracted itself from the confrontation with Moreau, and marched eastwards with amazing speed to check him in open battle. His total forces behind the Tidone still numbered only 22,000, and he decided to stay his hand until the afternoon of the 18th, by when the divisions of Olivier and Montrichard would arrive to build his troops up to their full available strength of some 33,500 men and allow him to resume the attack. This delay, so he hoped, would also permit Lapoype's brigade from Moreau's army to descend from the upper Trebbia against the allied right flank, and for Moreau himself to appear on the enemy rear. Still suffering from his wounds, Macdonald toured his forces along the Tidone in the morning. He found the enemy quiet and his troops now in good order.

Now that the initiative and advantage

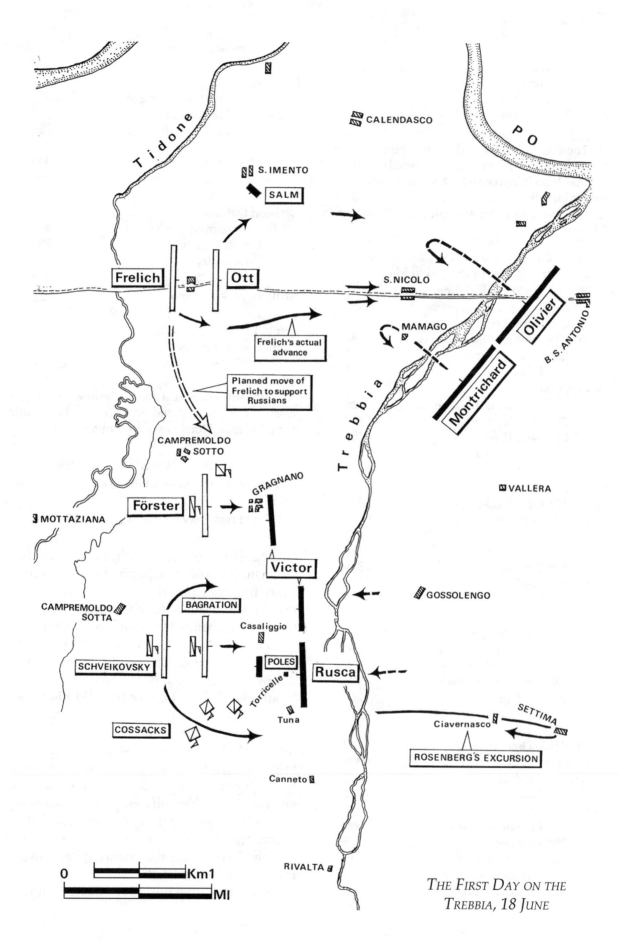

TIDONE

PO

CALENDASCO

S. IMENTO

SALM

Frelich   Ott

S. NICOLO

Frelich's actual
advance

MAMAGO

Planned move of
Frelich to support
Russians

Olivier

Montrichard

B.S. ANTONIO

Trebbia

CAMPREMOLDO
SOTTO

VALLERA

GRAGNANO

Förster

MOTTAZIANA

Victor

GOSSOLENGO

CAMPREMOLDO
SOTTA

BAGRATION

Casaliggio

SCHVEIKOVSKY

POLES   Rusca

Torricelle

SETTIMA

Tuna

Ciavernasco

COSSACKS

ROSENBERG'S EXCURSION

Canneto

0   Km1

MI

RIVALTA

*THE FIRST DAY ON THE
TREBBIA, 18 JUNE*

98

seemed to lie with the allies, Suvorov and Chasteler hatched an ambitious plan of attack, whereby the allies would sweep from the Tidone and all the way across the Trebbia to the Nure, and by increasingly weighting their attack on their right, cut off the French from the Apennines and force them towards the Po. It was a deliberate application of the 'oblique order' of Frederick the Great.

Suvorov dictated the character of the tactics in general, which were based in the main on columnar formation for the approach, and deployment into line for combat. 'When the enemy retreats, the cavalry and Cossacks set after them immediately, supported by infantry, which in this case advances not in line but in column, without losing time... The cavalry attacks in two lines in chequer formation, leaving intervals between the squadrons so that the second line can break through the gaps in case the attack of the first line is thrown back. The order "Halt!" is forbidden—that's just for the parade ground. In battle the only commands are "Attack! Cut! Thrust! Hurrah! Drums and Music!"'

The army was to be arranged in three columns, numbering from right to left, or south to north:

FIRST COLUMN

The Russian advance guard under Major-General Prince Bagration. Two battalions of Jäger, four grenadier battalions and two Cossack regiments, supported by six squadrons of Austrian dragoons. Bagration was to cross the Tidone at Breno, advance by way of

THE TREBBIA, LOOKING FROM THE RIGHT BANK TOWARDS RIVALTA

99

Campremoldo Sopra to force the Trebbia behind Casaliggio, and continue through Ciavernasco and Settima to the Nure at San Giorgio. 'The field-marshal was of the opinion that this column was to form the main attack.'[17]

The Russian division of Schveikovsky and the Austrian dragoon regiment of Lobkowitz were to follow in support.

SECOND COLUMN

The Russian division of Förster, consisting of seven battalions, one regiment of Cossacks, and the Austrian Levenehr Dragoons in support. Divided into two sub-columns, which were respectively to

—cross the Tidone, force the Trebbia in front of Gossolengo, then act in support of Bagration;

—cross the Tidone at Mottaziana, force the Trebbia behind Gragnano, and advance to the Nure by way of Vallera, San Bonico and I Vaccari.

THIRD COLUMN

A predominantly Austrian formation consisting of two divisions

The seven battalions, six Jäger companies, six squadrons and the Cossack regiment of the division of Ott to advance along the axis of the highway, cross the Tidone, force the Trebbia and capture Borgo San Antonio, and continue the advance via San Lazzaro and Montalto to Ponte di Nure.

The eight battalions of the division of Frelich were considered as a mobile reserve, initially to move up behind Ott's command, but then (a crucial point) to veer sharply to the south to give added weight to the Russian attack on the right.[18]

Chasteler completed his plan at ten in the evening of the 17th, and asked Suvorov to determine the passwords for the challenge and response. After a moment's thought the field-marshal replied: '"Theresa," in memory of the great Empress of Germany, and "Kolin," which is the name of a victory which Field-Marshal Daun gained over the Prussians under Frederick II on 18 June 1757.'[19] This shows an interesting regard for Austrian sensibilities (see page 26).

The cloudless morning of 18 June arrived, and found the allied troops so exhausted by the previous day's marching and fighting that the departure was postponed from seven to eleven. During the lull Suvorov inspected his men, and 'it was moving to see how the venerable field-marshal rode along the line, and was greeted by a general shout of martial jubilation by his moustachioed warriors.'[20] Suvorov climbed the church tower of Sármato to view the ground to the east, and the patrols reported to him that the main forces of the enemy had fallen back from the Tidone to behind the Trebbia, but were still keeping strong concentrations on the near side of the Trebbia at Casaliggio, Gragnano, Mamago and San Nicolo.

The battle opened on the southern sector, as the plan provided. Bagration's column forded the Tidone, and marched with some difficulty—but probably also unseen—through a close-set country of ditches, rivulets, vineyards and acacia thickets. Just after one in the afternoon the Russians were close enough to see the enemy drawn up in order of battle at Casaliggio. Suvorov ordered the troops to halt to recover a little from their exertions in the heat, then sent them forward again at two. The attack came in against the Polish Legion of Dabrowski deployed to the south of Casaliggio, and the Russians advanced so swiftly and silently that the men of the Polish outposts had their throats cut before they could so much as open fire. There were a few moments of crisis when an unengaged Polish battalion advanced from Tuna against the Russian rear from the south, but this brave unit was itself cut off and forced to surrender. The work of the Russian Jäger and grenadiers was seconded on the flanks by the Cossacks, and by Colonel Joseph Nimptsch and two squadrons of the Austrian Karaiczay Dragoons who intercepted the Poles before they could reach the higher ground to the south, and took 230 of them prisoner.

The fighting on this sector assumed altogether greater dimensions when the French adjutant-general Gauthrin divined Suvorov's intentions from the weight of the Russian attack, and succeeded in bringing the main forces of the divisions of Rusca and Victor back to the left bank of the Trebbia, where for a time they threatened to overwhelm Bagration's command.

Bagration relates that 'our men fell back unwillingly, while the atheists were seized by exuberant pride and advanced to the accompaniment of music, the beating of drums and loud cries of: *Vive, République, vive! Liberté, Égalité! Vive! Vive! En avant!* Chains of skirmishers extended across the front of their column and along its flanks, and their cannon sowed death in our ranks.' At that moment Suvorov arrived at speed from the left. '"Halt!" cried Aleksandr Vasilevich, and at that instant the line of retreating troops stopped, and our concealed battery spewed cannon shot into the faces of the enemy. The French wavered in a state of shock, and stood for a while as the cannon shot, shells and canister from our hidden battery coursed through them. "Press on! *Stupai, Stupai!* With the bayonet! Hurrah!" yelled Aleksandr Vasilelvich. Our men rushed on in a body with Suvorov, our father, in the lead.'[21]

The Russian right wing was massed in depth, if not in any great width, and Rosenberg himself took charge of the reserve division of Schveikovsky, directing some of the troops to prolong Bagration's left wing, and the main force to support Bagration's right in the neighbourhood of Tuna and Torricelle. Finally, as a French historian puts it, 'Rusca had to recross the Trebbia so as to take up a good defensive position and cover his left wing. He

FIELDS BETWEEN MAMAGO AND GRAGNANO, SCENE OF FÖRSTER'S BATTLES

101

executed this manoeuvre in good order.'[22]

The battle was now unfolding down the whole west bank of the Trebbia, and the right wing of the division of Victor was caught up in the fighting which developed in front of Gragnano. The action on this sector began with a clash half-way from the allied crossing of the Tidone between the Molchanov Cossacks and the Levenehr Dragoons on the one side, and several squadrons of French cavalry on the other. The allied horse succeeded in pushing the French back on their infantry, and from five in the afternoon the Russian lieutenant-general Förster exploited this success by a steady advance with his infantry which finally threw the French from Gragnano and across the Trebbia.

Altogether the grand push on the allied right might have fulfilled all the hopes of Suvorov and Chasteler, if their calculations had not been thrown out by developments on their left or northern flank towards the Po.

Down on this sector the French advance brigade of Salme was standing well forward of the Trebbia, at Sant' Imento, to the north of the highway. Salme remained in this exposed position until towards 2.30 in the afternoon, when the divisions of Olivier and Montrichard crossed the Trebbia and marched to support him—they were fresh, apart from the exertions of the march, and Melas concluded that he now had the main weight of the enemy facing him, and that 'military principles, and my overview of events and circumstances' compelled him to depart from Suvorov's plan of attack, and so retain the reserve division of Frelich for his own purposes, instead of releasing it to support the Russians on the right wing.[23]

Ott's division opened the much-delayed Austrian attack towards six in the evening. He chased the weak brigade of Salme from Sant' Imento, and with the help of Frelich's massed grenadiers he forced the two newly-arrived French divisions back across the Trebbia. It was an important local success, but it fell far short of the battle-winning role which Suvorov had in mind for Frelich on the right wing.

Some curious incidents passed during the night. Rosenberg took personal charge of two battalions of Russian grenadiers and led them across the Trebbia above Gossolengo. His motives are unclear. Captain Gryazev commanded one of the companies and comments that 'it would be rash to guess what impelled him into this enterprise, which could well have been entrusted to a senior regimental officer. Since I am not privy to the secret intrigues of our senior commanders, it may be assumed that he did not wish to abandon us to our fate in what was bound to be a very critical operation.' The Russians picked their way through the sleeping Poles on the far side, and penetrated as far as Settima—or half-way to the Nure—completely undetected:

> We arrived in silence at the village at midnight… and here we learned from the local people that the French rearguard [sic] was located nearby in a field. Our hearts beat with joy, though we did not know in what strength the enemy might be. We found the enemy lying in heaps with no sentries on watch. We drew in our two flanks, then fired a volley, while our two pieces opened up with canister. We had them surrounded and we threw ourselves on them with the bayonet, killing them all except for a few who escaped in the darkness. All their weapons, ammunition, knapsacks and equipment fell into our hands, and we destroyed it all rather than have to carry it away. This rearguard had been responsible for guarding a number of prisoners, who were drawn from a variety of regiments, and these people now approached us through the darkness, and we could recognise them by their shouts of joy… The prisoners had been locked in a village wine store and kept under guard. When the firing broke out they assumed that Russians must have arrived. The guard promptly fled, whereupon the prisoners smashed open the door and came to join us.[24]

We may assume the joyful shouts of the prisoners had something to do with their place of detention.

Rosenberg formed his grenadiers into a square, and wrapped himself in his cloak to snatch a little sleep. No news came to him from the main body, and after the peasants had regaled the Russians with food and some rather

102

fine wine, the grenadiers set off for the Trebbia at about three in the morning. They passed once more through the unconscious Poles, and re-crossed the river to the neighbourhood of Casaliggio. Four squadrons of the Karaiczay Dragoons had also established themselves on the far bank, but they had to abandon their bridgehead when they came under heavy fire from French infantry. The purpose of their expedition, like that of Rosenberg, remains a mystery.

Downstream from Mamago the French fancied they heard the distant rumble of Moreau's artillery fire (in fact the sound of Austrian artillery caissons). Without reference to their officers, the sergeants of three battalions got their men to their feet, and at 9.30 in the evening the French splashed and crunched over the six-hundred metre wide bed of the Trebbia to the west bank, where they caught an Austrian battalion unawares. Melas arrived on the scene, organised a counterattack by two of his companies, and summoned up support from the Russian division of Förster. The cry of 'Kavallerie vor!' likewise brought Prince Johann Liechtenstein and the six squadrons of the Lobkowitz Dragoons into the fight,

> and so in the course of a few minutes a perhaps quite unprecedented tussle broke out in the middle of the bed of the Trebbia. Everyone was yelling to everyone else. The troops were too closely engaged to open fire, and in the darkness and the crush they struck out blindly at all and sundry with swords, musket butts and spontoons. The artillery poured fire into the clumps from both banks, and because the moonlight was not sufficient to enable the gunners to take proper aim, or distinguish friend from foe, they killed them indiscriminately.[25]

The efforts of the Austrian, Russian and French officers brought this mindless action to an end at eleven at night.

The allied troops were ready to face the new battle that the next day would surely bring, and

> it was remarkable to observe how the men had endured the discomfort of one of the hottest day of summer and fought on with a quite extraordinary courage, as if they were

inspired by a common spirit… after setting out their sentries they laid themselves down on the banks of the Trebbia, exhausted from the combat, and slept as soundly as if they had been ten thousand miles distant from the enemy, instead of less than one thousand paces.[26]

These men were unaware how very far short the battle had fallen of the expectations of their chiefs. If we except Rosenberg's foray overnight, the allies had come nowhere near their objectives along the distant Nure, and by first light on the 19th the right bank of the nearby Trebbia was still wholly in the hands of the enemy, who were making ready to resume the offensive. No support had been forthcoming from Melas to enable Suvorov to implement his great right-flanking lunge, and communication between the two commanders came to an end.

THE SECOND DAY ON THE TREBBIA, 19 JUNE

Early on the morning of the 19th the Austrians detected French infantry massing on the far side of the Trebbia, and Melas ordered a battery of twelve pieces to advance to the near bank and drive them away. The French were goaded into retaliation, and at seven in the morning two of their battalions made their way across the Trebbia somewhere on the stretch between Rocco and Malpaga, under orders to seize the troublesome battery. They reached a dried-up channel of the river undetected (probably thanks to the bushes which grew on the pebbly islands), but they were discovered resting there by an Austrian officer on reconnaissance. He arranged to have two cannon brought up to a site from where they could take the French in enfilade, and at eight in the morning the Austrians opened a rapid fire of roundshot and canister. Every round threw up pebbles and splinters of stone, and only half the French survived to regain the east bank.

Otherwise the Austrians spent the early hours inactive. Melas explains that he waited anxiously for hours on end to hear what Suvorov had in mind, and only towards the end of the morning did he learn from Lieutenant-General Ott that Chasteler had sent him a *Disposition*,

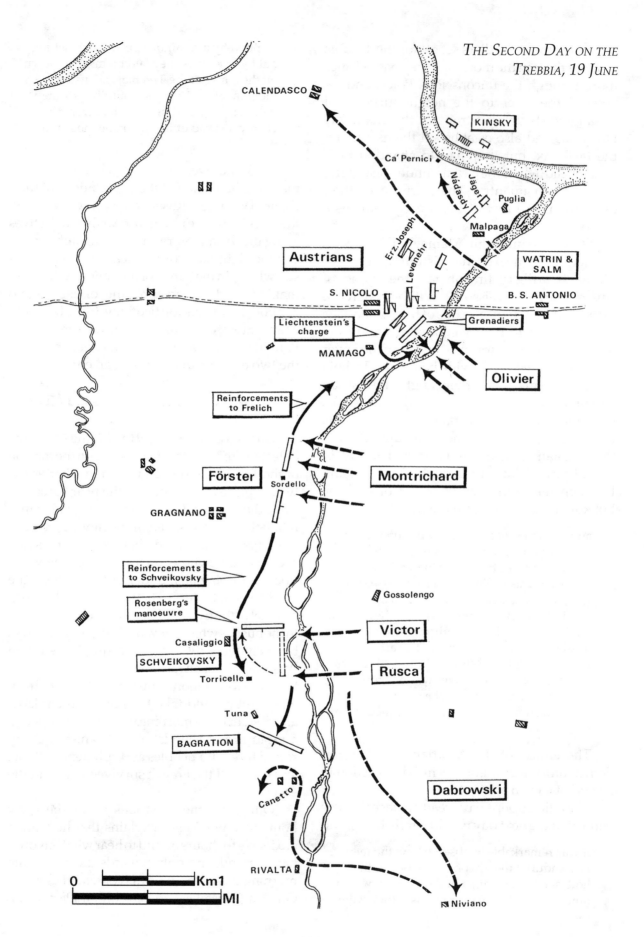

CALENDASCO

KINSKY

Ca' Pernici

Jäger

Puglia

Nádasdy

Malpaga

Erz. Joseph

Levenehr

Austrians

WATRIN & SALM

S. NICOLO

B. S. ANTONIO

Liechtenstein's charge

Grenadiers

MAMAGO

Olivier

Reinforcements to Frelich

Förster

Sordello

Montrichard

GRAGNANO

Reinforcements to Schveikovsky

Gossolengo

Rosenberg's manoeuvre

Victor

Casaliggio

SCHVEIKOVSKY

Rusca

Torricelle

Tuna

BAGRATION

Canetto

Dabrowski

0   Km1

MI

RIVALTA

Niviano

whereby the combined army was supposed to attack in exactly the same way as envisaged for the 18th, namely in three main columns, and with the division of Frelich being sent to support the Russians on the right wing. The operation was supposed to have begun at six in the morning, or five hours before. Now that the timetable was so badly astray, Melas saw no harm in allowing his troops to set up their cooking pots and eat their first meal in four days.[27]

Along the Russian sector upstream the first light of dawn had shown considerable movement among the enemy. The sun had scarcely lifted above the horizon they assembled a battery of ten or a dozen cannon opposite the division of Förster. 'They opened up with the guns all of a sudden, and kept up a heavy fire— perhaps they fired up to two hundred rounds— but without persuading us to move a single man… The enemy nevertheless appeared happy enough with this feint, and they marched off in such numbers up the Trebbia to our right that the movement seemed like a retreat. During their whole progress they were shot up by our cannon planted along the Trebbia, which frequently had the effect of throwing them off their line of march.' Otherwise the Russians

Rivalta

were as slow to bestir themselves as the Austrians. Suvorov finally made his appearance at eleven in the morning, and he was in the process of giving verbal orders to the Russian column commanders when his whole army was overtaken by a general attack on the part of the enemy.[28]

Macdonald's army was advancing in six mostly widely-separated columns on a total frontage of fourteen kilometres. Compared with the action on the 18th the new battle was extended considerably to the south by a wide left-flanking movement on the part of Dabrowski's Polish Legion, which marched by way of Niviano to cross the upper Trebbia opposite Rivalta—this was the 'retreat' which the Russians had noted earlier in the morning. Downstream the divisions of Rusca and Victor were to wade the Trebbia side by side (the only example of a concerted attack) and assault the allied centre in the neighbourhood of Torricelle and Casaliggio. The divisions of Dabrowski, Rusca and Victor together numbered up to 15,000 troops, and came under the overall command of Victor.

Downstream again the division of Montrichard (up to 5,700 troops) was assigned to pass the river and attack in the neighbourhood of Gragnano, at the potentially vulnerable junction of the Russian and Austrian forces. To his right the division of Olivier (up to 5,300) was to hit the Austrians squarely between Mamago and the highway. Nearest the Po the combined reserve and advance guard under Watrin and Salme (about 7,000) would move on Caldenasco and turn the allied left flank. Macdonald still hoped that Moreau would be coming at the allied rear, and that the detached brigade of Lapoype would advance from the Apennines down the upper Trebbia and arrive on the allied right flank.

As for Macdonald's purpose in general, he explains that 'during the night I decided to take the offensive, regardless of the numerical superiority of the enemy. I had fine troops, and the French character is better suited to the attack than the defence—and the army was eager to attack. It would probably never cross the minds of the enemy that we would get in our blow first.'[29]

Chasteler was standing with Bagration when he espied an enemy column (Dabrowski's Polish Legion) making for a crossing point facing Rivalta about four kilometres beyond the southern extremity of the allied right. Chasteler urged Bagration to get on the move, and the prince moved smartly up the left bank of the river with the Russian advance guard. Meanwhile the Poles waded the river, climbed the high and steep left bank (a spur of the Apennines), seized the little walled village of Rivalta from Russian outposts and advanced as far north as Canneto. The Poles were well supported by their artillery, and Dabrowski galloped among his companies calling out: 'Poles, show no mercy to the oppressors of your fatherland!'

Between Canneto and Tuna the Poles encountered Bagration's command, advancing at speed from the north:

Field-Marshal Suvorov was present, and he was a model of composure when he observed the various movements of the enemy, as they marching across the Trebbia in columns. A single word… was enough to set the Russians hastening to meet the attack at every point. The advance guard under Prince Bagration set itself against the enemy [Polish] column which had divided in two and was rushing on, and his Jäger and grenadiers went into the attack with the bayonet, receiving powerful support from the artillery. The pulks of Cossacks were in loose order and swarmed around the enemy flank and rear. [20]

The Poles were thrown back across the Trebbia with heavy loss, and Dabrowski owed his life to a history book (on the Thirty Years War) which intercepted a Russian bullet.

The French army was now breaking across the river downstream. Rusca had detached four of his battalions (the 55th demi-brigade, and the first battalion of the 97th) to support Dabrowski, and he had been making heavy weather of crossing the Trebbia under the fire of fourteen pieces of Schveikovsky's artillery, which was throwing up showers of pebbles and cutting whole companies apart. At about noon, however, the 55th returned from Dabrowski to its parent division, and the French now had the

106

means of exploiting the gap of 1,500 paces which had opened up in the allied deployment when Bagration moved to his right to counter the Poles. Rusca's troops irrupted from the river bank and advanced across a field of rye to the neighbourhood of Tuna and Torricelle, from where a battery of their horse artillery shot up the grenadier regiment of Rosenberg (of Schveikovsky's division) in flank and rear.

It was the middle of the afternoon, and the sun was beating down as fiercely as ever. General Rosenberg in person went to report the crisis to Suvorov, and found the old man prostrated by the heat and sitting on a stone. Bagration had just arrived from the right wing, and claims that Suvorov received Rosenberg with some displeasure: "Just try to move this stone. You can't, can you? Well, it's just as difficult to dislodge the Russians!" The field-marshal turned to Bagration:

'Tell me now, Petr, how is it going?' 'Badly, Your Excellency,' I answered. 'We are tired out, it's difficult to get the muskets to fire [they were becoming fouled], the enemy are strong…' Here Aleksandr Vasilevich interrupted me: 'God have mercy on us! That's not at all good, Prince Petr! Bring up my horse!' He mounted and rode on to my line of battle. For a time I was preoccupied with my command, and did not notice that he had ordered Cossack and Jäger units up at speed from the unengaged reserve. Then we rode together to my troops. The warriors saw their father Aleksandr Vasilevich, and they were resurrected as if they had had a visitation from the Holy Spirit. The French attack gained consistently in strength, but then, thanks be to God, something miraculous happened! Our rate of fire increased, our muskets somehow became more lethal, and the men, who had been demoralised by exhaustion, now revived. Everyone came to life, imbued with new

TORRICELLE

107

vigour! Aleksandr Vasilevich ordered the drums to beat, and in an instant the scattered ranks of my men coalesced. 'Prince Petr,' said Aleksandr Vasilevich, 'we shall strike and be after them! That's the way to beat the enemy!' Upon my command my whole line hurled itself forward. The French were thrown back, and overcome by the bayonets and lances in a massacre that few of them escaped with their lives.[31]

This was not the full story, as may well be imagined. Austrian sources have Rosenberg acting with considerable more resource, by wheeling back part of the division of Schveikovsky by ninety degrees to form a new front facing south against the breakthrough. Moreover Bagration's troops had arrived in the first place because Chasteler had sent an officer to tell him to return from the scene of his action against the Poles and come at the French breakthrough from the rear. Finally Chasteler in person betook himself north to the division of Förster, which was standing in front of Gragnano, and proceeded to extract four battalions from the second line and march them in column to the threatened right centre.

Chasteler's four battalions passed just to the east of Casaliggio and hit Rusca's right flank at four in the afternoon, at about the same time as Bagration assaulted his left. Bagration's Jäger and grenadiers had been hastening north at the double, and they were seconded as usual by the Karaiczay Dragoons, who threw themselves into the French and helped to take four hundred prisoners.[32] Rusca's division gave way after twenty minutes, but then retreated across the Trebbia in relatively good order under cover of its supporting artillery, and succeeded in holding the far bank against several Russian counterattacks.

Chasteler's march would have been impossible if the division of Victor had made any progress against Casaliggio. The French had established themselves on the left bank at noon, but their further efforts were halted by the left wing of the division of Schveikovsky and part of Förster's division, and after holding their ground for a time in the heat of the day the exhausted troops trailed back over the Trebbia.

The last shots on this part of the field were exchanged at seven in the evening.

The French forces destined to attack the allied left centre were composed of two disparate elements—the division of Montrichard and its lazy commander, who were pining for the easy life they had enjoyed in Tuscany, and the much more energetically-led division of Olivier.

Olivier was ready to attack at ten in the morning, according to Macdonald's instructions, but the operation had to be delayed for a good hour because Montrichard's division was typically slow to arrive. Luckily for the French, the massing of their troops along the east bank was concealed by trees and bushes, and the Austrians remained off their guard, resting and preparing their meal. Some time towards noon a body of French cavalry burst from the trees, and splashed through the Trebbia at such speed that it was able to gain the west bank almost unscathed and scatter the Austrian outposts. Behind them Olivier's infantry slid down the bank, crossed the islands and channels at the run, then pushed along the axis of the highway to capture two guns and the village of San Niccolo from the division of Ott, which was engaged in its third day of combat.

The Austrians might have caved in altogether, if Montrichard's troops to the south had attached with equal panache. Olivier was left unsupported, and his division was now caught off balance by a counterattack that was delivered against its left flank by a force of unengaged Austrian cavalry (one squadron of the Erzherzog Joseph Hussars, two divisions [pairs of squadrons] each of the Levenehr and Lobkowitz Dragoons) under the immediate leadership of Lieutenant-General Prince Johann Joseph Liechtenstein.

This force had been standing in the Austrian rear as a kind of third line, and the sound of the first cannon shots carried to Liechtenstein when he was lunching with a group of officers. He suspected nothing untoward, and prompted by duty rather than alarm he mounted horse and rode off to investigate. Almost at once he found himself in a mass of fleeing troops and vehicles, with the enemy close behind. He returned and placed himself at the head of his cavalry:

The general flight prevented us from progressing along the highway, and so I led my force to the right through the vineyards, where we encountered some particularly awkward obstacles in the shape of a series of ditches, which the troopers had to jump—but they were keen, and they had their reward when we attained our objective. I emerged from the vineyards at the head of the column of cavalry, about eight hundred to one thousand paces from the Trebbia, then deployed and proceeded to attack the flank and rear of the enemy who were chasing our fleeing army.[33]

The French at once broke off their pursuit, and the first unit of the Austrian infantry to come at them was the grenadier battalion of Wouwermanns under its acting commander Captain Ludwig L'Olivier (like Chasteler, one of the last bearers of the Netherlandish tradition in the Austrian army). The grenadiers advanced with sounding music, and, as Liechtenstein experienced, they had to contend not so much with the French as with the hedges and ditches among the vineyards. The contingent from the regiment of de Ligne became particularly entangled, and Lieutenant de Montfleury had to clear the way for his men through the bushes and vines by mighty swipes with his sword. The grenadiers finally reached the bank of the Trebbia when the French were in the process of turning about a pair of captured 12-pounders, and Montfleury led an attack which carried on some way across the river before the grenadiers were overtaken by altogether greater events.[34]

One of the reasons why Liechtenstein's intervention had been so effective was that the whole of the left flank of the French division of Olivier had been exposed by the failure of Montrichard's division to the south. Montrichard's troops had been taken under violent fire while still crossing the Trebbia in widely-separated columns. The 5th light demi-brigade deployed in line on the far bank, but its further advance was halted by an Austrian battery and by a battalion of Austrian grenadiers which dropped one hundred of the French in its first volley (Gachot identifies the Austrians as the Wouwermanns grenadiers, which is a possibility, though subsequent events make it

unlikely, and Liechtenstein's account has the Wouwermanns battalion advancing from San Nicolo to the north, which makes more sense[35]). Counterattacks by the Russian division of Förster and the rest of Frelich's Austrians now had Montrichard's troops fleeing across the Trebbia and north-east towards Piacenza, and the combined allied force closed in on Olivier's flank to complete his defeat.

The press of French fugitives actually threatened to overwhelm the Wouwermanns grenadiers in the bed of the Trebbia, but the Austrians held firm in closed ranks until Förster's Russians broke through to help them. The grenadiers and the Russians then fell back to the west bank and consolidated there.

The reports of the French breakthrough on the Russian right (above) made Melas hesitate to order a full-scale advance to the east bank, and the thing was made altogether impossible by the news that an enemy force had turned his left flank in the direction of the Po. This was the doing of the hitherto unengaged French advance guard (Salme) and reserve division (Watrin), which had forded the Trebbia towards noon, broken through the screen of Austrian outposts, and progressed in two main columns to the Ca' Pernici and as far as two farm complexes in front of Caldenasco. The bold Watrin (the most aggressive and independently-minded of the French middle-ranking commanders) would have pushed on towards the Tidone and cut in against the allied rear if a great clamour from the main battle had not told him that something was going wrong.

Melas dispatched Liechtenstein to eliminate this nuisance with nine companies of infantry, a couple of hundred Cossacks, one squadron of the Lobkowitz Dragoons and one division of the Erzherzog Joseph Hussars. This force came at the French from the south at the same time as Watrin and Salme were being shot up from the north by a battery of artillery which Colonel Kinsky had brought up from the Mantua siege army and planted on the far side of the Po. The guns were escorted by five companies of infantry and a gang of armed peasants. Under this double pressure Watrin and Salme retreated in good order across the Trebbia, leaving three hundred of their men prisoners in the hands of the Austrians.

The actions on the lower Trebbia were the last of the battle, and the firing along this stretch of the river died away at nine in the evening. 'The combined Imperial army remained on the ground where it had been fighting. The banks of the Trebbia and the bed of the river itself were strewn with bodies, and all the farm houses behind the front were packed with wounded.'[36]

The French lining the hedges on the east bank had repulsed every attempt on the part of the allies to force the passage, but when their surviving generals reassembled at Macdonald's quarters the confusion was so great that they were unable to give him any accurate returns of their divisional strengths. In fact the French had only 7-8,000 battleworthy troops with which to face 27,000 allies. Macdonald records:

There was now news of Moreau and his Army of Italy, or of the detachment [Lapoype's] which was supposed to be arriving from Bobbio to come at the enemy right wing from behind. It was obvious from the deployment of the Austro-Russian forces to our front that they had no worries for their rear. We were much weakened, we had hardly any generals left, and we were almost completely out of ammunition. A powerful army stood to our front, while the route leading to our rear was under fire from the guns in Piacenza citadel and another large battery [Kinsky's] on the far side of the Po… We were certain to be attacked the next day, and if we were beaten everything was lost. I had done enough to effect the junction, and there was no point in any further wasted effort. I had to conserve the surviving two-thirds of our army for the effort needed to extricate ourselves from this awkward situation, and to seek our fortunes elsewhere.[37]

At ten in the evening Macdonald gave the orders for the retreat. While the French infantry and cavalry redoubled their camp fires, the engineers set about building a new bridge across the Nure to carry the army well clear of the citadel of Piacenza, which was firing random shots into the night. The artillery and the baggage carts set out once the crossing was complete, and the rest of the army departed from midnight in some confusion.

To the allies it seemed that this bitter contest would have no end. Suvorov resolved to press home his advantage by a new attack, and the allied columns began to wade the Trebbia at four in the morning of 20 June. The troops had to step between the French dead and wounded to reach the far bank, but when the emerged from the riverside trees they found that Macdonald's army had gone.

Over the three days of fighting the allies had lost about 6,000 men from all causes. The Austrian lists includes the losses sustained during the pursuit on the 20th, and amounts to 254 killed, 1,903 wounded and 500 missing, a total of 2,657. In detail:

Infantry regiments:	
Nádasdy	565
Mittrowsky	198
Frelich	348
Grenadier battalions:	
Pertusi	106
Paar	109
Weber	62
Morzin	29
Wouwermanns	102
Schiaffinatti	37
Light Troops	
Mihanovich free bn	260
6th Banater Croats	115
Dragoon regts	
Lobkowitz	107
Levenehr	76
Karaiczay	62
Württemberg*	2
Hussar regt	
Erzherzog Joseph	152
Artillery	64 [38]

Russian Losses
681 killed, 2,073 wounded, missing unrecorded.

*(does not appear in the list of columns; its involvement must have been marginal)

The only verifiable figures related to the French losses are those of the 7,183 untransportable wounded found by the allies in Piacenza, and the further 200 in Parma, from which it is fair to assume that with the dead, the transportable wounded and the missing the

110

total could well have reached 12,000.

In general terms the actions on the first two days of fighting, on 17 and 18 June, had been shaped by the march of the reinforcements as they came panting up the highway to strengthen one combatant or the other. Just as the successive reinforcements brought up by Chasteler, Bagration, Melas and Suvorov checked Macdonald on the Tidone on the 17th, so the arrival of Montrichard and Olivier prevented the allies from sweeping across the Trebbia to the Nure on the 18th. The battle of the 19th was fought when almost all of the available forces were present on the field from the start.

Suvorov later told William Wickham that at the Trebbia the French had 'fought most *ably* and obstinately.'[39] This must relate to the tactical level, rather than the management of the battle as a whole. Macdonald, who was already probably inferior in numbers, scattered most of his attacking columns too widely, and his divisional commanders never gained enough depth beyond the western bank of the Trebbia to effect any manoeuvres of mutual support, if indeed they intended any at all.

There was much more ensemble on the side of the allies, at least among the divisional commanders, as witness the way Bagration and Rosenberg helped one another out during the various crises on the right and centre, and the support which Förster gave to Melas on the left. At the higher level we nevertheless find an almost total lack of accord between Melas and Suvorov. There was some excuse for the lack of preparedness among the Austrians on the morning of the 18th, but much less for their immobility and lack of vigilance on the 19th, when the troops of Olivier burst among them while they were at their ease among their cooking fires and piled muskets. On both days Melas denied Suvorov the division of Frelich, whose support for the Russian right was an integral part of the general plan of attack.

Melas was handsome in the acknowledgements he made to the cavalry commander Lieutenant-General Liechtenstein, and the sharp-eyed and active Major Joseph Radetzky in his capacity as general adjutant.

Radetzky was living up to this promise nearly fifty years later, but the suspicion must remain that Melas needed to build up the reputation of a rival to Chasteler, who was now identified irredeemably with the Russians.

Melas confided to a friend his belief that the Russians under Suvorov had been 'entirely beaten,' and mentioned that the Russians asked him for 2,000 muskets, which he suspected were replacements for weapons which had been thrown away during the battle.[40] The last comment probably has a ring of truth, for there had been occasions when the Russian discipline disintegrated on a mass scale. At times like that Suvorov's leadership never showed to better advantage. Suvorov had spent three days in the saddle on an ordinary Cossack horse, and Fuchs recalls one of those episodes when his appearance at the right time and place transformed the face of affairs. General Derfelden happened to be with Fuchs, and he turned to him with the comment: "Well, that's something that must be new to you. I have served under that incomprehensible man for thirty-five years, and I have come to recognise that he is like some kind of holy totem. You just have to carry him around and show him to the troops, and victory will be guaranteed. Time and time again a plan of his appeared to me a muddle, but the way it turned out proved the opposite. Catherine was right when she said she was sending two armies to Poland—one an army of troops, and the other—Suvorov." [41]

A greater achievement still was at the operational plane, for by marching at such speed from Alessandria Suvorov had brought Macdonald to battle when and where it was impossible for him to receive any support from Moreau.

Paul too recalled the last reign when he congratulated the field-marshal on his victory in the words which Suvorov himself had used to Catherine after his storm of Izmail: 'Glory to God! And to you be glory!' Suvorov's immediate reward was a miniature of the Emperor, with the command to wear it as a token of what a sovereign could owe to a subject who had made his reign illustrious. On 19 August Paul elevated Suvorov to a Prince of the Russian Empire with the suffix 'Italisky,' as recognition of the commander who in the course of four month had 'liberated the whole of Italy from its godless conquerors, and restored rightful governments and the course of law.'[42]

THE END OF MACDONALD

We left the allies on 20 June, when they had crossed the Trebbia to fight a new battle, but found that they had to convert their advance into a pursuit. Out on the left the Austrians entered Piacenza, and discovered that the town was piled with thousands of untransportable wounded, among them the generals Olivier, Rusca and Salme. Melas retained the division of Frelich in the town, and sent the division of Ott to support the pursuit.

The chase was headed by the Karaiczay Dragoons and one battery of horse artillery, and they made excellent progress until they ran into a substantial rearguard which was posted behind the Nure at San Giorgio. This force comprised cavalry, some determined infantry, and a number of guns that were served so well that they repulsed the Austrian dragoons and dismounted two pieces of the horsed battery. Bagration then arrived on the scene with the main body of the advance guard, which Chasteler deployed for a set-piece attack (the Jäger regiment of Bagration on the upper Nure to the right, the Jäger regiment of Miller out to the left towards San Paolo, and the four battalions of grenadiers in four lines against San Giorgio in the centre).

Chasteler had scarcely issued the necessary orders when Suvorov appeared at the head of the divisions of Schveikovsky and Förster (which had united at Gossolengo), and ordered the attack to proceed. It started badly, for the fine 17th light demi-brigade (the old regiment of Auvergne) beat back the converging attack of the Russian Jäger with heavy fire. However the Russian grenadiers battered their way into the nearest houses of San Giorgio by their frontal assault, and then with the help of the Russian main force they cleared the entire village. Almost the whole of the 17th demi-brigade (the surviving 29 officers, 1,070 men, with three colours, four cannon and two howitzers) fell into the hands of the allies.

After this unexpected fight the Russians continued the pursuit as far as Castel di Montanaro. Over to the left the Austrian division of Ott advanced by way of San Lazzaro and Montale, but it encountered a whole French division deployed on the right bank of the Ponte Nure in front of Nure, and was held at bay until the French broke contact.

The allies pushed on to the neighbourhood of Fiorenzuola, and they rested there on the 22 June after their six days of continuous effort, beginning with the march from Alessandria. Suvorov had exerted himself at least as much as any of his soldiers, but he was buoyed up by his triumph, and he wrote to Bellegarde that on the next day he would start back west to join him, 'and so we can bring the enemy between two fires on the 26th at San Giuliano or Bosco, and crush them if they are still to be found there. That's our manoeuvre! I pin my hopes on you— and ask you to rely on me. We will deal with Moreau in the same way as we dealt with Macdonald.'[43] Captured correspondence had told him that Macdonald's army was in such a bad way as to offer no independent threat to the allied combinations in northern Italy, and he therefore left the further pursuit to the reinforced Austrian division of Ott, which now consisted of 7,000 infantry, 2,000 cavalry and fifteen pieces of artillery.

Macdonald as usual scattered his forces, notably by throwing out the division of Montrichard to the east, which led to French troops surrendering by penny packets at Bologna on 3 July, and at Fort Urbano on the 10th. The rest of the troops were meanwhile falling back west over the Apennines, and had put up a fight only on 24 June, when they overwhelmed one battalion of Warasdiner Croats and the squadron of Bussy Chasseurs under Major Pastory, who sought to block their way to the mountains at Sassudo. Macdonald's main force consolidated at Pistoia on the 28th, and remained there early July, when it began its march to the western coast. By now detachments to the Mantua siege army had reduced Ott's command to 5,900 men, and he left the pursuit to an advance guard under Major-General Klenau, who worked with the armed peasants to purge all of Tuscany of the French.

The remnants of Macdonald's army retreated to the coast and re-formed along the Riviera di Levante under *général de division* Gouvion Saint-Cyr. Their old chief Macdonald was still feverish and coughing up blood—the consequence of his mauling by the Bussy Chasseurs in June, and he was shipped off to France in near-disgrace.

The garrisons which Macdonald had abandoned in southern and central Italy proved incapable of holding out against local counter-revolutionaries, and the efforts of British and Russian squadrons and (as at Ancona) Austrian land forces. This was an indirect but important consequence of Suvorov's career of victory, and a vindication of the insistence of Francis II on striking at the seat of French power in northern Italy.

MOREAU AND SECOND MARENGO

Suvorov had unfinished business somewhere to the north of Genoa. By detaching Victor, Montrichard and Lapoype to support Macdonald, Moreau had weakened his command successively to 14,000 troops. All the same he had a useful superiority over Bellegarde, who was facing him with just over 11,000 men, and commentators with their all-seeing view might hold that Moreau should now have advanced with speedy resolution to crush the Austrians. Moreau nevertheless made the logical assumption that Suvorov was acting like a reasonable general, and would be waiting nearby to reinforce Bellegarde, and not chasing off east to do battle with Macdonald.

Moreau's troops emerged from the Genoese mountains into the plain on 14 June, and began to advance cautiously down both banks of the Scrivia. On the 20th the second battle of Marengo opened when the division of Grouchy attacked San Giuliano and Cascina Grossa to the west of the river. Bellegarde recaptured the two places, but he became so extended in the process that he was unable to hold his ground when the division of Grenier intervened towards sunset. Having

lost 2,260 troops, or about one-third of his force, Bellegarde recoiled to the west behind the safety of the Bormida.

Before midnight Moreau learned that his efforts had been in vain, for the Army of Naples had been defeated on the Trebbia. He now had to abandon all hope of uniting with Macdonald in the northern plain, and was left with nothing to show for his expedition except interrupting the allied siege of the citadel of Tortona.

PLANS AND SUSPICIONS

On 23 June the main force of the allies turned back west and camped on the scene of the fighting along the Trebbia, now reeking after days of midsummer heat. Suvorov himself took up quarters in Piacenza in the Palazzo Scotti, and slept in the same room where Bonaparte and Massena had lodged before him. Speedy marches brought the allies to Stradella on the 24th, to the Scrivia at Castelnuovo on the 25th, and to San Giuliano on the 26th as Suvorov had planned, but by then it was clear that Moreau had escaped up the Apennines towards Genoa.

On 27 June Suvorov shifted his army south-west to the right bank of the Orba, from where he could cover the renewed blockade of Tortona citadel by Major-General Alcaini's 3,000 Austrians, and the active siege of the citadel of Alessandria by Bellegarde and another 10,000 Austrians. The Austrian lieutenant-general Hadik was observing the passes from Switzerland with 13,000 troops, while a further Austrian corps of 10,000 men under Lieutenant-General Kaim arrived to guard the exits from the Maritime Alps and Ligurian Alps in a wide arc to the west of Turin. All the time Kray and 10,000 Austrians were keeping up the blockade of Mantua away to the east.

Suvorov had covered himself against every reasonable contingency, and he still had the Russians at his immediate disposal. He now wished to maintain the tempo of offensive operations by driving over the Ligurian Apennines against Genoa, which was the last French bridgehead of any consequence in Italy. Chasteler noted in his journal that 'the united Imperial army... was assembled at Pozzolo

113

Formigaro as early as 26 June, and it could have reached the crest of the Apennines in four or at the most five days, and dislodged the corps of Moreau—which numbered less than 12,000 troops—and either thrown it into Genoa or driven it back to Savona.' Chasteler calculated that Macdonald's troops could reach Moreau in Genoa by 5 or 6 July at the earliest. In fact Macdonald's forces arrived on the Genoese Riviera in dribs and drabs only between 8 July and the end of the month, and even then the combined forces amounted to scarcely 24-25,000 troops.

Chasteler was dismayed to find that the great opportunity had to be abandoned on account of the repeated commands from Vienna, which insisted that nothing further must be done until the base of Austrian power in Italy had been secured by the capture of Mantua and the citadel of Alessandria. Chasteler shared Suvorov's disappointment to the full, 'and I had in fact to bring to bear all my influence on the field-marshal, and finally—with the greatest effort on my part and the greatest possible unwillingness on his—dissuade him from advancing on Genoa, in compliance with the order from Vienna.'[44]

Even now Chasteler did not grasp how deep-rooted was the aversion of Francis and Thugut to offensive operations as such, and to any notion of accepting liberated Piedmont as a full partner in a crusade to clear the enemy from Genoa and the Riviera di Ponente, and to carry the war into France itself. On 11 July Chasteler put forward a new plan of operations.[45] He explained that the allies had by now cleared the whole territory between the Po and the mountains of the Tyrol and Switzerland. This rich land stood at the allies' disposal, together with great quantities of ordnance and 20,000 Piedmontese regulars and militia, and the Austrian troops who would be set free when Mantua and Alessandria (as Chasteler was confident) fell by the end of the month. The capture of the fortified posts of Tortona citadel, Serravalle and Gavi would open the direct avenues to Genoa, which would be exploited by 20,000 troops, while a further corps of 20,000 men struck from Coni (Cuneo) across the Colle

di Tenda to the sea at Saorgio, and then conceivably advanced along the corniche as far as Nice, though much would depend on the quantity of supplies and pack animals which could be marshalled to support the thrust over the mountains.

The essential points of Chasteler's plan were therefore the direct advance on Genoa over the Ligurian Apennines, and a right-flanking thrust over the Ligurian Alps that would cut the French landward communications to Genoa and set the allies on the coastal path to France.

Suvorov returned to the scheme on a number of occasions, and most immediately in a letter to Francis on 13 July, and again towards the end of the month (after Chasteler had been wounded) when he worked up a detailed version with his new Austrian chief of staff Major-General Anton Zach. According to the latter plan all the Austrians would be diverted to the right-flanking column, and all the Russians directed on Genoa. The suspicions of Melas were aroused, and he wrote to a friend: 'for reasons that you will readily understand they have changed the repartition of the troops completely, by assigning the right wing to the Austrians and the left wing to the Russians. It comes down to the fact that they have private objectives concerning Genoa, and talk openly about profiting from its plunder.'[46]

Francis and Thugut set themselves against any schemes of the kind, and the Emperor had already written in unequivocal terms on 10 July that Suvorov must think of nothing but reducing Mantua, Coni, and the citadels of Alessandria and Turin, and securing the Alpine passes between France and Italy. Any other employment of his troops was out of the question.[47]

On 7 August the Russians captured the fort of Serravalle under the Ligurian Apennines. From the operational point of view if was not of major significance (below), but it had the potential of clearing the Russian way to Genoa in more than just the military sense. Melas now had good reason to believe that the Russians' intentions extended beyond pillage, and he wrote to Thugut the next day that

114

Field-Marshal Suvorov seems to have arrogated to himself the authority to institute a separate political regime in Genoese territory, and that is why he is set on taking possession of Genoa exclusively by Russian troops. I am not yet in a position to supply Your Excellency with further specific detail, but I can state with reasonable certainty [probably from intercepted correspondence] that all necessary measures have already been taken to organise the Genoese state in such a way that for a considerable time into the future it will be totally subject to the influence of the Russian Cabinet, and identified with its interests. [48]

A couple of weeks later Melas learned that the contest for political influence was spreading to Tuscany, a grand duchy which for decades had been ruled by members of the house of Habsburg-Lorraine, and which the Austrians considered part of their sphere of influence. In 1799 Suvorov gained a foothold there through one of his confidants, the Russian lieutenant-colonel Egor Tsukato, whom he sent to organise the anti-French rebels in the neighbourhood of Arezzo, where the leaders were on historically bad terms with the authorities (of whatever persuasion) in Florence, the Tuscan capital. In the middle of August a courier from the provisional government of Arezzo set off with a confidential message for Suvorov, but was detained on the way by Major-General Klenau, who was pushing up the Riviera di Levante towards Genoa. Klenau realised at once that important political issues were at stake, and he applied to Melas for advice. He wrote that he would hold the messenger up for a few days in order to gain time,

and I will give him a letter to deliver to Your Excellency, so that you may assess him for yourself. He is the greatest fanatic in Arezzo. I have known him for a long time, and as he puts some trust in me he spoke without reserve. From this I learned that the people of Arezzo harbour an inveterate hatred of the Florentine Senate, an antagonism which now threatens to disturb the public order—and perhaps with external assistance. He let slip that the people of Arezzo have made a treaty with the Russian Court, which gives them

reason to hope for support of every kind. [49]

In October, without any prompting from the Austrians, William Wickham became convinced that the Russians were plotting to set up an 'Italian league' that would be under their influence (see page 261). There is no direct evidence of such arrangements and deals in the Russian documents which have so far seen the light of day, but the indirect testimony is telling, and the management of negotiations of this kind would have fallen well within the competence of Suvorov's political counsellors Fuchs and Trefort.

On their side the Russians had well-founded suspicions of the Austrian designs concerning Sardinia-Piedmont, and relations between the allies were aggravated by the peevish, interfering and bad-mannered ways of the ruling trio in Vienna—Emperor Francis, the foreign minister Thugut, and General Tige as acting head of the Hofkriegsrath. Suvorov knew that in military affairs it was necessary to seize Fortune by the forelock, if she were not to skip away; how absurd it was that Vienna was seeking to dictate the conduct of operations from a distance, when many decisions could only properly be taken on the spur of the moment: 'I was in Milan when I received from Vienna the answer to my report that I had arrived in Verona. I was already in Turin when they wrote to me concerning Milan.' [50]

Austrian generals nominally under Suvorov's control as commander-in-chief were referring directly to Vienna, and Tige in his turn was sending orders to them without notification to Suvorov. The position was becoming intolerable, and Suvorov wrote to Paul on 6 July:

The timorousness off the Hofkriegsrath, its envy of me as a foreigner, the intrigues of the individual double-dealing generals who correspond immediately to that organisation, which directed operations until recently, and the impossibility of putting anything into execution before I have made due report to Vienna—which is one thousand versts distant—all force me to ask Your Imperial Highness for my recall, if the state of affairs does not change. I wish to be assured that my bones will be laid to rest in my Fatherland, and that I will be there to pray to God on behalf of my Emperor. [51]

On receiving this letter Paul wrote to his ambassador Razumovsky in Vienna ordering him to demand a formal statement from Francis, and to point out that Suvorov's goodwill could never be in doubt, and that he understood his trade as well as any minister or diplomat. This message only spurred Francis into writing to Suvorov on 14 August to remind him that his Russian master had placed him totally at his disposal, and that he had every confidence that Suvorov would obey his future directives.

These and other divergences of interest and manner ultimately assumed a scale which drove Paul from the alliance. In the military context the more immediate effect was to fix the main Russo-Austrian field force in the plain south of Alessandria for more than month, from 27 June until the second week in August, and so lose the impetus which had carried the allied forces from the Adda to the approaches to Genoa, liberating two capitals (Milan and Turin) and wrecking two French armies in the process.

Suvorov had no alternative but to detach sufficient Austrians from his mobile forces to build up Kray's blockading army around Mantua to 29,000 troops. Again, the restraining orders from Vienna prevented him from making active use of a potentially valuable increment of Russian troops which reached Piacenza in the middle of July. This was a contingent of 8,400 combatants under Lieutenant-General Maksim Vladimirovich Rehbinder (1730-1804), namely:

Musketeer regiments:
    Rehbinder
    Mansurov
    Fertsch
Combined grenadier battalions:
    Plamenkov
    Budberg

Shengilidzev
Jäger regiment Kashkin
Don Cossack regiments:
    Kurnakov
    Posdeev (second regiment),

together with one company of pioneers, twenty-two pieces of medium artillery and eighteen of battalion artillery. The immensely capable Rosenberg took command of the newcomers, while Rosenberg's original corps passed to Derfelden. The Russian forces in northern Italy were now made up of thirty five-battalions of infantry and eight regiments of Cossacks, on a nominal establishment of 27,000 troops.

The new troops assembled at Piacenza on 15 July, and were ordered to prepare for inspection by Suvorov on the next day. Nobody slept a wink all night, for the soldiers were busy making themselves respectable, and they were in a state of high excitement. On the morning of the 16th the troops were drawn up on the plain south of Piacenza, awaiting Suvorov under the gaze of the thousands of townspeople and French prisoners who were lining the ramparts.

> He arrived in the heart of our corps, halted, fastened us with his eagle eye, and yelled out: 'Good day brothers! Warrior heroes! Old comrades! Good day to you!' And the response of the soldiers burst out like a storm irrupting from a mountain gorge: 'And good day to you, our little father!'

Suvorov then put the troops through a mock battle. It lasted less than an hour, but it was enough to impress the many foreigners in the field-marshal's suite with

> the youth and agility of the soldiers, their happy and joyful appearance, their firm step, and how the countenance of every one of them expressed—as clearly as if it had been written in letters—the word: *Invincible!* [52]

116

1. Anon., 1801-3, IV,109
2. Stutterheim, 1812, II,vi,83
3. KA CA 1799 VI 23, Tige to Melas, 24 June
4. Suvorov to Rosenberg, Alessandria, 13 June 1799, Fuchs, 1825-6, II,298
5. KA FA Italien 1799 XIII 1, Chasteler's Journal
6. KA, MMTO, Deposition of Lieutenant-Colonel de Best
7. Gachot, 1903, 248
8. Macdonald, 1892, 91
9. KA CA 1799 VI ad 30, Melas, 'Relation über die unterm 17ten und 18. Juny dieses Jahres vorgefallenen Gefechte, und der am 19ten erfolgten Schacht an der Trebia,' undated
10. Masson, 1859, 343
11. KA MMTO, Deposition of Colonel Nimptsch
12. Masson, 1859, 344
13. KA FA Italien 1799 XIII 1, Chasteler's Journal
14. Stutterheim, 1812, III,vi,13-14
15. KA FA Italien 1799 XIII 44, MacDermott, 'Militärisches Dage Buch'
16. Macdonald, 1892, 92-3
17. KA CA 1799 VI ad 30, Melas, 'Relation über…'
18. 'Disposition' for 18 June, Meshcheryakov, 1949-53, IV,155-7
19. KA FA Italien 1799 XIII 1, Chasteler's Journal
20. KA FA Italien 1799 XIII 44, MacDermott, 'Militärisches Dage Buch'
21. 'Ratnik,' 1844, No. 8, 350-1
22. Gachot, 1903, 251
23. KA CA 1799 VI 18, Melas to Tige, Ponte Nure, 20 June; KA CA 1799 V ad 30, Melas, 'Relation über…'
24. Gryazev, 1898, 51-2
25. Stutterheim, 1812, III,vii,13-14
26. KA FA Italien 1799 XIII 44, MacDermott, 'Militärisches Dage Buch'
27. KA CA 1799 VI 18, Melas to Tige, Ponte Nure, 20 June; KA CA 1799 V ad 30, Melas, 'Relation über'…
28. KA FA Italien 1799 XIII 44, MacDermott, 'Militärisches Dage Buch'
29. Macdonald, 1859, 96
30. KA FA Italien 1799 XIII 44, MacDermott, 'Militärisches Dage Buch'
31. 'Ratnik,' 1844, No. 8, 353-4
32. KA MMTO, Deposition of Colonel Nimptsch
33. KA MMTO, Deposition of Lieutenant-General Liechtenstein
34. KA MMTO, Deposition of Captain L'Olivier
35. KA FA Italien 1799 VI ad 169, Liechtenstein, 'Attestation,' undated
36. KA FA Italien 1799 XIII 44, MacDermott, 'Militärisches Dage Buch'
37. Macdonald, 1892, 97-8
38. KA FA Italien 1799 VI 30 A, 'Totale'
39. Wickham, 1870, II,209
40. KA FA Italien 1799 V ad 289, Melas to Camillo Lambertie, 29 July
41. Fuchs, 1827, 187
42. Milytuin, 1856-8, II,605
43. Fuchs, 1825-6, II,379
44. KA FA Italien 1799 XIII 1, Chasteler's Journal
45. KA FA Italien 1799 VII 56, Chasteler, 'Vorschlag zur Fortsetzung der Operazionen… in Italien'
46. FA Italien 1799 V ad 289, Melas to Lambertie, 29 July
47. KA HKRA Deutschland und Italien 1799 VII 19, Francis to Suvorov, 10 July
48. FA Italien 1799 VIII 85, Melas to Thugut, Novi, 8 August
49. KA CA 1799 VIII ad 127, Klenau to Melas, Berchetto, 19 August
50. Suvorov to Razumovsky, Alessandria, 12 July 1799, Meshcheryakov, 1949-53, IV,198
51. Suvorov to Paul, Alessandria, 6 July 1799, Lopatin, 1986, 342
52. 'Ratnik,' 1844, No. 7, 37-8.

6

THE SIEGES

Fortress warfare in general receives short shrift from the military historians—it proceeds by arcane rules, and its tempo rarely corresponds with that of operations in the open field—but in justice to the Austrians in 1799 we ought to establish why they set such great store by reducing the strongholds in northern Italy, and how they were able to capture them as rapidly as they did.

An enemy garrison in a fortified perimeter offered a standing challenge to political authority and military possession. Thus the Austrians could never claim to be fully masters of Milan or Turin until they had evicted the French from the citadels. A stronghold might deny a convenient river passage (the citadel of Alessandria), or provide a *point d'appui* for an army emerging from mountains into open plains—which is why the French put up such an obstinate defence of the citadel of Tortona, or the Austrians diverted so many troops to recover Mantua. The garrison of any unreduced fortress standing in the rear of an otherwise victorious army was a base for forays against lines of communication, unless contained by superior forces.

By the accepted standards of the eighteenth century the allies made remarkably short work of sieges that would reasonably be expected to extended into weeks or into months. The objective in siegecraft was to make one or more breaches in the fortress rampart by cannon fire or (less frequently) by mining, and bring infantry close enough to those gaps to be able to storm them at acceptable cost. According to conventional rules this necessitated a trench attack by successive parallels (support lines) and zig-zags (approach trenches), while the artillery eroded the means of the defence by lobbing explosive mortar bombs and howitzer shells into the interior of the fortress,

dismounting the guns by counter-battery fire, and finally by breaching the rampart by firing point blank from the outer edge of the ditch.

The fortresses attacked by the allies in 1799 usually surrendered long before the attacks had run their full course. The commentator Jomini was normally reluctant to give the attackers any credit on this account, and he claimed that the fortifications were in a ruinous state, the garrisons consisted of the debris of defeated field corps, and that 'finally the Directory and the commander of the Army of Italy appointed governors who were not up to the task, being either expert but lacking in energy, or having energy without the necessary skills.'[1]

The allies were in fact managing their sieges in some particularly astute ways. Suvorov was willing to intimidate the French garrisons by putting on showy preparations for a storm, as at the citadels of Brescia or Alessandria, but he knew that there was a big difference between attacking simple walls held by Asiatics or Poles, and a bastioned fortress defended by Western European regulars. Razumovsky wrote to him that in Vienna 'people await the capture of the citadel of Turin with impatience—and they expect you to take it in your usual style, by storm. It would not be a bad way of instilling terror into the French.' Suvorov however replied: 'We must first conquer the mountainous part of Italy as far as the Riviera—that is the way to terrify the French, but not by storming the single citadel of Turin.'[2]

The allies began their sequence of sieges with the inadequate park of heavy artillery which had been supplied from Vienna. The Austrians therefore decided to concentrate these scanty resources against one selected fortress at a time, and shock the defenders by a prodigal but brief rain of shot and bombs. This accelerated artillery attack proved its worth against Pizzighettone. The siege park was then turned against the citadel of Milan, after which the near-bloodless capture of Turin city yielded the great Arsenal with its effectively unlimited stores of artillery and ammunition, which Chasteler employed against the citadels of Turin and Alessandria and the other places where the French were still holding out.

The allies also showed an intelligent sense of priorities in their negotiations with the fortress governors. It was more useful to the allies to win time than to capture the garrisons of low-grade troops, which would have to be fed, escorted and accommodated, and so they almost invariably offered lenient terms to the French, by which those people would be allowed to return home on the promise not to bear arms against the allies for a specified period.

The most notable of the sieges in question were those of:

PESCHIERA

This fortress was sited on both banks of the Mincio, where the river flowed from the south-eastern corner of Lake Garda, and it was one of the first fruits of the Austrian victory at Magnano.

The fortifications were cramped and overlooked, and the Austrian mortar bombs therefore caused considerable havoc when General Kray's siege corps opened fire on the night of 5/6 May. Colonel Couteaux capitulated the next day, and promised that his 1,200 troops would not serve against the allies for six months. The Austrians took possession of one hundred cannon and mortars, eighteen copper pontoons and large quantities of ammunition—all of which were shipped down the Mincio and brought to bear against Mantua. The allies also gained the mastery of Lake Garda, and a secure communication with the Tyrol.

PIZZIGHETTONE

Pizzighettone stood on the left bank of the Adda, and consisted of seven irregular bastions with a wet ditch; a bridge connected the main fortress with the Fort Gera crownwork on the right bank.

Major-General Hohenzollern attacked the place with half a dozen battalions from Lieutenant-General Kaim's special siege army, and he employed the corps reserve artillery, and an assortment of captured pieces which had been brought together by the artillery major Friedrich Schimpf. There were no engineers available, and so the operation was directed by Lieutenant-Colonel Albert Johann de Best of the General Staff, who tells us that he decided to bluff the enemy in order to conceal his lack of resources for a regular siege: 'I drove on the construction of the batteries in such a way that we were able to open fire [on 8 May] after forty-eight hours. The commandant rejected the first summons, and so I connected the batteries by a parallel, and then opened fire with all batteries and with the greatest possible violence, which duly brought about the surrender of this fortress.'[3]

That was on 11 May, after one of the fortress magazines was blown up. The 650 troops of the garrison were made prisoners of war, an account of the commandant's first defiance. Hohenzollern found ninety-five cannon and large stores of gunpowder in the place, which made it possible for him to proceed to the siege of the citadel of Milan.

THE CITADEL OF MILAN

The citadel was a powerful bastioned pentagon surrounding the old Sforza Castle.

The accelerated siege began on the night of 21/22 May, when Major Philipp de Lopez of the Austrian engineers opened the first parallel unusually close to the fortress. The reason was again the lack of the means for a conventional siege. The French replied with a heavy fire in the course of the 22nd, but the Austrians were able to respond with sixty cannon and mortars on the next day, whereupon the garrison of 2,200 troops capitulated on the undertaking not to serve against the allies for a year. Austrian casualties amounted to only fifty men, and the garrison yielded 119 pieces of artillery along with considerable ammunition.

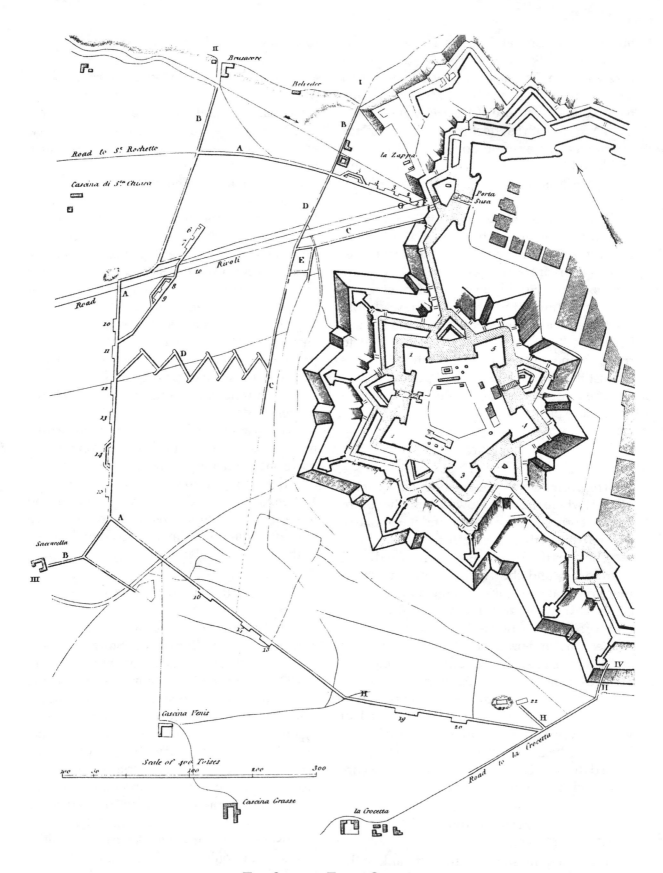

The Siege of Turin Citadel

THE CITADEL OF TURIN

This was probably the strongest regular fortress in Italy, with its five regular bastions with counterguards, ravelins and redoubts, outer lunettes and an elaborate system of countermines. It was defended by General Fiorella with a garrison of 3,337 troops, many of them ill-affected Piedmontese and Swiss.

The siege was undertaken by the corps of Lieutenant-General Kaim, who brought together for the purpose 5,740 Austrian troops, 300 Austrian and Piedmontese gunners and bombardiers, 392 Austrian miners, sappers and engineers, and about one hundred pieces of artillery. A formal siege would have taken two months,

> but we had to force the speedy surrender of the fortress if we were to secure Piedmont, and exploit the victories of our army. He [Major de Lopez] saw that we had too few men to capture the place by the usual rules of attack, and he maintained (and insisted throughout the siege) that we must accept a degree of risk, and exploit the haste with which the enemy had thrown themselves into the citadel. This we would do by giving them no time to cover themselves with traverses, shoulder works and so on, or to prepare their countermines.[4]

The Austrians opened the first parallel on the night of 10/11 June. Progress was delayed by the heavy rains as much as anything else, which forced the troops to bale out their trenches. The siege artillery came into devastating operation on 18 June—it ravaged the parapets and embrasures, it set many of the interior buildings ablaze, it blew up two of the magazines, and it threatened to explode the great quantities of gunpowder which had been stored haphazardly in various locations. The Austrians opened their second parallel on the night of 19/20 June at pistol shot from the covered way, and Fiorella capitulated at ten the next morning, by when 306 of the defenders had lost their lives. The garrison was bound not to serve against the allies until exchanged for an equivalent number of prisoners. Austrian casualties amounted to just eighteen killed and twenty wounded.

Inside the citadel the Austrians found 374 cannon, 184 mortars, 60 howitzers, and a reputed 250 tons of gunpowder. Suvorov later told Lieutenant-Colonel Sir Henry Clinton that during the battle of the Trebbia 'he received a positive order from Vienna to abandon the siege of the citadel of Turin, and confine himself to the defence of the Po; that he was fortunately saved from a new act of disobedience by a courier bringing him an account of the actual surrender of the citadel, and that in that fortress he found a prodigious artillery, which enabled him to convert the blockades of Alessandria, Serravalle and Tortona into regular sieges.'[5]

THE CITADEL OF ALESSANDRIA

The citadel was an oblong fortress of six bastions situated on the left bank of the Tanaro. It was built in the same style as the citadel of Turin and was considered to be almost as strong.

The garrison in 1799 consisted of probably well over 3,000 spirited troops under the determined *général de brigade* Gaspard Amadée Gardanne. There is nothing in Gardanne's career to suggest that he was anything but devoted to the Republic, but on 8 June we find Melas writing mysterious to Vienna: 'the hope I expressed in my report of the 5th, concerning the surrender of the fortress of Alessandria through bribery, has vanished completely, now that General Seckendorf [Major-General Friedrich Seckendorf] has been recalled to Acqui according to orders. The fall of this vitally important fortress must now wait upon the further operations of Lieutenant-General Bellegarde.'[6]

Alessandria was 'vitally important' because it was situated so advantageously at the meeting of the rivers and routes in the plain of north-west Italy. Gardanne launched sorties on 28 June and 8 July, which left no doubt that he was determined to resist, and Bellegarde was forced to open a full-scale siege with up to 10,000 troops, which included Russian infantry (very active workers) and Piedmontese engineers in addition to the Austrians of the main body. The first parallel was opened on the night of 11/12 July against the north-eastern fronts (Bastions

IV-VI), and the second parallel established on the night of the 17/18. The initial instalment of the captured artillery from Turin opened fire at three on the morning of the 12th, and the allies were able to proceed from the successive parallels by flying sap, and 'they made a breach by a novel way of firing their shot by reduced charges, but with much greater effect, whereby they sited their batteries at the foot of the glacis, and the shot skimmed over the top of an outer

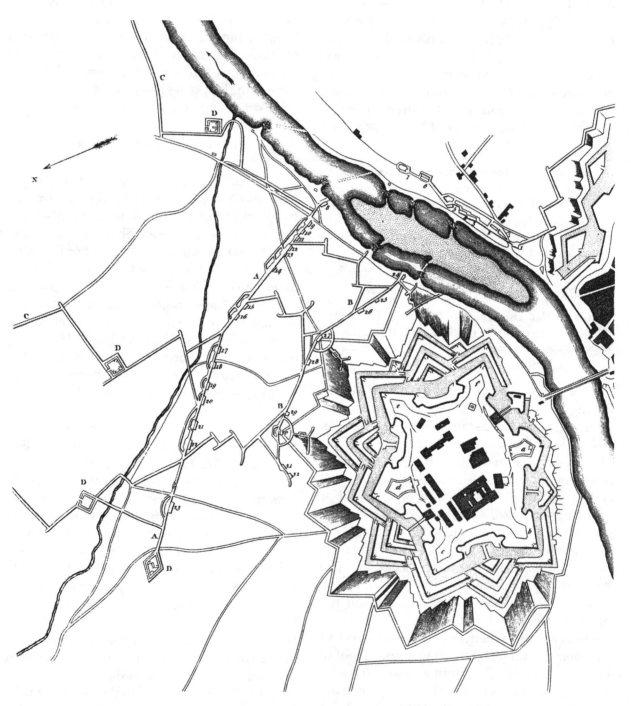

The Siege of Alessandria Citadel

122

rampart to hit the main rampart behind.'[7]

Gardanne surrendered on 21 July, by when the Austrians had expended 25,404 roundshot, and 16,350 mortar bombs and howitzer shells. The French troops (unusually) were made prisoners of war, but the general himself was at once released on parole in recognition of his brave defence.

The French casualties cannot be established with any certainty, and calculations of the number of troops who marched out to captivity range from 2,384 to 3,500. The Austrians had lost seventy-five killed and 262 wounded. Among the latter was Major-General Jean Gabriel Chasteler, Suvorov's chief of staff, who was hit in the left side by a canister shot on the evening of 17 July. Chasteler defied a gloomy prognosis to be fit again for service by 5 September, but he was in disgrace in Vienna, and disowned by Suvorov, and was forced to leave the theatre of war.

MANTUA

The fall of the citadel of Alessandria set free up to 10,000 allied troops, but three times that number of Austrians was tied down by the siege of Mantua. One of the reasons for this great commitment of force was strategic, for, in spite of all the conquests which had been made, there was still no fortified base for the Austrian army in Italy. Moreover Mantua was essential to the integrity of the line of the Mincio, if the army ever had reason to defend it.'[8] In addition Mantua was extraordinarily difficult to blockade, let alone subject to an active siege. The great strength of the place consisted in its girdle of lakes, whose waters were fed by the Mincio, and by the outworks on the far side of the lakes which guarded the access to the causeways. This geometry compelled the investing forces to occupy a vast perimeter in order to seal off the fortress from the outside world.

The Austrians under old Field-Marshal Dagobert Wurmser had held Mantua for eight months in 1796 and 1797, and since then the French had taken care to strengthen the outworks. Behind the shelter of the lakes the town fortifications consisted of a medieval wall, with a few primitive bastions. The defenders were numerically strong, at 12,402 troops, but a quarter of the complement was made up of unreliable auxiliaries, and the remainder consisted of under-strength and raw French demi-brigades which were unfit to take the field. The commandant Philippe François de Foissac-Latour counted as one of the best engineers of the Republic, 'but he had little experience of leading troops... as a product of the engineering corps, he placed an implicit trust in rules which are incontrovertible in theory, but very often fail to hold good in warfare. He was convinced that operations in a real siege proceeded with the same regularity as in a demonstration, while neglecting the importance of chance and the morale of the troops. He therefore concluded that a fortress was untenable once there was a breach in the main rampart.'[9] The 20,000 townspeople were devoted to their Austrian masters, and communicated intelligence to the besieging force by signals, while the armed peasants of the neighbourhood helped the Austrians to eke out their troops around the wider perimeter of the blockade.

General Kray began the investment on 7 May with an initial 11,971 troops; Major-General Hohenzollern arrived with his corps after the citadel of Milan had fallen. Proceedings were interrupted when Macdonald emerged on the scene with the Army of Naples. Hohenzollern's command was almost wiped out at Modena on 12 June, and Kray was forced to line the north bank of the Po with his armed peasants and all the available regulars.

After Suvorov had eliminated Macdonald from the theatre of operations, he detached Lieutenant-General Ott to reinforce Kray to a total strength of 29,043 troops, including 281 gunners and bombardiers under Lieutenant-Colonel Anton Reisner. Kray adopted the new Austrian technique of an accelerated trench attack, supported by powerful artillery, and he concentrated his resources on the western and southern sectors, where the lakes were at their narrowest and the outlying defences appeared to be weakest. In particular the Pradella

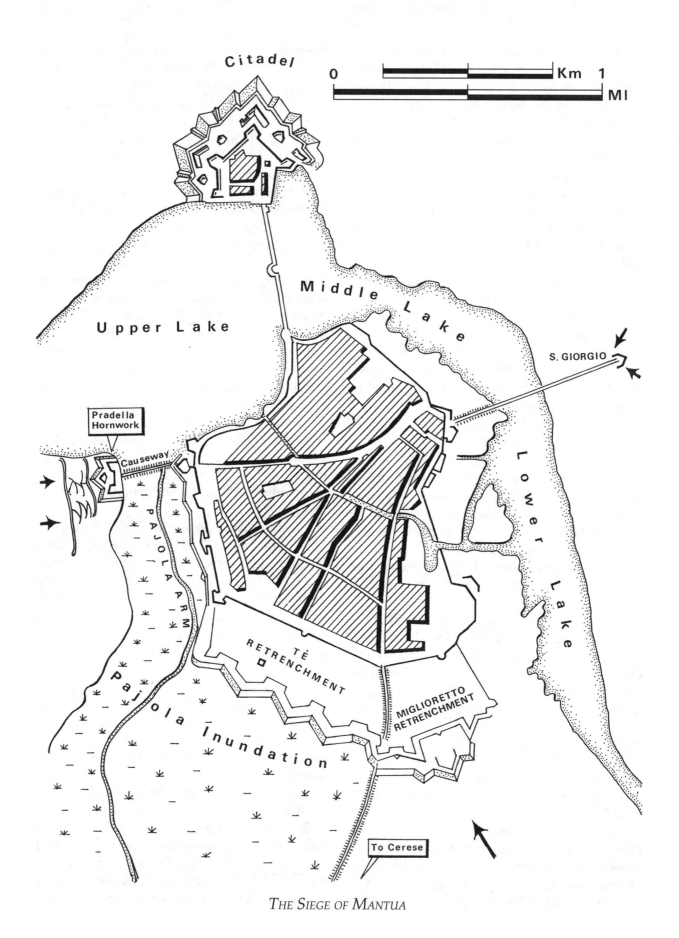

Citadel

0   Km 1

MI

M i d d l e   L a k e

U p p e r   L a k e

S. GIORGIO

Pradella
Hornwork

Causeway

L
o
w
e
r
L
a
k
e

PAJOLA ARM

P a j o l a   I n u n d a t i o n

TÉ
RETRENCHMENT

MIGLIORETTO
RETRENCHMENT

To Cerese

The Siege of Mantua

Hornwork seemed to be particularly vulnerable, while the adjacent stretch of the town wall was in a very neglected state.

The siege proper began on 10 July, when the Austrians stormed the fortified Cerese bridge, and the nearby bridge and sluice of the Pajola arm of the Mincio; the besiegers now had the means of draining the Pajola inundation, and thus of making their approaches on a wider frontage. Kray knew that 14 July (Bastille Day) would be a great occasion for the French, and he promised to hold his fire while the garrison devoted itself to its festivities. The defenders duly discharged three salvoes of blank fire in celebration, while French orators read out the Declaration of the Rights of Man in the public squares, and Foissac-Latour and 150 of his officers sat down to a great meal in the Ducal Palace.

As a wily Hungarian Kray had said nothing about other kinds of siegework, and so he opened a first parallel against the Thé suburb on the following night, when the French were in a state of stupefaction. The Austrians dug their second parallel on the night of 18/19 July, and on the 23rd they opened fire with one hundred cannon and mortars against the Thé entrenchments, the Pradella Hornwork and the town bastion of Alexis. On the night of 24/25 July the French beat off an assault on the Thé and the palace-castle of Migiliaretto, but the pressure on the defenders was mounting, and in order to concentrate his resources Foisssac-Latour evacuated the isolated lunette of San Giorgio on the night of 25/26 July. The Austrian saps were now dangerously close to the Pradella Hornwork, and this too was abandoned by the French, on the night of 26/27 July

Foissac-Latour was confident that he could prevent the Austrians making any further progress, by blowing a gap in the causeway to the rear of the Pradella Hornwork, but all the explosion did was to produce a crater which offered the enemy ready-made cover nearer the town. The besiegers established cannon and mortar batteries in the abandoned Pradella, and brought the town's Porta Pradella under heavy fire. The garrison was now sealed up in the town behind the fast-crumbling fortifications, and Foissac-Latour accordingly capitulated on 30 July.

Two hours after he had signed the document a surge of water on the Upper Lake carried away more than sixty feet of the contested causeway, and flooded into the Pajola marshes. It was too late.

The terms of the surrender were characteristically lenient, and allowed the French (and as many of the Cisalpines and Swiss as desired to accompany them) to depart for France. The garrison had lost 600 men by desertion, 706 who had been captured in the course of the siege, and 2,347 who had died of disease or enemy action; 7,649 survivors evacuated the fortress, leaving behind 800 untransportable sick and wounded, 675 pieces of artillery, and provisions which could have fed the garrison for another six months. The besiegers lost 2,095 men from all causes. Kray was free to join the main army with 17,201 of his troops, and with his gift for lucky timing he arrived just before Suvorov gave a new battle—at Novi.

THE CITADEL OF TORTONA

This rocky stronghold was diminutive, in comparison with the sprawling lake fortress of Mantua, but no less strong in its way, and almost as disruptive to the allied schemes. It was garrisoned in 1799 by *chef de brigade* Gast and 1,200 troops, and as long as they held on they offered the French forces lurking in the Ligurian Appenines a potential support for offensives into the plain. By the same token Suvorov would never be free for operations elsewhere until he had eliminated this threat to his rear.

Tactically the citadel was a hard nut to crack. It was situated at the south-eastern corner of Tortona town, and rose nearly one hundred metres above the surrounding countryside. The work had been rebuilt completely in 1745, in the reign of Victor Amadeus III, and bore the name 'Fort San Victor.' It was formed of two irregular crownworks, and an oblong inner work of four bastions. Many of the cannon were sheltered under full cover in tiers of casemates, while the ditches were hewn as much as twenty metres deep in the living rock. Not only was the fort immensely strong in itself, but the siege approaches would have to be made over 'such stony ground that every cannon shot had the effect of a round of canister, while the trenches had to be dug five feet deep below the surface of the ground, and their parapets raised to a height of ten or twelve, to avoid the plunging fire from the fortress, which lay at such a frightful elevation.'[10]

The allies had occupied Tortona town and placed the citadel under blockade in May, and they had managed to do nothing more of consequence before Moreau irrupted from Genoa at the time of the Trebbia campaign, chased the blockading force away, and stuffed the citadel with enough provisions to last a year. The leading Piedmontese engineers now advised Suvorov that the citadel could not be taken in less than five months, but the Austrian engineer major Philipp de Lopez was able to persuade him that energetic measures would reduce it in five weeks. On the strength of this assurance the siege was opened in the first week of August. De Lopez directed the engineers, and Major Swortnik the gunners, and the unspecialised labour of the siege fell upon eleven-and-a-half battalions of Austrian infantry.

As the target of his attack de Lopez selected the left face of Bastion San Maurizio at the north-west salient of the inner citadel, for it was unprotected by the two outlying crownworks, and could be assailed directly by the gunners and engineers. On the night of 5/6 August the besiegers opened their first parallel on the hill of San Bernadino opposite; they completed the trench before first light, but not without taking casualties from the French canister fire which flogged the hilltop. The proceedings were endangered when a new French commander, Joubert, descended from the Genoese mountains in still greater force than his predecessor Moreau. This time the French did not penetrate as far as Tortona, but Major-General Alcaini, as overall commander of the siege corps, had to withdraw almost all his infantry from the trenches.

The work on the siege batteries nevertheless continued without interruption, and the guns opened fire on the night of 15/16 August. The troops were back at work the next day, and they dug, or rather hacked out, the second parallel on the following night. Further progress was painful in the extreme, for the Austrians had to carry earth uphill in baskets to give their trenches and batteries some cover from the fire of musket balls, mortar bombs and showers of stones from pierriers, while the Austrian miners (who intended to blow in the counterscarp) were working through solid stone. All the time the rocky hill reverberated in the August heat. The state of equilibrium between besieger and besieged was recognised in an elaborate capitulation on 22 August, whereby hostilities were suspended until 11 September. If the citadel were not relieved by that date, then the French would march out to freedom, binding themselves only not to serve against the allies for six months—as indeed happened.

The remote little fortress-town or Coni, or Cuneo, remained as the only stronghold still held by the French in Piedmont, and Suvorov's work of liberation could now be regarded as complete.

NOTES TO CHAPTER 6

[1] Jomini, 1820-4, XII,53-4

[2] Suvorov to Razumovsky, 6 July 1799, Fuchs, 1825-6, II,473

[3] KA MMTO, Deposition of de Best

[4] KA MMTO, Deposition of Mittrowsky

[5] Reported in Wickham to Grenville, Schaffhausen, 12 September 1799, Wickham, 1870, II,209

[6] KA CA 1799 VI 12, Melas to Tige, Turin, 8 June

[7] Jomini, 1820-4, XII,51-2

[8] Stutterheim, 1812, III,ix,31

[9] Jomini, 1820-4, XII,35

[10] KA MMTO, joint Deposition on behalf of de Lopez.

Prince Bagration and his Jäger

AUSTRIAN INFANTRY IN THE PRE-1798 UNIFORM

7

AGAINST JOUBERT

By now we have run a little ahead of our story. Suvorov had deployed his troops across the western plain and the Alpine foothills in such a way that he could cover the sieges of the citadels of Alessandria and Tortona, observe the avenues from Genoa, the Maritime Alps and the Swiss Alps, and concentrate for battle if necessary, He therefore established his headquarters at Bosco Marengo in the centre of the western plain. From 26 July the Austrians of Melas and Derfelden's Russians (the original Russian contingent) were encamped to the east at Rivalta Scrivia, to block the French access to the beleaguered citadel of Tortona, while Bagration with the Russian advance guard at Pozzolo Formigaro served as an outpost towards the Genoese Apennines to the south. Rosenberg with the second Russian contingent (the one brought to Italy by Rehbinder) was stationed at Broni in the Stradella choke point. Suvorov was therefore in a position to bring together 45,000 troops at short notice in the plain between the Scrivia and the Bormida.

Suvorov positioned further corps on a wide perimeter to counter French incursions from the semi-circle of mountains. Lieutenant-General Bellegarde was standing at Gamalero up the Bormida valley, Lieutenant-General Kaim with 14,000 Austrians covered Piedmont in the direction of Savoy and Dauphiné, while 11,000 Austrians were still with Lieutenant-General Hadik, who had posted his subordinates Strauch and Rohan on the avenues from Switzerland. Finally Major-General Klenau and his lone corps of 5,000 Austrians had emerged from Tuscany, and were now at Sarzana, sealing up the exit from the Riviera di Levante.

The citadel of Alessandria surrendered on 21 July, and the fortress of Mantua on the 30th, which set free altogether 30,000 troops for operations in the field. Chasteler's last work for Suvorov was to overcome the pain of his wound, and draw up a revised plan for the two-pronged offensive, which he submitted to Suvorov on 1 August. Kray's disposable forces from Mantua were to be brought up with the greatest possible speed, so as to enable the allies to move on 10 August. The immediate objective on both fronts was the mountain crest, though Chasteler put more emphasis than before on the thrust to the western Riviera and Nice: 'I repeat that the army which masters the summits of the Maritime Alps also commands the Riviera. Anyone who knows the terrain will be aware that these peaks are easier to reach from the Piedmontese side than from the Riviera.'[1]

Three days later the allies had to put aside all such plans to confront a new crisis.

THE COMING OF JOUBERT

Suvorov was the unknowing author of the vengeance which the French Republic now wished to visit on his head. Month upon month of disappointments and defeats, above all in Italy, had discredited the old leadership of the Directory, which fell from grace in the coup d'état of 30me Prairial. The new chiefs Barras and Sieyès were dedicated to pursuing the war more energetically, and their credibility was enhanced by the fact that the date of their coup (18 June) coincided with the opening of the Battle of the Trebbia, the outcome of which justified them in identifying Macdonald, Victor, Montrichard and Lapoype with the old order, and summoning them to Paris to render account.

Bernadotte as the new Minister of War had ambitions to become a second Carnot, and he requisitioned men, money and provisions to build up armies that would carry the war back to the enemy. By the beginning of August the French combatants amounted to 150,000 men, which was admittedly well short of the 270,000 intended, but the new Directory pressed for decisive measures, and on two of the theatres (Switzerland and Italy) it had leaders who were willing to put them into effect. There were four armies altogether:

The Army of the Rhine (20,000 troops). This was a feeble body, scarcely up to maintaining a defensive before it was reinforced,

The Army of the Danube (70,000). Commanded by the enterprising Massena, the Danube Army was well placed to attack Archduke Charles (weakened by the departure of the two corps of Bellegarde and Hadik to Italy) and drive him from Switzerland,

The Army of the Alps (15-19,000). Its commander Championnet was supposed to take the offensive from the French Alps into Piedmont; in the

JOUBERT

event his forces were too few to amount to more than a nuisance, and in the second half of August this formation became the left wing of the Army of Italy,

The Army of Italy (40,713). The reformed Directory invested most of its hopes in the reinforced army in the Ligurian (Genoese) Republic and its new commander Joubert, who was ordered to take the offensive, and triumph where Schérer, Moreau and Macdonald had so signally failed.

Still only thirty in 1799, *général de division* Barthélemy Catherine Joubert (1769-1799) was a pure product of the Revolution, and well suited to point up the contrast with people like the mercenary Schérer and the semi-criminal Macdonald. He had been devoid of all military experience when he enlisted as a private soldier in 1791, yet rose to the rank of *général de brigade* in 1795, and won golden opinions from Bonaparte in Italy in 1796. Bonaparte now prized Joubert as a reliable man to leave in the European theatre, when the best of the French troops were campaigning in the Orient; the Directory valued him as a soldier who would bolster its military credit while being innocent of political designs.

In person Joubert was tall, spare, and not particularly eloquent, in spite of his earlier ambitions to become a lawyer. The Austrians had come to respect him as a bold and active enemy, and if he had survived the battle of Novi there can be little doubt that he would have been numbered among the Marshals of the Napoleonic Empire. Soult could detect in him one shortcoming, which he would surely have overcome with experience, and that was his desire to plunge into the thick of combat at the head of his troops—'a virtue, certainly, in a subordinate, but something different in a commander in chief. As leader of an army he would jeopardise his troops if he took the same risks as before'[2]

At a time when the allies were divided in both the military and the political dimensions, the French utilised the lull in operations to concentrate the forces which had been scattered along the Genoese rivieras. It was a coming-together in more than just the geographical sense, for 'a happy sense of brotherhood' now reigned in the Army of Italy; the experienced

Moreau showed no resentment at being ousted from command, and Joubert was glad on his side to accept Moreau's offer to stay with the army and help in any way he could. [3]

On 4 August the allies learned that Joubert had reached Genoa, and that Moreau had handed over the command of the Army of Italy. A mood of excitement, extraordinarily enough, now spread among the allied generals. Suvorov testified that

> for several weeks now the enemy army along the riviera had been demoralised and racked by hunger… with the arrival of Joubert as the

new commander it was inspired with new courage. He had come to prominence at the time of the Piedmontese revolution, and he had long enjoyed the complete trust of the army. Moreau had been beaten in every action since the crossing of the Adda, and his replacement by Joubert convinced every soldier that the war would take a new turn. Joubert did still more for the army when he referred to its old reputation for courage, and held out the prospect of a single battle that would transform its present miserable life in the mountains. [4]

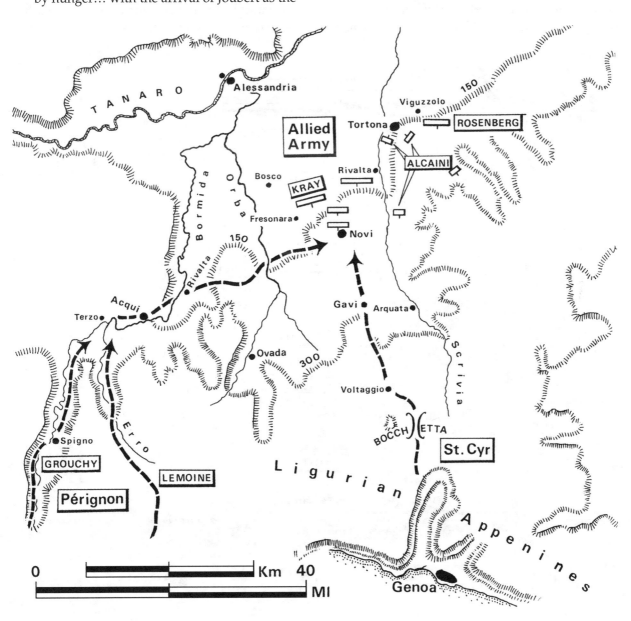

JOUBERT'S OFFENSIVE

Joubert had disembarked with about 5,000 conscripts, who were badly clothed and equipped. His new army even now amounted to little more than 40,000 men, and his cavalry was particularly weak, at about 2,000 poorly-mounted troopers, which would put him at a disadvantage if he ventured into the north Italian plain. His great assets were the restored morale of his troops, and the quality of his senior officers. Moreau was happy to serve the new chief, as we have seen, and four future marshals held important posts or commands: Emmanuel Grouchy as a divisional commander, Louis Gabriel Suchet as chief of staff, and the two wing commanders—Catherine Dominique Pérignon (left wing) and Laurent Gouvion Saint-Cyr (right wing).

The consensus among these generals was that Joubert must stay his hand until Championnet had time to come up on the far left wing with the so-called Army of the Alps, which was well below strength, but would have augmented the total force to about 57,000 troops. However Championnet would be unable to arrive before 20 August, and Joubert believed that he must obey his orders from the Directory and advance down from the Genoese mountains without delay. Even so he was not going to be fast enough, for he did not know how skilful was Suvorov at re-concentrating his forces, and

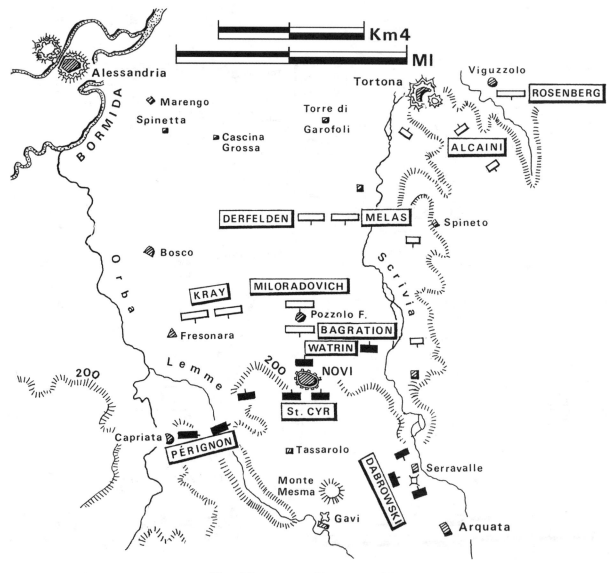

The Massing of Forces at Novi

132

he did not think it possible that Kray would make such short work of Mantua.

Suvorov and Melas were aware in general terms of Joubert's brief from the Directory, but they had more immediate concerns in mind. On 2 August Prince Bagration had set out with an advance guard consisting of 2,100 troops and twelve pieces of field artillery, and planted himself before the triangular rock castle of Serravalle which barred (as its name suggests) a choke point in the valley of the upper Scrivia. Two of the Russian battalions were assigned to carry out the attack, and Melas commented sourly that 'Suvorov was very conscious of the fact that the Austrians had besieged and taken a very great number of strongholds, and every time displayed courage and truly astonishing speed. He was determined to besiege some fortification or other with Russian troops alone, and he settled on the castle of Serravalle.'[5]

Bagration found some excellent battery positions on the steep Monte Buffo immediately to the west of the castle, and after his guns had been manhandled to the top he opened fire on 6 August. The French artillery was silenced almost immediately. Suvorov was present when the guns effected a wide breach the next day, and he made preparations for a storm. This was enough to persuade the commandant to surrender his garrison of 185 troops in the evening. The arrangements were completed on the 9th, when Suvorov detached four companies of the Austrian regiment of Stuart to garrison the castle, and moved his headquarters forward from Bosco Marengo to Novi, where the ground began to rise towards the Genoese Apennines.

By 10 August it was clear that the French activity in the mountains signified more than reconnaissances in force, and by the evening of the 12th the enemy were obviously bent on reaching the plain in two main bodies. The routes of the two French wings were dictated by the direction and capacity of the mountain roads:

Right (eastern) Wing. Here Saint-Cyr commanded the divisions of Watrin, Dabrowski and Laboissière. He advanced over the Bocchetta Pass, and he was now descending by way of Voltaggio and Gavi; the French blockaded the four Austrian companies in Serravalle Castle, and the division of Watrin hastened ahead in the direction of Novi.

Left (western) Wing. Under the overall command of Pérignon, the divisions of Grouchy and Lemoine advanced on parallel routes down the valleys of the Spigno and Erro against the Austrian corps of Bellegarde. They evicted his troops from Terzo on the Bormida, and veered west to approach Novi by way of Acqui, Rivalta Bormida, Capriata d'Orba and Francavilla.

Melas wrote to Vienna on 13 August that 'the enemy pressed on with their [locally] superior forces, which prompted us to abandon the mountain exits to them, and by pulling back our outposts lure them into the plain, where we could fight to much better advantage… and frustrate the enemy designs by putting our superiority in artillery and cavalry to effective use.'[6] The wording suggests a decision taken under the pressure of circumstances, but Suvorov rightly emphasised that he had been 'long determined to await the enemy in the plain between Novi and Alessandria, if they plucked up the courage to take the offensive.'[7] For that reason he had rejected the opportunity to strike at Saint-Cyr while the Frenchman was waiting unsupported for Pérignon (who had much further to go) to join him in the neighbourhood of Novi.[8]

On 13 August the two French wings re-established a loose contact (by leave of Suvorov and Melas) in the low hills between Capriata and Novi. 'Towards noon a number of French appeared on the hills—how their columns multiplied! Every now and again an outburst of firing could be heard from various spots, and it would last for a few minutes. Our outposts fell back calmly, drawing the enemy towards our main army, which was arrayed below. In front of our line of battle we caught glimpses of our father Aleksandr Vasilevich, rushing from one place to the next.'[9]

General Kray was hastening up with his 17,200 disposable troops from Mantua to support Bellegarde (who was falling back from Fresonara), and thus build up a strong right (western) wing of the allied army. Derfelden's corps of Russians made up the centre of the allied deployment, and the left (eastern) wing comprised the main Austrian concentration of

20,000 troops on the Scrivia at Rivalta, blocking the direct route to the French garrison in Tortona citadel. The Austrian corps of Alcaini was besieging the fort, covered by Rosenberg with the smaller of the two Russian corps. All of this made sense in the context of the scheme to allow the French into the plain and do battle with them there.

The emphasis had changed by the evening of the same 13 August, for the French advance had lost something of its impetus. Melas explains 'the enemy were still scattered and divided, since it had been impossible for them to bring their attacking columns into the plain at the same speed and at the same time. It was decided to attack the columns in question before they could unite, and so destroy them in detail.'[10]

Kray's troops had reached Alessandria on 12 August, after long and hard marching from Mantua, and they were now expected to pick themselves up again and attack the western grouping (Pérignon's) at Capriata at two in the morning of the 14th. The enterprise was a physical impossibility. It was already first light on 14th before Kray could set off from Alessandria, and his march came to an end when his troops reached those of Bellegarde at Fresonara in a state of prostration from the heat. On his own initiative he proposed a new attack for the 15th (below).

Thus in the morning of 14 August the French were able to occupy the walled town of Novi and consolidate their main forces on the hills to the north. However the vigorous Watrin kept up the momentum of the original advance by pushing his division directly towards Tortona down the spur which descended beside the Scrivia to Bettole di Novi. This isolated, unsupported thrust was in keeping with the independent way Watrin had behaved on the last day of the Battle of the Trebbia, but it gave Suvorov every reason to believe that the main French force would abandon the Novi camp and plunge on to relieve Tortona.

In fact Joubert was disinclined to follow Watrin's example, for he had accompanied his wing commanders Saint-Cyr and Pérignon to the edge of the hills, from where they counted enemy formations to the equivalent of 36,000 troops in the plain, together with further groupings in the distance which could not be made out clearly through the heat haze. This amounted to a considerable shock. Joubert had at first hoped to find no more than 8,000 troops between himself and Tortona, but there could no longer be any doubt that he was facing a whole wing of an army, including Kray's troops from Mantua, which for unknown reasons had fallen to the Austrians much sooner than had been expected. Saint-Cyr and Pérignon argued with new conviction that Joubert must recoil into the mountains and wait for Championnet to arrive with the Army of the Alps. Joubert was only half convinced, and replied that he would postpone his final decision.

Suvorov made (uncharacteristically) a personal reconnaissance of the French deployments. He sent forward two battalions of Russian Jäger, who lay down in the barley, and behind this screen he rode up and down in front of his troops, conspicuous in his white shirt and pantaloons. The view from the plain was uninformative, and Suvorov and Melas could not establish the numbers of the French, though they knew that a column (Watrin's) was making for Tortona down the Scrivia, that another column had occupied Novi, and that the column (Pérignon's) which had been advancing against Lieutenant-General Bellegarde had drawn over to its right towards that town.

By the late morning of 14 August the march of Kray's exhausted troops was coming to an end well short of their target. It was not from any lack of goodwill or energy on the part of their chief, and Kray wrote to Suvorov at 11.15 a.m. that he had decided to throw the united forces of the Austrian right wing (the two corps of Kray and Bellegarde) into a right-flanking attack on Novi at first light on the 15th, whereby he hoped to hit the French when they were on the march to Tortona and so cut their communications with Genoa. This message crossed with a letter which was sent to Kray by Suvorov's chief of staff Zach from headquarters at Pozzolo Formigaro at 9.45:

> The enemy have taken Novi. The column [Pérignon's] which had been acting against Lieutenant-General Bellegarde has now

mostly crossed the Orba and united with the enemy column at Novi, which means that only a screen remains along the left bank of the Orba. If Your Excellency throws it back and marches at once on Novi, you will not only take it with no great difficulty, but reduce the enemy to a frightful state of disorder.

The enemy's aim is to relieve Tortona—one of the columns is advancing by way of Novi, and the other across the Scrivia against Sarzano and Monte Goldone.

Write to tell me of your intentions and your time of attack, and we will advance simultaneously from Rivalta di Scrivia. The field-marshal is asleep; I am riding to see the general [Melas].[11]

Suvorov finally bestirred himself, and he wrote to Kray later in the day:

I am more than pleased with your proposal to attack the enemy with all your forces at first light tomorrow the 15th. I draw the enemy left wing particularly to your attention—you must fall on it with the greatest possible determination, and throw it back by way of Novi to Serravalle—namely from the valley of the Lemme to that of the Scrivia, and do all you possibly can to cut if off from Gavi.

I will follow this attack with the [Russian] troops positioned at Pozzolo Formigaro, and will also notify the [Austrian] army at Rivalta—I rely on you always as my heroic friend.

Kray wrote in confirmation at eight in the evening, and later the same evening Suvorov sent copies of the correspondence to Melas, and explained that

when this enterprise progresses towards its successful conclusion, an element of the column [Watrin's] marching from Serravalle along the Scrivia to Tortona may be cut off, and therefore be thrown against the army or corps [Rosenberg's and Alcaini's] at Tortona and Viguzzolo; I therefore ask Your Excellency to be on the alert to meet the fugitives from this shattered column, and send a detachment against them from the hills.

Would you please also notify this to the generals Derfelden and Rosenberg and Major-General Alcaini. [12]

The plan of action for 15 August was incomparably the most subtle to have been evolved under the authority of Suvorov. Joubert's reputation and most of his conduct so far indicated that he would abandon the Novi camp and be on the move again to relieve Tortona citadel, and Suvorov intended to turn the man's impetus against him by allowing the French to come on a certain distance (though not as far as originally intended) and turn their flanks. The most active role fell to the 27,000 or so troops of the combined Austrian right wing under Kray, which was to march from Fresonara, turn aside from the Novi road at Basaluzzo, and move at speed to attack the French rearward elements behind Serravalle, 'and by this rapid manoeuvre cut off the enemy from their only possible path of retreat over the Bocchetta Pass by way of Gavi.' The other jaw of the pincers was represented by the 5,700-odd troops of the advance guard under Bagration, assigned to thrust 'to the left of Novi' and unite with Kray in the area of Serravalle.[13]

For the time being the other allied formations were to hold their present positions. Melas was still down the Scriva with the Austrian left wing (8,800 troops) blocking the way to Tortona at Rivalta: 'The only task for the army corps at Rivalta was to take part in the attack by sending individual detachments against the [enemy] right flank, but otherwise wait on the success of the action.'[14] Derfelden was positioned behind Pozzolo Formigaro with the 9,850 troops remaining with his corps after Bagration was detached with his advance guard (5,705). Rosenberg with the rest of the Russians (8,270) was still in the neighbourhood of Viguzzolo containing the garrison of Tortona citadel from the east, while the Austrian siege corps under Alcaini (5,260) had detached some of its units to Spineto and other locations to the south to confront any French forces marching to the relief.

Forces at Novi

Allied Army, Field-Marshal Suvorov

(Strictly according to the strengths listed on 24 July. The numbers present by 15 August would have been slightly less, and are in any case subject to the variations listed below. Reliable Orders of Battle for this period are as 'rare as hens' teeth', as George Nafziger has commented)

Austrian Corps, General Kray

Right Wing, Lieut-Gen Bellegarde
Infantry regiments:

Sztáray	3 bn	2,517
Gyulai	2 bn	1,370

(3 bn according to Stutterheim)

Huff	2 bn	1,500
Kheul	2 bn	1,690
Lattermann	2 bn	1,339
Nádasdy	3 bn	3,380
Dragoon Regt Kaiser	6 sq	888

(4 sq according to Stutterheim)

Hussar Regt. Erz. Joseph	3 sq	836

(as for the full regt of 8 sq; Stutterheim places 3 sq with Bellegarde, and 4 with Ott)

Screening Force, far right, Maj-Gen Seckendorf

Infantry Regt Oranien:	2 bn	1,417
Szluiner Croats:	1 bn	1,074

(Stutterheim lists an additional bn with Ott)

5th Hussar Regt;	3 sq	524

(for the full 6 sq, 3 of which were with Melas)

Left Wing, Lieut-Gen Ott
Infantry regiments:

Deutschmeister	3 bn	3,380

(2 bn according to Stutterheim)

Vukassovich	2 bn	1,277
Terzy	3 bn	2,700

(2 bn according to Stutterheim)

Mittrowsky	3 bn	1,548
Szluiner Croats:	1 bn	1,074

(for the single bn listed on 24 July)

Dragoon Regt Erz. Johann	6 sq	906
Hussar Regt Erz. Joseph	4 sq	

(see above)

Total:	27,420

(According to the unit listings and strengths of 24 July. Actual variations would include the 3 sq of the 5th Hussars with Melas, which brings the total down by about 260).

Russian Corps, General Derfelden

Advance Guard, Maj-Gen Bagration
Jäger regiments:

Bagration	2 bn	571
Miller (formerly Chubarov)	2 bn	618

Combined grenadier battalions:

Dendrygin	405
Lomonosov	409
Sanaev	430
Kalemin	484

Cossack regiments:

Denisov	476

(but only 250 effectives according to Denisov)

Sychov	495
Grekov	476
Semernikov	501

Austrian Dragoon

Regt Karaiczay	6 sq	840
Total:		*5,705*

Russian Division/Brigade, Maj-Gen Miloradovich
Musketeer regiments:

Jung-Baden	2 bn	1,217
Dalheim	2 bn	1,266
Miloradovich	2 bn	1,237
Total:		*3,720*

Under the immediate direction of General Derfelden

Grenadier regt Rosenberg:	2 bn	1,132

Musketeer regiments:

Schveikovsky	2 bn	1,140
Förster	2 bn	1,229
Tyrtov	2 bn	1,152
Baranovsky	2 bn	1,474
Total:		*6,127*

Austrian Corps, General Melas

(Division Frelich; brigades Lusignan, Loudon, Mittrowsky, Nobili, Liechtenstein)
Grenadier battalions:

Pertusi	339
Goeschen	627
Weissenwolff	673
Morzin	693
Schiaffinatti	508
Paar	324
Hohenfeld	221
Weber	275
Fürstenberg	n.a.

Infantry regiments:

Fürstenberg	3 bn	2,081
Stuart	2 bn	

Minus the four coys in Serravalle Castle

Dragoon regiments:

Lobkowitz	6 sq	591
Levenehr	6 sq	667

5th Hussar Regt;   3 sq
See comment concerning the Seckendorf screening force,
above

Total: 8,575

(Again on the strengths of 24 July; at Novi the loss of
the Stuart infantry was probably compensated by the
approximately 360 troopers from the 5th Hussars)
Austrian and Russian Totals: 44,347 infantry, 7,200
cavalry

Grand Total: 51,547

(All with the above provisos; the number of the
artillery and sappers is unknown)

FRENCH ARMY, GÉNÉRAL DE DIVISION JOUBERT

LEFT WING, GÉNÉRAL DE DIVISION PÉRIGNON

Division Grouchy
    Brigade Grandjean
        26th Light demi-brigade
        39th Line demi-brigade
        92nd Line demi-brigade
    Brigade Charpentier
        93rd Line demi-brigade
        99th Line demi-brigade

Total: 5,620

Division Lemoine
    Brigade Garreau
        5th Light demi-brigade
        26th Line demi-brigade
        80th Line demi-brigade
    Brigade Seras
        20th Light demi-brigade
        34th Line demi-brigade
    1st Hussar Regt

Total: 6,410

Infantry Reserve of Left Wing
    Brigade Clausel
        29th Light demi-brigade
        74th Line demi-brigade
    Brigade Partouneaux
        26th Light demi-brigade
        (N.B. Listed by Jomini and Saint-Cyr both here
        and with the division of Grouchy, above)
        105th Line demi-brigade

Total: 4,875

Cavalry Reserve of Left Wing, Richepanse
    1st Cavalry regiment
    3rd Cavalry regiment
    18th Cavalry regiment
    12th Dragoon Regt
    2nd Chasseur Regt

Total: 1,002

RIGHT WING, GÉNÉRAL DE DIVISION GOUVION SAINT-CYR

Brigade Colli
    14th Line demi-brigade
    24th Line demi-brigade
    68th Line demi-brigade
Attached Polish Troops
Total: 3,878 (Jomini), 4,260 (Saint-Cyr)
Division Laboissière
    Brigade Quesnel
        17th Light demi-brigade
        63rd Line demi-brigade
    Brigade Gardanne
        18th Light demi-brigade
        21st Line demi-brigade
    6th Hussar Regt
Total: 3,645 (Jomini), 3,976 (Saint-Cyr)
Infantry Reserve of Right Wing
    3rd Line demi-brigade
    106th Line demi-brigade

Total: 2,420

Cavalry Reserve of Right Wing, Guérin
    19th Chasseur Regt
    16th Dragoon Regt
    19th Dragoon Regt

Total: 425

Division Watrin
    Advance Guard Brigade, Calvin
        8th Light demi-brigade
        15th Light demi-brigade
        27th Light demi-brigade
        Two Line demi-brigades, numerical
        designations unknown
    Brigade Arnaud
        12th Light demi-brigade
        30th Light demi-brigade
    Brigade Petitot
        62nd Line demi-brigade
        78th Line demi-brigade
    25th Chasseur Regt
Total: 4,535 (Jomini), 6,040 (Saint-Cyr)
probably an over-estimate; he includes, for example, the
17th Light Demi-Brigade, which was actually in the division
of Laboissière)
Division Dabrowski
    17th Line demi-brigade
    55th Line demi-brigade
    1st Cisalpine
    Polish Legion
    Polish Cavalry
Total: 2,130 (Jomini), 2,340 (Saint-Cyr)

Army Total: Jomini puts the French combatants at 32,843 infantry and 2,087 cavalry, or a total of 34,930, which therefore corresponds closely with the figure of 34,000 mentioned by Saint-Cyr in his text (p. 227), if not his tables (35,487 infantry, 1,765 cavalry, total 37,252). No figures are available for the artillerymen.

It is evident that the French were inferior in quantity of infantry, and very weak in cavalry—a disadvantage to some degree offset by the broken terrain. The French as a whole were exhausted and thirsty, and so short of food that by the time of the battle they were reduced to eating leaves and grass.

NOVI, 15 AUGUST

During the night of 14/15 August four squadrons of light horse under Major Dobay cleared the way for Kray's advance by pushing back the outposts of the French left wing. Before first light Kray set his corps in motion by two wings, marching in multiple columns on half-company frontages. Kray in person accompanied his left-hand or eastern wing, which stood under the immediate command of Lieutenant-General Karl Ott. Lieutenant-General Friedrich Bellegarde commanded the powerful right-hand or western wing. To cover the far right-hand flank of his advance Kray detached Major-General Friedrich Seckendorf to take the route leading up the right side of the Riasco valley with a mixed force of regular infantry, Croats and hussars.

The first shots of the battle were exchanged at 3.20 in the morning. Much sooner than expected the advancing Austrians ran into the main force of the enemy left wing, provoking what is described as 'a great patriotic clamour' in the French camp. In the light of the rising sun the allies 'could see at once how the heights to the right and left of Novi were occupied by long blue lines... their position was admirably chosen for a day of battle. They were sited on heights whose slopes descended to the plain, and from where they could detect our slightest movement.'[15]

It was now clear that far from attacking a vulnerable flank of the French when they were already in motion, Kray had initiated an assault on an army which was still in position on advantageous ground. Joubert had not counted on fighting here (he had still been trying to make up his mind whether to advance on Tortona or retreat on Genoa), but in most respects his present positions were admirably suited for receiving an attack.

Monte Mesma is an outlying plateau of the Genoese Apennines, forming an oval complex drawn out on the long axis between the valleys of the Scrivia to the east and the Lemme to the west. The plateau reaches its highest points to the south at Monte Mesma proper (445 m) above Gavi, and Colle Ratto (426 m) above the Scrivia valley to the south-east. The northern edge of the plateau extends in a wide arc from Serravalle to the neighbourhood of Francavilla; it is much lower than the corresponding southern arc, but descends steeply to the northern plain in fertile slopes, which even now are covered by vineyards, orchards and little patches of woodland. In tactical terms the position was prolonged to the south by the salient formed by Novi town, which in 1799 was enclosed by a strong medieval wall furnished with battlements and a deep ditch.

It is more helpful to consider the French deployments in terms of the individual divisions rather than the parent wings. Out on the right (east) the adventurous Watrin was still standing on the lower ground towards Bettole di Novi. The northern edge of the plateau behind him was held by Laboissière, while Novi town was garrisoned by Gardanne. Lemoine occupied the long edge of the plateau extending west from behind Novi, and the western side of the plateau was secured by the division of Grouchy, and the infantry (Clausel and Partouneaux) and cavalry (Richepanse) reserves of the left wing. The position was therefore strong, in terms of warding off an attack, but in the case of a retreat it was a potential death-trap, for the deep-cut valley of the Braghena stream and the steep banks of the Riasco formed a continuous barrier across the rear.

We return to Kray's command, which in twenty minutes deployed from its columns into two lines and set itself at the steep slopes of the western plateau. On the wing of Lieutenant-General Ott the successive efforts of Major Mamola's Szluiner Croats, the regular infantry of the first line and Kray's powerful artillery succeeded in pushing back the division of Lemoine from the edge of the heights before the French could put themselves in order. To the right Bellegarde's wing made even better progress, for his assault arrived at a time when Grouchy's troops were standing unprepared and well back from the slopes

The advance of Kray's first line lost impetus when the troops had to re-form from line into column to negotiate the tangled terrain and steep gradients of the vineyards. The delays inevitably told to the advantage of the French, who were now coming to their senses. The

infantry reserve under Clausel and Partouneaux was already located very conveniently for the enemy in compact masses near Pasturana, and Pérignon as overall commander of the left wing directed this uncommitted force against Bellegarde. The French cavalry under Richepanse had been disconcerted by Seckendorf's push up the Lemme-Riasco valley, and he had been in the process of falling back towards Pasturana to avoid being cut off. This force too joined in the general counterattack.

Moreau was in charge of the centre, closer to Novi, and was meanwhile responding to the advance of Ott. Saint-Cyr (commanding on the right) sent the brigade of Colli to Moreau's aid, and before long the Austrians were coming under pressure from both their front and from their left flank. Joubert in person had helped to

View from the Braghena valley towards Pasturana

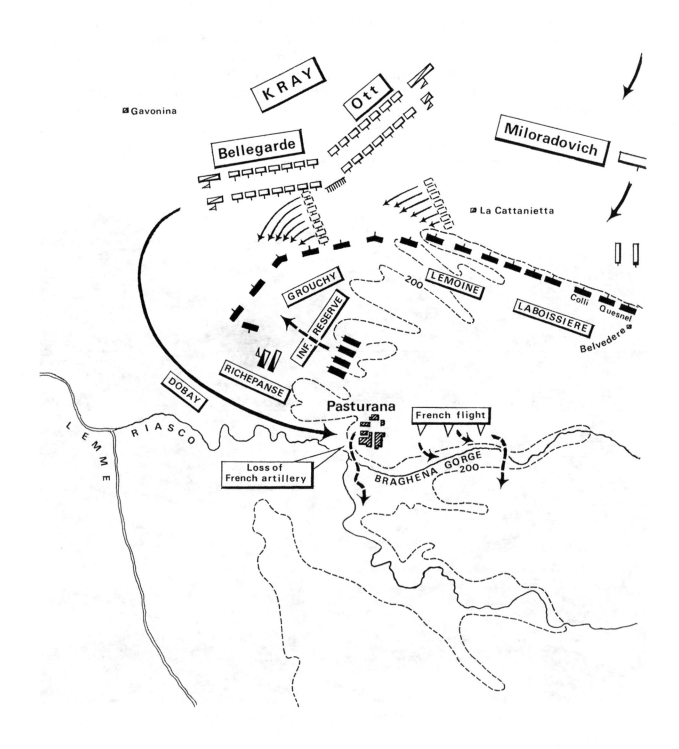

KRAY

◨ Gavonina

Ott

Bellegarde

Miloradovich

◨ La Cattanietta

GROUCHY

200

LEMOINE

INF. RESERVE

LABOISSIERE

Colli

Quesnel

RICHEPANSE

Belvedere ◨

DOBAY

Pasturana

French flight

L
E
M
M
E

R I A S C O

Loss of
French artillery

BRAGHENA GORGE
200

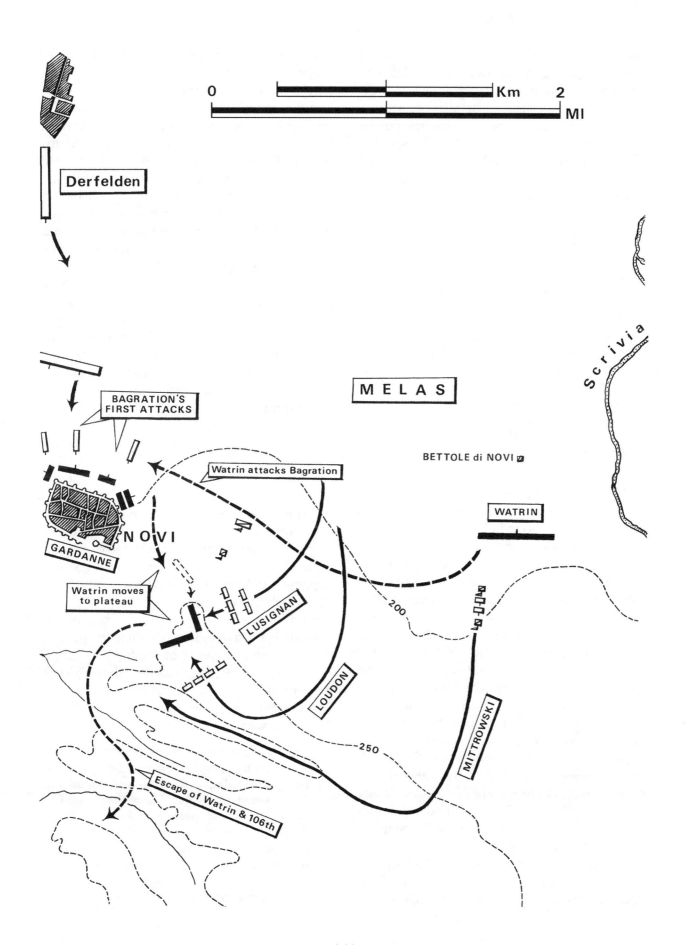

0   Km   2

MI

Derfelden

MELAS

**BAGRATION'S
FIRST ATTACKS**

BETTOLE di NOVI

Watrin attacks Bagration

WATRIN

N O V I

GARDANNE

Watrin moves
to plateau

LUSIGNAN

200

LOUDON

250

MITTROWSKI

Escape of Watrin & 106th

S c r i v i a

141

rally the fugitives during the first panic, and he was now leading the 26th light demi-brigade in a counterattack when an Austrian volley threw him from his horse, mortally wounded. MacDermott records that 'we saw the enemy carrying away a body escorted by chasseurs. It was covered with a cloak decorated in blue and gold, and taken to Novi… it transpired that this was their commander in chief Joubert.'[16]

Kray persisted in his attacks, but

the terrain was cut into transverse terraces, which proved impassable to our fearless infantry. Only after sustaining terrible losses could the heads of the columns [two great columns, according to the contemporary Austrian maps] make their way up the narrow passages, and then the troops found it impossible to deploy into line. The enemy at the top were formed up into several lines, and were able to deliver repeated counterattacks. Our troops stormed forward with a courage which verged on desperation, but to no avail against the obstacles presented by nature and the advantageous position of the enemy.[17]

One last effort by Ott's troops was turned back by the 26th light demi-brigade and the 105th at the Casa Bianca, and the entire first line of Kray's wing was soon falling back in disorder down the slopes.

By nine in the morning Kray had just succeeded in rallying the debris of his first line behind his second when the order came from Suvorov to renew the assault, this time with the assurance that the main army would be attacking in support. Only the main features of what happened next can be retrieved from the contradictory accounts. Ott and Bellegarde attacked Lemoine and Grouchy with the same initial success as before, but the help from the Russians was not forthcoming (they were being beaten back from Novi, below), and the French reserves were free to turn all their attention to the Austrians. The brigade of Partouneaux made for Ott's left flank, while Clausel and the cavalry under Richepanse once more took Bellegarde's command under attack.

Partouneaux was not content with his second success, and he led a number of his battalions down to the plain without support. In this open and level ground the French became a target for Major Dobay with his four squadrons of horse (two squadrons each from the Erzherzog Joseph Hussars and the Kaiser Dragoons). Dobay hit the French before they had time to form to meet his attack, and he chased them back to the plateau, Partouneaux himself being overhauled and captured before he could reach the shelter of the high ground. Kray and Bellegarde had by now deployed forty cannon in a single line, and they were able to shoot up the enemy French infantry every time they tried to show themselves along the crest.[18]

Kray was disinclined to throw the Austrian right wing into a further general assault until he had further evidence that the main army was doing its part. However the heights facing the Riasco valley to the south were now held weakly by the French, and Bellegarde took the opportunity to detach Dobay in this direction with his four squadrons and one battalion of the excellent Hungarian infantry regiment of Sztáray; this little force infiltrated to the wooded heights above Pasturana, with consequences that were to be of some interest towards the end of the battle.

The reader will be wondering why so little has so far been heard of Suvorov, the hero of our story. The same thought occurred to Bagration, who by the original scheme of things was supposed to have cut around the French right flank with the advance guard and join Kray at Gavi. Now the French were immobile on the plateau, instead of moving down to the plain as expected, and the noise of the fighting on the right, together with repeated appeals from Kray, prompted Bagration to address himself to Suvorov at headquarters at Pozzolo Formigaro. Bagration said afterwards:

one of my adjutants came to see me on the way with the report that the field-marshal was lying wrapped up in his cloak and fast asleep. This seemed impossible. The notion passed through my mind that he could actually be dead, and I spurred on. A number of the generals were standing in a circle in front of the column of Derfelden's corps. I hastened towards them, and not far from the group I saw that extraordinary man bundled up in an old cloak on the ground. I had scarcely got out a few words in answer to Derfelden's questions when Aleksandr Vasilevich threw his cloak aside, sprang up and declared; "God—how I must have slept! Like a stone! Now it's time for action!" It was clear that Suvorov had not been asleep at all, but had been listening to the conversation of the generals and the various reports that arrived from the scene of the fighting, and had been ruminating deeply on how to conduct the coming battle. He asked me how the combat had gone, then took in the enemy position with a rapid glance, and ordered Miloradovich and me to open the battle immediately.[19]

At ten in the morning Bagration advanced his Jäger and grenadiers directly against Novi. The French now had an excellent target. 'In the centre of the position they had placed three frightful batteries on the slopes of the hill; these now vomited forth flames and incessant thunder like an erupting volcano. They were deployed in such a way that the heaviest calibres were sited on the crest, the medium half-way down the hill, and the light pieces at the bottom.[20]

The Russians drove back Gardanne's brigade through the outlying ditches, gardens and suburbs of Novi, but the high and solid town wall proved to be impervious to the Russian field artillery, and Bagration accordingly shifted the axis of his attack to the right of the town (as the Russians saw it) to hit the edge of the plateau to the west. The broken ground forced the Russians to move in compact columns—easy marks for the tirailleurs (skirmishers) who were concealed in the vineyards and farm buildings—while the supporting fire from the Russian artillery ceased, for the pieces were still down on the plain, and the barrels could not be elevated sufficiently to reach the high ground with their shot and shell.

The Russians were checked frontally by Quesnel's brigade and the division of Laboissière, and hit in their left flank by two waves of attackers—Gardanne's troops surging from Novi, and then the division of Watrin, which was eager to gain its revenge for the defeat on the Trebbia, and which now came from the far French right and struck boldly across the plain.

The early morning of the 15th had found the greater part of the allied army deployed in depth as far back as the neighbourhood of Tortona, ready to bar the way to any French who might be seeking to escape after Kray and Bagration had cut across their rear. By the late morning both Kray and Bagration were instead engaged in battles of attrition on their respective sides of the plateau, and Suvorov concluded that he must commit all the troops within reach to an all-out attack on the French positions.

The brigade of Miloradovich was already on the way. It had been standing in front of Pozzolo Formigaro, and it now arrived on the scene of Bagration's action to build up the Russians fighting to the west of Novi to a strength of some 9,400 troops. The Miller Jäger and the Lomonosov and Sanaev grenadiers succeeded in containing Gardanne's thrusts from Novi, but every Russian frontal attack against the edge of the plateau was still breaking up in disorder.

There had so far been no chance for the Don Cossacks to get into action. Denisov's own regiment was no more than 250 strong at the outset of the battle, and in spite of his representations it had been placed in a position where it was exposed to the fire both of the French infantry and the cannon from Novi town. 'Alarmed by the shot striking the ground nearby, my horse made two or three large leaps to the side, and once reared up so high that I was nearly unsaddled. There were already up to sixty dead or wounded among my men, but the regiment stood in silence.'[21]

Denisov put an end to this useless sacrifice by ordering his regiment to fall back by bounds, which tempted numbers of the French to exploit their apparent success. Captain Gryazev and his badly shot-up company of the Rosenberg Grenadiers were looking on, and saw the Cossacks put on 'a very pretty display of tactics—they skirmished with the enemy tirailleurs, moving skilfully to entice the enemy further and further from their line, and then, choosing the right moment, they rushed together yelling in their usual style and cut of large bodies and surrounded and captured them.'[22] The Cossacks chased after the French who tried to escape, and it was good to see how they lassoed them and dragged them behind their horses, or skewered them with their lances at full gallop.

By now the approach of green columns across the plain signified that all the rest of Derfelden's corps (about 6,100 troops) was arriving from Rivalta. This accession of force enabled the Russians to make a new assault, which beat back the division of Watrin and reached the Belvedere Hill, but their ranks wilted once more under the fire of the tirailleurs, and the survivors fell back down the hillside. Melas wrote that 'upon this General Baron Kray made a new advance, and received a reinforcement in the shape of two [unidentified] battalions of Russians. He still could not break through, and so the field-marshal with his usual determination insisted that General Derfelden as well as Bagration and Miloradovich must deliver a new assault against the heights behind Novi.'[23]

The multi-tiered French battery to the west of Novi opened up again, and 'the canister and shot fell on us in showers. The missiles snatched away many a brave comrade, or exploded in the ground and threw up an impenetrable dust. Both sides thundered away unceasingly, and the sound re-echoed from the hills to still more frightful effect. We made out way towards the hill to the accompaniment of the groans of the wounded, and between the piles of the dead.' Gryazev relates that the Rosenberg Grenadiers advanced half way up the slopes, but recoiled in the face of a fire of musketry at point blank range. They were saved from destruction by Suvorov, who ordered them to veer to the right, and then fall back downhill.[24] The last general attack was beaten back at three in the afternoon, and this time the French tirailleurs and grenadiers chased the Russians as far as Pozzolo Formigaro.

Rosenberg (8,270) was standing to the east of Tortona, and beyond recall, which had left the Austrian corps of Frelich (8,800) at Rivalta as the only unengaged formation remaining at the disposal of Suvorov. Melas had chosen to remain with Frelich's troops rather than accompany Kray on his flanking movement, and the order to march had reached him soon after the same command came to Derfelden's Russians. The Austrians struck south up the Scrivia—either because Suvorov had ordered them to do so in the first place, or because the direct path to Novi was taken up by Derfelden (the accounts by Melas are contradictory).

As they looked over to their right the Austrians could see that the plain between Novi and Pozzolo Formigaro was covered with fugitives and confused knots of struggling French and Russians—the aftermath of one of the failed assaults—and at 11.30 in the morning Suvorov's adjutant Colonel Lavrov reached Melas with the order to move directly against Novi and launch a frontal attack. Melas was disinclined to break his teeth against the French where they were at their strongest, and 'meanwhile a detailed examination of the enemy position revealed that their right flank was the key to the whole, and therefore the proper target for the attack. I concluded that I must depart from the field-marshal's orders.'[25]

Melas was concerned to secure himself against any French forces which might descend from the upper Scrivia, and so he detached a 'first column' (two fusilier battalions of Stuart and two squadrons of the Lobkowitz Dragoons) under the command of Major-General Johann Nobili in the direction of Serravalle. Nobili crossed to the east bank of the Scrivia, and chased the French outposts through Cassano Spinola and Stazzano as far as Arquata. He was aided by Lieutenant-Colonel Dworschak and the garrison of Serravalle Castle, which made a sortie from their lofty perch into Serravalle town.

The main force continued on its way up the west bank of the Scrivia. Major-General Anton Mittrowsky was marching closest to the river with a distinctly over-commanded little party, namely two squadrons of the Lobkowitz Dragoons and two fusilier battalions of the regiment of Fürstenberg. The rest of the force consisted of nine battalions of grenadiers, which arrived in any untidy heap about two kilometres to the east of Novi early in the afternoon. Here Melas told off Major-General Lusignan with five of the battalions (Paar, Fürstenberg, Weber, Pertusi, Morzin) to make for the edge of the plateau close behind Novi. Major-General

Alexander Loudon continued on his way with the remaining four battalions (Hohenfeld, Schiaffinatti, Weissenwolff, Goeschen), and after two kilometres or so of marching he ascended the plateau in the company of Mittrowsky's dragoons and fusiliers, who had turned aside from the river.

We last encountered Watrin when he had moved his division from its original position on the far French right, and struck against the left flank of Bagration's columns as they advanced against Novi. By this time Watrin had returned to the right and climbed to a new station on the edge of the plateau south-east of the town, where a slight re-shuffling of his troops enabled him to place himself squarely in the path of Lusignan's grenadiers.

Franz Joseph Lusignan (1753-1832) hailed from an old family of Aragon, and his career hinted at a certain impulsiveness, for he had been captured at Rivoli in 1796, and taken prisoner again in the following year. He now brought the two battalions of his second line up in close support of the three battalions in the front, and set them at the slopes of the plateau:

> I grasped at once that in such an attack any delay or half-heartedness would have been fatal, and in order to deny my brave troops any time for reflection I dismounted, drew my sword, placed myself at their head, and began to ascend the hill under a hail of canister and musket balls. The enemy were putting up a hard fight, which augmented our casualties, but they were unable to withstand the desperate intrepidity of our troops. The hill was stormed and captured in fine style without a musket shot being fired.' [26]

So writes Lusignan. In fact three successive attacks by his grenadiers failed to dislodge the French from the vineyards and farmhouses where they were making their stand. What finally persuaded the enemy to fall back was the arrival of the rest of the Austrians, for Loudon and Mittrowsky had ascended the plateau unopposed, and Loudon's four battalions of grenadiers were now striding along the edge to take Watrin in flank, while Mittrowsky was infiltrating along a little valley against the French rear. Watrin's first line fled, carrying his second

line with it, and the Austrians might have pushed straight on to Novi if Saint-Cyr had not interposed the 106th demi-brigade, which advanced resolutely against the Austrian grenadiers and the supporting Levenehr and Lobkowitz Dragoons. Lusignan tells us that he

> advanced with such speed that I got several paces ahead of my grenadiers, and suddenly found myself completely unaided just twelve or fifteen feet from the enemy. I became the object of their undivided attention, and was thrown to the ground by two musket balls, one of which took me in the left arm, and the other which penetrated some way into my left ankle. I tried to get up, but two French cavalrymen set upon me at the same instant. One of the cut at me from the right—I was fortunately able to ward off the blow with my sword, but the other gave such a mighty cut to my head that it sliced through the gold-laced hat and plume, bit deep into my skull, and laid me out flat on the ground. My brave grenadiers were following close behind, but they were too late to save me. The enemy seized me by the hands and feet and dragged me off more dead than alive.[27]

After this check the Austrian grenadiers resumed their advance to sounding music, and by five in the afternoon they were pressing the outnumbered French back to Novi. Watrin judged that it was time for his division and the 106th demi-brigade to take their leave. His troops slipped adroitly past the advancing Austrians, and while the path of escape was still open they crossed the headwaters of the Braghena and reached safety on the far side of the Riasco.

Watrin had moved only just in time, for the two French flanks were now being beaten in. Over to the west Kray renewed his attack between three and four in the afternoon, on this occasion with the guarantee that the main army would be assailing the French right:

> I made the necessary arrangements [reported Bellegarde]. The troops had been under fire for hours on end, with nothing to drink—for there was not a drop of water to be had in the entire neighbourhood—and were exhausted by ceaseless exhaustion on one of the hottest days of the summer. It therefore gave me immense satisfaction to see how the men took

fresh heart from the example of our general [Kray], and pressed forward with every show of eagerness and courage. The enemy were holding their ground with equal bravery, but our troops attacked at the double to sounding music, and unhesitatingly climbed the steep slopes and drove the French from their position.[28]

Outside Novi the Austrian grenadier battalion of Paar pushed the 68th demi-brigade from the high ground by the upper gate. The French were keeping up a heavy fire from the windows of the nearest houses of the town, but on their fourth attempt the Austrians penetrated Novi at the same time as Derfelden's Russians broke in from the east and north. Most of Gardanne's men contrived to fight their way

out, but several hundred more were cut off in the course of the street battle and sought refuge in the houses.

By about 5.30 in the afternoon the French were giving way on every sector, and all cohesion broke apart when the two wings made for the steep river valleys across the rear of their position. The right wing fared best, for the division of Watrin had disengaged in the way we have just seen. The brigade of Quesnel and that of Gardanne were falling back from the neighbourhood of Novi, and made off in the direction of Tassarolo. The right wing as a whole was ultimately reassembled by Moreau, but it lost contact completely with the left, of which there was not the slightest news until 18 August.

The French left wing was being funneled

THE MEADOWS ALONG THE RIGHT BANK OF THE RIASCO. MAJOR KEES
ATTACKED FROM RIGHT TO LEFT IMMEDIATELY IN FRONT OF US

146

towards the picturesque little town of Pasturana overlooking the valley of the Braghena, which here formed a pronounced gorge. Bellegarde was pushing back Grouchy, while Ott advanced against Lemoine and Colli. To the left of Ott again Major-General Karaiczay was poised to unleash the pursuit with two and a half squadrons of his regiments of dragoons, three squadrons of Colonel Revay's 5th Hussars, two battalions of Russians (the reinforcements sent by Suvorov, above) and two pieces of horse artillery. Revay had been keeping his eye on the farm complex of Belvedere, a key position on the French centre, and as soon as he saw it abandoned by the enemy infantry he detached Major Steingruber with one of the squadrons to overhaul the French. Revay and Karaiczay then joined to lend support to Steingruber, while the infantry of Bellegarde and Ott closed in from the right, and Bagration came up with the advance guard from Novi and executed an outflanking movement against Pasturana from the left.

The whole of the French left wing was now piled up in and around Pasturana, while the artillery of the right wing, which had lost touch with its infantry, was brought at a gallop diagonally across the front of the advancing allies to arrive on the scene of general chaos: 'in the village there now ensued a frightful massacre, in which the Russians gave no quarter. The only French to save their lives were the ones who fell into the hands of the troops of Kray.'[29] The French were pressed back down the winding main street, through the central square, and out on the far side along the last stretch of the street to the sharp left-handed descent to the Braghena gorge. In the process Grouchy had been unhorsed in the central square while seeking to rally his troops by waving an abandoned colour; when the flag was snatched from him in the course of the mêlée he raised his hat on his sword as a new sign of defiance, but he was hacked down and captured. His fate was shared by Pérignon (another future marshal), who was wounded in the body and the forearm, and by a cut which left a spectacular diagonal scar across his left forehead.

While the issue of the battle was still in doubt, Bellegarde had detached a little force out on his right flank to infiltrate along the right bank of the Riasco towards Pasturana (two squadrons each of the Erzherzog Joseph Hussars and the Kaiser Dragoons, and the third battalion of the regiment of Sztáray, above). Major Kees assumed the command after Major Dobay was wounded, and he now struck to mortal effect against the French while they were struggling down the steep path to the bottom of the gorge; his detailed dispositions are unknown, though it is likely that the positioned the infantry in the Palazzo which overlooked the first bend in the road, and advanced his cavalry along the little plain immediately beside the deeply-cut bed of the Riasco.

Some of the French cannon were abandoned by their civilian drivers. Others were overturned in the panic, and the press of men, guns and vehicles was ultimately so great that General Colli was captured along with up to 2,000 of his troops and twenty-one of his guns.[30]

> The night terminated the action [writes a Russian soldier]. Our army put itself in order, and pulled a little way back. Everything fell quiet. The moon shone brightly, though the powder smoke was hanging in the air. We had only two or three cartridges left in our pouches; we sent for more and filled out pouches with them. We lay in a contented calm, and two men out of every three were allowed to go to sleep. Everyone thanked the Lord God from the bottom of his heart for having preserved him from death. It was eleven or twelve at night. The silence continued to reign, and we luxuriated in the opportunity to snatch some rest. Musket shots rang out all of a sudden—one, two, then a mighty crescendo—and then there was silence again.[31]

The outburst was occasioned by fugitive French who had hidden themselves in Novi and were now trying to break out. The Russians worked through the town again, routed out the last of the French, and set to work wrecking the houses and belabouring the inhabitants. Suvorov put an end to the sack by beating assembly, and he concentrated the Russian grenadier battalions in the main square in parade order before having them told off for security duty. There were French dead scattered about the town, and outside their bodies lay in profusion, with the faces contorted into the most hideous expressions. 'They were atheists, and it was evident that even at the moment of their deaths they had failed to invoke the name of Our Lord God, and thus perished as outcasts.' The countenances of the Russian dead, by contrast, were calm and settled.[32]

In the battle of Novi the allies lost about 8,200 men from all causes, of whom the Austrians accounted for some 5,800 and the Russians 2,496. The estimates of the French losses range between 6,500 and 6,643, and about 4,500 of these were lost on the left wing. The dead of all parties were buried in three mass graves, to the east of Bertole, to the south of Novi, and to the north of Pasturana.

> Such was the termination of this terrible battle, long, so disputed, and so bloody; and which in these three respects was without parallel in this campaign, or indeed in the whole war. It has been shown that 15,000 men, about a fifth of the combatants were disabled this day, and fortunately there are scarcely two or three similar examples to be found in the wars which have afflicted Europe for two hundred years past... Combining all the circumstances of this battle, it may be said that it was of the first order, as in it two great armies were engaged for more than twelve hours on the whole extent of their front; that it was one of the most remarkable combats of infantry, which have taken place since the invention of firearms. [34]

This was also one of those rare battles which was unsought by all the combatants, being precipitated by a series of misapprehensions, some of which endured long after the event. These now claim our attention.

If the distant fortress of Mantua had held out just a few days more, Kray would have been in no position to join the allies, and a campaign of a totally different order would have been fought out in the plains to the north. The sight of the allies on 14 August broke Joubert's initial confidence, and he still had not moved his troops from the plateau when they came under attack by Kray early on the 15th. Once Suvorov was fully awake, he grasped that his scheme of elaborate manoeuvre had gone awry, and that the only thing that mattered now was to open a general assault on the plateau. He therefore committed the successive formations of Bagration, Derfelden and Frelich to the battle. Without this drastic measure Kray would surely have succumbed, for the fighting on his sector was far more intense than elsewhere, and that day would have been remembered as a costly allied defeat.

The commentator Jomini assumed wrongly that Suvorov had intended to take the position under a general attack from the outset,

> but for some unfathomable reason all the attacks were assigned to arrive at different times, so that the allies made their various pushes in succession, without ever having enough force to break through... We cannot count this victory as one of Suvorov's finer feats of arms. His right wing went into action three hours before his centre, and eight hours before his left, and the French should therefore have been able to crush it at their leisure. The fact that this did not come to pass was due to the death of Joubert.[35]

Melas too remained under a misapprehension. He never knew about the debates among the French generals which caused them to hang back on the plateau, and he believed that Suvorov had missed the opportunity for an altogether more decisive action: 'I do not wish to talk about the blunder we made at Novi, when we ought to have let the enemy descend to the plain. They would have been eliminated for the rest of the campaign, and we would not have lost half the number of our brave troops, whom I love as my brothers and children. What is more, we could have advanced to the Var [the border river with Provence], which is out of the question for the present year.'[36]

Novi was a joint victory, but one in which the chief burden had been borne by the Austrians. Suvorov wrote to Emperor Francis on 5 August and enclosed the report of Melas, 'to which I must add one circumstance, which General Baron Melas is unwilling to mention on his own account, namely what I owe to the extraordinary enthusiasm of the Austrian troops, and the unparalleled exertions of their admirable commander who contributed so decisively to the victory by his repeated and selfless exertions.'[37]

For Emperor Paul the victory at Novi represented the last good news he was to receive from the southern theatre. He awarded the Order of St. Andrew to Derfelden, and bestowed the Alexander Nevsky on Bagration, and he wrote most handsomely to Suvorov: 'I do not know which is the more agreeable—for you to win battles, or for me to reward your victories. We both fulfil our duty. Me as Emperor, and you as the first commander in Europe.'[38]

NOTES TO CHAPTER 7

[1] KA FA Italien 1799 VIII 20 _, Chasteler, 'Vorschlag zu denen bevorstehenden weitere Operationen in Italien,' to Suvorov, Alessandria, 1 August

[2] Soult, 1854, II,152

[3] Jomini, 1820-4, XII,97

[4] KA CA 1799 VIII 164, Suvorov, 'Relation der Schlacht bei Novi am 15ten August 799,' Asti, 25 August. See also the admiring comments of Melas in KA CA 1799 VIII ad 24, 'Relation uiber die am 15ten August 799 vorgefallenen Schlacht, bei Novi,' 20 August

[5] KA CA 1799 VIII 1, Melas to Tige, Borgo, 1 August

[6] KA CA 1799 VIII 15, Melas to Tige, Pozzolo Formigaro, 13 August

[7] KA FA Italien 1799 VIII 164, Suvorov, 'Relation'

[8] Stutterheim, 1812, IV,x,20

[9] 'Ratnik,' 1844, No. 6, 256-7

[10] KA CA 1799 VIII ad 24, Melas 'Relation uiber...,' 20 August

[11] Zach to Kray, 9.45 a.m., 14 August 1799, Hüffer. 1900-1, I,281

[12] KA FA Italien 1799 VIII ad 155, Suvorov to Melas, Pozzolo Formigaro, 14 August. Among the enclosures Kray's letter to Suvorov at 1.15 a.m. on 14 August is mis-dated '13 August,' as is evident from the sentence in Suvorov's reply quoted above, concerning Kray's proposal to attack 'tomorrow the 15th.'

[13] KA CA 1799 VIII 16, Melas to Tige, Rivalta, 14 August. This document indicates clearly that Bagration's advance was supposed to be up the Scrivia valley. The letter of Melas to Archduke Charles of 16 August (Hüffer, 1900-1, I,283) is highly misleading, in that it talks of Bagration leaving Novi 'to the left,' i.e. advancing to the west of the town, a direction that would have brought him into immediate confrontation with the French, who by this time were expected to be marching to the relief of Tortona citadel.

[14] KA CA 1799 VIII ad 24, Melas 'Relation uiber...,' 20 August

[15] KA FA Italien 1799 XIII 44, MacDermott, 'Militärisches Dage Buch'

[16] Ibid.,

[17] KA FA Italien 1799 VIII 164, Suvorov, 'Relation der Schlacht,'

[18] KA FA Italien 1799 VIII ad 164, Bellegarde, 'Relation,' undated

[19] Quoted in 'Ratnik,' 1844, No. 6, 259

[20] Gryazev, 1898, 66-7

[21] Denisov, 1874-5, XII,33

[22] Gryazev, 1898, 68-9

[23] KA CA 1799 VIII 19, Melas to Tige, Novi, 15 August

[24] Gryazev, 1898, 69. Suvorov's active and expert interventions are also detailed in 'Ratnik,' 1844, No. 6, 260

[25] KA CA 1799 VIII ad 24, Melas, 'Relation uiber...'

[26] Lusignan to Melas, Pavia, 10 September 1799, Hüffer, 1900-1, 353

[27] Ibid., I,354

[28] KA FA Italien 1799 ad 164, Bellegarde, 'Relation'

[29] Stutterheim, 1812, IV,x,37

[30] For the fighting at Pasturana see the depositions of Nimptsch, Rakovsky and Revay in KA MMTO; KA FA Italien 1799 VIII ad 164 F, Revay's account; KA FA Italien 1799 VIII ad 164 E, Karaiczay, 'Relation'; KA FA Italien 1799 VIII 164 C, Bellegarde's 'Relation'; CA 1799 VIII ad 24, Kray, 'Relation,' 17 August; KA CA 1799 VIII ad 24, Melas, 'Relation uiber...'

[31] 'Ratnik,' 1844, no. 6, 262

[32] Ibid., No. 6, 264

[33] Writing immediately after the battle Melas put the loss of Kray's wing at 5,171, and that of the Austrian left wing at 736, and the staff and the artillery reserve at 42, making a total of 5,949; this figure includes 1,320 missing, or whom 700 (mostly wounded) were in the hands of the French, and the rest, or 620, were likely to return, which would bring the total down to 5,349. Stutterheim's total is 5,754, made of 5,145 on Kray's wing (710 killed, 3,260 wounded, 1,175 prisoners and missing), and 583 on the left wing (89 killed, 410 wounded, 84 prisoners and missing). Both sets of figures in any case represent eight or nine times as many men being lost by Kray than Melas.

[34] Anon., 1801-3, IV,218-9,223

[35] Jomini, 1820-3, XII, 103

[36] KA FA Italien 1799 V ad 289, Melas to Lambertie, 2 October

[37] KA FA Italien 1799 VIII 164, Suvorov to Francis, 25 August

[38] Paul to Suvorov, Fuchs, 1835-6, III,268

8

FRUSTRATION

In the euphoria of victory one of Suvorov's Austrian devotees exclaimed that 'such a happy success on the part of the combined army must inspire every right-thinking man to still greater deeds!'[1] That was to prove premature.

In the first place the allies made no attempt to destroy the disordered French before they could reach the refuge of the mountains. The opportunity was there. It was true that the troops of the former French left wing (Pérignon's old command) made for the upper Orba and Erra, and were very soon out of reach. However the right wing under Saint-Cyr was in a potentially disastrous situation. It had extricated itself from the immediate neighbourhood of the battlefield mostly unscathed, but it was driven off the direct route to Genoa (by way of Gavi and the Bocchetta Pass), and the remaining path of escape up the Scrivia to the east was blocked at Arquata by the Austrian major-general Nobili with the two battalion strong regiment of Stuart and one division of the Lobkowitz Dragoons (i.e. the garrison of Serravalle Castle and the components of the 'first column' of Melas). Nobili defied all the efforts of Dabrowski through the morning of 16 August, so that in the afternoon Saint-Cyr was forced to commit the whole of the division of Watrin before he could smash his way through.[2]

As the sun descended in the evening of the 16th it revealed the Ligurian mountains in all their bulk, and also great numbers of French who were climbing towards the summits and then disappearing from the Russians' sight. Rosenberg's troops were impatient to be after them, but no order to pursue came from Rosenberg himself, 'and on this account the whole corps became infuriated against him. "How can this be?" we muttered. "How can we be so close to the enemy and not be allowed to finish them off?... letting them slip from our hands like that is not the Russian style."'[3]

On the following day Suvorov brought his troops back to the positions they had occupied before their victory. Successes on the tactical plane was now less important to him than pushing ahead with the much larger scheme of conquering the entire Riviera di Ponente and arriving at the southern gateway of France. The grand design was postponed from one day to the next by a variety of nuisances and distractions. On 16 August Suvorov had to accept that the advance must be put off for five days, to allow time to assemble the mules to transport his supplies over the mountain tracks. Orders arrived simultaneously from Vienna for the Austrian corps of Klenau (reinforced to a strength of 9,000 by Austrian troops from Mantua, and now pushing up the Riviera di Levante towards Genoa) to turn back towards Tuscany and the Romagna. Suvorov was to detach Lieutenant-General Frelich to take command of the corps, whose unstated purpose was to consolidate Austrian influence in central Italy.

Suvorov wrote to Francis on the same 16 August to assure him that he would put the Emperor's wishes into immediate effect. He was sorry to see the forces at his disposal weakened by so many thousand troops, but he was still confident that before the end of the campaign he would be able to secure the borders of Piedmont along the mountain crests and down to the sea at Nice.

The next day brought the news that the French had taken the offensive in south-eastern Switzerland, retaken the Valais and the Little Cantons from the Swiss rebels, defeated Hadik's outlying detachments and seized the Simplon and St. Gotthard passes. On 18 August Suvorov sent Kray marching north with 10,000 troops to lend immediate help, and on the next day he set

150

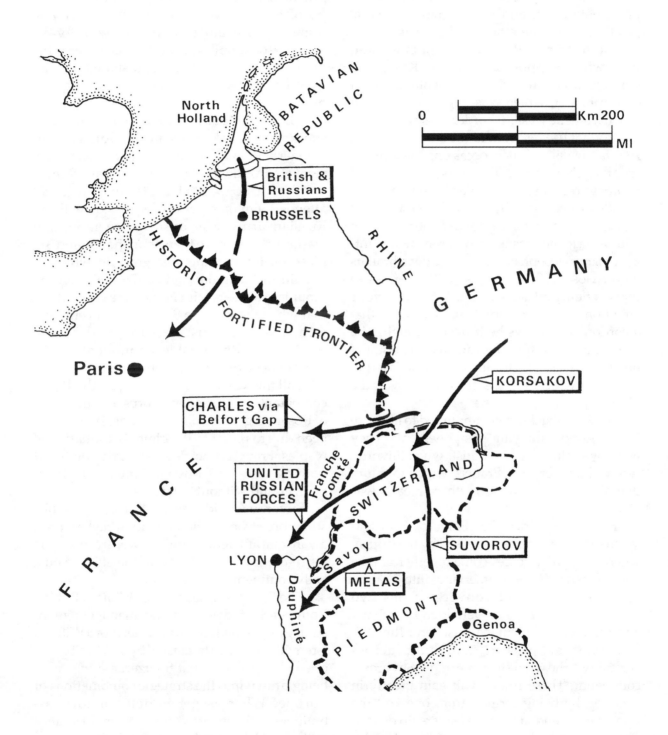

off with Derfelden's corps for Asti, leaving Tortona under blockade.

Suvorov reached Asti on the 20th. This little town was cradled in the foothills of the Piedmontese Alps, and offered Suvorov a central position from where he could still launch his invasion of the Riviera di Ponente, and meanwhile support Hadik and Kray, and perhaps do battle with the feeble corps of Championnet, which was beginning to push down from the western border passes. Suvorov made what use he could of the enforced delay. As was usual on such occasions, he put his troops through strenuous drills and manoeuvres, and assembled them in great parades to celebrate the recent victories and distribute honours. He extended the process of education to the chastened Austrian lieutenant-general Karl Joseph Hadik, whose detachments had just lost the Swiss passes. 'With reference to those enemy attacks… I must draw your attention to a well-founded military axiom, that a cordon can always be broken through. The attack can throw his forces against any point of his choosing, while the defender, who is left in uncertainty, scatters his troops all over the place.'[4]

All the setbacks so far amounted to no more than a run of annoying postponements. They were overtaken on 25 August, when Suvorov received a letter from Francis, which told him that his campaign on the southern theatre was at an end.

Francis explained that Emperor Paul had fallen in with a scheme proposed by the British, whereby Russian forces come together to take the offensive from Switzerland into France. These forces would converge from two directions—the corps of Derfelden from Italy, and the corps of Lieutenant-General Rimsky-Korsakov at present marching across Germany—the whole to come under Suvorov's command. 'These troops will gain greatly in cohesion by being formed from one and the same nation, and, under the leadership of such a brave commander as you, my esteemed field-marshal, who can doubt that they will go forth and attain the objectives which the allies have set before them?'[5]

Melas was to remain in northern Italy with the greater part of the Austrian forces, while the Russian corps of Rosenberg was to march south. The invasion of the Riviera would have to be put off for a little while, and (so reasoned Francis) it might prove altogether unnecessary, for the shortage of supplies would probably force the French to retreat anyway, and spare the allies from having to make bloody assaults against mountain-top positions.

The first impulse of Suvorov in his state of shock was to take off with his Russians for Switzerland without a moment's delay. He recovered a little, and 'whether out of attachment to Italy and the good military fortune which had attended him there, or because he knew that a Russian army was unsuited to mountain warfare'[6] he wrote to Francis on the 28th and 31st pleading for two months' grace in which to remain in Piedmont and settle affairs on the mountain borders with France. He pointed out that when the move to Switzerland eventually went ahead it must be supported by the Austrians with suitable equipment and a complement of staff officers, and prosecuted with all the Russian forces—not just the 12,500 combatants of Derfelden's corps, but the corps of Rosenberg (originally Rehbinder) which had been due to revert to its original destination of Naples. Francis conceded these last points but nothing else—the Russians must march on Switzerland without delay.

Suvorov would have protested, if possible, still more strongly than he did, if he had been aware that amateur strategists were responsible for re-deploying the forces of the alliance on a truly continental scale.

The British prime minister William Pitt the Younger had devolved the management of strategy upon his foreign minister, Lord William Grenville, who was fascinated by the possibilities opened by the fact that Switzerland was now being drawn into the strategic combinations of Europe. Whereas generations of fortress-builders had converted the borders of France with the Netherlands and the German states into an 'iron frontier,' the Jura border with Switzerland was defended only by little places like the Fort de Joux and Salins, and offered a

152

path by way of Franche-Comté to Lyon and the neighbourhood, where royalist sentiment was strong. British finance had sent Korsakov's auxiliary corps of a nominal 45,000 troops in march across Germany. The British had planned to link this force with a Prussian army in a drive across the lower Rhine, but now that Prussia refused to be tempted out of her neutrality these troops could be diverted in a useful way to Switzerland, there to link up with the 20,000 further Russians being brought up from Italy by Suvorov. Grenville's friend William Wickham was at the same time to raise a force of 20,000 freedom-loving Swiss, which would bolster the ideological credibility of the great enterprise.

By Grenville's arithmetic 45,000 Russians coming from Germany and another 20,000 marching from Italy amounted to 65,000 troops, which ought to be more than sufficient to clear Switzerland and carry the war into France, quite independently of the Swiss patriots. Powerful flanking support would be furnished by the Austrian army of Archduke Charles, which would leave northern Switzerland once Korsakov's Russians were comfortably in place, and advance across the upper Rhine nearby. The Austrians staying in Italy under Melas were no longer to advance on France by way of the Riviera, but would enter further north from Savoy, and thus be closer at hand to the Russian drive through Franche-Comté. Grenville still had at disposal one million pounds in cash, which would otherwise have been spent on subsidising the Prussians, and he used the sum to open a further front in the war—an expedition by British and Russian forces to North Holland, which might set the allies on a path to Paris from the north, and would at the least offer a powerful diversion.

The strategy ultimately foundered on crucial issues of numbers, geography, direction and timing. When Lieutenant-General Aleksandr Mihailovich Rimsky-Korsakov reached the headquarters of Archduke Charles at Zürich on 12 August he was taken aback to learn that he was supposed to spearhead the liberation of Switzerland and a full-blooded invasion of France; he pointed out that his troops amounted to 28,000 effectives, and not the 45,000 which

had been supposed, and that he lacked provisions and transport. The most militantly anti-French areas of Switzerland were now under occupation by the French, after a series of bloody actions, and all the efforts of Wickham succeeded in raising justly 2,000 patriots. The entire force, together 18,000 Austrians left behind under the command of Lieutenant-General Hotze, amounted to 48,000 men.

As regards the geography, Francis and his foreign minister Thugut agreed to the final scheme on 31 July with one important proviso, namely that Archduke Charles should make his main effort (with about 60,000 troops) across the Rhine in the neighbourhood of Philippsburg and Mannheim, in other words further downriver than Grenville had planned; an intermediate corps of 25-30,000 Austrians, together with a few German troops, was supposed to advance on the Belfort Gap, but this amounted to nothing like the powerful and immediate support which the Russians needed. Thugut argued in justification that it would be impossible to subsist a combined army of 140,000 troops in the narrow confines of Swabia and Switzerland.

The timings were to fall out in such a way that Archduke Charles and his Austrians left Switzerland too early, and Suvorov arrived from Italy too late, which left Korsakov and Hotze in very extended positions to face the 76,000 troops of Massena. The scheme nevertheless appealed to Francis and Thugut because it had come to them from the British by way of Paul, and they could now call on Suvorov to remove himself from Italy in the name of the solidarity of the alliance. Thugut chose his confidant Major-General Franz Joseph Dietrichstein to carry the appropriate message of the Emperor to Archduke Charles, who was an experienced military man, and might present a danger to the plot.

Dietrichstein presented the letter on 7 August. Charles tore open the seal with impatience, and a first reading showed him the potentially fatal implications. Dietrichstein tried to dismiss the archduke's presentiments, but two days later he found him as uneasy as ever. Charles pointed out that the Russians even at their nominal strength would amount to scarcely half the Austrian forces in Switzerland: 'I don't know how they will manage, especially if we take ourselves off any distance.' Dietrichstein replied that when Charles considered the matter he would be likely to fall in with Vienna's plan, and

> particularly if we separate the armies as soon as the weather, the season and the physical resources permit, and in such a way that the Russians do not complain too loudly that we are abandoning and sacrificing them. We can trail down the Rhine and make various manoeuvres which will persuade friend and foe alike that we still intend to do something serious, and so distract the French and Russians to some degree while our forces are gradually taking up winter quarters. I believe that in the present state of political uncertainty it is necessary to bring the campaign to an end before we arrive in French territory.[7]

The reservations of Charles were shared by Lieutenant-General Hotze (commanding the Austrian forces remaining in Switzerland), the new British military representative Major-General Lord Mulgrave, and Lord Minto as the new British ambassador in Vienna, all of whom expressed their concern. Thugut was determined that Archduke Charles must remove his army forthwith. At the end of August the over-extended Russian corps of Korsakov therefore took over the former Austrian positions from the lower Aare along the Limmat to Lake Zürich, while the remaining corps of Hotze assumed responsibility for the extremely long stretch from that lake to the Grisons.

Suvorov was left with a very narrow margin of time in which to bring his troops from Italy to Switzerland. Pitt and Grenville had sent the original plan to Paul on 8 June. Paul communicated his agreement to Vienna, where Francis and Thugut settled on their fatally amended version by 31 July, the date on which the Emperor dispatched Dietrichstein with the new orders to Archduke Charles. Paul had meanwhile written directly to Suvorov, and the authorities in Vienna delayed communicating with Suvorov on their own account until the unwelcome message was well on its way— probably with the intention of throwing the responsibility of the whole scheme on Suvorov's Russian master. It is striking that the Hofkriegsrath wrote on 13 August to inform Suvorov's Austrian chief of staff Zach about the change of plans, but enjoined him to tell nobody about it. Francis finally brought himself to send his fateful order on 17 August, and it was received by Suvorov only on the 25th, as we have seen.

Suvorov believed wrongly that Archduke Charles had been personally responsible for the haste in moving his army from Switzerland, and he communicated his alarm in a letter of 30 August. Relations between the two had already been exacerbated by petty quarrels as to who had the authority to dispose of the intermediate forces in the Tyrol and southern Switzerland. Thus Suvorov came to know Charles not as a fellow-victim of Thugut, but as a stiff and remote individual who was quick to take offence.

NOTES TO CHAPTER 9

[1] KA FA Italien 1799 XIII 44, MacDermott, 'Militärisches Dage Buch'

[2] For the early stages of this interesting action see KA FA Italien 1799 VIII 164 H, Nobili's 'Gehorsamste Bericht'

[3] 'Ratnik', 1844, No. 6, 265

[4] Suvorov to Hadik, 22 August 1799, Meshcheryakov, 1949-53, IV,267

[5] Francis to Suvorov, 17 August 1799, Milyutin, III,380

[6] Lieutenant-Colonel Weyrother, 'Tagebuch des Herrzuges der Russen unter dem Oberbefehle des Herrn Feldmarschalls Suworow,' Hüffer, 1901-2, I,36

[7] Dietrichstein to Thugut, 9 August 1799, Ibid., I,260

9

THE ASSAULT ON THE ALPINE RAMPARTS

SWITZERLAND AS A THEATRE OF WAR

For month after month every clear afternoon on the north Italian plain had brought into view the peaks of the Alps as they marched across the northern horizon. This was the direction in which Suvorov now had to turn his army.

Mens' imaginations were quickening to the experience of campaigning in that part of the world. Not many years had passed since travellers had averted their eyes from the horrors of the Alps, but now the perception of the landscape was under the influence of Romantic sensibility. In 1799 a French officer could call on his readers to admire the unsuspected beauties that were being discovered in Switzerland,

> for no other country in Europe can show forth so much grandeur, such a variety of majestic and smiling landscapes. Nowhere else may you encounter so many marvels within such a small compass—mountains reaching to such a prodigious height that their peaks are formed of everlasting glaciers and their slopes covered with snow for nine months of the year; frightful precipices, and deep gorges down which crash those torrents which unite their waters in the spacious valleys of the Rhine and the Rhône.[1]

Fuchs once saw Suvorov standing entranced at the sight of those inaccessible peaks, where the wandering clouds and wet mists were shot through every now and again with rays of golden sun and rainbows. 'Such visual miracles wrested from the old man a cry which might have come from the whole army: "Why was I not born an artist? Oh for a terrestrial Vernet to come here, and set down for posterity that unique, fleeting moment which is our existence!"'[2] (Joseph Vernet [1714-89] was a celebrated painter of seacoasts).

More prosaically Suvorov the strategist pondered on the fact that the hitherto separate theatres of war in southern Germany, south-eastern France, north Italy and the western provinces of Austria now demanded to be considered as a coherent whole.

In the horizontal, or east-west plane, the opening of Switzerland turned to the advantage of the allies, for the Alps of the Vorarlberg and the Tyrol to the east presented much more formidable barriers that did the wooded hills of the French Jura—a truth that was grasped by Grenville, and by the French statesmen and soldiers who began to regret that they had invaded Switzerland in the first place. 'In previous times,' commented Carnot, 'we could leave the Swiss frontier from Huningue to Geneva safely uncovered, for we could rely on the cantons to keep their pledge of neutrality; now we must commit 40,000 troops to that part of the world, whether to occupy Switzerland, or to guard the neighbouring depots which have no fortresses to protect them.'[3]

In the vertical (north-south) aspect Switzerland offered passages between the regime of the Rhine on the one hand, and that of the Po on the other. Once an army was in possession of Switzerland it therefore had the facility of acting in northern or southern Europe at will. As Soult phrased it, 'in the previous campaigns Switzerland as a neutral interposed a bloc between the war in the Italy and the war on the Rhine. Now that we occupied Switzerland it became the inevitable pivot of operations—for offensive purposes to connect the armies operating on the two sides of the Alps, and on the defensive to fill the gap by which the enemy could not only have taken those two armies in the rear, but taken in rear the line of the Rhine itself.'[4]

For centuries past the business of fighting in mountains had devolved on Jäger, miquelets,

Croats and the like—men whose upbringing, trades or brigand-like ways suited them for that specialised work. Here again the campaigning in 1799 called forth new perceptions, for regular soldiers from the lowlands now had to accustom themselves to combat across upland forests, steeply-sloping pastures, screes and crags, and at altitudes that could leave men gasping for breath. 'On such a theatre more than any other there is a call for tireless activity, a courage which takes inspiration from the obstacles it must encounter, and a sustained vigour—or even obstinacy—in the attack and on the defence.[5]

According to Clausewitz the Austrians furnished some of the Russian units with crampons for the storm of the St. Gotthard Pass. The French seem to have been using them as a matter of course, and a Russian writes that 'for a long time it was a mystery to us soldiers how the French tirailleurs, and indeed the French troops as a whole were able to advance or retreat over the mountains like wild goats... finally on the day of battle in the Muotatal [30 September or 1 October] we discovered the reason. It was a very simple device. They had extra soles, rather like sandals, into which they hammered and fixed spikes, and which they fastened to their shoes by straps.'[6]

The Austrian army was no stranger to mountain warfare as such. However Switzerland was virgin military territory, and had never been subject to the same kind of topographical analysis as, for example, the Piedmontese Alps. While the allies had the sympathy of nearly all the mountain people, who provided guides willingly, the priorities of a cattle drover were not necessarily those of a

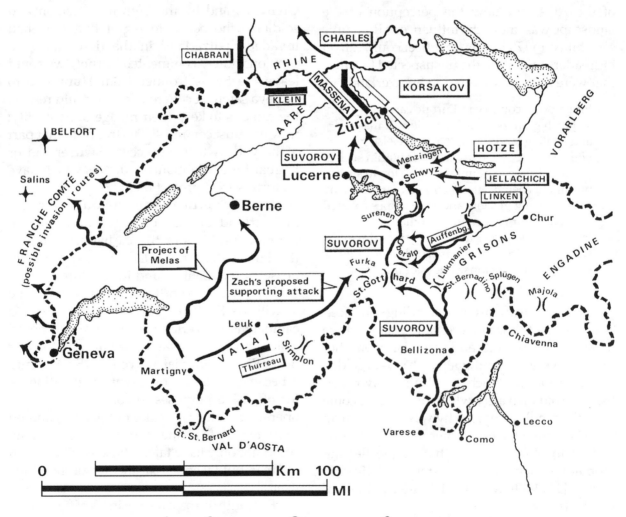

ALLIED SCHEMES FOR OPERATIONS IN SWITZERLAND

156

military commander, and thus it remained to some degree a matter of conjecture how long a column would take to cross such and such a pass, and what state the troops would be in when they completed the passage. The problem was complicated by the fact that as many individual paths had to exploited as possible, if the entire army was not to be strung out inordinately along a single track.

The immediate tasks for Suvorov were to resolve the general shape of the coming campaign in Switzerland, and determine how his little army was to reach the theatre of war. He knew that the French held the whole of western and central Switzerland, and an eastern salient which was bounded by the water barriers of the lower Aare, the Limmat, Lake Zürich and the Walensee to the north, and the mountains overlooking the long curves of the valleys of the Linth and Vorderrhein (upper Rhine) to the east. The allied forces already in Switzerland were thrown out in an arc around the perimeter of this salient:

the recently-arrived army of Lieutenant-General Korsakov (28,000, or 26,000 after the detachment mentioned below) was concentrated to the north-west of Zürich along the right banks of the Limmat, the lower Aare, and the Rhine near Waldshut,

Prince Alexander of Württemberg with 2,500 Austrians and Swiss and 2,000 detached Russians held the long and low-lying north shore of Lake Zürich, supported by the hastily-improvised flotilla of the Austrian lieutenant-colonel James Ernest Williams, an English-born seafarer, who had been recruited personally by the late Austrian Emperor Joseph II in Ostend, and commanded Austrian craft on the Danube and Rhine and in the Adriatic.

The Austrian lieutenant-general Johann Konrad Hotze commanded the left or eastern wing of the allied forces with a total of about 18,000 troops. Eight thousand of these troops stood under his immediate command and guarded the middle Linth, which formed a near-continuous line with the Walensee. Local control of the rest was exercised by Lieutenant-General Linken, who held about 4,500 men troops under Major-General Franz Jellachich in reserve at the nodal point of Sargans, and the remaining 5,500 or so (brigades Simbschen and Auffenberg) along the great valley of the Vorderrhein as far

as Disentis to cover the Austrian-occupied canton of Grisons (Graubünden); the brigade of Major-General Simbschen (about 3,500) could be regarded as an integral part of Linken's force, while the brigade (2,000) of Major-General Auffenberg was assigned to co-operate with Suvorov when the Russians emerged from Italy.

Colonel Gottfried Strauch had been attached to Hadik's corps with 4,570 troops quite independently of the Austrian command in Switzerland. He had just been dislodged from the St. Gotthard by the French, and forced down the middle Ticino valley (Val Levantina) in the direction of Bellinzona.

The planning for the campaign was a cumulative and co-operative process. Suvorov put together his first ideas at Asti, and dispatched them to Hotze, Jellachich and Linken on 5 September, asking for their comments. The reply of Lieutenant-General Friedrich Hotze was awaited with particular eagerness on two accounts. Suvorov had met him on campaign against the Turks, and knew him as an enterprising officer. He was moreover a native of Switzerland, and well acquainted with the topography of that part of the world.

Hotze answered in useful detail on 10 September, though he put the total forces of the French and their Swiss auxiliaries at 60,000, which was an underestimate of about 16,000 men.[7] Suvorov replied on the 13th to confirm the receipt of the letter and expressed his

> complete approval of the proposal you sent to me, with sincere thanks. I find it in total conformity with those sound principles which indicate that one should fall with united forces on the most vulnerable side of the enemy... I shall therefore conform completely with your plan, and would ask you to talk it over with Lieutenant-General Korsakov; I am acquainting him with your plan and of my complete approval, and directing him to co-operate meticulously.[8]

Three groups of forces were to converge according to the scheme of operations just agreed:

1. Korsakov from the North

Korsakov was already locked in direct confrontation with the French across the Limmat in the neighbourhood of Zürich, but he must wait to deal his blow until all the other forces had arrived in close support.

2. Hotze from the East

The forces of Hotze were directed against the salient of the French positions. His principal body would force the line of the lower Linth, which covered almost all of the eighteen-kilometre wide tract of low-lying ground between Lake Zürich and the Walensee (at that time the Linth had not yet been diverted into the Walensee), while the division of Major-General Jellachich advanced along the south side of the Walensee and evicted the French from the middle Linth between Näfels and Glarus. The joint force of Hotze and Jellachich would then advance west to evict the French from the heights behind Menzingen—thus opening a corridor between lakes Zug and Zürich—and veer right towards Zürich town.

Lieutenant-General Linken was to take personal control of the brigade of Simbschen, climb the mountains which separated the Vorderrhein from the remote Sernftal, descend that valley to the upper Linth, and lend support to the operations of both the main force of Hotze and Suvorov. The remaining brigade, that of Auffenberg, would wait at Disentis for the coming of the Russians.

3. Suvorov from the South

Suvorov was to march with the Russian forces from north Italy, and he got down to work with his staff to examine how he could best reach the great rendezvous across the mountain barriers which stood in his path.

Four routes, or sets of routes, stood at the disposal of any commander who wished to advance from north-west Italy into Switzerland:

1. If he struck half right, or north-east, he could take the road to Como, march by way of Gallerate and Saronno around Lake Como (perhaps embarking his artillery for the sake of convenience) and reach Chiavenna. From there the road over the Majola Pass, down the Inn valley through the Lower Engadine to Landeck, and then by way of Bludenz to Lake Constance offered a militarily secure though extremely roundabout route, which Suvorov in fact chose for his field artillery.

2. Alternatively the force could make north from Chiavenna by the difficult but practicable route up the Val San GiaComo by way of Isola to the Splügen Pass (2,113 m), from where a short descent would bring it to the Hinterrhein and the goodish road leading to the Vorderrhein above Chur, and thence by an easy march to Sargans and the main concentration of the corps of Hotze. The Splügen route could have accommodated 6-pounder cannon, and it was proof against enemy interference. Clausewitz, Jomini and most other commentators of the period believed that Suvorov was at fault in rejecting this alternative, and the Comte de Venançon (a Piedmontese in the Russian service) calculated that even allowing for the necessary rest days Suvorov could have reached Como from Asti on 15 September, Chiavenna on the 18th, Sargans with the advance guard on the 24th and with the whole army on the 25th. Concealment and security gave the Splügen route to the Hinterrhein the preference over the route which branched off to the east from Bellinzona and took the San Bernadino Pass (2,065 m, not to be confused with the Great St. Bernard, below).

3. We turn west to the Simplon Pass, where Napoleon constructed a magnificent road between 1801 and 1805. In 1799 the passage was a poor mule track, and did not come into realistic consideration for a whole army. Zach however suggested to Suvorov that it would be useful to detach 8,000 troops on wide left-flanking move from the Valle d'Aosta over the Great St. Bernard (2,469 m) well to the west of the Simplon; they would descend to the valley of the upper Rhône at Martigny, then march east-north-east up the valley by way of Leuk, liberate the oppressed people of the Valais en route, and arrive by way of the Furka Pass (2,431 m) to the rear of the St. Gotthard Pass just when that feature was being assaulted by a further 8,000 troops under Suvorov. 'After weighing up carefully all the arguments for and against the proposal of General Zach, the field-marshal came down against splitting his force into two separate columns… however the idea of the offensive march by way of the St. Gotthard and Altdorf against the rear of the enemy army standing on the Limmat appeared to him to be eminently practicable.'[9]

On 27 August General Melas had suggested a bold variant, whereby the Russians would advance from the Great St. Bernard up through western Switzerland in the direction of Berne, deep in the French rear, which might compel Massena to fall back from the Limmat in order to cover his line of communication. This was a scheme on the grand scale, but it would have carried Suvorov too far away from the rendezvous with Korsakov and Hotze, who needed all the support they could get after Archduke Charles made off with the main force of the Austrians.

4. The final choice of the St. Gotthard route was dictated by several considerations. Most immediately it corresponded to Suvorov's instinct for direct action by his united forces, and he was happy to accept the price of fighting the French who were certain to be emplaced there. In addition the St. Gotthard was known as the best and the most heavily-frequented pass giving access between Germany and Switzerland on the one side, and Italy on the other, and the route counted as an excellent pack road, being paved with granite cobbles, though it was inaccessible to wheeled vehicles. The Austrian officers were probably happy to support the decision for the St. Gotthard presented a classic 'key to the country,' in the strategic thinking of the time:

> The St. Gotthard is situated in the high Alps which separate Italy from Switzerland. It forms the highest feature of this range, and from here the waters spread in every direction. The Rhône rises on its western flank, and hastens down to Lake Geneva, and thence to the Mediterranean. Its southern foot is bathed by the Ticino, whose waters reach the Adriatic by way of Lake Maggiore and the Po. The sources of the Reuss unite on its northern slopes, and flow to the Rhine and the North Sea. The Inn rises not far to the east of the pass, and feeds the Danube which in its turn reaches the Black Sea.[10]

The plan for the assault on the St. Gotthard evolved in full detail only when Suvorov's troops were approaching their objective, but a number of features were already present in the outline plan which Hotze sent to Suvorov on 5 September. Thus the Austrian major-general Franz Xaver Auffenberg with four battalions (2,000) would climb from Disentis to the head of the Maderanertal, and descend to Amsteg in the Reuss valley, thereby threatening the French communications with their base at Altdorf at the same time as Suvorov assaulted the St. Gotthard from the front. As for the date, Hotze adopted the proposal of Colonel Strauch that the attacks by Suvorov on the St. Gotthard,

Auffenberg on Amsteg, and Hotze on the Linth should arrive simultaneously on 19 September.

Suvorov replied to Hotze from Novara on 13 September, and endorsed the plan in enthusiastic terms (above). His only reservation concerned the timing, for the French had pushed from the St. Gotthard down the Ticino a couple of days before, and they might be already at Bellinzona. If that proved to be the case, he would have to clear them out of the way before he could arrive at the St. Gotthard, which might delay his attack.

As for the further avenue by which Suvorov proposed to arrive at the rendezvous at Zürich, his exploratory circular of 5 September to Hotze, Korsakov and Linken suggested routes around both sides of Lucerne. Suvorov came to know from a separate source (below) that the Schächental-Chinzig route to the east of the lake was practicable but difficult, and Hotze assumed that the field-marshal would take the southern route alone, by way of the Surenen Pass (2,191 m) and Engelberg, which is why he proposed to retrieve Auffenberg's column after it had done its work in the valley of the Reuss.

As late as 16 September Suvorov toyed with the idea of leaving the St. Gotthard under guard, and (instead of striking north down the Reuss) taking the rest of his force on a very wide circuit out to the east and the north by way of the Vorderrhein valley to rendezvous with Hotze; there would have been no French forces in the way, once he had captured the St. Gotthard and the nearby Oberalp Pass. However such a route would have been much longer than keeping on north down the Reuss, and would not have struck into the rear of the French positions— which is probably why Suvorov gave way to Weyrother on this point.

Once we have Suvorov committed to the avenue of the Reuss, we touch upon the much-disputed question of how he then proposed to get around Lake Lucerne, once he had arrived at Altdorf at the head of the lake. The issue deserves some attention, for the nationalistic Russian historiography represents Suvorov as arriving at Altdorf and finding, contrary to the assurances of his Austrian staff, that no path led around the eastern lake shore. The story gained credibility from the reminiscences of the Swiss commissary Schoke in the 1830s, but it has no other substance.

Suvorov knew before he entered Switzerland that if he intended to pass to the eastern side of the lake he would have to do so by a roundabout route which led up the Schächental and then over the Chinzig Pass. On this subject it is worth quoting the Swiss colonel Ferdinand de Roverea:

Hotze asked me to establish direct contact with Lieutenant-General Aleksei Gorchakov, whom believed to have more influence than Korsakov. I betook myself to Zürich, where Gorchakov [a divisional commander in Korsakov's army] made me very welcome, and initiated me into the projects of his uncle, who was preparing to enter Switzerland by way of the St. Gotthard and make for Lucerne by way of the cantons of Uri and

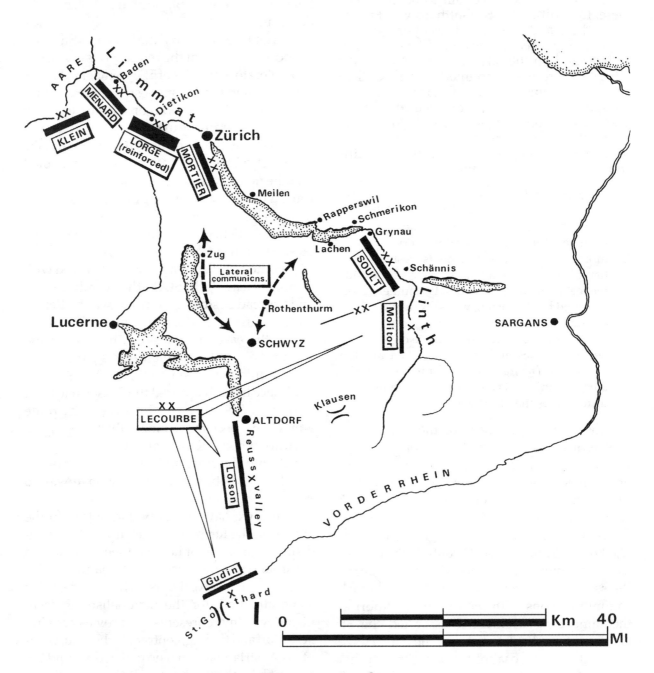

FRENCH DEPLOYMENTS IN SWITZERLAND

Unterwalden. I took it upon myself to prove that it was physically impossible to reach Unterwalden from Altdorf by land, and almost as impossible to make the passage by water from Flüelen to Stansstad without a great number of boats. A courier was sent at once to Tortona and informed the field-marshal about the nature of these obstacles, and to indicate the Schächental passage as mandatory.[11]

In Taverne Suvorov was likewise made aware that the path to the east of the lake was not at all easy, 'because the column would have to traverse by just one route, in single file.'[12] In view of these well-known difficulties Hotze thought that Suvorov would after all prefer to take the Surenen route, as we have seen.

It is surprising that the story of Suvorov's ignorance has persisted even in the face of indirect evidence. The Austrians and the Swiss on the northern side of the Alps were doing everything they could to inform him of the practicability of the various routes. Written communications were frequent and easy (a letter from Hotze reached Suvorov in Novara in three days, and his further correspondence arrived in just two when Suvorov was approaching the St. Gotthard). These written messages were supplemented by verbal reports by the Austrian captain Sarret, Lieutenant-Colonel Sir Henry Clinton and the émigrés Hanseau and Varicourt, all of whom were sent by Hotze in addition to the commission he gave to Roverea.

On his way across the Alps Suvorov was accompanied by an excellent Swiss guide in the person of Captain Antonio Gamma, whose brother Gaudenzio owned inns on both sides of the watershed at Taverne and Wassen—and Swiss inn-keepers have traditionally considered it part of their duty of care to keep travellers well briefed on the practicability of roads. Antonio himself was so well informed of conditions in the area of Altdorf that he was able to steer Suvorov to lodgings in one of the few intact houses, and it is inconceivable that he and the field-marshal should never have discussed where the army was supposed to be going. Suvorov blamed the Austrians for a great deal, but he makes no mention of the supposed blind alley in his correspondence, and he remained on good terms with Lieutenant-Colonel Weyrother ('Pavlovich'), who would have borne the prime responsibility for any such débâcle.[13]

We may dismiss totally out of hand the related story to the effect that Suvorov had expected to find the Austrian lieutenant-colonel Williams' flotilla waiting for him at Flüelen to transport him across the lake. Williams' flotilla was known to be operating on Lake Zürich, not Lake Lucerne, and there was no means by which the boats could have been transported from one body of water to the other.

More disturbing was the narrow logistic margin of the coming campaign. The route over the St. Gotthard was good of its kind, but accessible only to pack animals, and Suvorov depended on the Austrians living up to a promise to assemble provisions for ten days and the necessary 1,429 mules at Bellinzona by 15 September. Even the full complement of pack mules could not have subsisted the army for more than a few days on the far side of the St. Gotthard, and Suvorov counted on supplies being assembled for him at Schwyz by the efforts of Korsakov and Hotze.

The allies had been in possession of the north Italian plan for months, and with the coming of harvest there had been no need to gather provisions for more than four days at a time. William Wickham feared that Suvorov had not been made sufficiently aware of the very different conditions in Switzerland, where the most fertile cantons were under French occupation. He wrote to him to emphasise that in the area where he proposed to operate 'the country offers *absolutely nothing* in terms of resources. Even in better times it is unable to sustain its own population, and whatever power controls it this coming winter, it can still bring forth nothing but hunger and misery.'[14]

Intelligence on the enemy was necessarily imperfect, for many of their forces were tucked away invisibly behind mountain ranges. The total came to about 79,200 infantry and cavalry and 5,000 gunners which exceeded the estimate of Hotze (above) by some 19,200 troops, but by a more realistic 7,100, if we exclude the remote division of Thurreau and the garrison and security division of Montchoisy.

161

FRENCH FORCES IN SWITZERLAND, MID-SEPTEMBER 1799

(all demi-brigades line, unless otherwise stated; the regiments of horse were much below strength, while the Helvetic Legion and demi-brigades were shadowy units, retained on the lists largely for propaganda reasons)

Massena commanded the main concentration of 34,000 men in four divisions, confronting Korsakov outside Zürich and along the lower Limmat and Aare

Division Mortier
    Brigade Drouet
        50th demi-brigade
        53rd demi-brigade
        57th demi-brigade
    Brigade Brunet
        100th demi-brigade
        108th demi-brigade
    Divisional Cavalry
        1st Dragoon Regt (2 sq equivalent)
        8th Chasseur Regt
Division Lorge
    Brigade Gazan
        10th light demi-brigade
        37th demi-brigade
    Brigade Bontemps
        57th demi-brigade
        102nd demi-brigade
        1st Helvetic Legion
    Divisional Cavalry
        9th Hussar Regt
        13th Dragoon Regt
Division Ménard
    Brigades Quétard and Neudelet
        1st light demi-brigade
        2nd demi-brigade
        46th demi-brigade
        17th demi-brigade
    Divisional Cavalry
        5th Chasseur Regt
Division Klein
    Brigades Goullus and Roget
        103rd demi-brigade
        2nd Helvetic demi-brigade
    Divisional Cavalry
        7th Hussar Regt
        8th Hussar Regt
        23rd Chasseur Regt
        2nd Dragoon Regt
Reserve, Humbert
    3,500 grenadiers (behind div. Lorge)

The Division of Chabran (9,700) was deployed on Massena's left flank down the Rhine from the confluence with the Aare to Basel
        14th light demi-brigade
        1st demi-brigade
        23rd demi-brigade
        1st Helvetic demi-brigade
        4th Helvetic demi-brigade
    Divisional Cavalry
        4th Hussar Regt
        5th Hussar Regt
        11th Dragoon Regt
        11th Chasseur Regt

To Massena's right the division of Soult (11,500-12,700) held the north-eastern French salient along the southern shores of Lake Zürich and the Walensee, and the left bank of the Linth.
    Brigade Mainoni
        36th demi-brigade
        44th demi-brigade
    Brigade Laval
        25th light demi-brigade
        94th demi-brigade
    Divisional Cavalry
        10th Chasseur Regt

The widely-scattered brigades of the division of Lecourbe (11,800) held the valleys of the Reuss and the upper Linth, and were now in possession of the St. Gotthard. The brigade of Molitor was stationed in the valley of the upper Linth so far from its parent division that it may be considered part of Soult's command.
    Brigade Gudin (on the St. Gotthard and Oberalp passes and the area of Andermatt
        109th demi-brigade
        67th demi-brigade
    Brigade Loison (along the Reuss valley)
        38th demi-brigade
        76th demi-brigade
    Brigade Molitor (on the upper Linth)
        84th demi-brigade
    Divisional Cavalry
        1st Dragoon Regt (at Schywz; the equivalent of a small squadron)

The division of Thurreau (9,600) was deployed in south-western Switzerland, and covered the entries from Italy to the Valais (Wallis); it was too isolated and thinly-spread to take an active part against Suvorov in 1799.

`Brigades Jacopin and Jardon
        28th demi-brigade
        83rd demi-brigade
        89th demi-brigade
        101st demi-brigade
        1st, 4th and 5th Helvetic bns
    Divisional Cavalry
        23rd Chasseur Regt

The division of Montchoisy (*division de l'intérieur*) (2,500) was deployed on garrison and security duties in the interior of Switzerland and could not be considered an active field force
        3rd bn of the 109th demi-brigade
        3rd Helvetic demi-brigade
        5th Helvetic demi-brigade
    Divisional Cavalry
        22nd Cavalry Regt
        12th Chasseur Regt

Out of these formations the one most immediately relevant to the coming campaign was the division of Lecourbe, which Hotze estimated at 10,000 (actually 11,800). The French happened to be planning an offensive of their own, in which Lecourbe's rôle was to leave a force to hold the St. Gotthard and strike down the valley of the Vorderrhein and (in association with Soult) at the same time across the upper Linth. These designs were overtaken by the storm that was about to break from the south.

Into Switzerland

On 1 September Suvorov informed his officers in outline of his proposals for the new campaign. The troops completed their fitting-out on the 7th, and on the following day the two Russian corps set out for the first stage of their march—Derfelden's column from Asti to Ceresole, and that of Rosenberg to Alessandria. Three days were forfeit when the French executed a reconnaissance in force from the Genoese mountains, which persuaded the Russians to rejoin the Austrians between the Bormida and the Scrivia.

The French fell back to Gavi on 10 September, and when their isolated garrison marched out of the citadel of Tortona on the 11th Suvorov knew that he could leave the security of the Italian theatre to the Austrians with a clear conscience. The Russian and Austrian armies parted company at Alessandria on the evening of 11 September, though Suvorov retained Lieutenant-Colonel Weyrother and eight other members of the Austrian General Staff. The Austrians at headquarters were nevertheless outnumbered by the forty-seven or so military and civilian personnel of Suvorov's Russian staff and suite.

Once the troops were fairly on the move the rate of marching was sustained at a furious rate of about forty kilometres per day. Forced marches were nothing new to the Russians, 'but what was surprising was that nobody fell by the wayside... if anyone's strength failed his comrades helped him out by taking his ammunition and carrying it themselves... Many of the officers no longer had their baggage or riding horses with them; for the first time in a Russian army they marched with their greatcoats rolled up and slung over their shoulders, and they carried a pack with contained their rations of bread.'[15]

On the second march beyond Alessandria the Russians 'began to see the gigantic Alps; in the blue distance their silhouettes seemed like huge clouds, but the closer we approached the more detail we could make out... their peaks were covered with snow and lost in the clouds. The range seemed to stretch without end.'[16]

On 15 September the leading troops entered Swiss territory at Ponte Treza, agreeably situated on a western arm of Lake Lugano, and Suvorov and Constantine celebrated by sampling the local spirits in the house of Vittorio Pellegrini (the present *Ristorante Gambrinus*, where the glasses are preserved). Shortly afterwards the first casualty of the campaign was incurred at Bedano, where a Cossack of the advance guard was wounded by a shot from behind a hedge. Suvorov urged his troops along the meadows of the pebbly Vedeggio stream and before the day was out they reached Taverne, after marches 'which for their length and continuance are almost without example.'[17]

At Taverne Suvorov toured the bivouacs and chatted with the troops in his old style, but 'our veterans noticed that Aleksandr Vasilevich was preoccupied with weighty thoughts, as could

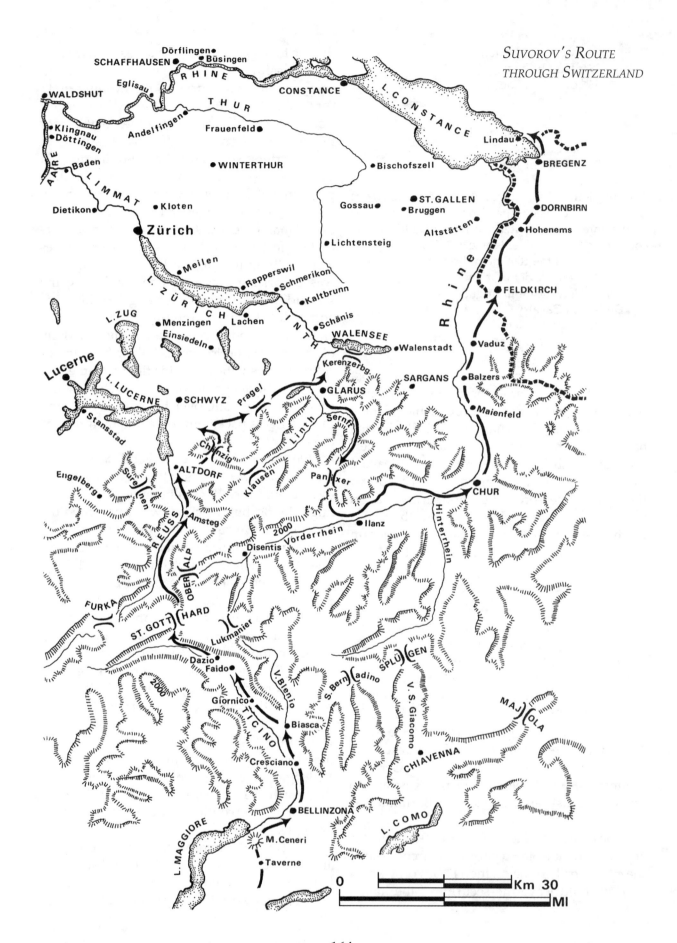

be read by the change in his expression. "How are things with him, our father?" we asked ourselves. "Is he well? Spare him, O Lord, and have mercy on us! We are fit for nothing without him!"'[18] What was wrong?

News had come from Bellinzona that only about 340 pack mules had been assembled there by the Austrians to support the further advance into Switzerland, and Suvorov could see for himself that there were no animals ready for him at Taverne. He wrote to Paul:

> I arrived here on the 15th, and so I kept my word. At some effort I accomplished in six days a march for which most people would allow eight. Today is the 17th, and there is no sign of a single mule, and no indicated of when any will be coming. All our haste was in vain. We have an important operation before us, and we needed surprise and impetus for the breakthrough—these advantages have now been lost.[19]

The blunder seems to have been due partly to the Austrian *Proviantmeister* Rupprecht who (according to Melas) took it on himself to halt the march of a train of Italian mules in Pavia, and partly to a failure to advance enough cash to the Austrian major-general Johann Döller and his officials, who were responsible for bringing together the mules as a whole at Bellinzona. The Austrians had indeed collected mules and drivers in some quantity, but the trains melted away again when the muleteers were left unpaid. The disgruntled Suvorov settled down for an indefinite stay in the house of the merchant Gaudenzio Gamma in Sigirino, just north of Taverne.

Without mules on the spot it was impossible to push even as far as Bellinzona, for the carriage road ended at Taverne, and only a track lay across the intervening Monte Ceneri (554 m). Instalments of mules arrived to a total of 1,170 by 18 September, but the ill-paid muleteers continued to desert along with their animals, and it was clear that the Russians still lacked the means of transporting the ammunition and the ten days' worth of biscuit (six days' consumption to be carried on the mules, and the other four in the mens' haversacks) for the dash to the rendezvous in northern Switzerland.

In this embarrassment Suvorov adopted a proposal by Grand Prince Constantine to dismount the Cossacks and put their horses to work as pack animals. This was a hard decision, taken over the protests of Suvorov's suite, for the horses were the personal property of the Cossacks, and not army issue. In the event 1,500 of the Cossacks were unseated, instead of the 2,500 as originally proposed, which left all the others available for mounted service. Each animal was to be laden with two sacks, the necessary canvas and ropes being obtained from the coverings of vehicles, and the packaging of the bales of commercial goods which were heaped up in the warehouse at Taverne.

On 20 September Suvorov assigned or re-assigned the units among the advance guard and the two component corps of his army in an order which held good for the rest of the campaign, except that the division of Förster was transferred from the corps of Derfelden to that of Rosenberg (as shown below) before the passage of the Chinzig Pass (i.e. by 27 September). The grenadier regiment of Rosenberg and all the regiments of musketeers and Jäger were on a establishment of two battalions. The strengths are of all ranks and as of 12 September. The previous provincial designations are entered in square brackets.

Advance Guard Maj-Gen Bagration
    Jäger regiments:

Bagration	506
Miller (formerly Chubarov)	496

    Combined grenadier battalions:

Dendrygin	339
Lomonosov	330
Sanaev	326
Kalemin	397
Advance Guard Total (excl. Cossacks):	2,394

Corps General Derfelden
Division Lieut-Gen Schveikovsky

Rosenberg Grenadiers	911

    Musketeer regiments:

Schveikovsky	921
Baranovsky	1,479
Kamensky (formerly Dalheim)	1,049
Divisional total:	*4,360*

Cossack regiments:

Sychov	480
Posdeev (of corps Derfelden)	462
Semernikov	431
Molchanov	464
Cossack total:	*1,837*

Advance Guard and Corps total: 8,591 infantry and Cossacks, excl. artillery

Corps General Rosenberg
Jäger regiment Kashkin	697

Division Maj-Gen Miloradovich
Musketeer regiments:
Miloradovich	1,043
Rehbinder	1,428
Mansurov	1,401
Fertsch	1,467
Divisional total:	*5,339*

Division Lieut-Gen Förster (reassigned from Corps Derfelden)
Musketeer regiments:
Förster	1,134
Tyrtov	891
Veletsky (formerly Jung-Baden)	957
Divisional total:	*3,982*

Cossack regiments:
Grekov	472
Denisov	449
Posdeev (of Corps Rosenberg)	482
Kurnakov	480
Cossack total:	*1,883*

Corps total: 10,901 infantry and Cossacks, excl. artillery

Totals:
Advance Guard and Corps Derfelden	8,591
Corps Rosenberg	10,901
Artillery	1,581
Engineers	212
Grand Total:	*21,285*

The complement of artillery was made up of twenty-five Piedmontese 2-pounder mountain cannon, as the only pieces fit for the Alps, and the surplus gunners were probably used to fill out the infantry. The documents give contradictory indications as to how the cannon were assigned to the divisions. Each column was led (in succession) by twenty-five Cossacks, one battalion of Jäger and one piece of artillery. The tail was closed up by the train of pack animals, escorted by one battalion. Fifty dismounted Cossacks marched with each division, while the remaining three hundred were retained in reserve.

At the same time Suvorov (almost certainly guided by Weyrother) produced a set of *Rules for Military Operations in Mountains*. This document emphasised that the predominating influence in such warfare was the narrowness of the mountain paths, which forced the troops to move by thin, straggling columns. It was impossible for the Cossacks to scout ahead in the usual way, and so a still greater responsibility than usual must fall on the officers who acted as column guides. The mules carrying the mountain artillery were not to be placed at the head of the column (where they would have impeded the march) or at the rear (where they were in danger of being left behind), but in the middle, from where they could be brought forward to lend fire support as necessary.

'We hardly need to mention that there is no need to attack a mountain top frontally, if we can get at it by side paths. If the enemy has been slow to occupy a height, then we must hasten to seize it...' Attacks were to be delivered on the frontage of a platoon, company or larger unit depending on the width of the mountain feature under attack. Once the skirmishers were halted by a superior force, the leading unit was to be put in a bayonet attack without delay, with the battalions in the rear following at intervals of one hundred paces. 'Heights cannot be seized by fire alone, because fire can do little harm to an enemy in possession. Bullets fired uphill mostly either fail to carry to the top, or fly over the summit, whereas fire from the top downhill is more accurate. This means that we must strive to reach the crest as soon as we can, to diminish the time under fire and hence our casualties.'[20]

On 19 September (the day originally assigned for the assault on the St. Gotthard) the corps of Rosenberg marched from Taverne to Bellinzona, while Derfelden's troops were still busy packing rations into 5,000 of the improvised sacks at Taverne.

On 20 September Suvorov, his chief adviser Lieutenant-Colonel Weyrother and the senior commanders met in council in Gaudenzio Gamma's house in Sigirino. They reviewed the numbers and locations of the French on the basis of the information provided by Hotze, and established the three groupings of the allied forces as being those of:

Korsakov (nominally 33,000 Russians) along the right bank of the Limmat between Zürich and the confluence with the lower Aare,

Hotze (nominally 21,000 Austrians) in extended positions along the middle and upper Linth, and

Suvorov's Italian army (20,000-odd Russians).

The conference protocol continues:

> The issue now arises as to how these three forces should be employed most effectively— first to liberate the Little Cantons, and then to exploit the initial success with speed to capture the whole of the Switzerland.
>
> To this end we establish as our first principle that the most speedy means of attaining the great objective is to concentrate the forces of each of the three elements... and break in against the front and rear of the enemy right wing with determination and the greatest possible speed. It is quite out of the question to sustain a large number of troops in the Little Cantons without the possession of Lake Lucerne [which was commanded by the French], and so we must not waste time by making detours or ponderous attempts at inter-communication.[21]

We can almost hear Suvorov speaking.

The meeting settled on 24 September as the revised date for the attack on the St. Gotthard:

Rosenberg with the smaller of the two Russian corps was to diverge from the Ticino valley, and execute a right-flanking movement that would take him up the Val Blenio to the Lukmanier Pass (1,914 m) and on by way of the Oberalp Pass (2,040 m) to arrive at Andermatt (Urseren) in the enemy rear.

Major-General Auffenberg with 2,000 Austrians from Linken's command was to descend on the French line of communication at Amsteg by way of the Maderanertal, in accordance with the original plan of Hotze,

The direct assault on the St. Gotthard was the responsibility of the advance guard and Derfelden with the larger of the Russian corps. The Austrian brigade of Colonel Strauch (4,570 troops) would be waiting at Biasca, and proceed with them to Airolo at the foot of the pass (2,108 m).

According to the ambitious timetable Rosenberg and Auffenberg would descend the Reuss valley to reach Altdorf on 25 September, and the whole Russian Army of Italy was to arrive at Schwyz on the 26th. There Suvorov would be in contact with Hotze, advancing from the upper Linth, and the Russians would be able to draw on the further six days' rations which were supposed to be waiting for them. The 27th would bring Suvorov's main force to Lucerne, while several thousand troops already detached by Derfelden would pursue any French falling back by way of Engelberg to the south of Lake Lucerne. The scene would be set for the allies to combined for the attack on Massena in front of Zürich.

On 21 September the Russians were in general movement. Rosenberg with the designated right-flanking force had already set out from Taverne on the 19th, and he now turned right from Biasca up the Val Blenio towards the Lukmanier Pass:

> We marched by narrow tracks which sometimes lay across high mountains, and sometimes descended into precipices, but often we could see no kind of path at all. We forded torrents where the water reached to our knees, and on two occasions to the waist. An endless haul up the highest mountain of all drained our morale and strength. Throughout these days the rain poured incessantly, while the nights were cold, dark and pierced with a north wind. We maintained a forced march from first light to nightfall, and many of the soldiers lost their footing on the mountain paths and fell head over heels to their deaths; many of the loads of baggage together with many of the horses were also lost over the side.[22]

On 23 September the corps completed the crossing of the snow-covered Lukmanier, and Rosenberg marched down to the valley of the Vorderrhein at Disentis, from where he would be able to execute his part in the scheme.

After five days of enforced inactivity at Taverne the troops of the main force under Derfelden formed up along the Vedeggio meadows before first light on 21 September, then set off by echelons into the streaming rain.

Having climbed Monte Ceneri, the Russians followed the track as it bent hard right. Down to their left they could make out the plain of the Ticino as it funnelled towards their immediate destination at Bellinzona, where the white crenellated walls of the medieval Sforza valley barrier reached down from the wooded slopes on either side. Suvorov lodged for the night in the house of the von Mentlen family, where he probably chatted with the gifted young Giuseppe Mentlen (1778-1827), who was to become a celebrated doctor, poet and historian. The field-marshal left a brace of pistols there as a return for the hospitality.

On the 22nd the head of Derfelden's column set out from Bellinzona at the accustomed hour of four in the morning. The Russians made slow progress, for the heavy rain lasted all morning, and the way up the Ticino valley was obstructed by networks of trellised vines, and by a bottleneck which formed in the narrow street of Crescentino. Suvorov was wearing his

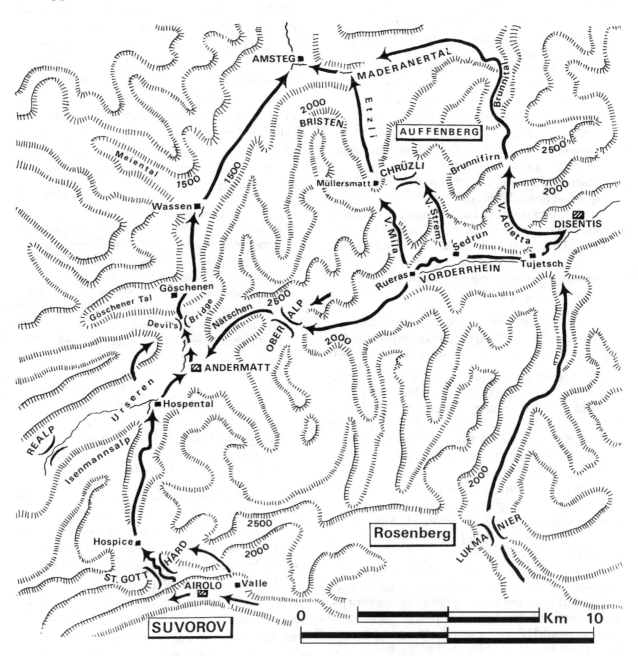

FROM THE ST. GOTTHARD TO AMSTEG

168

customary garb of white shirt and breeches, and no cover except his broad-brimmed hat and a threadbare old cloak which he threw across his shoulders. On the way to Biasca he was cheered to meet the Austrian colonel Gottfried Strauch, whom he knew to be a determined and resourceful fighter, with much experience of warfare in these parts. The Russians pressed on to their next night's halt at Giornico. A clearing of the skies in the evening tempted them to hold their clothing up to dry against their bivouac fires, but a series of squalls of icy rain during the night soaked the soldiers and their uniforms all over again.

On 23 September Suvorov and Strauch continued on their way up the great Ticino valley, passing two battalions of Austrian fusiliers and one of Banater Croats, who were veterans of six months of combat in the mountains. The march from Giornico to Dazio was deliberately slow, to allow Rosenberg time to get into position behind the St. Gotthard, but when Suvorov halted on the way to watch his troops he saw that some of the men were already limping, and that many of the sacks on the suffering mules and Cossack horses were spilling their loads or slipping. Suvorov halted for the night in the crowded little town of Faido, where he lodged in the house of the Capuchin

THE MONASTERY AT FAIDO

169

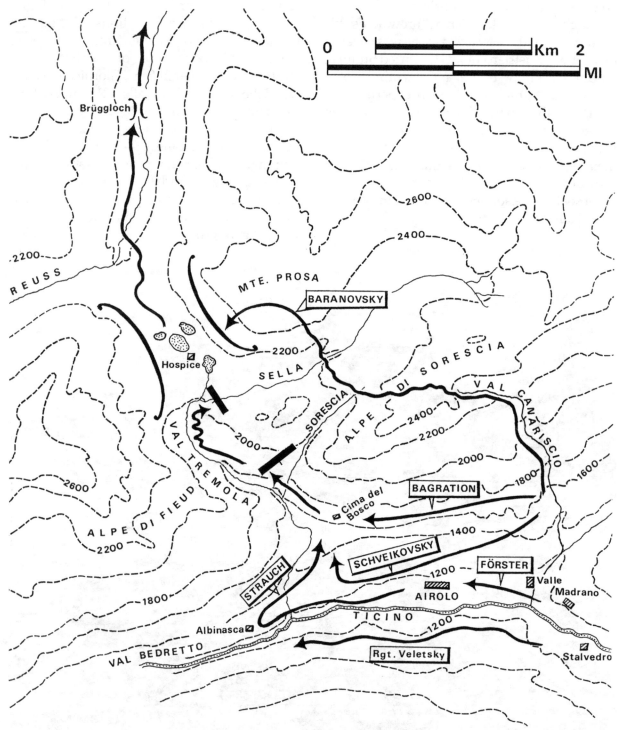

Suvorov's Assault on the St. Gotthard, 24 September

monks.

The Storming of the St. Gotthard

In so far as it suggests a gap or valley between heights, the word 'pass' is a misnomer for the St. Gotthard passage, which was a way straight up the side of a mountain and over one of its saddles. The heights in question were the snow-capped peaks which overhung the Ticino valley to the right, as Suvorov saw it from Faido. From there the pack road continued through Dazio, wound between rocks to the widening of the Ticino valley floor at Airolo, then after one hour's distance at a walking pace crossed the river by a wooden bridge and began the ascent to the pass.

The first bends carried the road up through a zone of scrubby pasture to the narrow gorge of the Val Tremola, which led to the summit. The path gained height by winding its way up the ravine between the near-vertical wall of the Alpe di Fiud to the left (west), and the rocky escarpments of the Alpe di Sorescia to the right. The name Val Tremola derived from the avalanches which thundered into the gorge, and the snow already accumulating on the path indicated that the Alpine winter was arriving unseasonably early. The relative difference in height between the valley floor at Airolo (1,179 m) and the summit (2,095 m) amounted to 916 m, and was the equivalent of a two-and-a-half hour climb for a man who was able to keep to the path, who was not laden with musket, accoutrements, ammunition and rations, and did not have to fight the French all the way to the top.

The summit was a curious little upland plain of horizontal slabs of rock, on which the water had accumulated in large ponds; the plateau was bare of all vegetation, but for centuries now travellers had been able to find shelter in the Hospice. The building which stood in 1799 was only two years old, having replaced a smaller house which had been swept away by an avalanche in 1775, and in its very short peacetime life it had been capable of storing commercial goods in its warehouses, sheltering up to forty horses in its stable, and accommodating guests of all conditions. The Hospice had been pillaged only recently by the French, but the Capuchin Prior and his brothers did their best to maintain the traditions of the place.

This part of Switzerland fell within the very wide area of responsibility of the division of Lecourbe (11,800). One of its brigades (Molitor's) was committed irrevocably in the area of Glarus on the upper Linth, but the other two stood immediately in Suvorov's path:

Brigade Gudin (3,801)
    67th demi-brigade (Chossat, 1,861), whose companies were in two battalions, dispersed in three groupings, namely:
    In the Ticino valley at Airolo.
    At Cima del Bosco to the north-west of Airolo near the entrance to the Val Tremola.
    At the summit of the St. Gotthard.

Every detailed account of the action has the components of the 67th split among the three locations in different combinations, but it is significant that Lieutenant-Colonel Weyrother, who had no incentive to diminish the French numbers in his record, states that his enemies had less than 1,000 troops actually engaged in the combat (below).

    109th demi-brigade (1,700), two battalions, at Andermatt and on the Oberalp Pass.
    Brigade reserve (240), three grenadier companies, one each of the 38th, 76th and 84th demi-brigades, at Andermatt.

Brigade Loison
    76th demi-brigade (800), two battalions, at Amsteg.
    38th demi-brigade (2,180), three battalions; first and second battalions at Amsteg, third battalion all the way up the Reuss valley from Altdorf to Wassen, with units up the Muotatal, Schächental and Maderanertal.

Divisional Reserve
    Nine grenadier companies (720) at Altdorf at the immediate disposal of Lecourbe.
(For the French numbers and locations the calculations of Hennequin (1911, 330-1) are the most thorough and convincing.)

It follows that the French had about 3,800

troops available to dispute the passage of the St. Gotthard and the Oberalp, with another 3,700 capable of arriving in support in the course of a number of hours. However Lecourbe's attention was caught up in the part his division was to play in the general offensive which the French in Switzerland were planning to launch on 25 September. Lecourbe was supposed to attack to the east and on a broad frontage; hence he planted his headquarters well down the Reuss at Altdorf, and the role chiefly assigned to the brigade of Loison was to descend from the Oberalp to Disentis in the valley of the Vorderrhein, and so prevent the Austrian brigade of Linken from going to the help of Hotze. In other words the French were looking east at a time when Suvovor's attack was going to arrive from the south.

Neither Lecourbe nor any other of the senior French commanders set much store by the rumour that had been circulating in Switzerland since 5 September, to the effect that Vienna had ordered Suvorov to leave Italy with 25-30,000 troops and march to support Korsakov at Zürich. As a precautionary measure Lecourbe had pushed fighting patrols down the Val Levantina (the Ticino valley below Airolo), which merely established that the Austrian brigade of Strauch was holding the valley in the neighbourhood of Biasca. From 20 September an accumulation of reports confirmed that Russian forces too were present in the Val Levantina, but Lecourbe merely put the 67th demi-brigade on a state of heightened alert, and saw no reason to stir from his headquarters in distant Altdorf. He wrote from there to Massena at nine in the evening of 24 September:

> It's quite true, my dear general, that considerable Russian and Austrian reinforcements have arrived today in the Ticino valley, and that three or four thousand were advanced yesterday as far as Dazio. There are persistent stories that General Suvorov is at Bellinzona, and that another elderly general [Lecourbe did not make the connection] is at Giornico. They cannot tell me whether he is Russian or Austrian. They also say that another large corps [i.e. Rosenberg's] is advancing on the Grisons. I have just learned that the enemy are attacking us at Airolo. I imagine it is no more than a reconnaissance.[23]

By then the St. Gotthard had already been lost.

The last of several allied 'Dispositions' for the assault was issued on the evening of 23 September. On the operational scale it adhered to the plan which had been established for over a week, whereby the main effort by Suvorov against the St. Gotthard was to be seconded by attacks by Rosenberg against the Oberalp Pass and Andermatt, and by Auffenberg's Austrians against the French line of communication down the Reuss at Amsteg.

At the tactical level the shape of the assault against the St. Gotthard was determined by the fact that the position was impregnable to an unsupported frontal attack up the narrow Val Tremola. Suvorov therefore allotted a crucial role to a right-flanking column, namely the Russian division of Schveikovsky, preceded by the Russian advance guard under Bagration, which were expected to climb to the right and take in succession the French positions at Cima del Bosco and on the summit of the pass. In detail the column was to follow the pack road to Piott or Salvedro, climb some distance up the mountain slopes, then continue their advance leaving Madrano, Valle and Airolo down to their left. On the way Bagration was to establish how many French might be ensconced at Cima del Bosco, a little mountainside settlement which command an excellent field of fire over the grassy slopes. If the location proved to be held by fewer than three battalions (in fact a good deal less), he was to detach four of his battalions directly over the mountain towards the St. Gotthard to cut the garrison's retreat. Lieutenant Giurczak of the Austrian General Staff was to lead Bagration's column, and recruit the necessary local guides in Faido.

It was thought necessary to plug the Val Bedretto (the western continuation of the Ticino valley above Airolo) against any French forces (i.e. the division of Thurreau) which might seek to attack the flank of the allies while they were operating against the St. Gotthard. Two battalions of the Russian regiment of Veletsky would therefore ascent the left-hand (southern) side of the Val Levantina, carry clear of Airolo and descend into the Val Bedretto. Here they would be reinforced by the main body of Strauch's brigade, which was to accompany the central column (below) along the pack road only as far as the ascent to the Val Tremola, and then carry on by itself into the Val Bedretto.

The central column comprised the Russian division of Förster and two battalions of the Austrian regiment of Wallis. It was to allow the two flanking columns to gain the lead, and thus facilitate its drive up the Val Tremola directly against the St. Gotthard.

All three columns were to be assembled in compact formations by midnight on 23/24 September, and the advance would start at three in the morning. Suvorov was confident that by the end of the day the St. Gotthard would have been taken, and the allies would be well down the far side of the watershed.

By five o'clock on the morning of 24 September scarcely even the troops of the

VIEW EASTWARDS OVER AIROLO (RIGHT) DOWN THE VAL LEVANTINA. THE ST. GOTTHARD MASSIF RISES TO THE LEFT (NORTH), AND THE CIMA DEL BOSCO IS THE LIGHT DOT ON THE SUNLIT MEADOW JUST BEYOND THE PRONOUNCED BEND OF THE MODERN ROAD TO THE LEFT CENTRE

Russian advance guard had assembled at Dazio. The columns set themselves in march only at dawn—or rather what little light filtered through the low-hanging clouds that veiled the mountains. After further inexplicable delays the advance proper began at about two in the afternoon, and was headed by Lieutenant Egor Nikitich Lutovinov and 250 Jäger, who now advanced with such speed that the French outposts evacuated Stalvedro and Airolo after no more than a spattering of fire. The French commander Leblond consolidated his forces behind a line of improvised defences (probably rocks and logs) which reached up from the valley floor to the Cima del Bosco. The French met the Russian attack with fire at close range, killing Lutovinov and dropping 150 of his men

as casualties. Colonel Pavel Andreevich Shuvalov brought up a number of companies as reinforcements, but he was disabled by a musket shot, and forced to hand over the command of the leading troops to Lieutenant-Colonel Tsukato.

The assault was already running many hours behind schedule, and Bagration's unsupported Jäger were sticking fast. Schveikovsky's musketeers should have been close behind, but most of them had descended to the pack road (another mystery of the day) in front of the division of Förster, and the two formations climbed slowly and hesitatingly towards the Val Tremola. This was the first mountain fighting most of the Russians had seen, and the 'great column immediately fell back towards the

ENTRANCE TO THE VAL TREMOLA, WITH CIMA DEL BOSCO ON THE FAR RIGHT, AND THE ALPE DI SORESCIA RISING IN THE LEFT CENTRE

[Ticino] valley, halted half-way, and was persuaded only after considerable exhortation to resume the pretty stiff climb up the mountain path. The consequence was that at the very outset of the operation we lost a great deal of the precious time which had been allowed for the ascent which remained.'[24]

Suvorov's anger was mighty, and had been transmitted in various legendary accounts. Masson was told by one of the Russian generals that

> The vigour of his army had been depleted by hunger, exhaustion and endless hardships. The soldiers grumbled, came to a stop, and refused to go any further. Suvorov had a trench scraped by the side of the path, and he laid himself down in it. 'Cover me with earth,' he said, 'and leave your general here! You are no longer my children, and I am no longer your father. There is nothing left for me but to die!' The grenadiers rushed forward, crowded around him, and demanded loudly to be permitted to climb to the summit of the St. Gotthard and evict the French. [25]

The story was denied emphatically by Arkady Suvorov and other Russian veterans, but Masson himself was inclined to believe it, because the episode would have been so much in Suvorov's character.

With some difficulty Weyrother persuaded Suvorov to recall Colonel Strauch with the third, or left-hand column which had been assigned to it up the Val Bedretto.[26] The French remained masters of the situation until the Austrians arrived to reinforce the efforts of Bagration against Cima del Bosco. When the allied pressure against this outlying position became irresistible, the French just fell back in an orderly fashion to the rocks behind the Sorescia torrent at the entrance to the narrowest part of the Val Tremola. The divisions of Schveikovsky and Förster were patently unwilling to press home their attacks up the gorge, for the French were firing to deadly effect from behind the shelter of the rocks and the heaped-up snow, and they 'noted that the first attack had been pressed with no great determination, and that the enemy were becoming demoralised on account of the difficult terrain and their unfamiliarity with

this kind of war. The French therefore stood and fought at every bend of the mountain path leading to the Hospice.'[27] Captain Gryazev recalled how 'every now and then our operations were halted by the wandering clouds which enveloped us and concealed the enemy positions, or by the billowing sulphurous smoke from the continuous firefight which darkened the sky and made us lose contact with one another.'[28]

The French made a new stand on the strongest position of all, where the pack road ceased its zig-zagging, and climbed steeply up to the right to deposit the attacking troops in a patch of level ground which lay within musket range of the French who were holding a rampart-like wall of rocks behind. The gorge was already deep in shadow when a commotion caused the French to look over their left shoulders and see troops descending from the eastern slopes towards the plateau of the Hospice. It seems that all of this time Major-General Mikhail Semenovich Baranovsky had been toiling over the mountains with the Baranovsky Musketeers, the Miller Jäger and a party of dismounted Cossacks.. Bagration was certainly under orders to detach a force of this kind in the course of his original march against Cima del Bosco, and the troops had probably climbed the extraordinarily steep eastern ridge by the Val Canariscio, crossed the shallow valley of the Sella, and emerged in an exhausted state on the south-western slopes of Monte Prosa immediately above the Hospice. The French at once disengaged from their fight down the Val Tremola, and escaped over the plateau while their path of retreat was still open.

As the main column approached the crest of the plateau the Russians were cheered by the sight of the tall Hospice building which rose amid the snows immediately to the right of the pack road. Suvorov was greeted at the door by the Prior, a man of seventy years, with a long beard, lively eyes, and a fine forehead crowned by a halo of white hair. 'And what a spectacle it was!… two elderly men, Suvorov and the Prior, greeted one another as warmly as if they had grown old and grey together.'[29] The Prior invited the field-marshal to share a simple meal. The

ABOVE, THE UPPER VAL TREMOLA. BELOW, THE VIEW WEST FROM THE FINAL FRENCH POSITION ON THE ST.GOTTHARD. THE RUSSIANS AND AUSTRIANS EMERGED FROM THE VAL TREMOLA NEAR THE BLACK ROCK TOWARDS THE TOP LEFT, AND WOULD HAVE COME UNDER INTENSIVE FIRE IN THIS LITTLE HOLLOW. THE ORIGINAL TRACK MAY BE SEEN ON THE FAR LEFT, AND AGAIN ON THE FAR RIGHT.

repast (potatoes and peas) was to Suvorov's liking, and after the two men had chatted in several languages Suvorov departed with the monk's blessing.

The Cossacks and the Jäger took the leading in chasing the French down the further valley which led gently down towards Hospental, and they first caught up with the French in the neighbourhood of the Brüggloch narrows, which formed one of the boundaries of Latin- and German-speaking Europe. In the darkness the Russians were unaware that the French screen consisted of no more than two obstinate companies of the 67th demi-brigade. 'The French were fighting for every step, from which it was reasonable to suppose that Rosenberg's column could not have reached its destination at Urseren [Andermatt] at the appointed time.'[30]

The valley terminated at a brow which overlooked the plain of Urseren, and a steep winding descent brought the Russians to the village of Hospental towards nine at night. The captains Gryazev and Panov of the Rosenberg Grenadiers halted to give their men some rest. 'In the heat of action we failed to notice the great efforts we had been putting forth. But now exhaustion took its toll, and we threw ourselves to the ground in a stupor, scarcely able to recall what we had done, or make sense of what was happening to us now.'[31]

The Russians were content to occupy the houses of Hospental, and they placed no more than an outpost on the stone bridge which spanned the Reuss torrent. They did not know that *chef de brigade* Gudin was just out of sight in the darkness with his remaining forces—the survivors of the 67th demi-brigade, the 109th (retrieved from Andermatt, below) and the grenadiers of his brigade reserve. The French grenadiers evicted the unwary Russian outpost from the bridge, but they were left unsupported by their fusiliers when the Russians began to advance *en masse* with thundering drums.

Gudin extricated his grenadiers without more ado. The Russians were present in Hospental in force, and because his retreat down the Reuss by way of Andermatt had been cut by the advance of Rosenberg (below), his only path of escape lay south-east over the Realp and

Furka Passes. Gudin slipped past the Russians in the murk, but speed was at such a premium that he was unable to take with him his complement of artillery—two cannon and a howitzer. Before abandoning them he made one last discharge into the Russian troops as they lay around Hospental. Weyrother comments that 'there had been no reason to think that any French were left in the neighbourhood. We must admire the steadfastness of the Russians, who showed not the slightest disorder, but answered the fire with the mountain guns they had with them, and calmly awaited the coming of the day.'[32]

Although he was a daring and charismatic leader, Suvorov never forgot the need for caution and 'balance.' Just as he had ensured his line of potential retreat across the Po before the Battle of the Trebbia, so now he took measures to secure the line of his advance into central Switzerland against any French interruption

THE ST. GOTTHARD HOSPICE

THE LANDSCAPE OF THE St. GOTTHARD PLATEAU

ABOVE, HOSPENTAL, LOOKING WEST UP THE REUSS. THE BLACK BLOB ON THE BANK BELOW THE CASTLE TOWER IS AN ABUTMENT OF THE ORIGINAL BRIDGE. BELOW, THE VIEW NORTH FROM THE EDGE OF THE HEIGHTS NORTH OF HOSPENTAL, WITH THE URSEREN VALLEY EXTENDING ON THE RIGHT. TO ACCOMPLISH THIS OUTFLANKING MOVE ON 25 SEPTEMBER, KAMENSKY CLIMBED SOME WAY UP THE THE SLOPE DIRECTLY TO THE FRONT, THEN MADE OFF TO THE RIGHT FOLLOWING THE CONTOURS.

179

HOSPENTAL, LOOKING WEST UP THE REUSS.

from the Valais. He sent back Strauch's Austrians to Albinasco to guard the St. Gotthard and the Val Bedretto, and he dispatched Major-General Veletsky with his regiment and that of Tyrtov to follow Gudin a little distance towards the Realp.

The fighting around Hospental ended some time after ten at night, and one hour later Suvorov wrote to Hotze and Korsakov:

> We were forced to make some difficult outflanking movements to gain the enemy positions on the St. Gotthard, which delayed our progress so considerably that we have only just arrived here, and cannot reach Urseren [Andermatt]. We will advance against Urseren at six in the morning and throw the French out, if they are waiting for us there, but we will still strive to reach Altdorf by the evening, according to the original plan.

On the back of the note to Hotze Suvorov penned a little verse, telling how the mules had at last arrived on 20 September, Rosenberg and Derfelden advanced on the 21st and 22nd, and the St. Gotthard taken by sword and bayonet on the 24th to accomplish the salvation of Switzerland:

Am 20ten sind die trag thier bereit
Den 21ten zieht Ros. zum streit
Den 22ten folgt Tiefeld [Derfelden] zur Schlacht
Den 24ten ist Gotthardsberg erobert durch Macht
Dann haben wir durch Säbel und Bajonette
Die Schweiz von ihren Untergang gerett. [33]

Major-General Veletsky was climbing the Isenmannsalp ridge on his way to the Realp when he looked behind him to the east and saw bivouac fires in the neighbourhood of Andermatt—it was impossible to tell whether they belonged to the troops of Rosenberg, who would have driven over the Oberalp Pass according to plan, or to French who might still have had the place in their possession. He sent word to Bagration and Förster, but they knew that they would be unable to call on their troops to make any further effort through the darkness and rain.

ROSENBERG AT THE OBERALP PASS AND ANDERMATT

By falling on the left flank of the French positions on the mountain ridge, the all-Russian division of Rosenberg formed a key element in the plan of attack. Rosenberg's troops together with those of the Austrian brigade of Auffenberg had already completed the taxing passage of the Lukmanier Pass and descended to the valley of the Vorderrhein, and now in the early hours of 24 September Rosenberg had to force the Oberalp against the opposition of the French and the elements.

The allies set out from their camp in front of Disentis at first light. The Austrians had to climb hard right to cross the range of mountains which separated them from the Maderanertal. A first column was ascending the Val Acleta in the neighbourhood of Disentis. A second column left the main force four kilometres beyond Tujetsch (Tavetsch) at Sedrun to make for the Chrüzli Pass by way of the Val Strem. At Rueras two kilometres further on the last of the Austrians headed up the Val Mila, while the Russian column divided in two, with the main body keeping to the pack road in the Vorderrhein valley, and the regiment of Mansurov taking a track which wound along the right-hand valley slopes by way of Givo, Mulinatsch and Milez and gained the Tiarms Pass at the rear of the dome-like Calmut mountain to the north of the Oberalp Pass proper.

The main force continued along the valley for another five or six kilometres to a point just beyond the Surpalitz farmstead, where the pack road began its snake-like ascent north-west to the Oberalp. Lieutenant-General Rehbinder advanced three regiments up the passage, while the advance guard under Major-General Miloradovich (Jäger regiment Kashkin and Cossacks) addressed the steep climb of the Piz Nurschalas to the left or south.

The Oberalp position was defended by just one of the two battalions of the 109th demi-brigade, but the French had eked out their forces in a skilful way. To have offered a strong forward defence on the pass itself would have exposed them to being outflanked at the beginning of any action, and so they had positioned their main body behind a patch of boggy ground which extended around the north shore of the Oberalpsee just by the eastern head of the lake. Outposts were thrown out to the north to give cover against an advance by way of the Tiarms

Pass, while a further chain occupied a ridge which reached down to the lake from the Nurschalas mountain.

The Russians attacked on a total frontage of three kilometres. To their right or north, the Mansurov regiment split into multiple columns to pass behind the Calmut mountain and emerge on the slopes above the head of the lake, where it was joined by the main force under Rehbinder which pushed over the Oberalp. To the left again the Kashkin Jäger under Major Sabaneev braved a volley to dislodge the French from the Nurschalas ridge, and continued their advance along the slopes leading down to the southern shore of the lake.

The French now showed their capacity for executing controlled retreats under pressure. They resisted the combined forces of the Mansurov regiment, Rehbinder and Miloradovich along the slopes on both sides of the lake, then down the four-kilometre length of the gently-sloping valley beyond, and finally negotiated the zig-zag path from the Nätschen mountain (1,842 m) down to Andermatt. This dignified little town with its tall houses was a supply base for the now-aborted French offensive, and Gudin consolidated there with the help of the remainder of the 109th demi-brigade.

The Russians arrived on the Nätschen crest at three in the afternoon in the same array in which they had been fighting, with Miloradovich on the left, Rehbinder on the axis of the pack road, and the regiment of Mansurov having rejoined from the right. The French had broken contact and made their presence known only by lobbing howitzer shells which burst harmlessly on the Nätschen. The story is taken up by a soldier of the regiment of Rehbinder:

> The afternoon was drawing on, the mountains were clouding over, and the mist hid the valley where the enemy were deployed. The brigade major [Aleksei Dmitrievich Zaitsov] had been sent to reconnoitre the enemy position. He now reported to General Maksim Vladimirovich Rehbinder that powerful enemy columns were standing in front of Andermatt and preparing for battle. Rehbinder commanded us to make our way down the hill as quietly as possible, and put ourselves in order just as soon as we reached the bottom. Major Sabaneev went ahead with the Jäger and the skirmishers from the line infantry [an interesting tactical detail], and he was followed by the whole corps in line. The mountain was terrifyingly high and steep, and we had to descend as best we

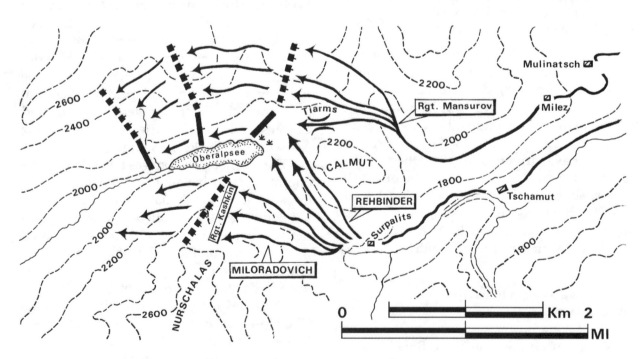

ROSENBERG'S ASSAULT ON THE OBERALP

182

could—creeping, clambering down or sliding. At the bottom we arrayed ourselves in silence, and we were still invisible to the enemy on account of the fog. We opened a volley fire upon command against one of the enemy columns, and then to the cry of 'Hurrah!' we threw ourselves on the French with the bayonet and got to work on them in the Russian style. They met us bravely and firmly, but at last their whole body was overthrown and routed at bayonet point.[34]

Gudin made off for Hospental, with results which have been reviewed, and Rosenberg entered into possession of Andermatt, where he found 370,000 cartridges, and enough flour to allow his soldiers to take three handfuls each. The Russians had captured forty-one prisoners and three pieces of artillery, and established that the French dead amounted to 180.

On this first day of active campaigning in Switzerland the forces of Suvorov had reached the immediate approaches to the St. Gotthard and Oberalp undetected, wrested these formidable barriers from the French, and were poised to irrupt into the heart of Switzerland. About 150 men had been killed or badly wounded in Rosenberg's corps, while Suvorov had lost some 1,200 troops from all causes. More serious on the operational plane was the loss of time. By now the allies ought to have been well down the Reuss, but they were unable to make good the hours wasted by the slow development of Suvorov's attack on the St. Gotthard, and Rosenberg's halt on the Nätschen above Andermatt.

The one outright failure was on the part of the Austrian brigade of Major-General Franz Xaver Auffenberg, which had been unable to reach its target on the French line of communications at Amsteg, where the Maderanertal ravine reached the valley of the middle Reuss. Auffenberg's 2,000 troops (the three battalions of the regiment of Kerpen, and the Third Battalion of the Gradiscaner Croats)

VIEW WESTWARD OVER THE ASCENT TO THE NURSCHALAS MOUNTAIN. THE KASHKIN JÄGER CLIMBED FROM LEFT TO RIGHT.

ABOVE, THE OBERALP PAS, WITH THE FOOT OF THE CALMUT MOUNTAIN TO THE RIGHT.
BELOW, THE OBERALPSEE FROM THE EAST.

The French blocking position at the eastern end of the Oberalpsee. Some of the original bog survives (bottom left), and the French made their stand where the ground rises from the car park and the entrance to the modern avalanche screen.

had set out from the Vorderrhein valley at first light on 24 September, and begun to climb the intervening ridge in the way just described. The Austrians encountered no French along the way, but the passage was unexpectedly long and difficult, and night was closing in by the time the columns reunited in the Maderanertal two hours' march from Amsteg.

Most probably the delay was occasioned by the right-hand column which ascended the Val Acletta, and which would have had to cross the Brunnifern glacier before descending the Brunnital to the upper Maderanertal. The other two columns probably met on the far side of the ridge at Müllersmatt, from where the path to the middle Maderanertal followed the relatively easy Etzli valley. Auffenberg decided to put off his attack until the following morning.

25 SEPTEMBER

THE URNERLOCH AND THE DEVILS' BRIDGE

Suvorov lodged for the night in Andermatt at a new (1786) house in the local style, of stone below, and timber upper storeys in the chalet style (No. 253 St. Gotthardstrasse). He was back with the corps of Derfelden early in the morning of the 25th, and set the troops in march from Hospental at six. He was making for the eastern end of the Urserental, where the wide flat valley

ROSENBERG'S VIEW FROM THE LOWER SLOPES OF THE NÄTSCHEN MOUNTAIN WEST OVER ANDERMATT AND THE VALLEY OF USEREN. HOSPENTAL IS AT THE TIP OF THE DARK WOODS REACHING DOWN FROM THE LEFT, AND THE ISENMANNSALP RISES IN THE LEFT CENTRE.

186

with its scattered chalets and images of pastoral peace terminated at yet another mountain rampart. Suvorov joined the corps of Rosenberg at Andermatt, and the Russians made for the only exit, which lay just fifteen minutes' march beyond—in other words a distance that should have been well within Rosenberg's capacity to reach on the previous evening.

If the French had chosen to make a serious stand, the difficulties of forcing a way through would have reached a degree approaching the absurd. The Reuss here reverted to its character of a mountain torrent, and hurled its blue-green ice water down a narrow and near-vertically sided slot through the mountain wall. In 1707 the Canton of Uri had completed a prodigy of civil engineering, by hacking a tunnel through the right-hand or eastern wall. This Urnerloch ('Uri Hole') was a low passage, 65 metres long, just 2.20 metres wide, and lit by a single hole which had been driven through the left-hand side to the Reuss gorge. At the far end the tunnel

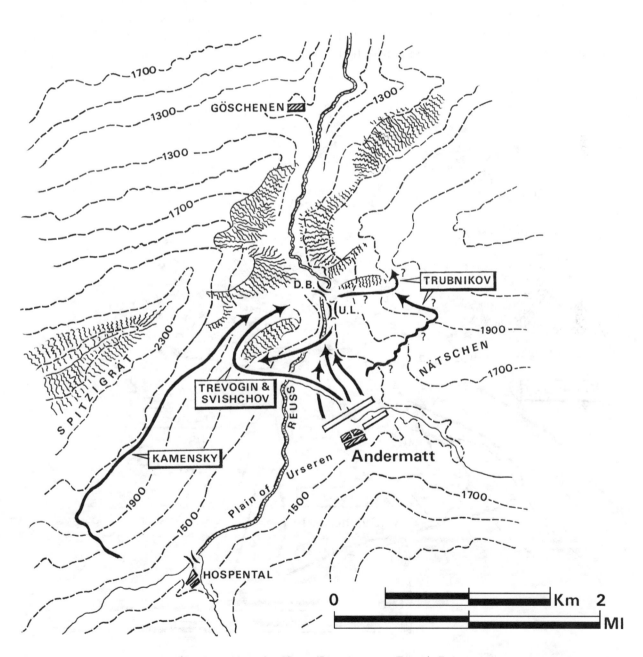

Approaches to the Urner Loch and the Devil's Bridge

187

gave onto a rocky amphitheatre which opened to the right under the name of the Schöllenenschlucht ('Schöllenen Gorge'). The Reuss torrent, the author of this nightmarish scene, coursed out of its slot in a jumbled cascade, cut hard right in front of the exit of the Urnerloch, and rampaged out of sight around a bend in the Schöllenenschlucht.

The rock walls enclosing the amphitheatre to the west and north fell vertically to the water, and those to the east were only marginally less steep, and gave a purchase to a number of brave and stunted trees. A few metres beyond the exit of the Urnerloch the pack road was projected over the cascade by the bold single-span arch of the Devils' Bridge (built 1595), and the path continued down the left-hand side of the gorge, borne initially on two arches which had been built onto the rock. The whole reverberated to the thunder of the torrent, and in the half-light, the spray and the drizzle the spectator was appalled rather than cheered by the incongruous pinks and pale greens of the rocks.

No other episode of Suvorov's campaigning in 1799 is attended with more historical uncertainties than the passage of the Urnerloch and the Devils' Bridge. Writing in the 1850s, when the event had only just slipped from living memory, Milyutin had to state that the accounts were so divergent as to lead one to

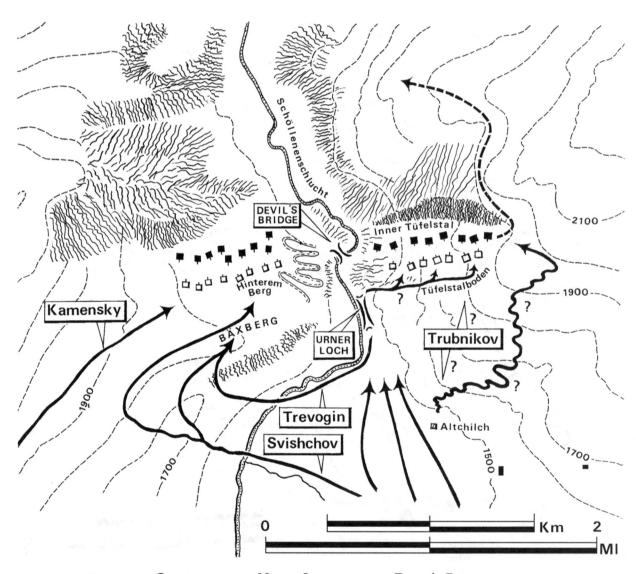

COMBATS AT THE URNER LOCH AND THE DEVIL'S BRIDGE

188

*THE SCHÖLLENENSCHLUCHT ABOVE
THE DEVIL'S BRIDGE*

believe that they related not to contradictory versions of the same events, but to different actions altogether. At one extreme we may rank the tradition that was initiated by the colourful and highly unreliable relation which Suvorov sent to Emperor Paul, and was perpetuated in popular biographies and the semi-fictional history of Gachot (1904). In contrast the Austrian staff officer Weyrother and the Russian grenadier captain Gryazev talk merely of the engineering problem of negotiating a broken arch below the Devil's Bridge (below), and relate nothing concerning a bloody action. An intermediate position is occupied by a veteran ('Ratnik,' 1844, probably Starkov) of the regiment of Rehbinder, who was undoubtedly present in person, but whose account was written long after the happenings, and may well have been influenced by legends and perceived truths.

In all probability the French would have been physically unable to concentrate more than about 2,400 troops as far up the Reuss as the Devil's Bridge, namely two battalions of the 38th demi-brigade, the depleted second battalion of the 76th and nine companies of grenadiers. The Rehbinder veteran states that the French positioned a cannon on the near (right) bank of the Reuss in the narrow space between the exit of the Urnerloch and the Devil's Bridge, while the contemporary map reproduced by Meshcheryakov shows French pickets deployed over the rocky heights on either side of the gorge. The defenders of the Devil's Bridge were in any event soon called away in succession to meet the threat which Auffenberg posed to their line of communication at Amsteg.

We now shall try reconstruct the sequence of events on 25 September. According to the Rehbinder veteran the first move on the part of the Russians was to detach a party of the Kashkin Jäger (200 men under Major Fedor Ivanovich Trevogin) and a battalion of the Rehbinder regiment under Colonel Vasily Ivanovich Svishchov to initiate a left-flanking movement by fording the Reuss to the left bank—an achievement in itself—and climbing the Bäxberg heights to reach a track which descended ultimately to the Schöllenenschlucht from the west.

The last contribution to the left-flanking movement was made by the exceptionally energetic Major-General Nikolai Mikhailovich Kamensky, who had bivouacked overnight with the two battalions of his regiment by Hospental. He gained the track in question some two kilometres to the west of the other parties, then hastened along it to join in the action.

A corresponding right-flanking move to the east of the gorge was undertaken by Colonel Iosif Petrovich Trubnikov with three hundred volunteers from the Mansurov musketeers. These man had proved their agility at the Oberalp, but it is unlikely that they would have been capable of the feat attributed to them in Meshcheryakov's map, which has them emerging from the northern exit of the Urnerloch, then at once turning hard right and scrambling up a cleft in the rock to deploy in an extended line across the Tuefelstalboden to do battle with the French pickets. It is impossible to identify the supposed route today, for the Urnerloch has been widened considerably and prolonged by an avalanche screen, but the slopes are everywhere so steep as to appear to be beyond the capacity of all but experienced climbers. More likely (as Reding-Biberegg suggests) Trubnikov gained the necessary height by ascending the Nätschen mountain, then took the uncontested Gütsch passage through the Grätli ridge. To sum up:

Left-flanking (W) Movements	Right-flanking (E) Movement
Trevogin and Svishchov Kamensky	Trubnikov

Down on the pack road the advance of the main army was spearheaded by Major-General Mansurov with the remainder of his own regiment and a number of skirmishers detached from the regiment of Rehbinder. They encountered a party of French outside the entrance to the Urnerloch, beat them back through the tunnel, and emerged into the Schöllenenschlucht, where they became targets for French infantry sniping from the cliffs on either side, and a 4-pounder cannon firing canister at point blank range from the near side of the Devils' Bridge.

Lecourbe was now present on the scene in person, along with reinforcements he had rushed up from the lower Reuss, but now that the Austrians were battling their way down the Maderanertal (below) he had to reduce his concentration behind the Devil's Bridge to five companies or less. The tactical impasse was finally resolved when Trevogin and Svishchov and the first of the left-flanking columns drove the French pickets from the Bäxberg and

THE DEVIL'S BRIDGE, AS REBUILT ON THE SAME LOCATION IN THE NINETEENTH CENTURY

A painting of the original bridge

descended against the enemy right flank and rear. At this the French threw their cannon into the foaming Reuss, crossed the Devil's Bridge and fell back down the path on the far side of the Schöllenenschlucht. They were hastened on their way when Kamensky appeared with his battalions further down the gorge, and (as the ranking officer present) took charge of the pursuit. By this time Trubnikov's command had cleared the pickets from the heights on the right hand side of the gorge, from where the French would in any case have found it difficult or impossible to take the passage under effective fire, owing to the excessive range and the

The Schöllenenschlucht above the Devil's Bridge, at low water. The tiny figures on the path indicate the scale of this grim landscape.

cramped fields of fire.

The French had abandoned the Devil's Bridge intact, but on the far side the Russian main force found its further way barred by a gap which had been effected in one of the arches which carried the path on the first stage of its descent down the left bank of the Reuss. The gulf was spanned by a few scorched beams and planks which probably only an acrobat could have negotiated in safety. We cannot establish who broke the arch and when, but it is likely that the masonry had been hacked away or blown up previously as a precautionary measure, and replaced by the timber structure which the French tried to destroy to cover their retreat.

The histories tell of the gap being scourged by deadly fire, and Suvorov urging on his soldiers by blows and shouts. In fact the field-marshal was fast asleep, and Weyrother did not care to wake him when he sent off messages to Hotze, Linken and Korsakov at eleven in the morning.[35] Possibly the fevered dreaming of Suvorov or more likely the intervention of Fuchs and Trefort is responsible for the fantastic stores ever since in circulation about officers dashing forward under fire, binding planks together with their sashes, or alternatively (like Major Prince Stepan Vasilevich Meshchersky) using his sash to help others across.[36]

The first troops to cross the bridge were the Rosenberg Grenadiers. As one of their captains Gryazev knew that the reports being made to Paul were false, and he set the record straight in his diary. His troops had entered the Urnerloch where 'complete darkness reigned. We held one another by the hand, and picked our way under that great mass of rock which seemed to weigh down on us, and discharged streams of water.'[37] By the time the grenadiers crossed the bridge the various flanking columns had done their work, and so the problems which were remained were of an engineering, not a tactical nature.

Austrian pioneers arrived on the spot, and took their time over measuring the gap and discussing what to do:

These leisurely proceedings annoyed the Russian troops, who were eager to get across as soon as possible and strike and beat the enemy. Maksim Vladimirovich Rehbinder lost patience, turned to his regiment and asked any men who were acquainted with carpentry to make themselves known. More than one hundred soldiers came forward in response to this appeal. Our men snatched the tools from the Austrian pioneers and got down to work.

The Russians brought up any serviceable pieces of timber they could find, and the improvised bridge was soon complete. '*Ja, fertig!*' pronounced the Austrian pioneers, '*Das ist gut!*'[38]

The leading Russian troops found that the way down the gorge was still clinging to the cliff face, but then it became a respectable hillside track, the mountains drew apart, and finally villages could be seen in the valley beyond. The pack road wound from one side of the Reuss to the other on its descent to Göschenen, and the French succeeded in blowing the little bridges along its course. There was a further check at Göschenen village, where some troops of the 76th demi-brigade were defending the church and the neighbouring chalets, but this time the French delayed too long in extricating themselves, and the party had to escape up the Göschener Tal to avoid being cut off. Suvorov rode past the scene of the little action and continued to Wassen, where he spent a restless night in the Hotel zum Ochsen (the present Hotel St. Gotthard), disturbed perhaps by an inaccurate report from Major-General Miloradovich that Auffenberg had been beaten up the Maderanertal from Amsteg and was retreating over the Chrüzli Pass to Disentis.

By now the pursuit was entirely the affair of two battalions which stood under the command of Miloradovich, and were progressing through the pine forest of Intschi, which covered the sides of the great gloomy valley that led down to Altdorf and Lake Lucerne. According to Weyrother 'the advance guard actually penetrated to within half an hour's march of Amsteg. They saw a number of [bivouac] fires in the valley there and on the heights behind the village, but they forgot all about General Auffenberg and mistook them for the fires of

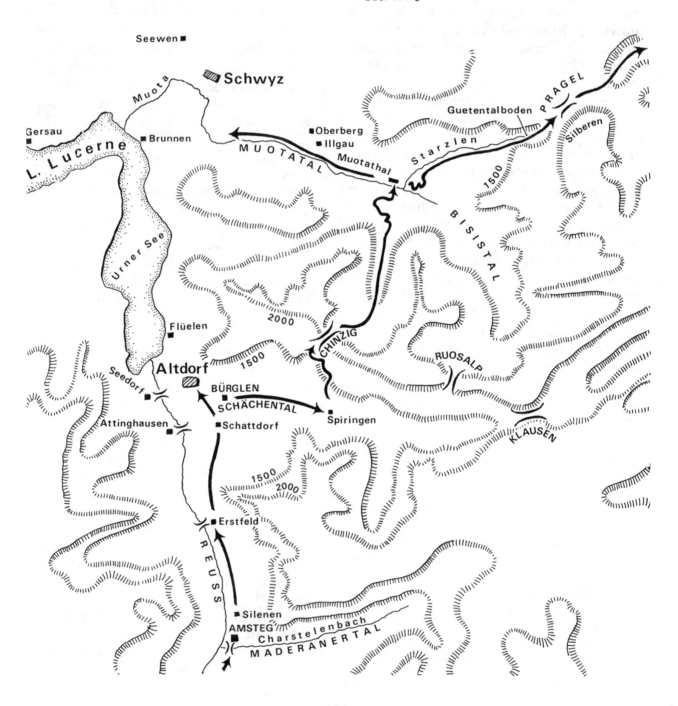

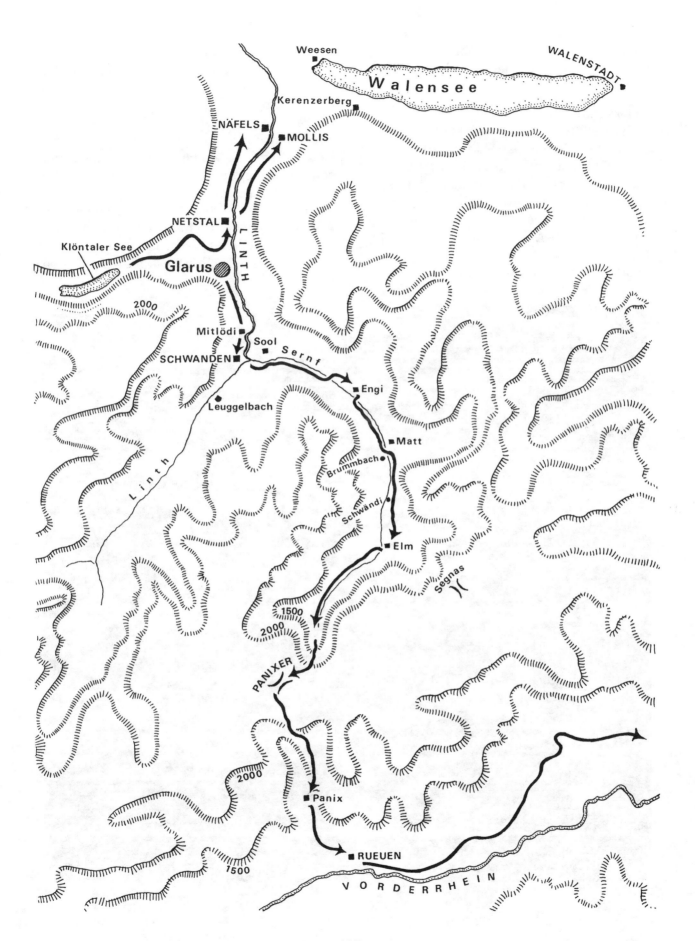

the French, and on that account concluded that it was too risky to attack.'[39] What had been going on in that part of the world?

AUFFENBERG AT AMSTEG

We left the Austrian brigade of Auffenberg overnight on the upper Maderanertal, having crossed the fearsome mountain ridge from the Vorderrhein, but being overtaken by darkness before it could reach the village of Amsteg. Auffenberg resumed his advance at first light on 25 September, and encountered the first French posts on the Charstelenbach half an hour's ordinary marching time from Amsteg.

The waters of this considerable mountain stream passed over and around rocks for the whole of its descent to the valley of the Reuss, and this barrier helped the French (two companies of the 38th demi-brigade) to hold Auffenberg at bay for a full four hours until the Austrians forced a passage over the wooden bridge to the north bank at Amsteg, just above the confluence with the Reuss. The French recoiled to a position outside Silenen on the lower Reuss, whereupon Auffenberg left two of his battalions in Amsteg and deployed the other two on the far (left) bank of the Charstelenbach on the slopes of the Bristen

THE CHARSTELENBACH ABOVE AMSTEG

mountain, ready to beat off the French when they poured down from the Devil's Bridge, and to receive Suvorov when he came up behind in pursuit. This probably explains why Auffenberg left the Charstelenbach bridge only partly demolished—sufficiently damaged to interfere with the French retreat, but not wrecked so completely as to be impossible to repair in good time for the passage of Suvorov's army.

The two Austrian battalions down at Amsteg came under attack between seven and eight in the evening by the two companies of French which had been beaten back towards Silenen, but were now coming on again with the help of reinforcements from Altdorf. Meanwhile the French blocking force was recoiling from the Devils' Bridge. The first of Lecourbe's troops to reappear in the neighbourhood of Amsteg were those of the single battalion of the 76th demi-brigade, with Lecourbe following in person with the panting grenadiers of his reserve, and lastly the two battalions of the 38th.

The pack road (unlike the later motor road and autobahn) descended the right (east) bank of the Reuss, and so for a time the French lapped around Auffenberg's position further up the Bristen mountain. The enemy launched three determined but vain attacks on this feature, then left it masked by two companies of the 76th, while the rest of their force crossed the partly-demolished Charstelenbach bridge, cleared the Austrian posts from Amsteg and continued on they way towards Altdorf. Auffenberg had succeeded in holding his position, and this last fight contributed to his not inconsiderable loss of eighteen killed, fifty-six wounded and 155 captured.[40]

We can never establish convincingly whether the falling-away of the French forces from the Devil's Bridge was due primarily to the activity of the Russian flanking columns on the heights to either side, or to the emergence of

THE REUSS AT AMSTEG

Auffenberg on the French line of communication down the Reuss valley. It is at least certain that the story of this remarkable day will remain incomplete as long as the two scenes of interest — at the Devil's Bridge and on the Charstelenbach — are considered in isolation.

26 SEPTEMBER

ALTDORF

At about six in the morning of 26 September the acting Russian advance guard under Miloradovich completed some business left over from the day before by pushing on to join Auffenberg, who had been waiting overnight on the heights south of Amsteg. The lone battalion of the 76th was covering the retreat of the remainder of Lecourbe's force (the battalions of the 38th, and nine companies of grenadiers) down the Reuss, and for the next few hours it engaged in a running battle with the allies as it retreated towards the head of Lake Lucerne.

The French set the remains of the Amsteg bridge ablaze, and opened a lively fire against the head of the allied columns from behind the Charstelenbach. This first position became untenable when the leading Russians scampered over the smoking timbers of the much-abused bridge and rushed into Amsteg. Below Erstfeld the valley on the right (east) bank of the Reuss opened out into a respectable little plain, and the 76th found its next defensible position behind the Schächenbach in front of the town of Altdorf.

The allied advance guard was now being reinforced from the main body of the corps of Rosenberg, which took the Schächenbach under frontal attack towards nine in the morning, while at the same time a number of small parties of Russian Jäger evicted the tirailleurs from Bürglen further upstream and began to turn the enemy left flank. The Russians were in the process of fording the stream when they were scourged by half a dozen discharges of canister from a cannon planted at the entrance to the Schächental, which gaped to the east. On the far side they received a further painful surprise in the shape of four companies of Lecourbe's grenadiers, who irrupted against them from Altdorf, and the check was sufficient to allow

the French to make good their escape through the town to the left (west) bank at Seedorf, on the plain of the lower Reuss just short of Lake Lucerne.

Lecourbe placed a party of infantry and his two light cannon in an improvised bridgehead fortification on the right bank of the Reuss opposite Seedorf, and he considered it his first duty to seal off the allies on the right (east) bank of the river, and prevent them from breaking through to the west to reach Lucerne by way of the Surenen Pass. On the far (eastern) side of the Reuss he still had his bridgeheads on the lakeshore at Flüelen, and in front of Seedorf. He destroyed the bridges at Attinghausen and Erstfeld, and the 2nd battalion of the 38th held the posts there and at Ripshausen.

Auffenberg's battalion of Gradiscaner Croats was indeed supposed to force the crossing and make for the Surenen Pass, but the first reconnaissances and soundings of the Reuss proved discouraging. The three battalions of Austrian regulars (regiment of Kerpen) remained in reserve at Schattdorf. The Russian corps of Derfelden was deployed on the right bank as far as the confluence with the Schächenbach, and the corps of Rosenberg from there downriver towards the lake.

The generals Rosenberg and Auffenberg and their staff had entered Altdorf at about noon. The Russian troops were exhausted and starving, and their officers were not above asking for bread for them at the few houses that were left standing after the great fire which had swept the town on 5 April. At Rosenberg's orders the local carpenter Franz Indergrund pulled down the Tricolour of Liberty, and the Russian soldiers set about cleaning their smoke-blackened hands on the silk of the offensive flag.

Suvorov and Constantine were meanwhile making a leisurely journey from Wassen. Suvorov halted to pray at the little chapel which lay hard under the grim little tower of the medieval Landammann Arnold der Ritter at Silenen, and they lunched at one of the chalets. Peasants came running to welcome their liberators all the way to Altdorf, where Suvorov dismounted at six in the evening to make his way through the blackened timbers to the centre of the town.

> He was wearing a fantastic outfit—a shirt, with an open black waistcoat and pantaloons unbuttoned down the sides; he was carrying a whip in one hand, and with the other he dispensed blessings to the people as he rode by, just like a bishop. The Landammann [head of the cantonal administration] Schmid and the venerable priest Ringgold came out to meet him in front of the Landhaus; from Schmid he asked the kiss of peace, and from the priest a blessing—which he received with reverently bowed head. He then delivered a speech in fairly broken German, in which he proclaimed himself the redeemer and saviour of the world, for he had come to free it from atheists and tyranny.[41]

Antonio Gamma then conducted Suvorov to one of the few surviving buildings in Altdorf, the massive gable-ended house (built 1550) of the old Landammann Stephan Jauch, where the field-marshal lodged on the third floor.

Suvorov was proud of what had been achieved so far, but his immediate concern was to reach the stores of provisions which Hotze and Korsakov were supposed to have ready for him at Schwyz, behind multiple mountain walls. His pack train of mules and Cossack horses was still labouring up all the way from Airolo, and the convoy might be disrupted at any time by French forces intruding from the west—from the Valais down the Val Bedretto, from the Furka and the Realp against Hospental and Andermatt, from the Susten Pass down the Meiental against Wassen, or from the Surenen Pass against Erstfeld. Suvorov had been able to spare only Colonel Strauch and his 4,500 Austrians to guard the Val Bedretto and the St. Gotthard, and two battalions of Russians to mask the Meiental. The flour captured at Andermatt had been consumed by Rosenberg's corps in twenty-four hours, just two of Suvorov's battalions had gobbled all the provisions found in Altdorf, while an attempted mass requisitions of foodstuffs in the neighbourhood produced just fifteen cattle, and no flour or bread. At Altdorf Russian troops were seen chewing on discarded animal skins in the tannery drains. By now the men had put forth six days of exertion with no shelter. Their muskets, bayonets and swords were rusting, and their lice-ridden clothing clung clammily to their shrunken frames.

With seemingly no consultation, and certainly very little hesitation, Suvorov resolved to turn aside from the lower Reuss and Lake Lucerne, march a short distance east up the Schächental, climb the Rosstock massif by way of the Chinzig Pass (2,073 m), and turn back west on the far side to gain Schwyz by way of the Muotatal. In detail the corps of Rosenberg was assigned to guard the right bank of the

The Jauch-Haus at Altdorf

199

lower Reuss until the main body was safely on its way over the Chinzig. Bagration with the Russian advance guard was to lead the way over the pass, followed by the Russian corps of Derfelden, which would thus have security in both rear and van.

27-28 SEPTEMBER

THE PASSAGE OF THE CHINZIG PASS

Bagration set ouf from Bürglen along the new direction of march at four on the drizzly morning of 27 September. Four hundred Cossacks of the Sychov and Posdeev regiments were in the lead—half mounted and the other two hundred on foot—supported by the Jäger regiments of Bagration and Miller.

After probably less than two hours' march up the Schächental Bagration's command turned left to begin the ascent to the Chinzig, passing to one side or other of the Gangbach cleft. The muddy tracks up the steep meadows gave way to the expanse of loose and slippery stones which led to the summit, which was passed at about noon. A relatively easy descent on the far side brought the party to a belt of continuous and thick forest which began at Lipplisbüel, where the crags closed in from either side to form the dark and narrow Hürital, leading to the head of the Muotatal near Muotathal village. Bagration reached Lipplisbüel in the middle of the afternoon, and was told that a French company was down below—partly by the Convent standing to the north of the village, and partly a little way up the Bisistal at the beginning of the path to the Klausen Pass.

The report underestimated the number of the enemy, but it was otherwise reasonably accurate. These people were in fact those of the sixth and seventh companies of the 38th demi-brigade, which had been sent by Lecourbe up the Muotatal on 26 September, in case the Austrians might seek to enter the valley from the south-east, namely from the upper Linth by way of the Ruosalp passage. News that an enemy column was about to break in from that direction therefore persuaded the local French commander, Adjutant-General Vautrin to turn his attention towards the Bisistal, leaving the

descent from the Chinzig to the south unguarded.

Back at Liplisbüel, Bagration directed his dismounted Cossacks to make a flanking movement through the woods to the right of the central path, and the horsed Cossacks to the left, while he brought his Jäger down the zig-zag track to the bluff which overhung the final and steep descent to Muotathal village. The Russian light infantry and dismounted Cossacks reached the floor of the Muotatal just above the village, and they passed to the right (northern) bank of the little river Muota by a covered bridge to the right of Fuggeln. The mounted Sychov Cossacks over to the left scrambled and skidded down the slope, turned left on reaching the plain, galloped along the left bank of the Muota, then forded to the right bank opposite Illgau to complete the encirclement of the French.

The peasants and the French soldiers had no reason to expect that a Russian army was about to descend among them from the southern mountain range. The French mistook the first bearded riders in their long brown coats as monks on a pilgrimage, while the local people were astonished to see the dark masses which proceeded to pour from the Hürital. A peasant was making hay at Hinter Iberg on the far side of the valley when he heard a sudden outburst of musketry from below. He at first assumed that the French were drilling as usual, but when he looked down he saw a company of the French in full flight to the west.

The Russians had caught the French when they were in the process of moving up the Bisistal. The 6th company had been in the lead, and it was now unable to extricate itself before the Russians closed off its retreat; the 7th company had progressed only a little way up the valley, and it made off down the Muotatal, pursued closely by the mounted Cossacks. Altogether about fifty French made good their escape (if only for the time being), leaving fifty-seven of their comrades dead or wounded, and another eighty-seven to surrender to the Russians.

Overnight Bagration placed outposts beyond the Kirchenbrücke and east of Jessenen along the Bettbach, while his main force bivouacked in the meadows by the Hoftrog and

200

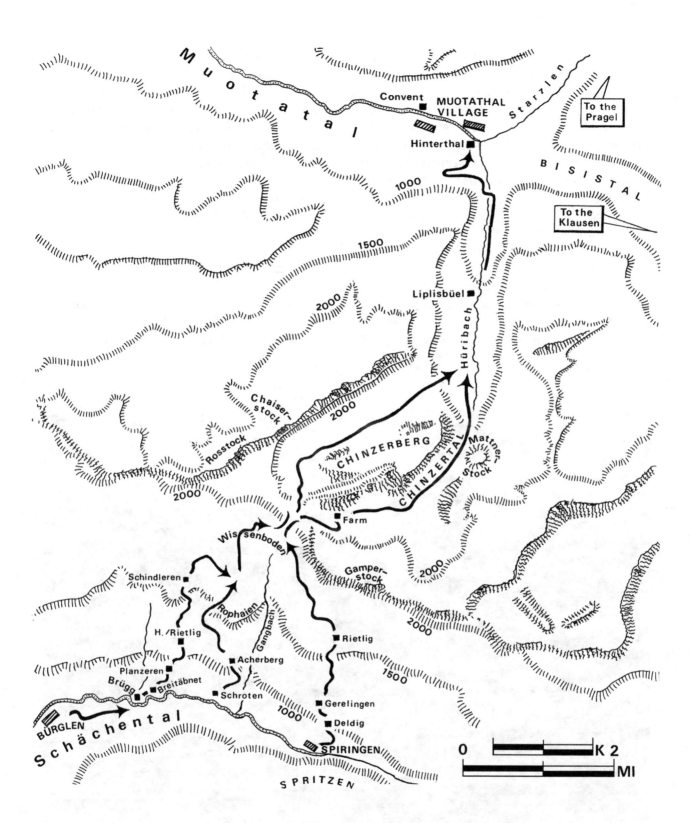

THE PASSAGE OF THE CHINZIG, 27-28 SEPTEMBER

201

Aabort farmsteads to the east of the Convent.

Towards the end of the fighting two to the Cossacks—complete with lances, sabres and pistols—had ridden hard uphill on their little horses to our peasant at Hinter Iberg. One of the Cossacks was an officer, and he opened his coat to show the large cross hanging on his chest and declared: 'We good Christians too, we enemies of French. You too, and so we are friends!' The peasant took him to his house, where they made up milk and flour into damp little cakes and gobbled them down half cooked. After nightfall the officer asked to be led to a point which gave a good view over the left bank of the Muota stream. They could see forty or fifty of the French at rest around a camp fire on the far side of the stone bridge. The officer brought up his men, and the peasant guided them down to the bridge, where he was asked to wait. 'The Russians crept forward like cats and soon disappeared into the darkness of the night. Nothing could be heard for a time, then all of a sudden shots rang out, followed by a frightful yelling, and soon after that Cossacks came back from various directions. Having returned to the near side of the bridge they washed their sabres, and said that they had cut down nearly all the French.'[42]

We return to Suvorov, who left his lodgings in Altdorf, and joined Derfelden's division and Auffenberg's Austrians for the march in Bagration's wake over the Chinzig. The column swung half-left under the Rosstock, and climbed the winding road up through the little old town

THE ASCENT OF THE CHINZIG PASS, LOOKING TOWARDS THE WISSENBODEN AMPHITHEATRE

of Bürglen. This was the heart of conservative Switzerland, and Suvorov's guide Captain Antonio Gamma drew the field-marshal's attention to the home of William Tell, a low and massively built house on the right.

The broad grassy plain of the lower Schächental narrowed beyond Bürglen at Brügg, from where the valley was prolonged into the mountains as a V-shaped passage, overhung with dark woods. The Russians turned aside from the path at intervals to form the columns by which the force was to attain the left-hand crest, which reached some 1,500 metres above the valley bottom. The routes in question were probably three:

1. Most immediately from Brügg along a spur which mounted by way of Breitäbnet, Planzeren, Hinter Rietlig and Schindleren,

2. From the path at Schroten, up through Acherberg and the left-hand (western side) of the Rophaien height,

> On emerging from the zone of pasture and trees both columns would have had to swing right to traverse the steep scree slopes of the Wissenboden at the head of the Gangbach amphitheatre to reach the Chinzig Pass.

3. The last column, accompanied by Suvorov in person, took the path which zig-zagged from Spiringen up through Deldig, Gerelingen and Rietlig. This route was the one which led most directly to the pass, and involved a short and relatively safe passage of the scree on the right-hand side of the Gangbach.

THE CHINZIG PASS—THE FINAL ASCENT

203

With the exception of the village of Spiringen all the locations mentioned above were chalet farmsteads which were connected by tracks snaking up through the pastures, and they and their neighbouring chalets were combed by the Russian soldiers, who were looking for this summer's production of cheese, and the few luckless cattle which they chopped up on the spot and devoured half raw.

Suvorov dismounted from his mule at Spiringen, and began the ascent in relative comfort, being borne upwards by Swiss peasants in a kind of sedan chair. He was escorted by Grand Prince Constantine, four generals, ten staff officers, eighteen guides or attendants and a party of Cossacks. Colonel Trocherko carried the box of Suvorov's jewels and decorations (the field-marshal is said to have beaten him for

negligence on the descent from the St. Gotthard).

The ridge which had to be crossed was at first invisible when the partly climbed the steep pastures from Spiringen, but to the rear the valley floor began to disappear into a gulf, and the view was dominated by the gigantic black scree of the eroded north face of the Spritzen mountain. A slight flattening of the slope between Furen and Rietlingen brought the crest in front clearly into sight, as a continuous saw-like wall of limstone crags, which presented no visible passage. The sight was hidden once more when the track led up through thick-set Conifers and hornbeam, but it emerged dauntingly close when the column came into the open and found itself under the rock wall amid rough, rock-strewn meadows. The path negotiated the foot of one of the buttresses of the ridge, and brought

On the Chinzig plateau, looking north-west towards the Rosstock-Chaiserstock massif

The first descent from the Chinzig, with the Mattner-Stock in the centre, and the Chinzerberg on the left. The road is modern.

the party to the rocks and scree at the head of the Wissenboden amphitheatre, where all the routes converged on the cluster of fang-like rocks which masked the narrow gap which was the pass proper (2,073 m).

Beyond the gap the leading troops spilled over a small plateau of windswept grass and rocks. The men were impressed by Suvorov's evident lack of concern for the situation of his army. In so far as any news had arrived, it was encouraging. An Austrian messenger (probably Captain Joseph Taza) announced that Lieutenant-General Linken with the left wing of the corps of Hotze had begun his part in the general allied offensive promisingly enough, by storming the French position at Glarus on 26 September and taking 1,500 prisoners. Shortly afterwards Suvorov's British companion

Lieutenant-Colonel Sir Henry Clinton could write to Wickham that as a consequence of this report 'the army will proceed to execute the remainder of the operations as formerly concerted… The marshal has applied to me to procure him some English ale; he says it is what keeps him alive. As you are likely to be stationary—at least I hope so—will you have the goodness to direct some dozen to be sent to your address?'[43]

Below the plateau two great rock mesas towered to form a great valley—the Chaiserstock to the left and the Mattner Stock to the right—while the available paths descended to one side or another of a central massif, the Chinzerberg. The physical dangers were over, and the Russians began to stream down towards the Hürital narrows in disorderly groups. Night

THE FURTHER DESCENT OF THE CHINZIG, LOOKING BACK TOWARTDS THE RIDGE

overtook the troops before many of them had progressed far, and they wrapped themselves in their coats, and nestled into what shelter they could find among the rocks. Suvorov probably spent the night in one of the stone-built shepherds' shelters (most likely the present Chinzertal farm) standing on a ledge above the Chinzertal.

All the rest of Derfelden's column was still strung out along the tracks leading to the pass, and most of the troops were immobilised in the darkness in a bone-chilling wind. Captain Gryazev and a group of fellow officers ultimately found their way over the pass by the feeble light of a lantern which they improvised from candle-ends and rolled-up paper from a book. They gained some relief from the cold, but had nothing to eat except some biscuits they carried in their pockets.

ROSENBERG ON THE REUSS

Rosenberg was still standing in the plain of the lower Reuss with rather more than half the Russian army. His responsibility was to mask the departure of the others, and cover the train of mules and horses that was even now winding down from the St. Gotthard.

So as to keep Lecourbe amused, Rosenberg assembled troops as if to force a crossing at Erstfeld and gain the Surenen Pass. Lecourbe responded by sending the third battalion of the 38th demi-brigade up the left bank to deny the passage to the Russians, and he mounted a demonstration on his own account, by throwing the remainder of his force (three companies of the 76th and four companies of grenadiers) against Altdorf from his bridgehead in front of Seedorf. Thus each party was launching a diversion against the other's left flank. The unexpected weight of the French attack chased the regiment of Fertsch from the neighbourhood of Altdorf at five in the afternoon. Rosenberg accordingly brought up the regiments of Tyrtov and Mansurov from his centre, together with the dismounted Cossacks. The odds were now turning in the Russians' favour, and they forced the French first from Altdorf, and then entirely back to the left bank of the Reuss.

On 28 September Rosenberg left Lieutenant-General Förster to hold the entrance to the Schächental south-east of Altdorf with a rearguard (musketeer regiments Fertsch, Tyrtov and Mansurov, and the Grekov and Denisov Cossacks) while the rest of the corps filed up the valley and over the Chinzig. The passage proved to be still more difficult than it had been for the corps of Derfelden, for it was attended with rain on the way up, and snow towards the summit, and the tracks were churned up by the thousands of troops who had passed on the day before. 'It became darker and darker,' writes a soldier of the regiment of Rehbinder, 'the clouds more and more dense, and the rain soaked us through and through until we were virtually pouring with water. We made our way through the opaque clouds, sometimes clambering over bare rocks, at others making our way through sticky clay.' The regiment reached the summit before evening, and bivouacked on the plateau.

The rain and the wind ceased, the sky cleared overhead and towards the west, though murky clouds still hung on the mountains to the east and south and there was a rolling of thunder. In front of us in the far distance we could hear intermittent musketry and artillery. The musket fire and thunder re-echoed through the mountains and gorges. 'How wonderful are Thy works, O Lord!' exclaimed one of the soldiers, an educated man who by misfortune had fallen among the rank and file… But the beauty of the landscape meant nothing to us when there was not a twig of firewood in the neighbourhood, when we were soaked to the skin, when our shoes were in a deplorable state and the officers' boots looked even worse. 'Clean your muskets! Get some fires going!'— Miloradovich was speaking in a loud voice as he walked through the ranks of the soldiers. We hastened to execute his orders. Before an hour was out we troops of the [corps] advance guard had a fire blazing— we had found a shed not far away and demolished it. Now we all set to work— repairing our shoes, drying uniforms and greatcoats, or baking flat cakes with the flour we had been given at Altdorf. Mikhail Andreevich [Miloradovich] came to our fire, espied a cake which was fully cooked, and proceeded to pick it up and eat it with gusto.

'My God! That's worth eating! Sweeter than pineapple! Now, whose cake was that?' they informed him. 'Many thanks, and now I'll give you some cheese in return.' And indeed he took out a little morsel of cheese and gave it to the soldier.'[44]

The train of mules and horses was labouring up behind. Even such experienced horsemen as the Cossacks were unfamiliar with the toll that the mountain roads was taking on the animals. Most of the horses had already shed their iron shoes on the good pack road over the St. Gotthard and down the Reuss, and now many of them injured their unprotected hooves on the Chinzig tracks, or vanished down the slopes. 'The Cossacks love their horses, and since they have strong ties of community the whole column came to a halt every time one of the horses had an accident. We issued a whole string of prohibitions, but nothing could get the convoy to hurry up.'[45] The Swiss officer Dufour came across the skeletons of a number of these animals when he re-traced Suvorov's route in 1833.

The Cossack regiment of Denisov was the first unit of the corps rearguard to follow the provision train. On the way up the Chinzig during the night Adrian Karpovich Denisov (now a major-general) looked back towards the Schächental and saw what seemed to be a constellation of stars. He was ill and exhausted, and the sight made no sense until an old Cossack explained that these were the bivouac fires of the rest of the rearguard, which was waiting until the ways up the pass were clear. The track now began to narrow to such an extent that Denisov's horse was in danger of falling over the edge at every step. Denisov was unable to dismount to the left in the usual way, for he would have stepped into thin air, while the face of the mountain was brushing his right side, and so he took the unstylish but sensible course of sliding over the rump of his horse and taking hold of the creature's tail.[46]

It was fortunate that Lecourbe did not re-cross the Reuss and enter Altdorf until the 30th, and by then the tail of the supply train and the Russian rearguard had reached the Muotatal.

The Muotatal

In the early morning of 28 September the Russians and Austrians who had huddled overnight on the Chinzig continued their journey down towards the Muotatal. Suvorov was in their midst, being carried by four sweating Swiss peasants. The glaciated glens running on either side of the Chinzerberg united beyond that massif in a magnificent forest of ancient larches, where the descending valley began to narrow towards the north. Suvorov's party halted briefly at Liplisbüel, a settlement of cabins scattered across a ledge-like meadow just above the final plunge down the Hürital narrows. Here Suvorov learned from a courier of Bagration's success on the day before, and we can imagine him urging his bearers to extra efforts to carry him down through the dense woodlands beside the Hüri torrent.

A bend of the track above Hinterthal gave Suvorov his first clear sight of the verdant valley of the Muotatal, and a few minutes later, at seven in the morning, he was at the gate of the Convent of the Franciscan nuns of St. Joseph, being welcomed by the Reverend Mother Waldburga Mohr. He entered, followed by Grand Prince Constantine and the generals Derfelden and Rehbinder. On the first floor of the north wing they viewed the great chapter hall and its long table, which might suit their debates very well. Suvorov was then ushered to the bedroom which had been chosen for him— a narrow room with a little bed, a simple toilet table and a tall cupboard.

The Convent of St. Joseph was sited amid meadows which rose on the right bank of the Muota stream. It was already an ancient foundation, having been established in 1280, and now formed an oblong, continuously walled compound. The narrow windows and the multiple high-pitched roofs endowed the Convent with an oriental air, and indeed the near-level floor of the valley, with its orchards and rich pastures represented the equivalent of a Shangri-la to the Russians and Austrians, who had spent most of the last week shivering in the mountains.

The officers showed the nuns and clergy every sign of respect, and paid well for everything they took from the local people—Constantine himself disbursed forty ten-rouble pieces for two beds of potatoes. The Russian soldiers too, or at least the infantry, were at first on their best behaviour, but they had exhausted the biscuit they carried with them, and when the loads were unpacked from the mules and horses it was found that much of the biscuit (of unleavened white flour) had rotted in the rain. The Muotatalers were demanding high prices for whatever remained in the valley after the depredations of the French, and so the starving troops resorted to force. The cheese distributed as rations was not to the Russians' taste, but tallow candles, dug-up potatoes and unripe fruit from the torn-down branches all went to feed the hunger of the troops.

Footwear was a still more urgent priority for many of the men. The French prisoners, the people of Oberschönenbuch and other places, and the Convent chaplain (who had been delivering a sermon of welcome) were all relieved of their shoes by the first Cossacks to arrive on the scene. When no more ready-made shoes were available, the Russian stretched the hides of the slaughtered cattle on the ground, stood on them in their foot rags, and cut the leather to the appropriate shape with their knives. The hides could also do service as food, when they were cut into little pieces, skewered on ramrods and roasted.

Six of seven kilometres west of the Convent the valley of the Muota stream narrowed into a twisting and heavily-wooded gorge, then emerged on the far side into the plain of Schwyz. This was where Suvorov hoped to find the supplies that would sustain him on his final bound to Zürich, and he intended to march in that direction as soon as all his forces were together in the Muotatal. By now the main force of the corps of Derfelden had reached the valley, while the leading troops of Rosenberg had already begun the passage of the Chinzig, and the last of the pack animals and the rearguard

The Convent of St. Joseph in the Muotatal

209

were expected on the 30th.

It will perhaps be useful to recall the main features of the plan of the general allied offensive, which Suvorov assumed was still in the process of execution:

The fresh Russian corps of Lieutenant-General Korsakov (28,000, or 26,000 after the detachment to Hotze), having completed its march across Germany, was to assail Massena behind the Limmat near Zürich,

Under the overall command of Lieutenant-General Hotze, the scattered Austrian forces still at hand in Switzerland (16,000, together with 2,000 Russians detached by Korsakov) were to break through the extended right flank of the French on the Linth and press on to Zürich; Hotze in person was commanding on the lower Linth between Lake Zürich and the Walensee, while Lieutenant-General Linken on his left was to break through on the upper Linth in the region of Glarus,

Suvorov with Auffenberg's Austrians (now depleted to 1,700) and the Russian Army of Italy would pick up the provisions supposedly deposited at Schwyz, and march to the rendezvous at Zürich. Suvorov was behind his already-delayed schedule, by which he should have been at Schwyz on 26 September, but that made him all the more confident that he would very soon have news of great victories won by Korsakov, Hotze and Linken.

Just to the east of the Convent and Muotathal village, the upper end of the Muotatal gave onto three valleys—the Hürital slot by which Suvorov had just descended, the Bisistal to the south-east (where Bagration had cut off the company of the 76th on the day before), and the great opening to the north-east which narrowed gradually to the top of the Pragel Pass, and from there gave access by way of the shore of the Klöntaler See to the upper Linth at Glarus.

Early on 28 September a captain of the Austrian general staff and a party of two hundred dismounted Cossacks and one hundred mounted Sychov Cossacks set off for the Pragel to demand the surrender of a body of French that was reported to be at Glarus. These folk were presumed to be survivors from the general disaster which must by now be overtaking the French in Switzerland, and the Cossacks were astonished to be halted by an enemy outpost up the Pragel. The Austrian captain called on the French to lay down their arms, but he was told that he and his force ought to be the ones to surrender, for Massena had routed the allies and taken 20,000 prisoners,

> but it is a good rule not to trust the enemy in such circumstances, and especially that enemy, much given to exaggerations. We had every reason to believe that our situation was excellent, and that we needed to take just one more step to unite with the corps of Lieutenant-General Hotze as intended. According to the reports from Schwyz no obstacle stood in our path, and so it appeared that all that remained was to advance in a decisive style and bring an overwhelming force to bear in an attack against the right flank and rear of the enemy position on the Albisberg—an attack which the enemy would be in no state to withstand.[47]

Down in the Muotatal individuals were nevertheless beginning to arrive with news of the same tenor as delivered by the French on the Pragel. A priest told how he had been chased by the French from Zug, and the cheese merchant Sebastian Schelbert, who had been returning from business in Germany, described a great battle he had witnessed around Zürich. Further and incontrovertible detail was provided by the mountain people, by a letter from Linken of the 27th, and by two of Suvorov's officers who had been dispatched in disguise to Schwyz, and had overheard French officers talking about their triumph in the inns.

It was now evident that Korsakov had been

broken by Massena at Zürich, that Hotze had been defeated and killed by Soult at Schänis, and that Linken had been beaten back from Glarus. How had such things been possible? What did they portend for Suvorov and his now unsupported troops in that remote valley in the heart of Switzerland?

NOTES TO CHAPTER 9

1. Colonel Louis Marès [1799], 1909, 23
2. Fuchs, 1827, 155
3. Quoted in Heuberger, 1988, 192. See also Marès [1799], 1909, 15
4. Soult, 1859, I,379-81
5. Marès [1799], 1909, 42
6. 'Ratnik,' 1844, No. 19, 374
7. Hotze to Suvurov, Kaltbrunn, 10 September 1799, Hüffer, 1900-1, I,355-7
8. Suvorov to Hotze, Novara, 13 September 1799, Ibid., I,361
9. Weyrother, 'Tagebuch.', Ibid., I,35
10. Stutterheim, 1812, IV, xi,4
11. Roverea, 1848, II,241
12. Captain Sarret to Hotze, Taverne, 16 September 1799, Hüffer, 1900-1, I,363
13. Stutterheim, 1812, IV, xi,24
14. Wickham to Suvorov, Schaffhausen, 9 September 1799, Wickham, 1870, II,439
15. 'Ratnik,' 1844, No. 10, 367-8
16. Ibid., No. 10, 368; Gryazev, 1898, 78
17. Anon., 1801-3, IV,241
18. 'Ratnik,' 1844, No. 10, 371
19. Suvorov to Paul, Taverne, 17 September 1799, Lopatin, 1986, 355
20. 'Pravila dlya voennykh Deistvy v Gorakh,' Taverne, 20 September 1799, Meshcheryakov, 1949-53, IV,331-4
21. Suvorov and Weyrother, 'Entwurff zum allgemeinen Angriff,' Taverne, 20 September 1799, Hüffer, 1900-1, I,367
22. 'Ratnik,' 1844, No. 10, 372
23. Gachot, 1903, 278
24. Weyrother, 'Tagebuch,' Hüffer, 1900-1, I,38
25. Masson, 1859, 366-7
26. On the retreat of the Russians and the summoning of Strauch see Stutterheim, 1812, IV, xi,29; Strauch's account in Hüffer, 1900-1, I,345, and the original version of Venançon's account in Ibid., I,529
27. Weyrother, 'Tagebuch,' Hüffer, 1900-1, I,38
28. Gryazev, 1898, 68
29. Fuchs, 1827, 29
30. Weyrother, 'Tagebuch,' Hüffer, 1900-1, I,40
31. Gryazev, 1898, 87
32. Weyrother, 'Tagebuch,' Hüffer, 1900-1, I,40
33. Suvorov to Hotze and Korsakov, Hospental, 24 September 1799, Hüffer, 1900-1, I,374
34. 'Ratnik,' 1844, No. 10, 375
35. Weyrother to Hotze, Linken and Korsakov, Hospental, 25 September, Hüffer, 1900-1, I,375
36. Suvorov to Paul, 14 October 1799, Meshcheryakov, 1949-53, IV,405
37. Gryazev, 1898, 91
38. 'Ratnik,' 1844, No. 10, 381
39. Weyrother, 'Tagebuch,' Hüffer, 1900-1, I,41
40. KA FA Deutschland 1799 IX 180, Auffenberg to Petrasch, 8 October
41. Dr. Lusser, quoted in Reding-Biberegg, 1895, 49
42. Quoted in Ibid., 72-3
43. Clinton to Wickham, Muotathal, 28 September 1799, Wickham, 1870, II,223
44. 'Ratnik,' 1844, No. 10, 383-4. The regiment of Rehbinder formed the advance guard of Rosenberg's corps, and the mention of the noise of combat from the Muotatal suggests that the regiment climbed the Chinzig on the date he states in the text, namely 27 September; on balance, however it is more likely that the description relates to the 28th
45. Weyrother, 'Tagebuch,' Hüffer, 1900-1, I,43
46. Denisov, 1874-5, XII,40. This passages indicates that Denisov took the third of the routes mentioned above, which is the only one with the mountain rising to the right and the gulf yawning to the left
47. Weyrother, 'Tagebuch,' Hüffer, 1900-1, I,42-3

10
The Débâcle

Korsakov

North of the Alps the French had lost very quickly the advantage they enjoyed from being the first to open hostilities. Their two armies, those of Jourdan and Massena, tried to encircle the Austrian army of Archduke Charles in southern Germany, but the scheme fell apart when Charles defeated Jourdan's Army of the Danube in a series of clashes at Ostrach and Stockach near Lake Constance between 20 and 25 March.

Now that the initiative lay in his hands, Archduke Charles opened an offensive in northern Switzerland on 21 May, and drove back Massena (as the new French commander in chief) as far back as the neighbourhood of Zürich. He attacked him there on 4 June, but he failed to achieve a decisive breakthrough, and even this partial success cost him heavily, for he had lost 3,400 men as opposed to the 1,600 of the French. Charles advanced to deliver a new attack on the 6th. This time the blow fell on thin air, for Massena had fallen back to a new and extremely strong position behind the Limmat on the Albisberg. Charles had already exceeded his instructions from Vienna by advancing as far as he had, and on 10 July he received an order from Emperor Francis commanding him to stay where he was until he was relieved by the Russian armies of Korsakov and Suvorov.

Lieutenant-General Aleksandr Mikhailovich Rimsky-Korsakov (1753-1840) was a type of senior Russian officer whom we have not so far encountered, namely one of those who had risen through largely nominal military service, and by diligent attention to the predilections of his sovereigns. He had witnessed the campaign in the Netherlands in 1794 in the circle of Louis de Bourbon Prince de Condé and the Comte d'Artois: 'these young idiots boasted that they had only to show their faces in order to annihilate the army of Sansculottes, and in their company he learned to underestimate the enemy.'[1] He likewise conceived a contempt for the performance of the Austrians, and a correspondingly high opinion of his own abilities. Korsakov reported to Empress Catherine that the well-disciplined Russians would make short work of the Republicans. He made the same point to the new Emperor. Paul was impressed further by the enthusiasm which Korsakov displayed for the new Prussian-style military regulations, and by an excellent slow march which the general (as a member of a musical family) had composed for the Semenovsky Guards.

In the spring of 1799 a force of 32,210 of the finest troops of the Empire assembled at Brest on the borders of Austrian Galicia, and they set off in three columns between 15 and 19 May. Korsakov assumed command of this brilliant host in place of the portly General Numsen, and in the course of the march the destination was changed from the Rhine to Switzerland, where the army was assigned a prominent role in the grand scheme to liberate the cantons and carry the war into France by way of the Jura. Seven or eight thousand troops of the émigré corps of the Prince de Condé followed in the Russians' wake, and gave further moral credibility to the enterprise.

While the senior Russian officers travelled from schloss to schloss independently of the army, drinking and dining hard, and fighting duels over the girls, the columns of troops on the whole kept excellent discipline as they progressed through Galicia (Koden, Wlodawa, Opatow, Wadowice), across Moravia, Bohemia by way of Kolin and Prague, and on the route through Germany (Waldmünchen, Kirn, Ubach, Neustadt, Schrobenhausen, Augsburg,

Türkheim, Memmingen, Ummendorf, Salgau, Moskirch) to reach Stockach after ninety days of marching.

On 12 August an advance party arrived at the headquarters of Archduke Charles at Kloten on the plain north of Zürich (the site of Zürich Airport), and three days later the first column came into position behind the Austrian right wing:

> The first impressions were those of astonishment and a kind of respect. Such was the impact of the martial bearing of those robust infantrymen, marching with ease under the heavy gear copied meticulously from that of the old Prussians under Frederick, the bizarre and savage appearance of those nomadic horsemen who brought before our eyes a living vision of the tribes who are scattered along the banks of the Don and up the valleys of the Caucasus, the harsh words of command, the speedy step of those dense battalions marching alternately to the mournful beat of their drums… and the lively rhythm of their clear and sonorous songs, whose verses were taken up in succession from the head of the column to the tail.[2]

Sickness, straggling and desertion had in fact reduced the total of the troops to some 28,000.

The Russians betook themselves to the outposts and spoke of giving battle without delay. Korsakov was disconcerted to learn that his Russians were supposed to take the leading role in clearing Switzerland and invading France (see page 153), but he was confident enough of the outcome of any battle; he 'listened to nobody and consulted nobody; he paid not the slightest attention to the depth of knowledge of Archduke Charles, and was unable even to assemble a staff. His army was the embodiment of chaos.'[3]

Archduke Charles knew that the Cossacks' instinct for plunder could not be restrained for much longer, and he was aware that Korsakov's force as a whole was incapable of independent action, all of which—together with the Russian generals' boasting—could have been tolerated in a joint army under his control, but threatened disaster now that he was under short notice from his political master Thugut to depart with

30,000 of the Austrian troops for Germany, and leave a key sector of the allied position entirely in Russian hands.

While the two armies were still together, Charles tried to turn the extreme left or western flank of the French deployment, by crossing the lower Aare at Döttingen and Klingnau just above the confluence of the Rhine. The Austrians advanced to the Aare after nightfall on 16 August, but found it impossible to anchor their pontoons to the rocky bed of this fast-flowing river, and they had to abandon the enterprise the next morning when the bridges were only half complete and all surprise was lost. Charles led his 30,000 men from the Kloten camp on 28 August, fully convinced of the 'fatal consequences' of his departure.[4]

The Forces at Zürich

(N.B. for the best modern account the reader is referred to 'Alpine Thunder: the Battle for Zürich, 1799,' by Wilbur E. Gray, in Empires, Eagles & Lions, #4, Chicago, 1993).

Russian Army, under Lieutenant-General Aleksandr Mikhailovich Rimsky-Korsakov

All Musketeer and Jäger regiments on an establishment of two battalions.

Division Lieut.-Gen Gorchakov

Brigade Maj-Gen Tuchkov
(in main position in front of the Sihl)

Musketeer regiment:		
Sevesk		1,354
Combined grenadier battalions:		
Selekhov		651
Rakhmanov		580
Potapov		584
Jäger regiments:		
Titov		703
Fock		730
Hussar Regiment:		
Lykoshin	10 sq	1,245
Ural Cossack Regiment:		
Borodin		467

Brigade Maj-Gen Essen
(at Wollishofen)

Grenadier regiment:		
Sacken	1 bn	770

213

Musketeer regiment:

Essen		1,327
Dragoon Regiment:		
Shlepev	5 sq	692
Artillery:		6 pieces
Grenadier Regiment:		
Ekaterinoslav		770
(in garrison at Zürich)		
Divisional total (with gunners):		*10,330*

DIVISION LIEUT.-GEN DURASOV

Brigade Maj-Gen Markov
(along right bank of Limmat down to Baden)

Musketeer regiment:	
Markov	1,085
Combined grenadier battalions:	
Treublut	608
Shapsky	586
Ural Cossack Regiment:	
Misinov	286

Brigade Maj-Gen Pushchin
(along right banks of Limmat and Aare from Baden to confluence with Rhine)

Musketeer regiments:	
Pushchin	1,254
Durasov	1,262
Don Cossack Regiments:	
Astakhov	486
Kumshchatsky	373
Tartar Mounted Regiment:	
Baranovsky	1,081
Artillery:	22 pieces
Divisional total (with gunners):	*7,080*

RESERVE DIVISION LIEUT.-GEN SACKEN

(along north bank of Lake Zürich, partly in support of Hotze)

Musketeer regiments:	
Razumovsky	1,340
Koslov	1,418
Przhibyshevsky	1,390
Izmailov	1,303
Artillery:	unknown
Divisional total (with gunners):	*5,670*

CAVALRY DIVISION MAJ.-GEN GUDOVICH

(along Rhine)

Cuirassier regiments:		
Tsarina	5 sq	729
Voinov	5 sq	725
Dragoon regiments:		
Gudovich	5 sq	665
Svechin	5 sq	648
Artillery:		28 pieces
Divisional total (with gunners):		*3,276*
Grand total:		*27,116*

(showing re-allocation for attack)

Division Mortier (4th)

Brigade Drouet		
53rd Line demi-brigade	2 bn	1,877
8th Chasseur Regiment	2 sq	377
Foot Artillery	2 coy	207
Brigade Brunet		
50th Line demi-brigade	3 bn	2,425
108th Line demi-brigade	2 bn	2,100
1st Dragoon Regiment	2 sq	172
Light Artillery	1 coy	60
Divisional Total:		*7,218*

Division Lorge (5th, heavily augmented)

Brigade Gazan		
37th Line demi-brigade	3 bn	2,411
57th Line demi-brigade	2 bn	
& grenadiers		1,133
13th Dragoon Regiment	4 sq	584
9th Hussar Regiment	4 sq	519
Foot Artillery	2 coy	152
Artillery artisans		5
Pontoon troops	3 coy	200
Brigade Bontemps		
10th Light demi-brigade	2 bn	2,312
1st Helvetic Legion		636
Light Artillery	2 coy	162
reinforcements from other divisions		
57th Line demi-brigade	2 bn	1,920
100th Line demi-brigade	2 bn	1,965
Artillery	1 coy	60
Brigade Quétard (from division Ménard)		
1st Light demi-brigade	2 bn	1,740
2nd Line demi-brigade	3 bn	2,635
Divisional Total:		*16,434*

Division Ménard (6th)

Brigade Heudelet		
103rd Line demi-brigade	2 bn	1,950
46th Line demi-brigade	2 bn	2,169
53rd Line demi-brigade	1 bn	449
23rd Chasseur Regiment	3 sq	386
9th Hussar Regiment	4 sq	519
Foot Artillery	8 coy	398
Pontoon troops	1 coy	117
Divisional Total:		*5,469*

Division Klein (Reserve)

Brigade Heudelet		
102nd Line demi-brigade	3 bn	3,106
Combined grenadiers	2 bn	1,200
7th Hussar Regiment	2 sq	303
5th Chasseur Regiment	4 sq	495

2nd Dragoon Regiment	4 sq	587
17th Dragoon Regiment	4 sq	501
Horse Artillery	1 coy	134
Divisional Total:		*6,327*

Grand Total: 35,448

ZÜRICH

Some fifty thousand allied troops were left holding an arc that extended from Basel by way of Lake Zürich, the Walensee and Sargans to the Grisons. Lieutenant-General Nauendorf and 5,400 Austrians were positioned along the long stretch from Basel up the Rhine to the confluence with the Aare. Korsakov's Russians were deployed along the right banks of the lower Aare and of the Limmat to Lake Zürich, with their main force heaped up near Zürich town. All the other troops stood under the command of the Austrian lieutenant-general Friedrich Hotze.

Hotze's wing now comprised about 16,000 troops—most of them Austrians, and the remainder 2,000 attached Russians, and the Swiss regiments of Bachmann and Roverea. The 'main' force (about 8,000 men) was strung out from Mellen on the northern shore of Lake Zurich to Uznach at the eastern end of the lake, and from there up the lower Linth and on to Wessen on the Walensee. The Austrian lieutenant-colonel Williams had improvised a flotilla of nineteen little boats on Lake Zürich, but he could not be expected to operate with the same success as earlier in the year on Lake Constance.

Hotze's subordinate Lieutenant-General Linken was in overall command of the remaining 8,000 or so troops (all Austrian), deployed at Sargans and towards the Grisons (see page 157). This figure excludes the 1,700 surviving men of Auffenberg now with Suvorov.

General André Massena enjoyed both superior numbers (76,000 available troops) and a central position. He had no inkling that the allies intended to attack him, but he determined to turn his advantages to good account by dealing simultaneous and concentrated blows by 56,000 of these men against three sectors of the over-extended allied deployment:

The main effort by 35,500 troops (divisions Mortier, Lorge, Ménard and Klein) against Korsakov in the neighbourhood of Zürich,

A subsidiary attack by the division of Soult (about 10,000 effectives) against Hotze's command on the lower Linth,

Finally two efforts on the right flank against the far-flung Austrian left, namely by the brigade of Molitor (3,000) on the upper Linth, and by the rest of Lecourbe's division (7,500) emerging by way of the Oberalp Pass into the valley of the Vorderrhein.

Astoundingly, Massena was acting without any accurate knowledge of the whereabouts of the army of Suvorov, which many presumed to be still in Italy, and yet his attack could scarcely have been better timed to dispose of Korsakov and Hotze before they could be reinforced.

Massena's attack on Korsakov was designed to pull the maldeployed Russian forces still further off balance. He directed the greater part of the division of Ménard to execute a feint at Stilli below Brugg well down the lower Aare, so drawing the Russian general Durasov north-west from his station at Baden. The division of Mortier (later reinforced from Klein's reserve division) was ordered to carry out a matching diversion against General Essen on the Russian left, by advancing along the Albisberg above Lake Zürich against Wollishofen. With the Russians thus being kept amused, Massena and his main force would advance against the Russian left centre and cross the Limmat at Dietikon-Fahre, where a bend of the river permitted a French battery to take the right bank under heavy fire. The near (left) bank was overgrown with dense brushwood, and the heavy fog on morning of the attack was going to give the French further cover for their concentration.

Between four and five on the morning of 25 September Lord Grenville's personal envoy William Wickham was awakened in Zürich by the sound of firing from the Limmat. Only a few streaks of light showed in the east, and in the darkness he could make out clearly the fuses of the howitzer shells which the French were lobbing from the far bank of the river. The

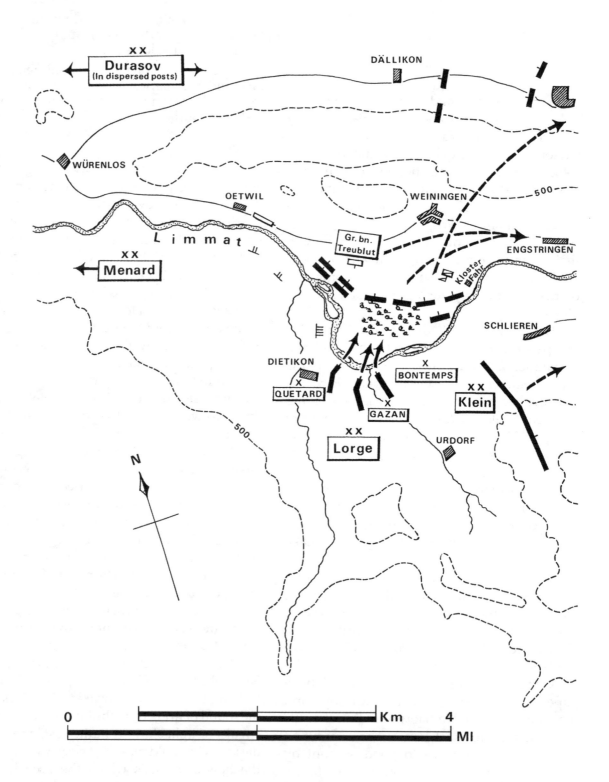

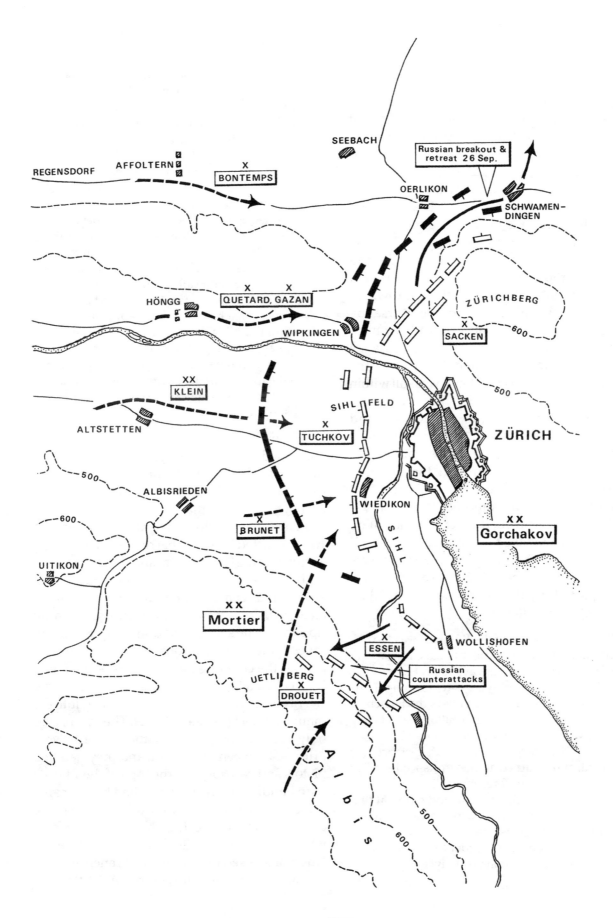

REGENSDORF

AFFOLTERN

SEEBACH

Russian breakout & retreat 26 Sep.

X
BONTEMPS

OERLIKON

SCHWAMEN-
DINGEN

ZÜRICHBERG

600

HÖNGG

X   X
QUETARD, GAZAN

WIPKINGEN

X
SACKEN

500

XX
KLEIN

SIHL FELD

ALTSTETTEN

ZÜRICH

X
TUCHKOV

500

ALBISRIEDEN

XX
Gorchakov

600

WIEDIKON

X
BRUNET

S I H L

UITIKON

XX
Mortier

WOLLISHOFEN

X
ESSEN

Russian counterattacks

UETLIBERG

X
DROUET

A
l
b
i
s

500

600

217

émigré colonel Lambert and the Austrian representative Major-General Johann Hiller were in no doubt that the French intended to cross in force at Dietikon, but until early in the afternoon Korsakov's attention was taken up almost wholly by the fighting south of Zürich at Wiedikon and Wollishofen, from where the Russians were launching clumsy but determined counterattacks up the Albisberg.

Already by 6.30 in the morning the French had made good their crossing at Dietikon, and the leading elements of the division of Lorge were fanning out towards Würenlos, Dällikon and Höngg. The bridgehead was wide and secure, and the French were now well based to direct their main thrust south-east towards Zürich. At two in the afternoon Korsakov perceived the true threat, and called on all available forces to meet the French outside the town. Even now he failed to occupy the commanding Zürichberg when it was still within reach, and he packed his troops into the narrow space of ground outside the Kloten and Winterthur gates, which left the Russians fighting at a disadvantage against the French, who were advancing through the outlying woods, vineyards, gardens, orchards and outbuildings. As the afternoon wore on 14-15,000 Russians crowded together in a square formation outside the town ramparts, just as if they had been engaged against the Turks. This impenetrable mass beat off every serious thrust on the part of the French, but was ravaged by the fire of the tirailleurs:

> The answering fire of the Russians was too mechanical and too regular to have much effect, and it seemed always subject to the orders of the officers who were directing it. In the intervals between the volleys the French horse artillery came up at a gallop, halted at twenty paces from the square, poured in torrents of canister, retired to safe distance to reload, and returned at the same speed—it was like effecting a breach in a living bastion… whole files fell under the frontal fire, while entire ranks were carried away from the flanks. The Russians trampled their dying comrades under foot in order to close up and reload by their platoons and divisions…[5]

All the counterattacks were in vain. Wickham reported that

> The hedges and vineyards all about the villages were full of wounded and dead Russians, though I do not recollect having seen five dead Frenchmen on the whole ground. This is easily accounted for from the nature of the country, which is particularly well calculated for the French manner of fighting, and from the mode of attack of the Russians who appear to trust only to the bayonet, against which the French never attempt to stand… It was a melancholy thing for those who could understand them to hear the soldiers on every side repeating the name of 'Suvorov,' and calling on him to come to their assistance. The really expected every moment that he would have appeared on the top of the Albis, on which side they knew he was approaching. At about nine in the evening all the surviving troops were shut up in the town with the baggage and wounded in a state of the most horrible confusion and disorder.[6]

Even now the Russians might have continued to put up a fight from behind the ramparts, if news had not reached them of disasters which had overtaken their Austrian and Swiss allies to the east.

The central sector of the allied deployment was protected by water barriers—Lake Zürich, a stretch of the lower Linth, and the Walensee—and the French assault therefore had a semi-amphibious character. For days now *général de division* Nicolas Jean Soult had dressed himself up as a private soldier and done outpost duty to investigate the positions of Hotze's troops behind the channels and marshes of the lower Linth. At 2.30 in the morning of 25 September twenty French of the advance party slid into the main channel opposite Schänis. They were clad only in shirts and breeches, their swords were gripped between their teeth, and they had tied pistols and cartridges to the tops of their heads with handkerchiefs. They reached the far bank, pulled up lightly-built rafts by ropes, and in the darkness and dense fog the equivalent of a whole battalion was ferried across before the Austrians raised the alarm. The French effected a similar passage downstream at Schloss

Grynau, and a crossing by boats from Lachen across the head of Lake Zürich to Schmerikon.

At four in the morning the noise of artillery summoned Lieutenant-General Hotze from his headquarters at Kaltbrunn. He found his troops at Schänis fighting well and in good heart, but a further alarm drew him towards Weesen on the Walensee, and this brave and active old soldier was shot dead when he ran into two battalions of French who were concealed in a wood. The whole of the valley was hidden in mist until late in the day, which facilitated the passage of Soult's main force, and the orphaned, demoralised and disorientated Austrians fell back towards Lichtensteig. The base of Williams' flotilla at Rapperschwyl was now untenable, and he had to abandon his boats, join his little

body of Austrians to the Swiss regiment of Roverea, and escape towards Rheineck.

The Russians had known and trusted Hotze, and the news of his death induced panic among the troops heaped up in and around Zürich. On the morning of 26 September Korsakov's army fled in disorganised mobs, abandoning to the French 5,200 men (mostly wounded) in the town, nine colours, nearly all their baggage and artillery, and whatever was left in the money chest after it had been plundered by the Cossacks.

Massena sent only 250 cavalry in close pursuit, but the Russians continued northwards with undiminished velocity though Eglisau and Winterthur, and eventually coalesced at the end of the month in the 'camp of Dörflingen' behind

Massena's triumph at Zürich

the shelter of the Rhine between Lake Constance and Schaffhausen. They were joined by Condé's royalists, a corps of 2,400 Bavarian auxiliaries and the 2,000 Swiss troops of the regiments of Bachmann, Roverea and Salis. Only on 6 October was an officer finally assigned to tour the army to establish how many Russians remained with the colours, and it emerged that 8,000 men had failed to survive the battle of 25 September.

Another 3,740 Russians were lost in a confused fight on 7 October, when Korsakov attempted to push the French back from the left bank of the Rhine. The Russians ran into considerably greater forces than they had expected, and the action ended with the loss of Constance town and the Russian footholds on the left bank.

JELLACHICH AND LINKEN ON THE UPPER LINTH

At the risk of running a little ahead of our story, it will probably be useful to complete the narrative of the disintegration of the allied offensive on the northern flank of the Alps. The forces in question were those of the Austrian far left or eastern wing, comprising the commands of Major-General Jellachich and Lieutenant-General Linken.

According to his instructions, Jellachich marched his troops from Sargans along the southern shore of the Walensee on 24 September, and reached Mollis, where the upper Linth widened into a little plain. He was (unknown to him) perilously close to the offensive of Soult which was about to break across the lower Linth, and he attacked dutifully on 25 September. The 84th demi-brigade held on successfully behind the Linth, then counterattacked in force on the 26th, its confidence bolstered by the victory of Soult over Hotze. At two in the afternoon Jellachich began to fall back towards Walenstadt, and so another body of Austrians was removed from the scene of operations in central Switzerland.

The campaign of Linken's 3-4,000 Austrians on the uppermost Linth no longer had any relevance to the scheme of the general allied offensive, which was already lost beyond redemption by the evening of 25 September, but it might have afforded direct assistance to Suvorov, by giving him an assured exit from the potential trap of the Muotatal. Linken's little command constituted the extreme left flank of the forces which had been assembling for the offensive, and its first objectives were to climb the mountain massif which reached up to the north-west of the great trench of the valley of the Vorderrhein, descend on the far side to eliminate the French forces scattered along the Sernftal, then swing to the right down the upper Linth to Glarus. Once at Glarus he was supposed to be in contact with the forces of Jellachich and Hotze, and ready to join in the progress of the allied left wing westwards to the rendezvous at Zürich.

On the appointed 25 September Linken's troops passed the mountains by the Segnas, Panixer and Kisten passes, and made their way down the near-precipitous slopes which reached down to the little Sernftal. The Austrians descended among thirteen astonished companies (1,300 men) of the 76th demi-brigade, which surrendered en masse at Wichlen. These men had come under the tactical command of *général de brigade* Gabriel Jean Molitor (the future marshal), who put the Austrian numbers at 9,000.

On 26 September Linken reunited his forces at Schwanden, and in a day of scrappy fighting he pushed back the 3rd battalion of the 84th demi-brigade behind the town of Glarus, which remained as a no man's land between the Austrians and the French. A first batch of reinforcements from Soult (the 1st and 3rd battalions of the 44th) encouraged Molitor to attack the Austrian positions at Sturmigen, Ennetbühls and Haltengütern on the 27th. He was beaten off, and in the evening he had to fight hard to contain a new Austrian push against Glarus. Both parties knew that the entrance to the Klöntal lay just on the 'French' side of Glarus, and gave access by way of the Pragel pass and the Muotatal to central Switzerland, but neither was aware of how crucial that was to be to the welfare of Suvorov's stranded army. Molitor still assumed that Suvorov was in Italy, while at noon on the 28th Linken received a message from an Austrian captain (penned a few hours

220

earlier from the southern foot of the Chinzig Pass), telling him that Suvorov was marching *west* out of the Muotatal on Schwyz according to plan.

Further reinforcements enabled Molitor to attack in the strength of five battalions at three in the morning of 29 September. The main force advanced along the road which led up the floor of the valley from Glarus to Mitlödi, while flanking columns took to the mountain flanks on either side. The Austrian troops under their veteran general were fighting well, but at ten in the morning Linken received the second of two reports from a spy (possible a double agent) which assured him that the Muotatal was now in the hands of the French. Suvorov appeared to be totally beyond reach, and, in the absence of any news from him or from Hotze, Linken ordered his troops to disengage and retreat up the Linth to the Sernftal, and ultimately back over the mountains to the Vorderrhein.

Thus the forces on which Suvorov relied for support had found their offensive anticipated by the enemy, and themselves driven back to the north and east by an average of thirty-five kilometres—a significant distance when we consider the intervening geographical obstacles, the massing of the victorious French, and the bad state of Korsakov's troops in particular. The French were thus in a position to bottle up Suvorov in the Muotatal-Pragel corridor by sealing up the western exit in the neighbourhood of Schwyz, and the eastern exit along the stretch from the Klöntaler See to Glarus.

Massena was alerted to the presence of Suvorov in Switzerland by a letter which reached him from Lecourbe on 26 September, informing him that a force of Russians was descending the valley of the Reuss from the St. Gotthard. Almost certainly in response to this message Soult ordered the division of Mortier to make for Schwyz by way of Einsiedeln by forced marches. On the night of 28/29 September the left-hand brigade (Brunet) staggered into Schwyz in a state of exhaustion, while the right-hand brigade (Drouet) reached Zug.

In the circumstances, the degree of moral domination which Suvorov had achieved over Lecourbe was remarkable. Lecourbe wrote again on 28 September that the troops of his division had once taken for granted that they would continue to win every encounter, but now their morale was so fragile that he would have to stay with them at Seedorf. On the 30th Massena accompanied the shaken Lecourbe on a reconnaissance up the Schächental, and they found no trace of the Russians except discarded muskets, stragglers and other material and human wreckage. These sights convinced Massena that Suvorov's army was now beyond the Chinzig Pass in the Muotatal, and he accordingly hastened to Flüelen, embarked on a boat of the Republican flotilla to make the journey to Brunnen, and galloped on to Schwyz to join Soult and order Mortier to push into the Muotatal with his available forces.

NOTES TO CHAPTER 10

1   Lewenshtern, 1900, CIII, No. 3, 489
2   Roverea, 1848, II,222
3   Levenshtern, 1900, CIII, No. 3, 489
4   Wickham to Grenville, 28 August 1799, Wickham, 1870, II,185
5   Masson, 1859, 363-4
6   Wickham to Grenville, Ravensburg, 30 September 1799, Wickham, 1870, II,228, 232.

11
COMBAT, EVASION AND TERMINATION

Clausewitz writes of the extremity of emotions in warfare, and the effect of the collapse of hopes which had been stretched to the utmost. He was not referring to any specific event, but the reality applies to the scenes at Suvorov's headquarters on 28 September 1799. When the bad news accumulated in ever more circumstantial detail the field-marshal paced up and down, clenching his fists and grinding his teeth in the effort to find the words the express his fury and frustrations. He finally broke out in his harsh voice and 'railed especially against Korsakov, the Austrian generals and Archduke Charles himself. His voice rose to a shout as he accused them of envy and treachery.'[1]

Suvorov summoned a council of war to review what had been established so far. Korsakov had been defeated and the whereabouts of his broken army was completely unknown. Hotze was dead, and his successor Lieutenant-General Franz Petrasch had recoiled to Lichtensteig. Weyrother writes that

> this blow was painful enough in itself, and all the more hurtful for Field-Marshal Suvorov because he had been confident of proceeding to that one final step that would immortalise his fame—a prospect now set at naught as if by a lighting strike. He was confronted with new difficulties, and there was no immediately obvious way of resolving them and reviving the operation which had been in mind… The course most appealing to the enterprising spirit of the field-marshal was to march to the attack by way of Schwyz and strike at the rear of the enemy as they advanced from the Limmat to the Rhine… he actually ordered it to be put into effect and mounted horse ready to set out. The alternative was to march to Glarus, from where, strengthened by the command of Linken, we could easily have forced out way through Weesen and Walenstadt to unite with

the entire corps of Lieutenant-General Petrasch. But this seemed to that tempestuous old man to smack too much of a retreat—a manoeuvre he always maintained was beyond his comprehension… Only after exhausting all the relevant arguments was it possible to extract from him the permission for the Austrian general Auffenberg to set out the same evening for the Pragel Pass, from where he would push forward to Glarus and, united with Linken, secure the exit from the Muotatal for the Russians.[2]

Major-General Auffenberg was present at the meeting, and had taken the leading part in representing that Suvorov's preferred advance by way of Schwyz would have decanted his army among his enemies without any support, and led to the capture of his entire force.[3] Auffenberg was now commissioned to advance his brigade over the Pragel, then break through the French to unite with Linken in the neighbourhood of Glarus on the 29th, thus securing the eastern end of the Muotatal-Klöntal passage. Auffenberg and his 1,700 surviving Austrians began the climb on the evening of the 28th.

29 SEPTEMBER

THE COUNCIL

Suvorov convened a full council of his generals on the 29th, and according to the Russian diarists and historians it was an affair charged with emotion. Two at least of the details thus transmitted are patent impossibilities, as we shall see, and it would have been fully in keeping with Suvorov's character to have stage-managed the whole event to impress his generals and posterity.[4]

Bagration was the first to enter the chamber, and he found Suvorov in his dress uniform, and striding up and down and declaiming against Korsakov: 'Parade-ground soldiers! … Doing up gaiter buttons! … What overweening self-confidence! … Good God! … There is nothing clever about being beaten. To have destroyed so many men in a single day! And what men they were!'[5] Bagration withdrew unseen.

Grand Prince Constantine and the rest of the generals arrived en masse some time later, and after a short silence Suvorov fastened the gathering with a quick fiery glance, and exclaimed in an unexpectedly cheerful tone: 'Korsakov has been beaten and his corps scattered! Jellachich and Linken have left us in the lurch [Suvorov could not possibly have known of Linken's retreat]. Our whole plan has been thwarted!' Suvorov raged against the Austrians for everything he had had to endure from them since he had entered Italy, and most recently Thugut's crime of whisking Archduke Charles from Switzerland, which had made the defeat of Korsakov inevitable, and was responsible for the plight of his own army. He recalled the five days lost waiting for the mules at Taverne, and drew a comparison with the situation of Peter the Great when he was surrounded by Turks and Tartars on the Pruth in 1711:

> What can we do now? [he continued] to go back is disgraceful; I have never retreated. To advance to Schwyz is impossible—Massena has over 60,000 troops, and all the men we have left amount to scarcely 20,000. We are devoid of provisions, ammunition and artillery… We can turn to nobody for help… We are on the verge of disaster! … All that remains for us is to rely on Almighty God and the bravery and self-sacrifice of my troops! We are Russians! God with us! Save the honour of Russia and its sovereign! Save the son of the Emperor!

Suvorov threw himself at the feet of Constantine, who raised him up and embraced him amid mutual sobbing. Derfelden assured Suvorov on behalf of all the generals that he could count on their courage and dedication, whereupon the field-marshal took on new life: 'Yes, we are indeed Russians, and with the help of God there is nothing we cannot overcome!'[6]

The Russian sources now describe the council as turning to the possible courses of action. The first to come under consideration was to implement the original intention of advancing on Schwyz, as proposed by the Austrian staff officers [which was the reverse of the truth]. Suvorov commented that he had believed that the scheme had been practicable on the day before, but he was now convinced that it was too dangerous.

More realistic was the notion of retracing the army's steps to Altdorf and back up the Reuss to Amsteg, from where the route up the Maderanertal and over the Chrüzli Pass led to the Vorderrhein. This was rejected, because Lecourbe stood in the way, and he was known to have been reinforced.

In these circumstances the council determined on [or rather confirmed] the course of breaking out of the eastern exit of the Muotatal-Pragel-Klöntal passage and uniting with Linken at Glarus [i.e. contradicting the sense of Suvorov's alleged opening statement]. For this purpose the Russian advance guard under Bagration and the division of Schveikovsky would support the efforts of the Austrian brigade of Auffenberg. The main body of the Russian rearguard under Rosenberg was completing its descent from the Chinzig Pass, and it must now secure the western exit of the Muotatal towards Schwyz, while the rest of the troops were filing away east over the Pragel.

Once united at Glarus, the army would march the short distance north to the Walensee, and make for Sargans by the road which led along the lake shore by way of Kerenzerberg. The army had rations for only five days, but these would now have to be eked out to ten, and the difference made up by whatever cheese or butter could be found along the way.

These points had already been determined on the 28th, and Weyrother tried to persuade Suvorov to march at once for Glarus, and abandon the pack animals still passing the Chinzig, for they had little worth carrying. It was in vain, for Suvorov and his generals needed the time to give full vent to their rancour against things Austrian.

AUFFENBERG ON THE PRAGEL

Auffenberg's 1,700 Austrian fusiliers and Croatian light infantry (the regiment of Kerpen and one battalion of Gradiscaner Croats) had struck out along the new direction of march on the evening before. The Austrians left the Starzlen brook above Muotathal village, and picked their way up through the woods which lined the steep right-hand side of the valley leading towards the Pragel Pass. Climbing more gently now they continued to the north-east, while the murmur of the Starzlen died away to their left, and the far side of the valley reared up as a mighty and continuous rock wall, streaked at intervals by the white threads and plumes of waterfalls. The Starzlen could be heard once again as the column neared the head of the valley, and after some two hours of marching the troops reached the left bank of the stream, and followed it through a zone of dank woods to where the landscape opened up into the amphitheatre of the Guetentalboden. It was very likely here that Auffenberg called a halt in the darkness and his troops bivouacked for the night.

First light on 29 September showed that the hollow was spacious and lined with fine stands of larch, but when the Austrians reached the far end they had to address themselves to a brutally punishing climb up a steep zig-zag path. The Pragel Pass proper—the Bärenloch—lay just beyond the top. The bare eroded rocks of the Silberen massif heaved themselves up to the Austrians' right. To their left the Miserenstock mountain spread out towards its base in pleated meadows which offered excellent positions to

THE ASCENT OF THE PRAGEL PASS

anyone who had it in mind to dispute the passage, and it was probably here, if not on the ascent from the Guetentalboden, that the Austrians exchanged their first shots with the outposts of the 84th demi-brigade that they are known to have encountered on the near side of the pass.

The Austrians pushed the enemy down the far side of the pass through a close-set country of bluffs and woods. A zig-zag descent brought them to gently-sloping meadows which merged with the long and narrow plain at the head of the mountain lake of the Klöntaler See.[7] However the French were disputing every inch of ground,

and the terrain told in their favour once the fighting reached the lake, for the only path hugged the northern shore, where it led under crags and woods which descended nearly vertically to the water. The numerical odds were also turning against the Austrians, for the 84th (of Lecourbe's division) was receiving its first reinforcements from the 44th (of Soult's division). Auffenberg therefore suspended his attacks for the day, and fell back a little way towards the Pragel, knowing that the leading elements of the Russian army would be at hand to help him on the 30th.

THE PRAGEL PASS—THE FINAL CLIMB

30 SEPTEMBER

ROSENBERG'S BATTLE IN THE MUOTATAL, THE FIRST DAY

By the end of September Suvorov's troops were engaged hotly on two fronts—in the east where the leading elements were fighting their way towards the eastern exit of the Muotatal-Pragel-Klöntal passage, and to the rear, where the corps of Rosenberg was in combat with the French who were now seeking to break into the Muotatal from the west.

In detail the Russo-Austrian forces were located as follows on the morning of 30 September:

Auffenberg's brigade of Austrians (down to 1,700 effectives) in action in the Klöntal,

Bagration with the Russian advance guard (2,500) arriving in support,

Suvorov with the leading corps (Derfelden's) and two Cossack regiments crossing the Pragel,

Rosenberg's corps about to do battle in the Muotatal.

The task of Rosenberg's corps was to hold the Muotatal until the rest of the army was safely on its way to Glarus by way of the Pragel Pass and the Klöntal. His main consideration was therefore to win time, which could be done only by fighting an action in some depth along the Muotatal from near the western narrows to

VIEW EAST FROM THE SUMMIT OF THE PRAGEL

226

the neighbourhood of Muotathal village. It would have been dangerous to deploy the main force forward, for then Rosenberg would have laid himself open to being turned by his right flank, where a path descended into the valley from Illgau to the north.

Rosenberg therefore decided to impose a delay on the French by forcing them to fight their up the length of the valley through a screen of outposts, while he held his main body close in front of the Convent. Here he could deploy his forces over an area of level ground measuring some 1,200 metres by 800, and fight to full advantage against the French when their advance encountered a choke point formed by a double barrier—to the north a projection of the steep and heavily-wooded Zinglenwald heights which forced the Muota into a pronounced bend, and the bushy-banked Rambach stream which ran to the river from the heights on the southern side of the valley.

Rosenberg positioned his troops accordingly. Out in front Major Ivan Vasilevich Sabaneev set out a battalion of the Kashkin Jäger and a sotnia of Cossacks as a light screen from the western narrows back to Ried, and up on the right at Illgau. Lieutenant-General Rehbinder commanded the advance guard proper (Rehbinder musketeer regiment, a further battalion of the Kashkin Jäger, and the dismounted Cossacks of the Posdeev and Kurnakov regiments) along the left or southern bank of the Muota from the Vordere Brücke back to the Kirchen Brücke. Lastly the main body (musketeer regiments Miloradovich, Förster and Veletsky) stood immediately before the Convent. The regiment of Tyrtov remained up the Hürital, to guard against any push by Lecourbe over the Chinzig Pass. Having done all he could, Rosenberg awaited events 'with that philosophical calm which distinguished him in all his actions.'[8]

At two in the afternoon thick swarms of French tirailleurs emerged into the valley from the narrows, followed by the main force of Mortier's 108th demi-brigade with thumping drums. Sabaneev's Jäger, who had spread out in two lines across the whole width of the valley, duelled with their French counterparts, and fell

back by stages until they reached Rehbinder and the advance guard on a level with the Rambach stream towards three in the afternoon.

Rehbinder opened a lively fire with his musketry and mountain artillery, then counterattacked so effectively that he not only recovered a cannon which had been lost during the first retreat, but gained a howitzer from the French. Rosenberg meanwhile held back his main force until he could be certain that the French were not sending a flanking column through Illgau—a delay which his enemies were willing to attribute to a long-standing feud with Rehbinder.

Finally at four in the afternoon Rosenberg advanced his six fresh battalions, while his dismounted Cossacks took to the slopes on either side and worked around the enemy flanks. By a French account the 108th had been 'put together from detachments from various demi-brigades, and its cobbled-together battalions did not have the same consistency as units from a single body.'[9] The French had already shown some signs of disarray during the fight with Rehbinder, and despite what are described as 'stern measures' they now fled in near-total disorder through the valley narrows and over the plain on the far side. Mortier rallied whatever troops he could at Ibach towards eight in the evening, then fell back to cover the immediate approaches to Schwyz. It is a measure of the French disintegration that a sotnia of Cossacks was able to gallop across the meadows as far as Ingebohl, near the angle of Lake Lucerne.

Rosenberg committed the full force of his available troops only towards the end of the action, or a maximum of about 7.000 after we deduct the wastage since the beginning of the Swiss campaign and the regiment of Tyrtov and other elements of the division of Förster still to descend from the Hürital. His losses on 30 September are unknown. The 67th demi-brigade (above) did not have the time to take part in the action, which would have put the French total at very much less than the figure of 8,000 quoted in the Russian sources. Mortier lost 143 killed and 241 wounded, and the nuns recorded that the Russians brought back some eighty prisoners to the Convent.

THE PUSH TO THE KLÖNTALER SEE

Auffenberg's troops spent a dismal night in the dense fog beyond the Pragel, and a still more unpleasant early morning when the French (the first and second battalions of the 84th demi-brigade, reinforced from the 44th) opened a counterattack. What happened next has been laden by Russian and French historians with so much unsupported detail that the facts are not easy to recover. It is known that Bagration arrived in the scene in the course of the day with the powerful Russian advance guard of elite troops—the two-battalion strong Jäger regiments of Bagration and Miller, the four combined grenadier battalions of Lomonosov, Dendrygin, Sanaev and Kalemin, and one regiment of Cossacks. If we combine the highly-coloured accounts of Gachot (1904) and Milyutin (1856-8), together with Milyutin's map, we have Bagration preparing to launch a counterattack in the Gampellegen hollow about half way down from the Pragel pass. We have Surovov arriving in person, and summoning the French in vain to surrender. Constantine too was present, and could not be dissuaded from venturing into danger with the forward troops.

According to these authorities Lieutenant-Colonel Tsukato was marching the Miller Jäger over the Schwialp spur to the left, or north. The grenadiers were deployed in line across the lower ground—the Lomonosov and Kalemin battalions on the left wing, and the Dendrygin and Sanaev battalions on the right—while Bagration led the Bagration Jäger in a further column up the slopes to the right. The flanking columns now closed in from either side. At the same time the grenadiers beat the charge and came at the French from the front. The encounter ended with the French being pushed down the plain at the head of the Klöntaler See, and then

THE KLÖNTAL

228

through the darkness along the track that led along the northern shore of the lake.

A different perspective is offered by the accounts of Auffenberg and Lieutenant-Colonel Sir Henry Clinton. Their recollections correspond so closely that the Englishman's account is here reproduced verbatim:

In the morning of the 30th the marshal began his march, and his advance guard arrived in time to support General Auffenberg in the attack he was preparing to make, but the enemy having been reinforced by part of the division of Soult from the other side of the Linth, and by the detachment which had been opposed to General Linken, who had retired from the height of Glarus, sent a summons to General Auffenberg to surrender, and without waiting for his answer, began a vigorous attack. As the road required their marching by a single file, the advance troops were ordered to retire to induce the enemy to commit themselves in a plain at the west end of the lake, where everything was disposed to take advantage of their orders, but two battalions of Russians which had been destined to gain both flanks of the enemy having shown themselves too soon, the greater part were enabled to effect a retreat, but in so great confusion, that they suffered themselves to be pursued, with considerable slaughter, along the narrow path, to the other extremity of the lake.[10]

This indicates that the action took place not in the neighbourhood of the Gampellegen hollow, but much closer to the lake.

In any event Molitor had lost sixty men killed and 120 wounded in this first clash, and the Reverend Mother entered in the Convent journal that 'a badly wounded French major from the 84th demi-brigade was brought down to us from the Pragel, and admitted to the Convent at the request of General Auffenberg. His name was Peter Bodoceur from Amiens, major and adjutant of the second battalion of the 84th. His attendant was a brave lad from Lower Alsace.'[11]

Glarus lay just seven kilometres beyond the further, or eastern end of the Klöntaler See, and even in their exhausted state the Russians and Austrians might have arrived there before daybreak on 1 October, if Molitor had not decided to make a stand. He chose his ground well, for the little patch of open ground at Seerüti, at the end of the lake, enabled his troops to take the allies under concentrated fire when the emerged from the lakeshore path. He spread tirailleurs across the clearing, while he packed 150 grenadiers into a loopholed chapel (since vanished) atop a mound, which afforded him a ready-made redoubt.

The first of the allied troops to show their noses were the leading Austrians of the Kerpen regiment, who appeared from a thicket of willows and were met by a mighty volley at point blank range. Bagration committed the Russian grenadiers in four attacks, all of which were beaten off, as was a final desperate assault by a company of volunteers, which left Constantine's aide-de-camp Colonel Lang mortally wounded. Streaming rain and heavy snow were now falling through the darkness, and although the full division of Schveikovsky closed up on the lake shore during the night, there could be no question of dislodging the French under these conditions.

Bagration had to be content with positioning parties out to the flanks, ready to open fire at daylight on 1 October. He dispatched three bodies altogether:

1. Local guides led Lieutenant-Colonel Tsukato with the Miller Jäger, four companies of Austrians and two sotnias of dismounted Cossacks on a long hike up a mountain valley which ran parallel to the lake, between the Schijen ridge to the north and the Mättlistock-Dejenstock ridge to the south. The hardest part of the trek was the climb from the plain at the western edge of the lake, but the most dangerous was when the party crossed the summit of the southern ridge and descended the steep grassy slopes of Planngen to reach its attacking position to the rear of the Seerüti clearing.

2. The Bagration Jäger and the combined grenadier battalions are known to have concentrated themselves on the immediate right flank of the enemy, which they probably reached by clambering up the narrow Bergwald which lined the foot of the Ober-Herberg rock face

above the Seerüti clearing. It was a much shorter route than Tsukato's, though much more exposed to detection.

3. Bagration's thoughts also turned to the southern side of the lake, and he ordered Gryazev to take a battalion of the Rosenberg grenadier regiment and try to find a way by which he could take up position on the French left flank. As a captain Gryazev was greatly flattered by this commission, and he took off with the second battalion of the regiment, together with an officer of the Austrian staff. They forded the Chlue stream, and made some progress along the lake shore until they reached a stretch (probably near the Bärentritt) where the mountains descended like a wall and the water was too deep to wade. Gryazev sent the Austrian to carry the bad news to Constantine, and reported in person to General Derfelden as the corps commander: 'I found him sitting by a fire drinking coffee; I related all the details of my mission, how far I had managed to go, and how I had found it impossible to push any further, and was forced to return. He heard me out with Teutonic phlegm, and then, in the same cold-blooded way, and without taking the cup from his lips, he remarked: "I was not the one who sent you; that is nothing to do with me."'[12]

The Russians could only wait in the cold and wet for the coming of the light.

Viewing west from the Rambach down the Muotatal. the most intensive fighting on 29 September and 1 October took place immediately to the front. A modern bridge spans the Muota on the right centre, and the white tower of Ried church may be seen above the apex of the barn roof on the left.

1 October

ROSENBERG'S BATTLE IN THE MUOTATAL, THE SECOND DAY

The Russians in the Muotatal passed a restless night, in the full knowledge that they would have to fight a new action on the next day. The same considerations weighed with Rosenberg as on 30 September, and he disposed his troops in much the same way, except that the musketeer regiment of Veletsky did the whole service of outposts and advance guard. It was positioned two kilometres in front of the main position and on both sides of the Muota, with one to its battalions on the right bank in front of the Bettbach to the east of Ried, and the other on the left bank behind the Tröliger Bach.

As before, the main body was packed in tightly in front of the Convent, in the zone between the Rambach stream and the group of chalets at Schachen. The regiment of Miloradvich was dispersed across the front in skirmishing order. The Kashkin Jäger and the regiment of Rehbinder formed the first line behind, if 'line' is not a misnomer, for these troops (like all the rest of the Russian infantry) were concealed behind barns and walls. The Don Cossacks extended the two flanks to the heights on either side. As the senior major-general of the Cossacks, Semen Ivanovich Kurnakov placed one or two of his available regiments to the right, and the Denisov Cossacks on the left. Adrian Karpovich Denisov mentions that the latter regiment was stationed by a wood of tall trees, and that he arranged with the commander of the nearby infantry to leave the ground in front unoccupied, so that the Cossacks would have a clear space over which to attack. The Grekov regiment, the remaining unit of Denisov's brigade, was up ahead with the outposts.

The regiments of Mansurov and Fertsch and the complement of mountain guns made up the second 'line,' which was grouped three hundred metres to the rear and just behind the Grossmatt barn and the other available cover. Closer to Schachen the regiment of Förster stood in reserve in the Widmen meadows near the Hundenen chalet, and finally the regiment of Tyrtov was still located up the Hürital guarding the descent from the Chinzig. This time Rosenberg probably had between 8 and 9,000 troops at his immediate disposal, or rather more than on 30 September.

Massena and Mortier had meanwhile gathered all the forces within reach in the neighbourhood of Schwyz—the inglorious 108th demi-brigade, the remainder of the division of Mortier (50th, 53rd, 57th and 100th demi-brigades), with two companies of the 38th, the 67th (recently disembarked from the lake) and two weak squadrons of the 1st Regiment of Dragoons. The numbers have been put between 3,553 (Gachot) and an altogether extravagant 15,000, with an estimate of 9,000-10,000 (Reding-Biberegg) making more sense. In any event Massena concentrated all the forces at his disposal with the ambition of destroying the Russians remaining in the Muotatal, though he asserted afterwards that 'the object of the attack was less to achieve a decisive result on that particular day, than to delay Suvorov's march. I was bringing up forces against him from every side, and I wished to give them the time to arrive at their various destinations.'[13] He aimed not only to enter the valley by the western narrows, as before, but to direct a powerful flanking column out to the left to descend from Illgau much closer to Muotathal village—which justified the precautions which Rosenberg had taken against this eventuality.

The fog dispersed at about nine in the morning of 1 October, by when the main body of the French had negotiated the narrows from Oberschönenbuch, repaired the stone bridge over the gorge of the lower Muota, and was ready to attack. The lone regiment of Veletsky opened the action with a lively fusillade, then fell back skirmishing, and held its position behind Ried until the French reinforced their advance guard and brought up their artillery.

For the next two kilometres the French advanced eastwards up the valley unchecked. Their tirailleurs pushed back the small parties of Russian infantry and dismounted Cossacks which tried to shoot them up from the mountain flanks, while the main force marched confidently with beating drums and sounding music. The Veletsky regiment had by now fallen back all

231

the way to the Russian reserve, and so the clash between the French and the Russian main force in front of Muotathal village was of great intensity from the first moments.

Mortier opened fire with his ten cannon and howitzers. Denisov's Cossacks were standing in line by the wood, and 'the shot flew into it and tore great chunks from its side, while it gave out crunching sounds from within and the trees began to totter. The danger could hardly have been more obvious, but the Cossacks stood immovable for as long as I saw fit not to order them to advance.'[14]

The French arrayed themselves in dense columns and pressed towards the bottleneck in front of the Convent. There were three concentrations of effort—one on the right (northern) bank of the Muota seeking to gain the northern mountain flank, another which skirted the corresponding heights on the southern side of the valley, and the third in the centre following the left bank of the Muota. Rosenberg brought up his second line in immediate support of his first, and the battle was joined along the Rambach stream, and on the north bank of the Muota up to the rocky hollow above Ober Rüteli. Officers were fighting like madmen, and enemy wounded were finished off without mercy. Massena writes of 'mêlées in which the troops were striking out

Rosenberg's Battle in the Muotatal, 1 October

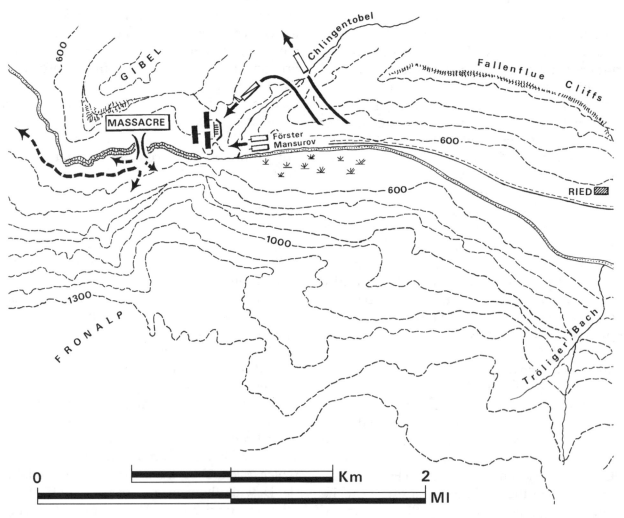

232

with musket butts and bayonets for hours on end. Cannon, colours, prisoners and patches of the field were taken and re-taken several times in the course of the day.'[15]

For a time the French enjoyed an advantage through the power of their artillery, which greatly outgunned the Russian 2-pounders, but the Russians began to push forward at one in the afternoon and 'nothing could withstand the steadfastness of the Russian attack.'[16] The third of the Russian attacks was aided by the Veletsky Musketeers, who had come up from the reserve, and worked their way around to the French flanks unnoticed by Mortier in the smoke. From about three in the afternoon the 108th executed a staged withdrawal by companies, which contrasted with its flight on the day before, but the 67th over to the left was beginning to disintegrate. A native of Illgau records that the Cossacks

rode forward with such impetus that they came together on the Rambach from both flanks. I noticed one of their horsemen who behaved magnificently. He was mounted on a white horse, and he rampaged down the path from Muotathal church till he reached the Rambach stream, cutting down everyone who stood in his way. The Rambach wood and the path leading through it were packed with fleeing French, whereupon the horseman

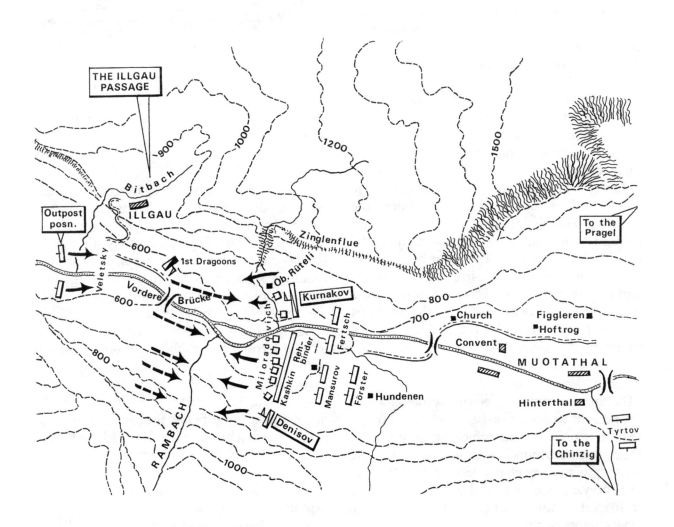

233

came at them from their rear, and defended the path until the rest of the Russians could arrive.[17]

A blast of canister at point-blank range enabled the French to disengage for a few valuable moments, while the little party of the 1st Dragoons enabled Mortier to cover his exposed left flank. The combat of the previous day had alerted him to the danger of being trapped in the western narrows of the Muotatal. Here the mountains closed in abruptly from the two flanks, and the wooded gorge fell near-vertically to where the Muota stream rushed through a hideous, winding slot-like channel of grey rocks. The only passage lay by way of the track, which crossed to the left (southern) side of the gorge by a narrow stone bridge.* Since morning the French sappers had been casting up a respectable earthwork atop a prominent mound—a south-eastern outcrop of the Gibel mountain—which rose in a commanding position on the right bank at the entrance to the narrows. Known variously as the Linggis Mattli or the Hinter-Iberger-Stutz, it now accommodated five pieces of artillery, while parties of infantry extended the line of defence as far as the mountain to the north.

The Russians would have stuck fast against this obstacle if a small column of infantry volunteers and two hundred Cossacks (possibly mounted) had not gained the left flank of the covering French infantry, rolled it up, and continued their advance over the mound and cut down the gunners. The main body of the Russians had been waiting in column of march, and Lieutenant-General Förster now launched it in the direction of the bridge. Within minutes the tactical reversal of the French was transmuted into a massacre.

THE OLD MUOTA BRIDGE, AS SEEN FROM THE WEST. IT WAS BUILT IN 1580, AND COLLAPSED IN MARCH 1800 AS A RESULT OF THE DAMAGE SUSTAINED IN 1799. IT STOOD 157 FEET ABOVE THE LEVEL OF THE MUOTA.

The timber covering and sides of the bridge had been destroyed by fire, leaving the narrow stone structure unguarded. An initial two battalions of French crossed safely, though in fair confusion, but the rest began to crowd together in a mass of infantry, dragoons, ammunition wagons and artillery pieces. Panic was augmented when two of the ammunition carts blew up. Men tottered over the edge, and in their terror they grabbed at their comrades, so that whole clumps fell over the side in a way that on two occasions left the bridge completely clear. It was just as dangerous to attempt to negotiate the gorge below the bridge, and some of the French who succeeded in reaching the far side found that they were unable to climb the rocks.

Major-General Denisov received orders to exploit towards the bridge with his wing of Don Cossacks. He was unwilling to risk his full two

---

*The abutments may be seen thirty metres above the present wooden bridge, which was built in 1810. The present road, which continues down the right bank around the Unter Gibel and on to Schwyz, was completed in 1864. In 1799 the way to Schwyz descended to the old bridge, and followed the left bank through Oberschönenbuch.

regiments in this difficult terrain, and so he detached Colonel Petr Matveeich Grekov with three hundred of the men, and came up behind with a party of his own regiment. Denisov could hear the Muota in its ravine long before he rode down the steep slopes and came in sight of the rushing waters and the bridge, which he found in a perilous state. On the far side he was joined by an Austrian officer and an officer of the Russian Jäger, both of whom could speak French, and he asked them to go out with waving handkerchiefs and call on the scattered enemy to give themselves up. Before long they returned with the French adjutant-general Lacour and a body of troops, who surrendered unconditionally. Denisov returned the Frenchman's sword, and sent him and his officers back to Rosenberg.

One minute later Grekov returned at the gallop with his Cossacks to report that he had emerged from the narrows into a broad valley, and seen fresh and powerful forces of the enemy advancing to the counterattack. Denisov sent the Cossacks back to the right bank of the Muota, to prevent them being caught on the near side of the bridge, but Grekov (who was not a professional gunner) was seized with the inspiration of turning one of the captured pieces against the French, and he piled the scattered cartridges in what seemed the most convenient place—in front of the muzzle. 'Just when I was most preoccupied,' writes Denisov, 'I heard the most frightful report and crash nearby… when I halted I saw Grekov spinning like a top, and several singed Cossacks lying on the ground.'[18]

Nobody was killed, and the main force of the Russians arrived before the French counterattack could reach the narrows. Wild scenes were now played out beyond the valley exit on the open ground towards Schwyz, 'which rang appallingly with the yells and screams of the dying, the wounded and the ferocious victors. The Russians pressed on with greater fury still and drove the French before them like children… The French believed that the whole Russian army was on their heels, and they fled without stopping or so much as a backward glance as far as Lauerz.'[19]

In the scramble Sergeant Makhotin and a knot of comrades fought their way through to a French officer and dragged him from his horse. The sergeant had to let go of his prize when he was assailed by a French officer from behind, but he found that he was still holding one of the man's epaulettes, which he deposited in his knapsack and showed later to Suvorov. The Russians fancied that the epaulette had been ripped from Massena himself, but it is more likely that the adornment belonged to his aide-de-camp Honoré-Joseph Reille, who is known to have been nearly captured.

A key role in Massena's original plan had been assigned to a left-flanking column of 1,200-1,500 men, which was supposed to march by way of Oberberg and Illgau and descend into the Muotatal from the north, in the way feared by Rosenberg. It was easy enough for the local guides to exploit the similarity between the names 'Oberberg' and 'Ober-Iberg,' and thereby misdirect the French away to the north-east. A villager of Hinter-Iberg writes that

the officer who commanded the column was a general, to judge by his richly-decorated uniform. He came into our room with his staff, spread a large map in front of him on the table, traced the paths indicated thereon with his finger. He spoke to me: 'I want to go by way of Illgau and hit the Russians in the flank and rear. You must show me the way!' I knew that such a path did exist, but I was disinclined to show it to him. I supported the Russians, and pretended to know nothing about it, in spite of all his appeals and questioning. The French officer became more and more impatient, and finally turned to me and pointed to the map: 'I know there is a path which climbs for some way, and then descends in the Russian rear. You know it as well, and you have to show it to me!' I gave another evasive answer, but I could see that the Frenchman did not trust me, and would use force to get me to show him the way. But he was given no time to carry out his threat. The shots and the noise came nearer and nearer… one rider galloped up after another, and a great commotion broke out. The officer bolted from the room, his troops got on the move, and he sent them at the double across the Chlingentobel stream to go to the help of the others.[20]

By six in the evening Massena and Mortier had reassembled their men in scattered groups to cover Schwyz, Seewen and Gersau—a defensive posture which indicates the extent of their defeat, and gives some clue as to the great victory which might have been Suvorov's, if he had followed his first instinct to attack with his available forces on 28 September. Rosenberg halted his main body in front of the valley exit, though a party of sixty Cossacks rode to the lake shore at Brunnen in search of food.

The valley floor was strewn with the bodies of men, horses and mules, and the Russians were leading Adjutant-General Lacour, ten other senior officers, and soldier prisoners by the hundred towards the Convent and Muotathal village. The captured pieces were spiked and buried, and whole wagon loads of unwanted French equipment were being decanted into the gorge.

The French owned to having lost 817 men from all causes and five of their guns, but Stutterheim puts the captured at 1,027, Venançon at 1,300, and the meticulous Convent journal at 1,500-1,600. The French prisoners had almost all been stripped of their footgear and much else besides. The nuns helped them out as best they could, and the captured officers were accommodated in the Convent, where Rosenberg dined the same evening with Lacour—unwittingly encouraging the rumour that Lecourbe himself had fallen into the hands of the Russians.

THE BREAKOUT FROM THE KLÖNTAL AND THE CHECK AT NÄFELS

We return to Bagration and the corps of Derfelden at the eastern end of the Klöntal. Early in the morning of 1 October a French patrol creeping about the heights above Seerüti encountered the Russian Jäger and grenadiers who had been positioning themselves for their assault. A violent firefight broke out among the rocks and trees, and the sound echoed and re-echoed from the mountains which lined the lake. Lieutenant-Colonel Tsukato's Miller Jäger and the Austrians assumed that they had heard the signal for a full attack, and they descended the Planggen meadows at speed, some of them

tumbling down the steep slopes.

Down by the Klöntaler See the Baranovsky Musketeers opened the push along the lakeshore track, which the French swept to the same deadly effect as on the day before, killing Colonel Tiller at the head of his men. The Rosenberg Grenadiers were coming up behind,

and soon the bodies of our dead warriors jammed the track, and especially the far end which led to the clearing. It was impossible to get through. We had to steel ourselves to the ordeal of dragging the bodies aside into the lake, and we advanced along the passage thus made and between the heaps of the remaining dead until we reached the open ground. Here we assembled and put ourselves in order under a hail of bullets, then speedily formed in alignment with the advance guard, and made straight for the enemy with the bayonet to the cry of 'Hurrah!' The enemy were formed up against parallel to the mountains, but they were taken simultaneously in their right flank by the Miller Jäger who came at them at the run.[21]

The French fell back behind their second line, which put up a stiff fight on rising ground. The second line in turn retreated to the first when the Russians were nearly upon it, whereupon the whole body of French disengaged, formed a number of columns, and made off down the mossy woods of the Löntsch gorge and through the hamlet of Riedern, where the mountains gave onto the open level valley of the Linth.

Suvorov followed the allied advance down the Löntsch on foot. Grand Prince Constantine feared that the field-marshal might become caught up in the fighting at the bottom, and prevailed on him to position himself out of harm's way on the isolated razor-back ridge south-west of Riedern. From here Suvorov had a good view of what was unfolding down the Linth valley to the north.

Suvorov had broken out of the Muotatal-Pragel-Klöntal passage, but if he were to retrieve something positive from the campaign he must fight his way through Molitor's troops to the Walensee, and so establish contact with Lieutenant-General Petrasch, who had taken command of the main Austrian force after Hotze had been killed at Schänis on 25 September.

Molitor knew what was at stake. He had abandoned the open and highly combustible town of Glarus as untenable, but he planned to fight in depth down the Linth, initially by holding up the allies at Netstal (so as to give isolated companies south of Glarus time to escape), then by putting up a determined resistance five kilometres to the rear at Näfels and Mollis. The Linth river was unfordable, and Molitor intended to turn this circumstance to his advantage by destroying the upper bridge at Netstal at an appropriate time, while doing his best to hold the lower bridge between Näfels and Mollis, so enabling himself to operate on both banks with equal facility.

In the middle of the morning the Russian advance guard arrived at the Linth levels beyond Riedern, and Constantine directed the leading troops to the left in pursuit of the French. The Russians fought their way through Netstal, house by house and garden by garden, and Major-General Nikolai Mihkailovich Kamensky succeeded in breaking through to the upper bridge with his regiment. The troops were about to cross when the wooden structure burst into flames, and the French musketry held them at bay until the thing collapsed into the water. A party of Cossacks swam to the right (eastern) bank and established a bridgehead, and at the urging of Lieutenant-Colonel Weyrother the

THE EASTERN END OF THE KLÖNTALER SEE. THE SEERÜTI CLEARING IS ON THE RIGHT CENTRE, FLANKED BY THE BERGWALD WOODS RISING TO THE OBER-HERBERG ON THE LEFT CENTRE. THE PLANGGEN SLOPES EXTEND IN THE RIGHT DISTANCE.

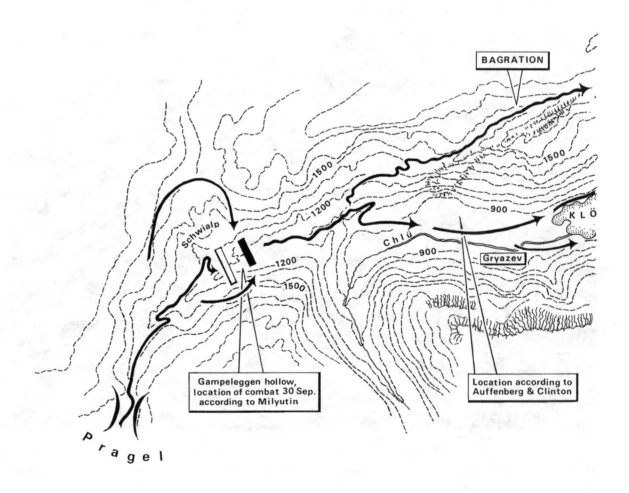

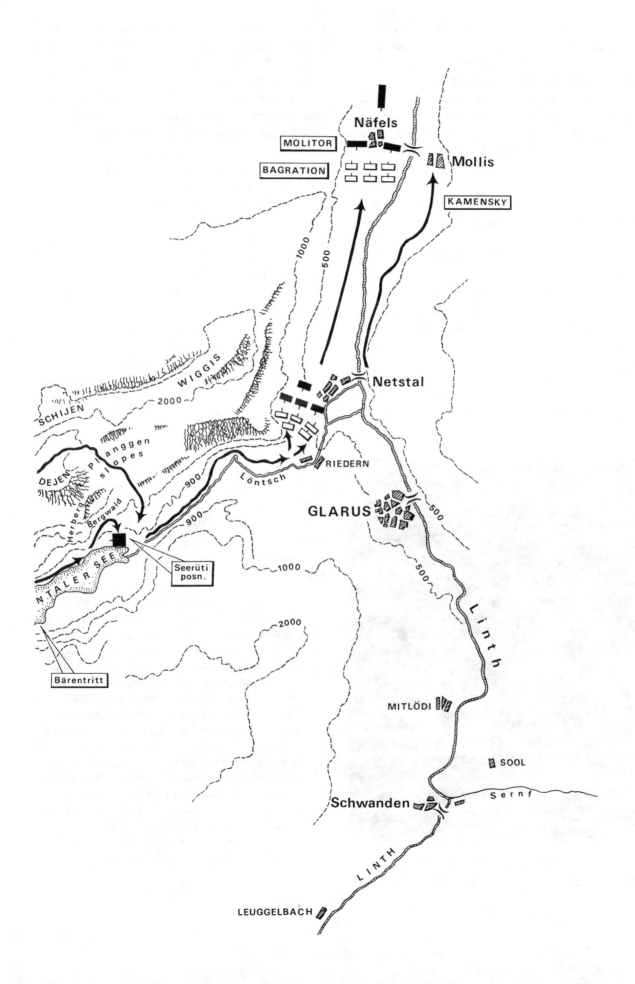

MOLITOR

BAGRATION

Näfels

Mollis

KAMENSKY

1000

500

WIGGIS

SCHIJEN

2000

Netstal

DEJEN Pfanggen slopes

Herberg

Bergwald

Löntsch

RIEDERN

900

900

GLARUS

500

NTALER SEE

Seerüti posn.

1000

2000

Bärentritt

Linth

500

MITLÖDI

SOOL

Sernf

Schwanden

LINTH

LEUGGELBACH

Russians set about building a trestle bridge—a difficult process which lasted until four in the afternoon, when Kamensky was able to cross with a battalion of his regiment.

Kamensky proceeded smartly down the right bank and seized Mollis, along with two cannon and 110 wounded who had been abandoned by the French. It was an excellent stroke, which turned the French flank and promised to open the way to the Walensee, but Weyrother was unable to prevail on the Russians to send any reinforcements, and the course of the fighting on the left bank (below) finally compelled the lone battalion to fall back on Netstal.

The Bagration and Miller Jäger, the grenadier corps, the Baranovsky Musketeers and the dismounted Cossacks had meanwhile inclined to the left and pushed in the direction of Näfels down the left bank of the Linth. This was by far the largest extent of level ground the Russians had seen since they had left Lombardy, but the plain was obstructed by farm buildings, ditches,

drainage channels, and lines of stone walls which extended all the way from the mountains on the west to the river in the east (most of the walls have now been removed, apart from a few which may be espied in the fields to the west of the present main road). It therefore took reinforcements from the division of Schveikovsky and four assaults for the advance guard to beat back the skirmishers, push through the little town of Näfels and advance onto the wooden bridge which extended for fifty-eight metres across the Linth.

The crossing changed hands at least once more, and when night was falling the newly-promoted *général de division* Honoré Theodor Gazan arrived at the head of a battalion of grenadiers, and enabled the French to push the allies back. The Russians were reinforced in their turn, but at nine at night the defenders were joined by the second battalion of the 94th demi-brigade under *général de brigade* Lochet, and they were able to open a general counterattack and bundle the allies back towards Netstal.

As far as Captain Gryazev could see, nobody on the Russian side was managing the action as a whole, and the only Russian general to show any initiative was Kamensky, who brought his battalion back from the right bank, and deployed his entire regiment together with two hundred volunteers (collected by Gryazev) to cover the retreat:

> The night was dark. We furnished ourselves with a great number of cartridges, stuffing our pockets as well as our cartridge pouches with them. We were pretty certain that the enemy were going to attack, and so Kamensky and I walked along the ranks, telling the troops to live up to the vital role which had fallen to them. It was important for the enemy not to discover what we were up to, and so we instructed them to remain silent and alert, and hold their fire until the order came. Our expectations were amply fulfilled. It was too dark for us to be able to see the enemy or make out their movements, but we could hear them coming nearer and nearer, and we waited patiently until we heard a loud and clear '*En avant! En avant!*' That meant the

Suvorov's house in Riedern, where he rested on the night of 1 October

French were almost upon us and that there was no point in waiting, and so we ordered our troops to open a rapid rolling fire… The effect was magnified by the sound carrying through the dark and silent night, and re-echoing endlessly from the surrounding mountains. The action was short and successful, and thereafter the enemy left us in peace.[22]

The number of troops engaged is as always difficult to establish, but probably amounted to 6,000-7,000 on each side. Over the last three days of action both parties lost about 400 men killed and 300 prisoners. Auffenberg put the losses among the Austrian troops by themselves at thirty killed, 139 wounded and 71 prisoners, and stated that he had captured six officers and 71 men.

The French accounts were more than typically high flown, and made much of the exploit of three hundred men of a 3rd Swiss demi-brigade, whose very existence is not easy to pin down.[24] Again the French historians write of an entire Russian company being blown up on the bridge at Netstal, whereas Weyrother, who was present on the spot, verifies that the structure was set alight and simply burned down.

THE LINTH PLAIN, LOOKING SOUTH FROM NÄFELS TOWARDS NETSTAL.
THE RIVER LINTH IS OUT OF SIGHT TO THE LEFT

ROSENBERG LEAVES THE MUOTATAL

At midnight on 1/2 October Rosenberg received an order from Suvorov to extract his corps from the Muotatal, and march with all possible speed to Glarus to reinforce the rest of the army—namely the corps of Derfelden and the advance guard under Bagration. Before he made his final arrangements Rosenberg dispatched Major Ukov with a patrol of Cossacks towards the Chinzig to investigate whether it might be practicable to take his corps by way of that pass and the Klausen, and thus down the upper Linth to the rendezvous. Ukov lost five of his men when he ran into the French at the Chinzertal farm, and he had to report that the Chinzig was firmly in the hands of the enemy. The corps would therefore have to follow in Suvorov's steps over the Pragel. To persuade the French that he had aggressive intentions, Rosenberg sent word to the town fathers in Schwyz to prepare rations of bread, meat and wine for a force of 12,000 troops that was about to arrive among them.

Overnight the Cossacks and the men of the Muotatal had been carrying the Russian and French wounded into the Convent, and burying the dead in groups of ten, complete with their uniforms and weapons, by torchlight on the valley floor. Early in the morning the French prisoners set off for the Pragel under the escort of a Russian battalion; each of them was given a piece of cheese, but 'it was pitiful to see how these people had to make their way over the rough Pragel track without shoes or stockings, and under a deluge of rain intermingled with snow.'[25]

The prisoners were followed by the train of pack animals, being chivvied along from the rear by a police detachment of grenadiers; the regiments of the main body of musketeers followed in succession, interspersed with dismounted Cossacks; one company of grenadiers escorted the walking sick and wounded, and the last elements of the column—the regiment of Rehbinder and a sotnia of the Kurnakov Cossacks—departed at three in the afternoon. They left behind Staff Captain Nikolai Ivanovich Seliavin, with a physician and a group of surgeons to look after the untransportable sick and wounded, who amounted to six hundred Russians and more than 1,000 French.

The first of the French to arrive on the scene were a trumpeter and two dragoons, who were bringing a message from Massena; the letter was accepted by a Russian lieutenant, and the trio rode away. At five in the afternoon five French officers made themselves known to the nuns at the Convent, 'and they could not have been more friendly and courteous towards us.'[26] The visitors found that the nuns and allies had taken good care of the sick and wounded of all the belligerents.

Rosenberg had gained a clear twelve-hour start over the three companies of French grenadiers who now ventured through the Muotatal and towards the Pragel; it was a scavenging expedition rather than a pursuit, and the French collected nothing more than one hundred stragglers, together with discarded muskets and ten pieces of the Piedmontese mountain artillery which the Russians had thrown into the ravines.

Just as had happened on his passage over the Chinzig, Rosenberg had the misfortune of following a path which had been already churned up by the rest of the army. Snow began to fall at ten on the first evening, which made the track even more difficult to find, and Rosenberg's troops had to spend two miserable nights and one full day on the crossing before they arrived at Glarus on 4 October.

THE COUNCIL AT GLARUS AND ITS CONSEQUENCES

Generations of Russians have been taught to believe that the events of the first week in October 1799 represented the last and most heroic stage in Suvorov's escape from a trap, and so indeed we might believe from the experience of his army when it fought off French divisions closing in from the flank and rear, and made the harrowing passage of the Panixer Pass. In fact Suvorov's move east to the Linth valley at the beginning of the month had positioned him to take the offensive with advantage, for the allies now had the potential to concentrate their forces, while the French were now the ones who were scattered with tenuous communications over a wide arc—in other words the reverse of the situation which had obtained in the second half of September.

After Auffenberg's brigade of 1,460 remaining Austrians made off by agreement for the Vorderrhein (below) Suvorov still had a force of 15,000 of so battleworthy Russians under his command, and stood within a few hours' march of the Walensee, where the path leading along the southern shore of the lake would have brought him into contact with the Austrian forces which were coming together after the general disaster of 25 September—Major-General Jellachich with about 5,000 troops, Lieutenant-General Linken with 4,000, and Lieutenant-General Petrasch (who had succeeded Hotze after the action at Schänis) with 5,000 immediately disposable men.

Petrasch had fallen back with the former corps of Hotze to Feldkirch, but he was now under instructions from Archduke Charles to do his utmost to join in a renewed offensive, and berated for his passivity. Charles assumed that the Russians would remain within reach, and once he had dispatched the appropriate orders he wrote to Suvorov from Donaueschingen on 3 October that he was setting the various Austrian corps in motion to take part in the general offensive. By then Jellachich had advanced his main forces to Walenstadt at the eastern end of the Walensee, and his light troops were advancing along the southern shore of the lake.

The Austrians and Russians could therefore have concentrated to the strength of at least 29,000 troops in the neighbourhood of Sargans, and provisioned and re-equipped themselves as necessary from the Austrian magazines at Feldkirch. At Sargans they would be not only defensively unassailable, but fully restored and able to think about pushing west to join the remainder of the allied forces in northern Switzerland. Korsakov's original army was in a worse state than any one suspected, but he could still call on the intact Austrian corps of Lieutenant-General Nauendorf (5,400 troops) and the newly-arrived Bavarian auxiliaries and French royalists.

The French were for the moment dispersed, and undergoing some confusing changes in command, and so it will probably be most useful to identify their three groupings in relation to the order in which Suvorov had already encountered them in the course of his campaign:

1. South-west Grouping. Division of Loison (formerly Lecourbe)

Six battalions: the main force of the 38th demi-brigade, and the 76th and 109th. This was the formation which had fallen back from the Devil's Bridge and down the Reuss valley; after considerable hesitations it was now moving up the Schächental and over the Klausen Pass towards the upper Linth.

2. Western Grouping. Division of Mortier

About twenty battalions: 50th, 53rd, 100th and 108th demi-brigades, and (from the division of Loison) the 67th and the third battalion of the 38th. These people were in a state of some shock after having been beaten by Rosenberg in the Muotatal on 30 September and 1 October. Mortier was sending three companies of grenadiers up the Muotatal and towards the Pragel, and Soult (as the new overall commander of the French right wing) placed him on defensive alert at Schwyz on the night of 2/3 October, and gave him contingency orders to fall back on Rotenturm and Einsiedeln. What Massena feared most corresponded closely to what Suvorov's Austrian staff officers had in mind (below)—a push by the combined forces of Suvorov, Jellachich and Linken, and a move across the Rhine by the reassembled forces of Korsakov and Hotze's successor Petrasch. A Swiss historian has commented that one would have the impression that it was not Suvorov who was cut off and beleaguered, but the French generals.[27]

3. Northern Grouping. Division of Gazan (formerly Soult).

Sixteen battalions: the 25th, 36th, 44th and 94th demi-brigades, and (from the division of Loison) the 84th demi-brigade. This was the French left wing, and some of its units had been engaged by the Russians and Austrians in the series of fights between the Pragel Pass and Näfels. Its three component brigades were now deployed in a defensive posture, with some doubt attaching to the allocation of units between the brigades of Laval and Lapisse (formerly Mainoni).

> **Brigade Laval**
> In deep reserve at Schänis and towards the Thur valley: one bn of the 25th demi-brigade, the 36th demi-brigade (three bns) and the 94th (three bns)

> **Brigade Lapisse**
> On the left bank of the Linth in the neighbourhood of Näfels and Niederurnen: two bns of the 25th demi-brigade, one bn of the 36th, the 44th demi-brigade (three bns) and two sq of horse

> **Brigade Molitor**
> At Mollis on the right bank of the Linth: 84th demi-brigade (three bns).

Subsequent events indicate that the 44th was the most responsive and alert of the French forces, while the 84th (most directly in Suvorov's path to the Walensee) was still a hard-fighting body but inevitably depleted by casualties and low on ammunition. A concerted advance by Suvorov's army (unlike the mismanaged, or rather unmanaged battle of the advance guard on 1 October) would almost certainly have reached its objective. Suvorov therefore responded enthusiAstically when the Austrians first pointed out this opportunity to him, and Weyrother wrote to Linken on the evening of 1 October that the army would march for Walenstadt on the next day, and that he (Linken) and Jellachich must join it there.

By the early morning of 2 October Constantine had learned of what was in the air, and he went straight to Suvorov to tell him that the army ran the danger of being delayed beside the Walensee and finally bottled up at Sargans, and that the only secure way to unite with the Austrians was by taking the extremely roundabout route which led over the remote Panixer Pass to the Vorderrhein, and then down the valley of that river to Maienfeld.

The generals met in council at eleven in the morning of 2 October (apparently at lodgings of Suvorov in a peasant house to the north of Glarus). After a prolonged discussion eight out of the ten voted for renouncing the rendezvous and all immediate prospect of active operations, and retreating southwards way of the Panixer.

Auffenberg was about to take the road to the Panixer later the same day, for his brigade had been assigned to rejoin the division of Linken, but before he departed he made one final attempt to persuade Suvorov to change his mind. The field-marshal was not to be moved, and 'his conduct of this occasion was directly contrary to his own better judgement, as well as to the repeated advice of the Austrian staff, of Lieutenant-Colonel Clinton, and of the Swiss officers who were with him, but the Grand Duke [Prince] and the Russian general officers insisted on it so strongly that the marshal was not able to resist.'[28]

On 3 October news arrived of Rosenberg's victory in the Muotatal two days before. Weyrother was so confident that Suvorov would return to the scheme for the offensive that he dashed off a note to Jellachich to tell him to come up from Sargans to join the Russians, who would be advancing on the 4th by way of Mollis to Walenstadt. He reckoned without the exhausted state of Rosenberg's corps, the demoralisation which now gripped that of Derfelden, and the ascendancy which the young thug Constantine had gained over a man to whom attacking and winning had been second nature. The answer arrived from Jellachich that he was awaiting Suvorov's army at Walenstadt, but the Russians proved to be beyond persuasion,

> and as a cloak for the collapse of their military spirit they replied that their troops were exhausted and had no cartridges (!!!), as if to romp across level ground demanded more exertion that retreating at speed over trackless rocks, and in circumstances which made action unavoidable, for the enemy would be sure to pluck up courage at the sight of our unexpected retreat, and not let our departure go unpunished.

The excuse of running out of ammunition was particularly odd coming from the field-marshal,

> who otherwise praised the advantages of cold steel to the skies, and who claimed that he alone was privy to the secrets of the bayonet, and that only the Russian troops were capable of employing that weapon. But he forgot about the principles he had once asserted with

such confidence, and this veteran, for all his experience, let himself be led by men whose brains were as devoid of military knowledge as their pates of hair.[29]

5 OCTOBER

THE RUNNING FIGHT UP THE LINTH AND SERNF

Rosenberg's victorious troops emerged from the Löntsch ravine early in the afternoon of 4 October. Now that all the Russians were together, Constantine insisted that the army must implement the decision taken at the council of war two days earlier, and march south without delay.

The pack animals and the greater part of the Cossacks set off the same evening under the commander of Major-General Miloradovich. The rest of the army wound out of Glarus from four on the morning of 5 October, with the remainder of Rosenberg's corps in the lead, followed by the corps of Derfelden, and the advance guard under Bagration (effectively now the rearguard) closing up the column. Bagration's force was made up of the same units as before—the Jäger regiments Bagration and Miller, the four combined grenadier battalions, and the Cossack regiment of Sychov—but it comprised just 1,899 out of the 3,000 troops who had entered Switzerland on 15 September. Bagration, once the impetuous leader of the advance guard, lost all interest in his command now that it was doing the work of a rearguard, and he virtually contracted himself out of the rest of the campaign.

Now the initiative passed to the French, whose three groupings of forces responded as follows:

1. Loison marched twelve companies of the 76th and 38th down from the Klausen Pass to approach the Russian line of retreat at Schwanden,

2. Mortier pushed three grenadier companies of the 108th (above) in Rosenberg's tracks from the Pragel down to Glarus,

3. As the divisional commander in most immediate confrontation with the Russians, Gazan ordered the main forces of his two leading

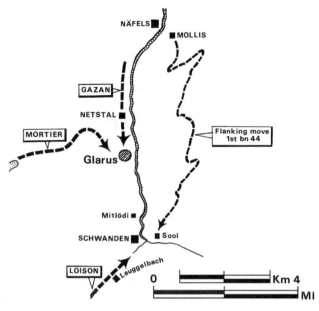

THE CLOSING TRAP

brigades (those of Molitor and Lapisse) to advance directly against Glarus on 5 October, while the first battalion of the 44th demi-brigade, or 560 troops, skirted the mountains to the east to position itself behind Schwanden, in the Russian deep rear.

Thus by 5 October a distinct converging movement was taking shape, with the main body of Gazan's division driving directly from the north, and units of all three divisions closing in against the Russian flanks and path of retreat.

Bagration set his troops in march at the same time as the rest of the Russian column, at four in the morning of 5 October. He left nobody behind to tend the fires in his abandoned bivouacs, and he gave no warning to the joint Russo-Austrian commissariat, so that the officials and the supply chest of 6,000-7,000 Austrian florins were captured when a squadron of the 10th Chasseurs entered Glarus at the head of Molitor's 84th demi-brigade at six in the morning.

Molitor's three battalions were joined in Glarus by Mortier's three companies of grenadiers who had descended from the Pragel, and at eight in the morning the united force advanced to do battle with Bagration's command, which was deployed across the narrowing valley of the upper Linth in front of Schwanden. The Russians were getting the worst of the engagement until the regiment of Veletsky hastened to their support form the tail of the main column, whereupon the Russian grenadiers launched a succession of attacks which drove the French from Mitlödi and back towards Glarus.

The main Russian army had meanwhile left the Linth valley at Schwanden, and was making south-east up the Sernftal towards the Panixer Pass. Now that the advance guard (confusingly functioning as the rearguard, above) had won some breathing space, it fell back through Schwanden with the intention of making a new

stand up the valley. Its margin was narrower than supposed, for the leading troops of Loison (the second battalion of the 38th) were arriving at Schwanden from the direction of the Klausen pass, which forced the Russians to put in a counterattack which drove the French back up the Linth towards Leuggelbach.

More dangerous still, the advance guard was in danger of being pinched out from the east by the battalion of the 44th which had been detached from Näfels, and which was trying to gain a rocky outcrop which commanded the Sernftal passage seven hundred metres to the east of Schwanden. There are no reliable accounts of the subsequent action, though it is

Matt church—the perspective of the French attackers

clear the Russian Jäger counterattacked towards Sool and were able to deny this important feature to the French long enough to allow the tail of the column to pass through.

The Russians had won themselves another short reprieve, which they employed to assemble outside Engi, where the rocky narrows opened into a pastoral upland valley. The French were soon upon them, and for the next two hours the Russian advance guard made a fighting retreat along the two-kilometre stretch of the valley between Engi and Matt, making what use it could of the folds in the grassy slopes which descended from either side. A replenishment of ammunition reached the Russians during a snowfall, and two hundred of their Jäger were emplaced in the high-standing Matt churchyard, which projected into the valley from the east as a ready-made redoubt, and from where the Russians could command the whole valley floor with their fire. The French brought their artillery to bear, and at eight in the evening their infantry stormed up the slope, over the wall and through the church to massacre the Russian sick and wounded who were lying at the foot of the altar.

The main force of the Russian advance guard blew up the bridge over the Sernf at Brummbach and fell back to the meadows behind Schwändi, only just short of the main army which was crowding around the chalets of the hamlet of

Suvorov's house in Elm

Elm. By now Bagration had 'ceased to concern himself with his duties, and had abandoned his subordinates to their fate. The result was that the hitherto invincible advance guard nearly came to grief during the retreat, and was lucky to be able to rejoin the main body. Although a certain Count Tsukato [Lieutenant-Colonel Egor Gavrilovich Tsukato] was assigned to the advance guard in the capacity of commander, he lacked the experience and temperament that were needed to plan and direct its operations effectively.'[30]

The leaderless advance guard had drawn the French onto Suvorov's army, and under the cover of darkness and a fall of thick snowflakes the French infiltrated to the adjacent heights and fired into the valley, keeping the Russians in a state of constant alarm. 'This circumstance augmented the demoralisation of the army, which was now transmitted [from the high command] to the officers and soldiers alike.' [31]

At two in the morning Suvorov therefore abandoned his lodging in the Freitag house in the narrow street of Elm, and he was escorted to a shepherd's hut beside the Sernf, 1,300 metres further up the valley.

6 - 8 OCTOBER

THE PASSAGE OF THE PANIXER PASS

From three in the afternoon of 6 October the elements of the army set off in succession up the

THE FIRST ASCENT FROM THE WICHLEN HOLLOW

track which led to the Panixer Pass. The corps of Rosenberg was the first to leave, with the division of Miloradovich at the head. The corps of Derfelden followed, pushing the train of mules and pack horses in front of it.

By the late afternoon the two corps had progressed sufficiently far up the pass to permit the advance guard under Bagration to withdraw from its perilous station in front of the entrance to the passage. These troops had been in action since first light, when a sotnia of 110 Sychov Cossacks charged into the mist and scattered parties of French who had been foraging in the neighbourhood of Elm. The Cossacks had won the infantry a period of grace, which the four battalions of grenadiers utilised to regroup in front of the entrance. Here they withstood

musket and artillery fire from the first battalion of the 44th demi-brigade until the evening, when they followed in the path of the rest of the army. The French ventured some way up the passage after them, but they posed much less of a threat that did the terrain and the elements. The St. Gotthard, the Chinzig and the Pragel had been a trial, but the Panixer was a killer in its own right.

We shall accompany the Russians on their *via dolorosa*. It began where a narrow gorge gave access to the Panixer path from the broad basin of the upper Sernf at Wichlen. The hideous rock abutment of the Rütersegg to the right matched the cliffs of the Unter Spienggen on the left, where they play of light after sunrise suggested the abode of evil spirits. A first climb up a slope

The head of the Jetzloch (right)

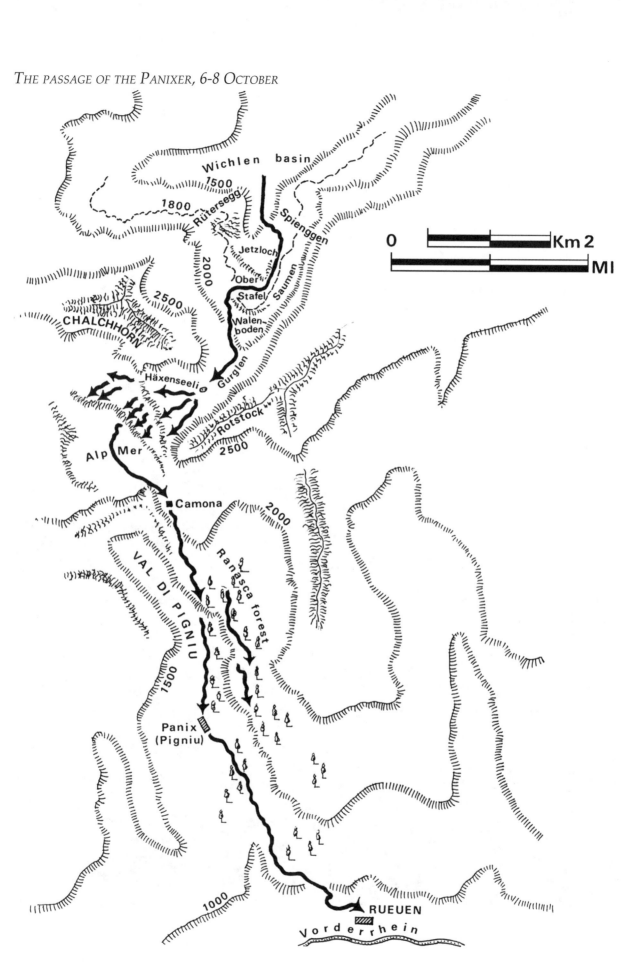

Wichlen basin

1500

1800

Rütersegg

Spienggen

2000

Jetzloch

Ober

Stafel

Saumen

2500

Walen-
boden

CHALCHHORN

Häxenseeli

Gurglen

Alp Mer

Rotstock

2500

Camona

2000

VAL DI PIGNIU

Ranasca forest

1500

Panix
(Pigniu)

1000

RUEUEN

Vorderrhein

0   Km 2

MI

*VIEW BACK FROM THE FINAL ASCENT, WITH THE HÄXENSEELI (TOP)
LOOKING LIKE A PEBBLE STREWN PUDDLE FROM THIS DISTANCE*

of black scree and over hillocks of turf and jumbled boulders brought the Russians to the great amphitheatre of the Jetzloch. The snowy-peaked Rütersegg massif barred to the view to the right; a rock wall—the first in a pair of giant steps—stretched across the front. The guides indicated that the Russians must take to the steep, winding and indistinct paths which led up to the left. Having gained height, the Russians picked their way along the Saumen slopes, passed to the left of the first rock wall and reached the broad and gentle hollow of Ober Stafel. A short descent brought the troops past a spouting waterfall (one of the sources of the Jetzbach) to the foot of the second rock wall; they turned to the right along the base of the rampart, negotiated the slope around its right to

the Walenboden basin, and set themselves to climb the steep Gurglen gorge.

All of this had to be accomplished through two feet of soft snow, which obliterated the tracks, and so sapped the strength that along some stretches it took a man half an hour to progress one hundred paces. At the upper end of the Gurglen the troops emerged into the rocky hollow which cradled the Häxenseeli ('Little Lake of the Witches'), a small body of water now seemingly hard frozen. According to legend successive parties of Russians ventured across the ice instead of taking to the sides of the basin, and were engulfed when the surface gave way, though the story probably owes more to the bleakness of the surroundings than to reality. Captain Gryazev writes of crossing a sheet of

THE FURTHER ASCENT, WITH THE ORIGINAL TRACK

252

snow, which could well be the lake in question, and then climbing a stretch of jumbled, dirty and stained ice, which might correspond to the crude path of shattered stones which led to the summit. Along this stretch Major-General Denisov felt just as ill as when he had been climbing the Chinzig, and he was forced to adopt the same technique of clinging to a horse's tail and having himself pulled upwards.

At the top 'a flash of sunlight revealed all of the Grisons and half Tyrol, but the trouble was that we could see no sign of a path beneath our feet which might lead us down the vertical slopes from the sea of snow where we were now standing. All we knew was that we must keep inclining to the left… everything appeared rounded off under its covering of snow, which

was polished to mirror brightness by the sharp wind.'[32]

According to Gryazev 'there was absolutely no shelter, nor a splinter of wood to light a fire to warm our frozen limbs. The carriages of the mountain guns and the lances of the Cossacks were useless for anything but to serve as firewood—very few of us were able to benefit thereby, and among them was our revered commander Prince Constantine, who was the first to think of this expedient.'[33]

The present-day walker is guided by signs to a place on the further edge of the summit plateau from where an open and very narrow path zig-zags down a bluff of black shale and decayed coppery-brown rock; the track descends to the flat-bottomed hanging valley of the Alp

THE WINDSWEPT SUMMIT OF THE PASS

Mer, along which the pebble-strewn bed of the meandering Muer stream (Aua dil Mer) snakes agreeably to the south-east. These landscapes give no indication as to the scenes in the early winter of 1799, when the troops wandered as individuals or in small groups all over the plateau of the pass and the slopes of the Rotstock mountain, and found that the descent to the Alp Mer lay down alternating rock ledges and sheets of snow. 'It was impossible to lead any of the animals, whether the beasts of burden or the riding horses; all we could do was to line them up along the edge of the precipice and push them from behind. What happened to them after that was a matter of chance—some survived unscathed, but many others broke their necks and legs and lay there disregarded along with their loads. But the men were in a still more pitiable state.'[34]

Weyrother wrotes that the locations that were totally impracticable were revealed eventually by the sight of men and horses falling to their death, and Grayzev saw one such party destroyed beside a waterfall that was carrying rocks and clods of black earth. The Russians were finally reduced to tucking up their coats and sliding down the snow from ledge to ledge. The slopes were 'as slippery as butter,'[35] and

THE UPPER ALP MER, LOOKING BACK TOWARDS THE SUMMIT

unless the men checked their descent they were in danger of being dashed against rocks or being carried over the lip of the next ledge. Each slide was over in a matter of seconds, but it might be followed by hours of prospecting along a rock ledge to identify the place for the next near-suicidal glissade.

The Alp Mer offered some respite, but it terminated at its southern end at the edge of a great cliff which overhung the mighty wooded Val di Pigniu. Just short of the precipice the track veered to the left and brought the Russians to the eastern slopes of the upper valley near the Camona farmstead. What is now a safe and well-marked path was then one of the most dangerous reaches of all, for the track was icy and obstructed by rockfalls, and the precipice to the right claimed about three out of every ten of the surviving horses and mules. All of the Piedmontese mountain cannon had by now been abandoned, buried or thrown over the cliffs. The cold abated a little when the Russians descended across an expanse of coarse and bumpy pasture (quickly churned into a sticky clay mud), and thence into the great Ranasca forest, which offered the first shelter of any kind, and extended gloomily towards Panix (Pigniu) village and the valley of the Vorderrhein.

Darkness descended in the later afternoon of the 6th when most of the army was still strung out over the pass. Denisov and his companions were overtaken by a blizzard on the summit, and he noted that young officers of the infantry

THE PENALTY OF A FALSE STEP. THE CLIFF ABOVE THE VAL DI PIGNIU

were the first to die, and that the lightly-clad French prisoners were suffering terribly:

I was at a loss to know how we could gain some relief—all attempts to find a way down from the mountain were in vain—but then I thought of having all the horses formed into a circle and tied together closely by the heads. We placed the weakest men in the centre, and so we remained till first light. As far as I remember three of the French died, but none of the Russians, though several of them had frozen limbs.[36]

Down below Gryazev managed to reach the Ranasca forest, where fires were being lit,

but I cannot say they did anything to restore our strength, because we had nothing left to restore… the fog prevented the smoke from rising, and so it spread out along the ground until its acrid smell became intolerable. I took off with one companion in the hope of finding somewhere better, and in the process I fell waist-deep into a stream [one of several which descended the slopes by deep-cut little ravines]. I carried on, but it was pitch black and I knew nothing of the way, and I stopped again in the depths of the wood in an extremity of exhaustion and distress. I threw myself down on a carpet of wet moss, but was racked by shivering in the cold and had to get up.

He finally succeeded in lighting a fire, which drew a number of wandering souls like himself, and he spent the rest of the night in their company.[37]

Suvorov was wrapped in a blue cloak inherited from his father (a rare concession to the cold), and Gryazev glimpsed him at about

THE FURTHER EDGE OF THE ALP MER. THE PERILOUS DESCENT TO THE VAL DI PIGNIU LAY UNDER THE DARK ROCKY OUTCROP ON THE RIGHT CENTRE.

noon on the descent from the pass. 'He was mounted on a Cossack horse, and I could hear him as he struggled to free himself from the grip of two sturdy Cossacks, who were walking on either side of him to hold him in the saddle and lead his horse. "Let me go!" he kept saying, "I can manage by myself!"'[38] We find him again in the middle of the afternoon, by when he had reached a clearing in the forest, and was dictating correspondence in the presbytery close by the square-towered church of the hamlet of Panix.

Suvorov remounted, and after a ride of an hour or so he gained the valley of the Vorderrhein at Rueun (Ruiz), where he lodged in the house of Lieutenant-General Schmidt de Grüneck, a veteran of the royal French service. As if in defiance of everything they had undergone, the field-marshal and his staff had their effects unpacked, put on their full dress uniforms, and went forth to receive the congratulations of the émigrés who had assembled at Rueun to meet them. All the valleys were dark by six in the evening, but distant lanterns could still be seen bobbing about in the mountains.

Denisov himself reached Panix in an appalling state, and was greeted by a gentleman who spoke excellent French and seemed to know him well. This was the French adjutant Lacour, whom Denisov had captured towards the end of Rosenberg's second combat in the Muotatal. Denisov believed that he owed his life to this gallant foe, who now had him fed with hot soup and wrapped in warm blankets. The last of the troops descended to the Vorderrhein on 8 October.

On 12 September, just before the Suvorov's

THE END OF THE TRAIL. PANIX VILLAGE

Russians entered Switzerland, they numbered 21,285. On 12 November an incomplete list put the losses from all causes (killed in action, missing, prisoners, sick and wounded) at 3,884, or 18.24 per cent, most of which must have been incurred during the period of active campaigning in Switzerland, from 21 September to 8 October. No figures were entered for the losses of the artillery and engineers, the infantry regiments of Baranovsky, Kamensky or Tyrtov, or the officers of the Cossack regiment of Denisov. However by extrapolating average losses of comparable listed regiments we may estimate an likely extra loss of some 528 officers and men, making a total of about 4,412, or nearly 21 per cent, still excluding the gunners and engineers, for whom there is no comparison. In detail the percentage unit losses from 12 September to 12 November were as follows:

Advance Guard	%
Jäger regiments:	
Bagration	17.90
Miller	20.36
Combined grenadier battalions:	
Lomonosov	47.27
Dendrygin	17.40
Sanaev	23.00
Kalemin	23.92

Corps Derfelden	
Grenadier regiment Rosenberg:	26.12
Musketeer regiments:	
Schveikovsky	22.23
Baranovsky	n.a.
Kamensky	n.a.
Cossack regiments:	
Sychov	2.50
Posdeev (of Corps Derfelden)	4.76
Semernikov	2.78
Molchanov	n.a.

Corps Rosenberg	
Jäger regiment Kashkin:	34.00
Musketeer regiments:	
Miloradovich	5.56
Rehbinder	44.53
Mansurov	45.89
Fertsch	34.00
Förster	21.86
Tyrtov	n.a.

Veletsky	38.55
Cossack regiments:	
Grekov	44.49
Denisov (excl. officers)	12.24
Posdeev (of Corps Rosenberg)	6.84
Kurnakov	5.62

Thus the Cossacks (except the regiment of Grekov) led a charmed life, and the brunt of the fighting was borne by the infantry, whose combatants (by the observations of Weyrother and a Swiss officer) had been reduced to some 10,000 when the army reached the Vorderrhein. About two hundred Russians had died from exposure or falls during the passage of the Panixer Pass; many of the survivors were spitting blood, and one hundred of them had been blinded by the glare from the snow.

The French did not go unscathed, to judge by the experience of the 50th, 53rd and 108th demibrigades (all heavily engaged in the Muotatal on 1 October), which between 12 September and 12 October suffered losses of altogether 46 per cent.[39] The Austrian brigade of Auffenberg had escorted 1,418 prisoners over the Panixer Pass—men who had been taken by the joint efforts of the Russians and Austrians in the combats between 24 September and 2 October.`

On 8 and 9 October the Russians made the short march down the Vorderrhein from Ilanz to the basin of Chur, and began to put themselves in order. Regiments of infantry were re-formed into battalions, and the Cossack regiments into squadrons, and the spirits of the men were recovering noticeably. This once prosperous part of the world had suffered heavily from the passage of armies, but it lay within easy reach of the Austrian depots, and the Austrians were able to provide the more urgent necessities, like the Russians' demand for 480,000 musket cartridges. Suvorov took up his lodgings in the bishop's palace at Chur, and was railing against Jellachich, Linken, Petrasch and even the unoffending Auffenberg. Some of the field-marshal's immediate military 'family' were wearying of Suvorov's changes of mood, and his favourite guide Captain Antonio Gamma insisted on rejoining his countrymen in the regiment of Bachmann.

By 11 October Suvorov's army was ready to be on the move again, and the troops marched through the smiling countryside from Chur to Maienfeld. On the way they devastated nearly all that year's vintage by stripping the grapes from the vines and boiling them up for soup. William Wickham met the horde on the march and found 'every soldier loaded with the plunder of the poor inhabitants of Uri, Schwyz and Glarus by whom they had been received as friends and deliverers, and who had rendered them the most essential services on their whole march. They were preceded by the Cossacks and the vanguard, which was already encamped on the plain between this town [Feldkirch} and Hohenems, where they turned their horses loose into the finest fields of Indian corn, of which they were plucking up large quantities by the roots to make roofs for the huts they were erecting for the army, though within ten minutes' march of a wood that would have furnished them in abundance with far better materials.'[40] All the same the Englishman had to concede that 'amidst all the difficulties and disadvantages under which they labour, they show a degree of bravery and intrepidity in the field, of patience under suffering, of docility and attention and submission to their leaders, that is without example in modern times.'[41]

On 13 October the Russians continued by way of Balzers and Vaduz to Austrian territory at Feldkirch, and found their field artillery and baggage which, being too cumbersome for campaigning in the high Alps, had been diverted through Chiavenna and the Tyrol. Suvorov himself had arrived with the advance guard on the 12th, and stayed at Feldkirch for two days, which gave William Wickham occasion to become acquainted with the field-marshal's infamous breakfast-cum-lunch-cum siesta. The experience began at eight one morning,

> when his whole behaviour was so extraordinary, that though I had been apprised of it beforehand, yet, had I not myself such evident proofs of the strength of his mind, I should certainly have taken him for a madman whose understanding was

gone—his knees were bent as if from old age, which was not the case when I saw him on business the night before—he walked about the room with his hands and his head hanging like those of an idiot, talking nonsense to everybody, mixed occasionally with shrewd and sensible remarks on all kinds of subjects, and occasionally very severe on the Austrians and the court of Vienna.

> The dinner, the whole manner of serving it, and above all the servants who attended, were so dirty and disgusting that General Jellachich, though a Croat, could not bring himself to eat a single mouthful, at which the marshal either was, or affected to be, much offended. After dinner, which lasted three hours, he went immediately to bed, and did not get up till four, nor see anybody till five in the afternoon; and it is in this manner that the best part of the day is constantly lost. [42]

Still following the plain of the upper Rhine, the Russians marched from Feldkirch to Dornbirn on 15 October. On the 16th they skirted the eastern end of Lake Constance, and arrived adjacent to the German island-town of Lindau.

Early the next morning the Swiss colonel Ferdinand de Roverea saw that the streets of Lindau were jammed with sleeping Russian soldiers who, bizarrely enough, had been unwilling to disturb the repose of the burghers by breaking into their houses. The first officer he encountered was Colonel Nikolai Ivanovich Lavrov, who offered to conduct him to Suvorov's lodging, and warned him not to be disconcerted by the eccentric questions that were likely to be put to him. Not long after Roverea arrived the field-marshal left his sleeping chamber to climb to his officers on the upper floor:

> The door facing me opened, and out came an old man of middling stature and scrawny frame. He wore a shirt of stout white cloth and carelessly buttoned breeches. A wretched little turned-up hat was perched on his head and tied under the chin. He seemed preoccupied, and kept screwing up his face in a way that accentuated the deep furrows in the features. While still muttering to himself he stopped and looked at me; I drew myself up in the manner of a simple orderly officer, and made ready to answer by name if he questioned me. But he passed on without a word and I

relaxed. He had scarcely entered his office when a heated exchange could be heard from within, and a few minutes later the colonel came down the stairs at some speed.

Lavrov explained that Suvorov was angry that Roverea had not been introduced properly. Roverea was ushered inside, and Suvorov received him

in the most gracious and considerate way you could imagine. He rested his hands on my shoulders… shut his eyes and pronounced in French: 'You are a good old Switzer who is fighting to free his country. You are my brother and my friend, and you can count on me to be the same to you. Tell your brave countrymen that I honour them… Be my friend!'[43]

The purpose of the series of marches north from Chur to Lindau had been to enable Suvorov's army to recruit its strength in security, and position itself to play a key role in a revived offensive. Constantine and the Russian generals had shown their abhorrence of anything of the kind in the council of war on 2 October, but Suvorov's confidence had revived during the descent from the Panixer Pass. Indeed the reason why he had halted briefly in Panix village on the 7th was to dictate notes which told Archduke Charles and the Austrian corps commanders that he intended to join Petrasch (successor of Hotze), and advance along the southern side of Lake Constance to unite with the army of Korsakov. The scheme probably originated with Weyrother, who was now working up a detailed plan.

According to the new proposals 3,000 Russians would be left to guard Feldkirch, and the remaining 10,000 effectives would open an advance in concert with the 15,000 Austrians reassembled by Lieutenant-General Petrasch. The night of 17/18 October was the appointed time, and the location was the stretch of the Rhine from Altstätten downstream to lake Constance. The country to the west was hilly rather than mountainous, but the columns would have to move quickly if they were to win the various valleys before the French could bar the way. The columns of Suvorov and Petrasch

were to converge at St. Gallen on the 18th, force the narrow passage between Bruggen and Gossau on the 19th, and unite at Wil with the Condé émigé corps and some 5,000 Austrians under Lieutenant-General Nauendorf, who would be coming from Constanz town and Bischofszell. Korsakov and the second Russian army would meanwhile have advanced across the Rhine to Frauenfeld (seconded if possible by a push by Archduke Charles across the Rhine at Andelfingen), and the 20th would see the opening of a joint offensive south-west by way of Winterthur towards the Limmat or the Aare.

On the evening of 12 October Weyrother explained the plans to Suvorov, in the company of two of the Russian generals and the Austrian major Ferdinand Bubna, as the representative of Archduke Charles. Suvorov followed the details with lively attention, and Wickham was persuaded that the Russian and Austrian forces would interact in a way that promised every chance of success.[44] Suvorov commended the scheme to Archduke Charles in a letter which was dispatched the same evening.

Two developments on 14 October precipitated the end of the campaign. Charles feared that the 25,000 troops of Suvorov and Petrasch would be unequal to meeting the 30,000 French who were now believed to be deployed at St. Gallen and beside Lake Constance. He wrote to Suvorov on that day with a proposal to tease the enemy concentration apart by advancing his Austrians across the middle Rhine at Büsingen, while diverting Korsakov's army around the northern side of the lake to join Suvorov at the eastern end. Thus all the Russians would be concentrated in a single force before the new operation began. Weyrother interpreted the Archduke's letter as an expression of whole-hearted support. To Wickham and Lieutenant-Colonel Ramsay, however, the offer of Charles amounted to no more than a promise of demonstrations, and fell far short of a proper commitment of the Austrian army.

At eight on the morning of the same 14 October Suvorov told Weyrother that his plan was 'fine' but not 'good,' for the Russians were still in a bad way, and by the time a few of them might have succeeded in beating their way through difficult country to Winterthur, Massena would have defeated Korsakov in the same style as at Zürich. Suvorov now instructed Weyrother to put together a brief and cogent letter to Charles, to tell him that the Russians were still exhausted and short of clothing and shoes, and therefore incapable of going over to the offensive. Korsakov must therefore come to join him by way of the northern side of Lake Constance, and only after all the Russians were together would Suvorov be able to take stock of their numbers and condition, and weigh up what to do next.[45] Superficially the proposal to unite with Korsakov safely away from the enemy corresponded with the new plan of Archduke Charles, which reached Suvorov shortly afterwards, but the last sentence betrayed an intention to be done with the campaign for good.

Suvorov, strikingly enough, was thinking of taking his army back to winter quarters in northern Italy, and the most that he was now willing to concede was to leave the corps of Rosenberg at Bregenz until 4 November, so as to provide some cover for the Austrian province of Vorarlberg. William Wickham had a direct interest in such matters, as the representative of Suvorov's British paymasters, and he pressed the field-marshal for an explanation. Suvorov replied that he wished above all to have a joint Austro-Russian army once more under his command, since 'without it I can do nothing, for my Russians, though in many respects the best troops in the world, are not fit to act by themselves…'[46] Such an army would again be his, if he could take his Russians back to Italy, from where the allied army could mount an invasion of France by way of Dauphiné the next year.

Wickham was not entirely satisfied, and was 'firmly persuaded that some notion of an Italian league, independent of and perhaps under circumstances hostile to Austria, supported by Russian troops and English subsidies, has materially contributed to determining the marshal to take his winter quarters in Italy.'[47]

Suvorov was not a simple soldier, but a political animal who had 'never yet taken a step

of any kind without having first learnt the Emperor's [Paul's] private opinion.'[48] It was therefore natural for the Austrians to trace the change in Suvorov's behaviour to Paul's personal representative, the young count Gustav Stackelberg, who reached the field-marshal on about 15 October. This was unjust, for Stackelberg joined Lieutenant-Colonel Henry Clinton in the last attempts to keep the campaign alive, and at the end of the month they called on Wickham to return to Lindau, as the one person who could exercise a positive influence on Suvorov. Stackelberg was appalled at the intrigues of Constantine, but was unable to speak out.

The Grand Prince was the soul of the nationalist party, and Wickham attached great importance to a long private conversation which Constantine held with Suvorov on the eve of the fateful 14 October. Wickham records that Suvorov invited him to see him afterwards, and 'whilst I was in the ante-chamber I learnt that the marshal had seen a vision in the night, which would prevent him from undertaking the projected enterprise. I had previously learnt that the Grand Duke [Prince] had absolutely insisted on his abandoning it.'[49]

Weyrother had known Suvorov as a straight-talking man in Italy, and he attributed his change of mind not to a sudden discovery that the army was in a bad state, but the influence of the clique which now had domination over him, and which was determined to be done with all campaigning in Switzerland. Weyrother took Suvorov and his suite to the water's edge at Lindau, and showed them that the hills on the southern side of the lake fell far short of the mountains they dreaded, but the Russians were still not to be persuaded.

Possibly something could have been achieved even now if Suvorov and Archduke Charles had met face to face, and discovered how much they had in common. On 18 October Charles wrote to Suvorov to invite him to a meeting at Stockach or wherever else might be convenient for him, and he attached so much importance to the encounter that on the 19th he sent his general-adjutant Lieutenant-Colonel Joseph Colloredo to Lindau to convey a further letter and reinforce the message verbally.

Colloredo arrived at Lindau on 20 October, but before he could gain access to Suvorov the invitation fell into the hand of the political counsellors Fuchs and Trefort, and General-Adjutant Colonel Kushnikov. Colloredo was kept waiting for three and a half hours, and by the time he was granted an interview it was clear that Suvorov had been briefed on what to say. He declared that his only concern was to give his army some rest, that he was not interested in meeting the Archduke, and that if Colloredo had anything to communicate to him he must do so on paper.

Suvorov's written reply could scarcely have been more dismissive. He declared that his sole objective was now to restore and re-equip his troops, and 'although I am impatient to become acquainted with Your Imperial Highness I would be disconsolate if I were to put Your Imperial Highness to the inconvenience of travelling to Stockach in person. I would hasten with pleasure to meet Your Imperial Highness, if only the state of my health allowed.'[50]

Korsakov's army was now completing its march around the northern side of Lake Constance, and between 18 and 21 October his Russians, together with 2,500 Bavarian auxiliaries, the Swiss regiments of Bachmann and Roverea and the Condé corps spilled over the area between Lindau and Bregenz. When he received the senior officers Suvorov's manner amounted to a commentary on their performance. He gave Korsakov a hug, but had nothing to say to him, which was seen as a suspension of judgment, 'but it was evident that this defeated general was less at ease with himself than would have been any private soldier who was content with the knowledge that he had done his duty. He wore a gloomy expression, and his thoughts came out in a disordered way which showed that the calamitous events at Zürich had broken his spirit.'[51]

The ultra-nationalists now crowded so closely around Suvorov as to make him virtually inaccessible. His two Gorchakov nephews, Lieutenant-General Aleksei and Major-General Andrei, now supplanted Lieutenant-General Schveikovsky as Suvorov's *général du jour*. Schveikovsky was acquainted with Switzerland from the time he had spent there before the war, 'all the others,' remarked Wickham, 'with whom I talked upon this subject were as ignorant of its points and bearings as if they had been all the time in Persia. They had not the least notion of the nature and value of the respective positions which the enemy had occupied, during their march. In one word, they seemed to me to have left all these matters to their guides, and to the Swiss and Austrian officers who accompanied them, as beneath the attention of a Russian general.'[52]

Aleksei Gorchakov and the ministers Fuchs and Trefort now determined who was, and who was not to be admitted to Suvorov's presence. Weyrother had to hand over the opening of correspondence to the cabal, but he was readmitted to Suvorov's confidence after only ten days, for the new Russian staff proved to be totally incompetent. Suvorov valued Weyrother amongst other things for his amusing companionship, and he put him to the test by calling on him to say grace at a dinner. The Austrian stumbled so badly that the field-marshal pronounced him 'a Carmagnole' (after a notorious Revolutionary rant), and Weyrother had to restore his legitimist credentials by shouting out *'Vivat l'Empereur!'*[53]

The Russians tarried for a few days longer at Lindau and the neighbourhood to put themselves in some kind of shape for the march to winter quarters, which were now to be in southern Germany. On 28 October Major-General Prince Esterhazy arrived from Vienna with sets of the cross and red and white silk ribands of the various grades of the Military Order of Maria Theresa—the Grand Cross for Suvorov and Constantine, the Commander's Cross for Bagration, and six of the Small Crosses for Suvorov to distribute as he saw fit. Suvorov and the other recipients were delighted, but the Russians had made up their minds and nothing could now alter their resolution.

If the Russians delayed even now, if was only because Aleksei Gorchakov had forgotten to make any arrangements to feed the troops and the horses. During the period of waiting the exchanges between Suvorov and Archduke Charles gave further evidence of the acrimony which tarnished the relations between those two great soldiers. On 28 October Suvorov dispatched a curious letter which gave an illusory hope of something better: 'Tomorrow I set off for my cantonments between the Iller and the Lech. The way to defend the Hereditary Lands [of Austria] is by unselfishly-motivated conquests, and gaining the goodwill of nations, and not by evacuating the Netherlands, or abandoning Italy along with two fine armies [references to the events of 1794-7]. He recalled his services to the House of Austria, and added 'I am not the man for feints, demonstrations or counter-marches; instead of those childish games I look for my guidance to *coup d'oeil*, speed and impetus… We have lost valuable time for the liberation of Switzerland, but it can be made up soon enough. Monseigneur, I urge you gather all your troops, except the detachments, for a short and vigorous winter campaign; you should inform me of your plans, so that they will match mine, and then, as soon as the roads are practicable, I shall be ready with all the troops under my command to act with Your Imperial Highness, forming a single spirit and a single body.'[54]

Archduke Charles replied on 30 October, and was crass enough to apply the word 'retreat' to the Russian departure, instead of the circumlocution 'withdrawal to quarters of repose,' which had become fashionable at Russian headquarters. Weyrother (now restored to favour) grabbed the letter before it could be intercepted by Suvorov's suite, and on reading it aloud to the field-marshal he omitted all the expressions likely to cause offence. Suvorov asked to have it read out again by an officer of the Russian staff, and the man naturally delivered all the words as they had been written. Wickham writes that 'the marshal as soon as he heard it flew into a violent rage, and immediately dictated a letter to the Archduke which, from what I have heard of its contents, was far more injudicious and more offensive than any of his former ones.'[55]

In reply Suvorov protested that the word 'retreat,' like the word 'defensive,' was one that had been foreign to him throughout his life. 'An old soldier like me can be tricked once, but will never be so stupid as to be tricked twice; I am unable to enter into a plan of operations which holds out no advantage to me. I have sent a courier to St. Petersburg, I will allow my army to rest, and I shall undertake nothing without the order of my sovereign.'[56]

Wickham nevertheless found the chief explanation for what was happening in 'the almost universal desire of the army to return to Russia and an evident dread of meeting the French, which I have observed increasing among every class of the officers since the unfortunate affair of Zürich.'[57]

HOMEWARDS

On 2 November Colonel Ferdinand Roverea and his regiment of Swiss set out for winter quarters in Germany as the advance guard of Suvorov's army. On the second day of marching he was overtaken by the field-marshal, who was travelling in a hired carriage and was escorted by a body of Cossacks,

one of whom as a mark of special favour carried a thunder box suspended from his neck, with his head through the circular seat. All of a sudden the party came to a stop and the escort held up their cloaks to serve as a screen around the carriage. It should have been easy enough to divine the occasion, which certainly did not call for witnesses or military honours, but Major Wagner was at the tail of the column with his old company, and he made his men halt and present arms… a dull sound told him what should have been evident to him from the beginning. This occasioned much ridicule at the time, and would certainly have led to endless jokes at our expense if Wagner had not suddenly cried out aloud: 'Well, my grenadiers, we have seen something no Frenchman has ever seen—the backside of the field-marshal!' The saying entered currency and the blunder was forgotten.[58]

The corps of Derfelden marched from Lindau on 3 November, and that of Rosenberg left the area of Hohenems and Bregenz on the following day. The Russians had still made no proper arrangements for the march, and 'within four days almost the whole of the Russian army was working through the country as destructively as a tornado. The troops marched wherever they pleased, they took up quarters as fancy dictated, and drove one another out of favoured locations.'[59]

On 6 November Suvorov established his headquarters in Augsburg, while his troops settled into the villages in the corridor between the Lech, the Danube and the Iller. The Cossacks were deployed along the Iller as a security cordon, which was a sensible precaution, though Massena had no intention of opening a fresh campaign at this late season of the year. Suvorov could therefore take his ease in Augsburg and enjoy to the full his reputation as a popular hero. His headquarters was never more crowded than on Sundays, when he relegated the Orthodox Popes to the role of acolytes, and officiated at the divine service in person. He wore his full dress uniform, which was covered with orders and decorations from shoulder to shoulder and down to the waist, and he remained the centre of attention, whether he stretched out flat on the floor, stood transfixed in religious fervour, or dashed among the 'choirboys' (regimental fifers) with a roll of paper to beat out the time on their shoulders and heads. The way from the chapel to the dining lay through a crowded vestibule, where Suvorov continued the performance. Roverea once saw him approach a venerable knight of the Order of St. Louis, who seemed to be down on his luck. 'The field-marshal's demeanour was humble. "My father," he said to him, "your blessing would be of great value. Do not refuse it to me!"'[60]

Outside, the streets the streets of this normally sombre city resounded to the clamour of roistering officers like Gryazev and his companions, who tugged at the house doorbells, and staggered drunkenly in and out of the city gates for the fun of putting the Austrian guards through their ponderous paces. The troops were busy selling the loot they had acquired on the march through Swabia, just as they had sold the booty from Italy and the Little Cantons in the Vorarlberg.

There was consternation when Suvorov ordered the Augustusbrunnen opposite the Rathaus to be demolished to make way for a guardhouse. The great fountain was the pride of the city, 'and it took repeated representations for the field-marshal to desist from breaking up the fountain, and then only after a service of twenty-four silver pieces was delivered to him at his demand. The guardhouse was set up beside the fountain anyway, and the city required to supply 120 pairs of fur shoes and 120 cloaks for the troops, and since the guard was never mounted we may presume that these items were diverted for other purposes.'[61] In nearby Memmingen Grand Prince Constantine observed no bounds whatsoever. He delighted in holding up the Austrians to contempt, and he beat soldiers who did not instantaneously pay the respects due to him.

On 13 November Suvorov wrote to Emperor Francis to inform him that he had received a letter from Paul dated 22 October, which required him to bring his army back to Russia. He would suspend his march only if Francis made a written request to him, together with an assurance that he had made representations to St. Petersburg. No order arrived from Paul for the Russians to leave at any particular time, but Suvorov anticipated events by setting his troops successively in motion between 26 November and 3 December. They marched in two columns—the one assigned a route by way of Regensburg, Pilsen and Prague, and the other a more southerly path through Linz, Budweis and Olmütz. The disorders continued unchecked, and Constantine excelled himself by pistolling a coach driver who impeded his descent on a hillside road; the man was not badly wounded by the shot, but he was nearly killed when he was belaboured by the officers of Constantine's suite. When he lodged for the night, Constantine delighted in having servants and soldiers summoned to his room, where he could beat them in person.

Francis replied (very tardily) to Suvorov on 28 November, asking him to postpone the Russians' departure, or at least contact Archduke Charles to make proper arrangements for supplying them on the way. It was too late, for

Suvorov left Augsburg on the same day, well before the Austrian Emperor's letter could arrive. He nevertheless took an extraordinarily long time on his journey to Bohemia, hoping perhaps that an unequivocal order from Paul would relieve him of personal responsibility. In fact Paul wrote to him on 1 December to tell him to suspend the army's return to Russia, while he awaited the reply of the Austrians to a number of his political demands.

Suvorov reached Prague only in the middle of December. The Austrian commandant called on the field-marshal in his house to make a courtesy visit, and was received by Suvorov in an open-necked shirt, which might be conceived as an insult. However Suvorov was unreservedly glad to see Lieutenant-General Bellegarde, an old comrade from Italy, and he talked once more of invading France by way of Dauphiné and marching on Paris to destroy that nest of atheists and restore the ancient royal dynasty to the throne.

Lord Grenville had suspected that his ambassador in Vienna Sir Morton Eden had absorbed too much of the Austrian ways of thinking, and he had replaced him by Sir Gilbert Eliot, Earl of Minto. The new envoy now travelled to Prague to meet Suvorov, and he described him in words that have unfortunately become one of the best-known portraits of the field-marshal. Suvorov appeared to be

> the most perfect Bedlamite that ever was allowed at large. I never saw anything so stark mad… I was full dressed of course, and although I did not expect him to be so, I was not prepared for what I saw. After waiting a good while an ante-chamber with some aides de camp, a door opened and a little old shrivelled creature in a pair of red breeches and a shirt for all clothing, bustled up to me, took me in his arms, and embraced me with his shirt sleeves, made a string of high-flown flummery compliments which he concluded by kissing me on both cheeks, and I am told I was in luck that my mouth escaped… He is always attended by one or two nephews [the Gorchakovs] who never take their eyes off him, and seem to me to keep him in the sort of subjection that a keeper generally does… He pretends or thinks at times, that he has seen

visions; and I have seen an official note written, or rather dictated, by him to Mr. Wickham, in which he says his Master, Jesus Christ, has ordered him so and so… Such are heroes, and thus the world is led, and such is name and fame. This is a correct picture of this mad mountebank.[62]

On 5 January 1800 Suvorov attended the Christmas Mass of the Orthodox Church in Prague. This was very nearly the last time that he was seen by an international public, for Paul was now bent on bringing the Russian army all the way back home. He was angered by the Austrian 'betrayal' of his forces in Switzerland, and at the British for sacrificing his contingent in North Holland; the Austrians moreover were interfering with his designs for Italy, and were proving careless of Russian sensibilities, as when they (very reasonably) advised French officers on parole to avoid locations where they were likely to be plundered by Russian troops.

THE END

The order to take the road to Russia reached the regiments in the middle of January. As a newly-promoted major Gryazev received the news with mixed feelings: 'On the one hand I regretted that I would not have the opportunity to correct the disorders in my [new] battalion, or command it on active operations, which were now at an end. At the same time I was more than glad that the return to our homeland would put an end to our hardships, and reunite us with our loved ones.'[63]

The army departed by instalments on 25 January, and progressed across Bohemia and Moravia to Teschen, where it divided into two columns—the division of Schveikovsky forming the right-hand column which marched by way of Tarnow, Zamosc and Vladimir, and Suvorov with the corps of Rosenberg as the left-hand column which was assigned a route leading to Brest by way of Krakow, Opatow and Lublin.

Suvorov was buoyed up by the news that Paul was not only putting him in command of all the troops in western Russia, but was promoting him to generalissimo, a rank without precedent in the Russian service. But the swiftest of horses could not outpace his age and the pent-up stresses of the campaign, which were catching up with him at last, and on 5 February he fell ill on the way to Krakow. On the 13th he relinquished command of the column of troops to Rosenberg, and journeyed on to his estate at Kobrin, where he arrived on the 20th. Suvorov was still in a bad way, but a stream of visitors from St. Petersburg told him of the plans that were being made for his reception there, complete with triumphal arches, salvoes of artillery, thundering drums and much ringing of church bells.

Suvorov left Kobrin for the capital at the end of March, unaware that Paul had tired not only of the war but of its hero. With that capriciousness which makes tyranny finally intolerable, the Emperor chose to take exception when he was told that Suvorov had appointed Förster and Schveikovsky as permanent *généraux du jour*, or standing senior duty officers; such posts were reserved for the service of emperors alone (Melas had run foul of Francis for much the same reason in Italy). Suvorov was still on the road when he learned that Paul was deeply offended, and that the great reception had been called off. For Suvorov the persons of his god and his Sovereign were scarcely to be distinguished, and the rebuke struck to his soul.

On 1 May Suvorov's carriage reached its destination in St. Petersburg, at the house of his son-in-law Dimitry Ivanovich Khvostov. Out of form Paul sent Prince Bagration to ask after his health. Bagration relates that he found Suvorov in bed:

> He was very weak and he lapsed into a coma. His attendants rubbed spirits on his temples and gave him smelling salts, which brought him to his senses. He looked at me, but the old fire no longer burned in his eyes. He continued to stare, as if trying to recognise me, then called out: 'Ah! You are Petr. It is good to see you!' He fell silent. He looked at me again, and I reported my commission from the Emperor. Aleksandr Vasilevich came to life again, but his speech was halting; 'Convey my respects… my deepest respects… to the Emperor… please do… Petr… ah!… so much pain!' He said no more and fell into a delirium.[64]

Suvorov returned to himself a little when he learned that Paul was sending a personal message, but when it was delivered to him he learned that he was forbidden to show himself at court. On 12 May a second and literally death-dealing insult deprived Suvorov of his adjutants, who were returned to regimental service.

Field-Marshal Suvorov died at two in the morning of 17 May 1800. The official newspaper passed over the event in silence, but the news spread throughout St. Petersburg and the citizens crowded onto the streets. The people again paid their tribute when they lined the route of Suvorov's funeral procession to the Alexander Nevsky Monastery, though the more astute courtiers stayed away from the event, as did almost all the diplomatic corps. After the service there was some difficulty about getting the coffin through the entrance to its resting place in a side chapel, whereupon a party of soldiers rushed to the front, seized hold of the coffin, and bore their hero aloft and through. 'No more nonsense!' they shouted, 'there is nobody who can stop Suvorov!'

CONSTANTINE

BAGRATION

Emperor Paul did not long survive the greatest figure of his reign. His tyrannical and arbitrary ways alienated more and more of his courtiers and military men, and he was murdered by a group of officers on 24 March 1801. His second son, Grand Prince Constantine Pavlovich, commanded the Russian Guard at Austerlitz and in the campaign of 1812-13. he was still capable of displaying the same brutality as in 1799, but he mellowed in some respects, and (under the influence of a Polish wife) became a surprisingly sympathetic Viceroy of Poland after the Napoleonic Wars. He refused to crush Warsaw when a revolution broke out there in 1830, when Suvorov would probably not have hesitated for a moment, and he died of natural causes in the following year.

Of all the Russian commanders Prince Petr Ivanovich Bagration had been the closest to Suvorov. In 1805, in contrast with his behaviour at the close of the Swiss campaign, he proved to be an expert and resourceful rearguard commander during the Russian retreat from Lower Austria to Moravia. After campaigning against the Swedes (1808-9) and Turks (1809-10) Bagration commanded the Second West Army in the opening weeks of the new French war in 1812. He was mortally wounded while defending the fieldworks on the Russian left wing at Borodino on 7 September, and died of the consequent infection seventeen days later.

Michael Friedrich Melas was left in command of the Austrians after Suvorov had been removed from Italy. He settled some uncompleted business by reducing the fortress of Coni, and he belied his years by taking the offensive in April 1800 and splitting the remaining French in two, driving one part on Genoa, and the other to Provence. Genoa fell on 4 June with Massena in it, but by then Melas was being forced to take measures against Napoleon Bonaparte, who had returned from Egypt, and was irrupting into north-eastern Italy with the newly-formed Army of Dijon. At Marengo (14 June) Melas gave Napoleon one of the greatest frights of his life, and failed to beat him by only the narrowest of margins. Melas never again exercised active field command, but Napoleon presented him with a fine Arab sword in recognition of his performance. He died in 1806.

Although Suvorov had never got on friendly terms with Melas, the same did not apply to his relations with his Austrian chiefs of staff. The connection of the Russians with Franz Weyrother did not end in 1799. He re-emerged in 1805 as chief of staff to Kutuzov in the campaign of Austerlitz, where his plan for the battle of 5 December is caricatured in Tolstoy's War and Peace as a pedantic Teutonic monstrosity. Weyrother knew and liked the

MELAS

CHASTELER

Russians, but he was at fault in failing to recognise that Kutuzov was not a Suvorov. Weyrother died not long afterwards, on 16 February 1806, possibly by his own hand.

The brave, idealistic and perilously short-sighted Jacques Gabriel Chasteler survived much better than might have been expected. He overcame his wound and his undeserved fall from grace in 1799, and proved his worth all over again in the campaigns in the Tyrol in 1805 and 1809. He ended his days on 7 May 1825 as a field-marshal and in the honoured post of the Austrian commandant of Venice.

A few thoughts come to mind. We see Suvorov when he was beyond his physical prime, yet powerfully creative in his ambition to frame a comprehensive response to the Revolution at every level. He matched its military prowess with energetic ways of war, and he confronted its ideology with principles of legitimacy and religion.

Tactical notions have a way of dying with their times and creators, but those of Suvorov survive much better than most, as long as we take them not at face value, as detailed prescriptions for action, but in the spirit in which they were probably intended—as the means of overcoming timorousness and inertia.

The stature of Suvorov as a leader is unchallengeable, and it was the product of example, firmness of will, gifts of communication, and a brutality which was tempered with empathy with the soldiers under his command. Two centuries after his last campaign his sayings on the subject were still to be discovered in fading paint on the walls of former Soviet military establishments throughout Eastern Europe. The Soviet order disappeared into history like the tsarist order before it, but Suvorov's work as an inspirer of troops will hold its relevance for as long as men prepare for war.

In Suvorov's own generation men of republican principles offered a tribute of their own, albeit couched in hostile terms: 'He was the best possible general at the disposal of the Russians and the allies as a whole. He had that force and intensity of will and character which can take the place of the most brilliant talents and of genius himself. If it had ever been given to men to halt the march of human progress, and subject Reason to servitude, then Suvorov and his Russians would have accomplished that abominable counter-revolution.'[65]

This certainly corresponds with the experience of French commanders in 1799. The *généraux de division* Schérer and Moreau were defeated in the opening stages of the Italian campaign, and a third of that rank, Sérurier, was caught up in the collapse of the French defence of the Adda and taken prisoner. The campaign and battle of the Trebbia produced a further crop of trophies: *général de division* Macdonald had been sabred outside Modena and was now wounded in the same culminating battle which left *général de division* Victor wounded, and the acting divisional commanders Olivier and Rusca and the *général de brigade* Salme not only bleeding but captured. At Novi the French commander Joubert was killed outright, which cut short a career of exceptional promise, while *généraux de division* Grouchy and Pérignon and *général de brigade* Partouneaux followed fashion by being disabled by wounds and falling in the hands of the allies. However none of these people was routed in

MORTIER

such convincing fashion as was Mortier by Rosenberg in the Muotatal.

The names by themselves indicate that Suvorov was by no means dealing with the second line of French commanders in 1799. Seven future marshals campaigned against him in that year, and only Saint-Cyr escaped the unhappy experiences which overtook Grouchy, Macdonald, Mortier, Pérignon, Sérurier and Victor.

The question is sometimes put as to who would have won, if Suvorov had remained in the southern theatre of war, stayed in good health, and encountered Bonaparte in 1800. Almost the most important issue concerns not the events of that year, but those of the high summer of 1799, presuming that Suvorov, Chasteler and Zach had been permitted to carry through their offensives against Genoa and its rivieras. If, as seems likely, Genoa and its rivieras had fallen, then it becomes a moot point as to which party would have been the first to take the new campaign into enemy territory. Even if Bonaparte had been quicker off the mark, his options would have been much reduced, and he would have been unlikely to have reached the north Italian plain unchallenged if he had still

chosen to make his passage by the Great St. Bernard.

The two mens' opinions of one another now become of some interest. Much later the considered judgement of Bonaparte, or rather Napoleon, was that Suvorov had 'the soul of a great commander, but not the brains. He was extremely strong willed, he was amazingly active and utterly fearless—but he was as devoid of genius as he was ignorant of the art of war.'[66]

Suvorov followed Bonaparte's career with the closest interest, and he once exclaimed to Roverea: 'That man has stolen my secret, the speed of my marches!'[67] He had written to one of his nephews in 1796:

> That young Bonaparte, how he moves ! He is a hero, a giant, a magician. He overcomes nature and he overcomes men. He turned the Alps as if they did not exist; he has hidden their frightful rocks in his pocket, and tucked up his army up the right sleeve of his uniform. The enemy scarcely catches sight his soldiers before he throws his troops at them like a thunderbolt from Jupiter, spreading terror in all directions, and crushing the scattered bands of Austrians and Piedmontese. My God, how he moves! The first time he assumed command he cut to the heart of tactics like a sword slashing through the Gordian Knot. He disregards the odds against him, he attacks the enemy wherever they are to be found, and he defeats them in detail. He knows that shock is irresistible—and that says it all. His enemies will continue in their old routine, subject to the scribblers in the Cabinet, but as for him, he carries his council of war in his head. His operations are as free as the air he breathes… My conclusion is this. That as long as General Bonaparte keeps his wits about him he will be victorious; he possesses the higher elements of the military art in a happy balance. But if, unfortunately for him, he throws himself into the whirlpool of politics, he will lose the coherence of his thoughts and he will be lost.[68]

In short, Suvorov did not underestimate Bonaparte, but Bonaparte underestimated Suvorov, and in the dimension most relevant to the events of 1800 Bonaparte would have been unlikely to grasp the speed with which Suvorov could concentrate his forces.

In the campaign of 1800, as it was actually fought, the unsupported Austrians reduced Genoa only on 4 June, but they were able to rearrange themselves to march against Bonaparte and bring him to within a trice of defeat at Marengo on the 14th, a day which the Corsican remembered as the closest and most crucial of his victories. The Austrians paid in the traditional way, by ceding territory, but a reverse for Bonaparte would have extended beyond north Italy, because he was now fighting as First Consul, and his political and military authority were both at stake.

Having journeyed so long in the company of Suvorov, it would be shameful for us to be classified as *Nichtswisser* and hatchers of *Unterkunft*. We therefore declare outright that Suvorov would have beaten Bonaparte in 1800, and can only regret that he never had the opportunity.

COSSACKS IN ACTION AT THE TREBBIA

NOTES TO CHAPTER 11

[1] Masson, 1859, 372

[2] Weyrother, 'Tagebuch,' Hüffer, 1900-1, I,43-4

[3] Auffenberg, 'Relation,' Ibid., I,62

[4] It is clear from the statements of Weyrother and Auffenberg, and confirmed by William Wickham (Wickham to Grenville, Wangen, 7 October 1799, Wickham, 1870, II,281) that the essential decisions were taken in a council on 28 September, and under Austrian influence, and not at the larger session on the 29th; Russian historians make much of Auffenberg's absence on the 29th, as a sign of Suvorov's disfavour, but in fact the Austrian was already on the Pragel.

[5] Milyutin, 1856-8, IV,101

[6] Ibid, IV, 268. Here I use Milyutin's reproduction of 'Ratnik,' the relevant number of *Moskvityanin*, 1844, being unavailable at the time this book went to press.

7   This spectacular location was a favourite with nineteenth-century landscape painters. The present dam at the eastern end of the lake has raised the water level considerably, and destroyed or submerged much of the scene of the fighting at Seerüti. The shore line in 1799 followed the 830 m contour, and the lake occupied about half its present extent; the water is deepest close to the northern shore, where the old shore line projected little further in 1799 than now, but the plain at the western end was double its present length, and (except for rocky bluffs like the Bärentritt) the southern shore was lined with meadows which are now under water. Something of the original appearance of the lake may be seen towards the end of winter, by when the demands of hydroelectric power have reduced the water to its former level.

8   Gryazev, 1898, 114

9   Marès, (1799), 1909, 236

10 PRO FO 74/27, Clinton to Grenville, Glarus, 2 October 1799

11 Quoted in Reding-Biberegg, 1895, 333

12 Gryazev, 1898, 106

13 Quoted in Hennequin, 1911, 365

14 Denisov, 1874-5, XII,42

15 Gachot, 1904, 358

16 PRO FO 74/27, Clinton to Grenville, Chur, 9 October 1799

17 Franz Bürgler of Illgau, quoted in Reding-Biberegg, 1895, 353

18 Denisov, 1874-5, XII,74

19 Commissary Fassbind, quoted in Reding-Biberegg, 1895, 353

20 Quoted in Ibid., 1132

21 Gryazev, 1898, 108

22 Ibid., 111-12

23 PRO FO 74/27, Clinton to Grenville, Glarus, 2 October 1799; Auffenberg to Petrasch, Chur, 8 October 1799, Hüffer. 1900-1, I,416

24 Reding-Biberegg, 1895, 125

25 Waldburga Mohr's 'Protokollum,' in Ibid., 335

26 Mohr in Ibid., 335

27 Ibid., 150

28 Wickham to Grenville, Wangen, 17 October 1799, Wickham, 1870, II,284-5. See also Auffenberg's 'Relation,' in Hüffer, 1900-1, I,64,66; Stutterheim 1812, IV,xi,35

29 Weyrother, 'Tagenbuch,' Hüffer, 1900-1, I,47

30 Gryazev, 1898, 118

31 Weyrother, 'Tagebuch,' Hüffer, 1900-1, I,48-9

32 Gryazev, 1898, 120

33 Ibid., 119

34 Ibid., 120

35 Denisov, 1874-5, XII,47

36 Gryazev, 1898, 122-3

37 Ibid., 21

38 This useful calculation is to be found in Reding-Biberegg, 1895, 98

39 Wickham to Grenville, Feldkirch, 11 October 1799, Wickham, 1870, II,258

40 Wickham to Grenville, Feldkirch, 17 October 1799, Ibid., II,262

41 Wickham to Grenville, Wangen, 17 October 1799, Ibid., II,272-3. Suvorov was lodging at the house of Josepha von Bauer, née von Funcken, at the present Marktstrasse no. 19

42 Roverea, 1848, II,300-1

43 Wickham to Grenville, Feldkirch, 12 October 1799, Wickham, 1870, II,160-1

44 KA Deutschland und Schweiz 1799 X 123, Suvorov to Archduke Charles, Feldkirch, 2.30 p.m. 14 October

45 Wickham to Grenville, Wangen, 17 October 1799, Wickham, 1870, II,277-8. See also Bellegarde to Thugut, Prague, 6 January 1800, Hüffer, 1900-1, I,522

46 Wickham to Grenville, Wangen, 18 October 1799, Wickham, 1870, II,290

47 Wickham to Grenville, undated, 'Dropmore Papers,' 1892-1915, V,508

48 Wickham to Grenville, Wangen, 17 October 1799, Wickham, 1870, II,273

50 Suvorov to Archduke Charles, Lindau, 20 October 1799, Hüffer, 1900-1, I,453

51 Gryazev, 1898, 194

52 Wickham to Grenville, Wangen, 17 October 1799, Wickham, 1870, II,281

53 Clinton to Wickham, Lindau, 29 October 1799, Ibid., II,306

54 KA FA Italien 1799 VIII 301, Suvorov to Archduke Charles, Lindau, 29 October

55 Wickham to Grenville, Augsburg, 3 November 1799, Wickham 1870, II,324

56 Suvorov to Archduke Charles, 1 November and 31 October 1799, in Hüffer, 1900-1, I,471, and Lopatin, 1986, 367-8

57 Wickham to Grenville, Augsburg, 3 November 1799, Wickham, 1870, II,324

58 Roverea, 1848, II,324

59 KA FA Italien 1799 XIII 43, 'Bemerkungen über die Beschaffenheit der russischen Armeen'

60 Roverea, 1848, II,329

61 KA FA Italien 1799 XIII 43, 'Bemerkungen über die Beschaffenheit der russischen Armeen'

62 Minto to Lady Minto, Prague, 3 January 1800, Minto, 1874, 107-8

63 Gryazev, 1898, 183

64 Bagration, in editorial notes to Gryazev, 1898, 187

65 Masson, 1859, 380

66 Quoted in Picard, 1913, 556-7

67 Roverea, 1848, II,322=3

68 Suvorov to Aleksei Gorchakov, 5 November 1796, Lopatin, 1986, 211-12

BIBLIOGRAPHY

SUVOROV'S CORRESPONDENCE

In order of publication. Also entered alphabetically under editors in main bibliography below

Fuchs, (Fuks), E., *Istoriya Rossysko-Avstryskoi Kampany 1799. G.*, 3 vols, St. Petersburg 1825-6 (for the correspondence in vols II-III). By Suvorov's cabinet secretary. One of the earliest and still one of the best of the documentary collections.

Milyutin, D. A., *Geschichte des Krieges Russlands mit Frankreich unter der Regierung Kaiser Pauls I. im Jahre 1799*, 5 vols, Munich 1856-8. Reproduces many of the relevant documents.

Hüffer, H., *Quellen zur Geschichte der Kriege von 1799 und 1800*, 2 vols, Leipzig 1900-1. Many letters to and from Suvorov included in this important collection of Austrian documents.

Meshcheryakov, G. P., *A. V. Suvorov. Dokumenty*, 4 vols, Moscow 1949-53. The standard collection, including much correspondence published for the first time. Meshcheryakov is nevertheless to be used with some caution, since he translated French and German originals into modern Russian, and omitted without notification many passages of military interest. The index by Z. M. Novikova is a work of scholarship in its own right, and proves invaluable for identifying individuals.

Lopatin, V. C., *A. V. Suvorov. Pis'ma*, Moscow 1986. A first-class annotated edition. Contains the best text of the *Art of Winning*.

N. B. The most accessible general biography of Suvorov is by Longworth, P., *The Art of Victory. The Life and Achievements of Generalissimo Suvorov 1729-1800*, London 1965.

MANUSCRIPT SOURCES

KRIEGSARCHIV (KA) VIENNA

Cabinets Akten (CA)

Feld Akten (FA)

Hofkriegsrätliche Akten (HkrA)

Kartensammlung, esp. the contemporary General Staff *Generalkarte des Kriegs Schauplatzes in Italien im Jahre 1799*; Maps H IV A 894-15 (Cassano and Lecco), H IV A 899-907 (Trebbia), H IV A 894-8 (Novi)

Depositions of the Military Order of Maria Theresa (MMTO)

N. B. These sources are cited only when documents are not reproduced in Hüffer (1900-1), or are printed there only in extract.

PUBLIC RECORD OFFICE (PRO) LONDO

FO (Foreign Office) 74/27, reports of Lieutenant-Colonel Clinton and Major-General Mulgrave

FO 74/28, reports of Lieutenant-General Ramsay

MAIN BIBLIOGRAPHY

Angeli, M. E., *Erzherzog Carl von Österreich als Feldherr und Heeresorganisator*, 6 vols, Vienna and Leipzig, 1896-7.

Anon., *The History of the Campaign of 1799, in Italy*, 4 vols, 2nd ed., London 1801-3. Astute and well informed.

Baumann, R., *Die schweizerische Volkserhebung im Frühjahr 1799*, Zürich 1912.

Blanning, T. C. W., *The Origins of the French Revolutionary Wars*, London 1986.

Blanning, T. C. W., *The French Revolutionary Wars 1787-1802*, London 1996.

Bousson de Mairet, E., *Éloge historique du Lieutenant-Général Comte Lecourbe*, Paris 1854.

Bunbury, H., *Narratives of Some Passages in the Great War with France*, (ed.) London 1927.

Burckhardt, F., *Die schweizerische Emigration 1798-1801*, Basel 1908.

Camenzind, A., *Maultiere machen Geschichte oder Suworows Krieg in den Schweizer Alpen im Jahre 1799*, Schwyz 1997. A good modern survey.

Charles-Lavauzelle, H., *Le Général Lecourbe*, Paris 1895.

Criste, O., *Erzherzog Carl von Österreich*, 3 vols, Vienna and Leipzig 1912.

Denisov, A. K., 'Istoriya Kazaka Voiska Donskago, Atamana Adriana Karpovicha Denisova,' *Russkaya Starina*, XI-XII, St. Petersburg 1874-5. Entertaining and informative.

'Dropmore Papers': Historical Manuscripts Commission, *Report on the Manuscripts of J. B. Fortescue, Esq., Preserved at Dropmore*, 9 vols, London 1892-1915. Esp. for the correspondence of Grenville.

Eggerking, T., *Moreau als Feldherr in den Feldzügen 1796 und 1799*, Berlin 1914.

Ehrman, J., *The Younger Pitt. The Consuming Struggle*,

London 1996.

Engelhardt, N. E., *Zapiski Lva Nikolaievicha Engelgardta 1766-1836*, Moscow, 1868.

Fasanari, R., *L'Armata Russa del Generale Suvorov attraverso Verona (1799-1800)*, Verona 1952.

Fuchs, (Fuks), E., *Istoriya Rossysko-Avstrysko Kampany 1799 G.*, 3 vols, St. Petersburg 1825-6. See 'Suvorov's Correspondence,' above.

Fuchs, E., *Anekdoty Knyazya Italyskago, grafa Suvorova Rymnikskago*, St. Petersburg 1827. This collection of stories complements usefully Fuchs' documentary collection of 1825-6. Both works are important sources.

Gachot, J. E., *Les Campagnes de 1799. Souworow en Italie*, Paris 1903.

Gachot, J. E., *Histoire Militaire de Masséna; la Campagne de Helvétie*, 1799, Paris 1904. The works of Gachot led me down many false trails until it became evident that they were essentially novels based on a modicum of fact. The descriptions of terrain, for example, are highly detailed but bear little relation to the actual ground.

Greppi, G., *Sardaigne-Autriche-Russie (1796-1802)*, Rome 1910.

Grayzev, Captain, (ed. Orlov, N.), *Italyansky Pokhod Suvorova v 1799 g., po Zapiskami Gryazeva*,

St. Petersburg 1898. By an officer of the Rosenberg Grenadiers. Detailed, reliable and most informative.

Günther, R., *Der Feldzug der Division Lecourbe im schweizerischen Hochgebirge*, Frauenfeld, 1896.

Hartmann, O., *Der Anteil der Russen am Feldzuge von 1799 in der Schweiz*, Zürich, 1892.

Hennequin, L., *Zürich. Masséna en Suisse*, Paris and Nancy, 1911.

Heriot, A., *The French in Italy 1796-99*, London 1957.

Heuberger, D., 'Die strategische Bedeutung der Schweiz aus der Sicht des Auslandes 1798 bis 1815,' *Revue Internationale d'Histoire Militaire*, LXV, Neuchâtel, 1988.

Hüffer, H., *Über den Zug Suworows durch die Schweiz, im Jahre 1799*, Innsbruck 1900.

Hüffer, H., *Quellen zur Geschichte der Kriege von 1799 und 1800*, 2 vols, Leipzig 1900-1. See 'Suvorov's Correspondence,' above.

Hüffer, H., *Der Krieg des Jahres 1799 und die zweite Koalition*, 2 vols, Gotha 1904-5.

Jomini, A. H., *Histoire critique et militaire des Guerres de la Révolution*, 15 vols, Paris 1820-4.

Keep, J. L., 'The Russian Army's Response to the French Revolution,' *Jahrbücher für die Geschichte Osteuropas*, XXVIII, No. 4, Stuttgart and Wiesbaden, 1980.

Keep, J. L., *Soldiers of the Tsar. Army and Society in Russia 1462-1874*, Oxford 1985.

Kray, P., 'Briefe des Feldzeugmeisters Paul Freiherrn von Kray de Krajova et Topolya an seinen Bruder Alexander von Kray,' *Mitteilungen des K. und K. Kriegsarchivs*, 3rd

series, VI, Vienna, 1909.

Langeron, A., 'Russkaya Armiya v God Smerti Ekateriny II,' *Russkaya Starina*, LXXXVIII, St. Petersburg 1895.

Leonov, O., Ulyanov, I., *Regularnaya Pekhota 1698-1801*, Moscow, 1995.

Lewenshtern (Löwenstern), V. I., 'Zapiski Generala V. I. Levenshterna,' *Russkaya Starina*, CIII, St. Petersburg, 1900.

Longworth, P., *The Art of Victory. The Life and Achievements of Generalissimo Suvorov 1729-1800*, London 1965.

Lopatin, V. C., *A.V. Suvorov. Pism'a*, Moscow 1986. See 'Suvorov's Correspondence,' above.

Lumbroso, G., *I Moti popolari contro I Francesi alla fine del secolo XVIII (1796-1800)*, Florence 1932.

Macdonald, J. E., *Souvenirs du Maréchal Macdonald Duc de Tarente*, Paris 1892.

Macksey, P., *Statesmen at War. The Strategy of Overthrow 1798-1799*, London 1974.

Marès, L., *Papiers de Marès; Précis de la Guerre en Suisse*, [1799], Paris 1909. Useful evaluation of Switzerland as a new theatre of war.

Massena, A., *Mémoires de Masséna*, Paris 1849.

Masson, C. F., *Mémoires secrets sur la Russie pendant les Règnes de Catherine II et de Paul 1er*, Paris 1859. Much useful detail, but heavily prejudiced against Suvorov and the Russians in general.

McGrew, R. E., *Paul I of Russia*, Oxford 1992.

Meshcheryakov, G. P., *A. V. Suvorov. Dokumenty*, 4 vols, Moscow 1949-53. See 'Suvorov's Correspondence,' above.

Meyer-Ott, W., *Johann Konrad Hotz später Friedrich Freiherr von Hotze, k. k. Feldmarschallieutenant*, Zürich 1853.

Milyutin, D. A., *Geschichte des Krieges Russlands mit Frankreich unter der Regierung Kaiser Paul's I im Jahre 1799*, 5 vols, Munich 1856-8. See 'Suvorov's Correspondence,' above.

Minto, *Life and Letters of Sir Gilbert Eliot, First Earl of Minto from 1751 to 1806*, 3 vols, London 1874.

Nafziger, G. F., Worley, W., *The Imperial Russian Army (1763-1815)*, 2 vols, Pisgah (Ohio), 1996.

Nostitz, F. A., *Der Westfeldzug Suvorovs in der öffentlichen Meinung Englands*, Wiesbaden 1976.

Petrushevski, A., *Generalissimus Knyaz Suvorov*, St. Petersburg 1884. The standard older biography.

Phipps, R. W., *The Armies on the Rhine, in Switzerland, Holland, Italy, Egypt and the Coup d'État of Brumaire*, Oxford, 1939, vol V of *The armies of the First French Republic and the Rise of the Marshals of Napoleon I*, Oxford 1926-39. This work would have been of greater value still, if not for the convoluted style and the limiting perspective (French generals considered mainly as future Napoleonic marshals).

Picard, *Préceptes et Jugements de Napoléon*, Paris 1913.

Ragsdale, H. (ed.), *Paul I - a Reassessment of his Life and Reign*, Pittsburg 1979.

'Ratnik,' (probably Starkov), 'Pokhod v Italiyu v 1799 godu. Razskaz Starika Suvorovskago Ratnika,' *Moskvityanin*, Nos. I, VI, VII, VIII, X, Moscow 1844. The valuable testimony of a soldier of the regiment of Rehbinder.

Rauchensteiner, M., *Feldzeugmeister Johann Freiherr von Hiller*, Vienna 1972.

Rauchensteiner, M., *Kaiser Franz und Erzherzog Carl. Dynastie und Heerwesen in Österreich 1796-1809*, Vienna 1972.

Reding-Biberegg, R., 'Der Zug Suworoff's durch die Schweiz,' *Der Geschichtsfreund*, L, Stans 1895. Still the most important single study of Suvorov's Swiss campaign. Reproduces virtually all the relevant French documents.

Regele, O., *Feldmarschall Radetzky*, Vienna 1957.

Reichel, D., 'La Guerre en Montagne dans l'Oeuvre Historique de Jomini,' *Revue Internationale d'Histoire Militaire*, LXV, Neuchâtel 1988.

Rodger, A. B., *The War of the Second Coalition: A Strategic Commentary*, Oxford 1964.

Roider, K. A., *Baron Thugut and Austria's Response to the French Revolution*, Princeton 1987.

Ross, S. T., *The Quest for Victory: French Military Strategy, 1792-99*, New York 1973.

Rothenberg, G., *Napoleon's Great Adversaries. The Archduke Charles and the Austrian Army 1792-1814*, London 1983.

Roverea, *Mémoires, écrits par lui-même*, 4 vols, Paris and Berne. By a colonel of one of the Swiss regiments. Encountered Suvorov towards the end of the Swiss campaign. 1848.

Saul, N. E., *Russia and the Mediterranean 1797-1807*, Chicago 1970.

Saul, N. E., 'The Objectives of Paul's Italian Policy,' in Ragsdale, 1979.

Schroeder, P. W., *The Transformation of European Politics 1763-1848*, Oxford 1994.

Sherwig, J. M., *Guineas and Gunpowder. British Foreign Aid in the Wars with France 1793-1815*, Cambridge (Mass.), 1969.

Soult, N. J., *Mémoires du maréchal-général Soult, duc de Dalmatie*, 3 vols, Paris 1854.

Stanislavskaya, A. M., *Russko-anglyskie Otnosheniya i Problemi Sredizemnomor'ya (1798-1807)*, Moscow 1962.

Stutterheim, J., 'Geschichte des Feldzugs der k. k. oesterreichische Armee in Italien im Jahre 1799,' *Österreichische Militärische Zeitschrift*, I-IV, Vienna 1812. A very useful source. Written in the author's typically lively style.

Suvorov, A. V., 'Suworow. Beiträge zu dessen Charakteristik nach bisher noch nicht editirten Schriftstücken des k. k. Kriegs-Archivs aus dem Feldzuge 1799 in Italien,' *Mittheilungen des K. K. Kriegs Archivs*, Vienna 1884.

Thugut, J. A., (ed. Vivenot, A.), *Vertrauliche Briefe von Freiherrn von Thugut Österr. Ministers des Äussern*, 2 vols, Vienna 1872.

Tuetey, L., *Sérurier, 1742-1819*, Paris 1899.

Vigel, F. F., *Vospominaniya F. F. Vigela*, 3 vols, Moscow 1864-6.

Vigel, F. F., *Zapiski*, 7 vols, Moscow 1891-3.

Vivenot, A., *Thugut, Clerfayt und Wurmser*, Vienna 1869.

Vivenot, A., Zeissberg, H., *Quellen zur Geschichte der Politik Österreichs während der französischen Revolutionskriege 1790-1801*, 5 vols, Vienna 1873-90.

Arkhiv Kniazya Vorontsova, 40 vols, Moscow 1873-90.

Wanner, G., 'Kriegsschauplatz Bodensee 1799/1800 und 1809,' *Militärhistorische Schriftenreihe*, LIX, Vienna 1987.

Wertheimer, E., 'Erzherzog Carl und die zweite Coalition bis zum Frieden von Lunéville 1798-1801,' *Archiv für österreichische Geschichte*, LXVII, Vienna 1886.

Wickham, W., *The Correspondence of the Right Honourable William Wickham from the Year 1794*, 2 vols, London 1870. Wickham was Grenville's agent in Switzerland, and his testimony is important for the later stages of the campaign of 1799.

Wiesendanger, E., *Die Schweiz im Kriegsjahre 1799*, Zürich 1899.

274

INDEX

A

Aare 154, 157, 162, 167, 213, 214, 215, 260
Acherberg 203
Acqui 121
Adda 23, 24, 30, 34, 39, 52, 57, 59, 60, 62, 63, 65, 66, 67, 68, 69, 85, 116, 119, 131, 268
Airolo 167, 171, 172, 173, 174, 199
Albisberg 210, 212, 215, 218
Alessandria 52, 68, 73, 76, 77, 79, 81, 84, 85, 90, 91, 111, 114, 115, 116, 117, 118, 119, 121, 122, 123, 129, 133, 134, 149, 163
Alexander 145, 149
Alp Mer 253, 254, 255, 256
Alpe di Fiud 171
Alpe di Sorescia 171, 174
Altdorf 158, 159, 161, 167, 171, 172, 181, 193, 197, 198, 199, 202, 207, 208, 223
Altstätten 260
Amsteg 159, 167, 168, 171, 172, 183, 186, 189, 193, 194, 196, 197, 198, 223
Andermatt 162, 167, 171, 172, 177, 181, 182, 183, 186, 187, 199
Apennines 52, 72, 84, 85, 87, 88, 89, 91, 92, 99, 106, 112, 113, 114, 129, 133, 138
Arezzo 115
Asti 38, 80, 84, 85, 86, 149, 152, 157, 158, 163, 244
Attinghausen 198
Augsburg 38, 212, 264, 265, 271

B

Balzers 259
Baranovsky 96
Basilicata 40
Belfort Gap 153
Bellinzona 157, 158, 159, 161, 165, 166, 168, 172
Bernadotte 129
Bettbach 200, 231
Bettole di Novi 134, 138
Biasca 167, 169, 172
Bisistal 200, 210
Bludenz 158
Bobbio 91, 110
Bocchetta Pass 133, 135, 150
Bögner 83
Bologna 84, 87, 89, 112
Bonaparte 8, 9, 12, 45, 48, 52, 53, 80, 130, 267, 269, 270
Borgo San Antonio 94, 100
Borgo Val di Taro 88
Bormida 52, 73, 79, 80, 85, 90, 91, 113, 129, 133, 163
Bosco Marengo 38, 129, 133
Bouzet 58, 59

Bra 84
Bregenz 261, 262, 263
Breitäbnet 203
Breno 99
Brenta 45
Brodanovich 47, 49
Bruck 44
Bruggen 260
Brummbach 247
Brünn 41, 44
Brunnifern 186
Brunnital 186
Bubna 260
Budweis 264
Bürglen 198, 200, 202, 203

C

Calabria 40
Cambio 73, 78
Camona 255
Campo Aviano 52
Campo Formio 8, 12
Campremoldo 94, 100
Candia 81
Canneto 106
Capriata 133, 134
Carmagnola 84
Carnic Alps 8, 44
Carnot 155
Carolina 8
Casaliggio 100, 103, 106, 108
Casatisma 81, 91, 92
Cascina Grossa 79, 113
Cassano Spinola 144
Casteggio 91
Castel di Montanaro 112
Castel San Giovanni 72, 92, 95
Castenedolo 58
Castiglione 52, 71
Cervesina 77
Ceva 52
Chabran 162
Chaiserstock 204, 206
Championnet 152
Chasteler 10, 21, 23, 25, 26, 30, 31, 36, 37, 38, 46, 48, 49, 53, 54, 58, 59, 63, 65, 68, 69, 70, 71, 72, 73, 78, 81, 82, 83, 84, 86, 89, 91, 92, 94, 95, 99, 100, 102, 103, 106, 108, 109, 111, 112, 113, 114, 117, 119, 123, 129, 149, 268, 269
Cherasco 80, 83
Chiavenna 158, 259
Chinzertal 207, 242
Chinzig Pass 160, 165, 199, 200, 202, 203, 220, 221, 223, 227
Chivasso 81
Chrüzli Pass 181, 193, 223
Chubarov 50, 73, 76, 77, 136,

165
Chur 259, 260
Ciavernasco 100
Cima del Bosco 171, 172, 173, 174, 175
Cisalpine Republic 8, 61, 68, 71
Coburg 48
Colle di Tenda 114
Colle Ratto 138
Colli 137, 139, 147
Colloredo 261, 262
Como 47, 62, 66, 158
Condé 12, 13, 41, 212, 219, 260, 262
Coni 80, 114, 126, 204
Constance 40, 212, 215, 219, 220, 259, 260, 261, 262
Constantine 23, 25, 34, 35, 73, 76, 77, 78, 79, 80, 82, 163, 165, 198, 204, 208, 209, 223, 228, 229, 230, 236, 237, 244, 245, 253, 260, 261, 262, 264, 266, 267
Craufurd 11
Crescentino 81, 168
Cuneo 80, 126

D

Dalheim 50, 76, 96, 136, 165
Danube 14, 16, 35, 39, 41, 44, 130, 157, 159, 212, 264
Dazio 169, 171, 172, 174
Deldig 203
Delmas 51
Denisov 30, 31, 35, 38, 41, 44, 50, 53, 59, 60, 62, 65, 69, 71, 79, 80, 81, 82, 83, 86, 136, 143, 149, 166, 207, 208, 211, 231, 232, 234, 235, 253, 255, 257, 258, 271
Derfelden 34, 35, 40, 111, 116, 129, 133, 135, 136, 142, 143, 144, 146, 148, 149, 152, 163, 165, 166, 167, 168, 181, 186, 198, 200, 202, 207, 208, 209, 223, 226, 230, 236, 242, 244, 245, 249, 258, 263
Dietikon-Fahre 215
Dietrichstein 9, 12, 26, 153, 154
Disentis 157, 158, 159, 167, 172, 181, 193
Dobay 65, 138, 142, 147
Döller 165
Donaueschingen 243
Dörflingen 219
Dornbirn 259
Durasov 214, 215

E

Eglisau 219
Egypt 9, 12, 45, 53, 267
Einsiedeln 11, 221, 243
Engadine 158
Engelberg 159, 167
Erro 133

Erstfeld 198, 199, 207
Essen 215
Esterhazy 50, 66, 262
Etzli 186
Eugene 18

F

Faido 169, 171, 172
Feldkirch 243, 259, 260, 271
Feldkirchen 44
Ferrara 52, 84, 88, 90
Fertsch 116, 166, 207, 231, 258
Fiorella 82, 83, 121
Fiorenzuola 112
First Coalition 7, 9
Florence 84, 87, 115
Flüelen 161, 198, 221
Fontana Pradosa 95
Förster 50, 73, 81, 96, 100, 101, 102, 103, 105, 108, 109, 111, 112, 136, 165, 166, 173, 174, 175, 181, 207, 227, 231, 234, 258, 266
Fort Urbano 52, 84, 112
Fossano 80
Francavilla 133, 138
Franche-Comt 153
Francis 13, 20, 22, 23, 24, 25, 26, 37, 39, 41, 44, 53, 58, 69, 81, 114, 115, 116, 117, 148, 149, 150, 152, 153, 154, 208, 212, 264, 266
Francis II 7, 26, 113
Frauenfeld 260
Frelich 46, 50, 59, 66, 69, 79, 92, 94, 95, 96, 100, 102, 105, 109, 110, 111, 112, 136, 144, 148, 150
Fresia 51, 67, 71
Fresonara 133, 134, 135
Fuchs 22, 31, 34, 37, 38, 70, 86, 111, 115, 117, 126, 149, 155, 193, 211, 262
Fuggeln 200
Furen 204
Furka Pass 158, 177

G

Galicia 26, 39, 41, 212
Gallerate 158
Gamalero 129
Gamma 161, 199, 203, 258
Gangbach 200, 203
Garda 40, 47, 52, 119
Gardanne 51, 77, 121, 123, 137, 138, 143, 146
Garofoli 73, 79
Gaudenzio Gamma 165, 166
Gavi 114, 150, 163
Gazan 162, 214, 240, 243, 245
Genoa 72, 80, 84, 85, 87, 88, 90, 270
Gerelingen 203
Giornico 169, 172

Glarus 158, 171, 206, 210, 211, 220, 221, 222, 223, 226, 229, 237, 242, 244, 245, 246, 259, 271
Gorchakov 19, 26, 34, 83, 86, 95, 160, 213, 262, 265, 271
Gorizia 52
Göschenen 193
Göschener 193
Gossau 260
Gossolengo 100, 102, 112
Gragnano 100, 101, 102, 106, 108
Grekov 30, 50, 60, 62, 65, 95, 96, 136, 166, 207, 231, 235, 258
Grenville 11, 13, 37, 38, 72, 126, 151, 152, 153, 154, 155, 215, 221, 265, 270, 271
Grisons 11, 24, 40, 58, 154, 157, 172, 215, 253
Grouchy 113, 132, 133, 137, 138, 139, 142, 147, 268, 269
Gryazev 13, 30, 35, 38, 41, 53, 77, 86, 102, 117, 143, 144, 149, 175, 177, 189, 193, 207, 211, 230, 240, 252, 253, 256, 264, 265, 271
Gua 48
Gudin 162, 171, 177, 181, 182, 183
Gudovich 118, 214
Gurglen 252

H

Hadik 84, 113, 129, 130, 150, 152, 154, 157
Hatry 46, 51
Häxenseeli 251, 252
Helvetic 10, 11, 51, 162, 163, 214
Hermann 13, 19, 28, 40
Hertelendy 65
Herzogenburg 44
Hiller 218
Hinter Rietlig 203
Hinter-Iberg 234, 235
Hinterthal 208
Hofkriegsrath 9, 23, 24, 26, 44, 48, 115, 154
Hoftrog 200
Hohenems 259, 263
Hohenzollern 46, 51, 59, 89, 90, 119, 123
Hotze 11, 40, 72, 153, 154, 157, 158, 159, 160, 161, 163, 167, 172, 181, 193, 199, 206, 210, 211, 214, 215, 218, 219, 220, 221, 222, 237, 243, 260
Hürital 200, 206, 208, 210, 227, 231

I

I, Paul 17, 27, 32
Ibach 227
Ilanz 258
Iller 263, 264
Illgau 200, 227, 231, 233, 235, 271
Inn 40, 158, 159

Intschi 193
Inzago 65
IV, Charles 10
Ivrea 83

J

Jassy 16
Jellachich 33, 157, 158, 220, 223, 243, 244, 258, 259
Jessenen 200
Jetzloch 249, 252
Joubert 10, 22, 126, 129, 130, 131, 132, 133, 134, 135, 137, 138, 139, 142, 148, 268
Jourdan 39, 212
Judenburg 44
Jura 152, 155, 212

K

Kaim 46, 47, 50, 58, 59, 66, 69, 80, 85, 113, 119, 121, 129
Kalemin 50, 96, 136, 165, 228, 258
Kamensky 50, 165, 179, 189, 190, 192, 237, 240, 258
Karaiczay 14, 15, 27, 30, 50, 91, 92, 94, 95, 96, 100, 103, 108, 110, 112, 136, 147, 149
Kashkin 116, 166, 181, 182, 183, 189, 227, 231, 258
Kerpen 183, 198, 224, 229
Khvostov 266
King Ferdinand 8
Kinsky 109, 110
Kisten Pass 220
Klausen 200, 243, 245, 246
Klenau 13, 49, 72, 84, 88, 89, 90, 113, 115, 117, 129, 150
Kloten 213, 218
Knittelfeld 44
Kobrin 16, 18, 266
Kolychev 13, 23, 38
Konchansk 18, 37, 38
Korsakov 13, 28, 41, 152, 153, 154, 157, 159, 160, 161, 162, 167, 172, 181, 193, 199, 210, 211, 212, 213, 215, 218, 219, 220, 221, 222, 223, 243, 260, 261, 262
Kosciuszko 16, 29, 32, 38
Kray 31, 40, 45, 46, 47, 53, 89, 90, 113, 116, 119, 123, 125, 129, 133, 134, 135, 136, 138, 139, 142, 143, 144, 145, 146, 147, 148, 149, 150, 152
Krems 44
Kurnakov 30, 116, 227, 231, 242, 258
Kushnikov 34, 262

L

Lacour 235, 236, 257
Lacy 9, 26
Lambert 218
Lambertie 23, 37, 38, 117, 149
Lambro 52
Landeck 158

Langenrohr 44
Langosco 81
Lapoype 129
Latour 123, 125
Lattermann 50, 136
Lavrov 23, 34, 144, 259, 260
Lech 40
Lecourbe 162, 163, 171, 172, 190, 197, 198, 200, 207, 208
Leiberich, von 8
Leoben 8, 44
Leopold 7
Lerici 87
Lichtensteig 219, 222
Ligurian 8, 72, 80, 87, 91, 113, 114, 125, 130, 150
Limmat 154, 157, 158, 162, 167, 210, 222, 260
Lindau 38, 259, 260, 261, 262, 263, 271
Linth 157, 158, 159, 162, 163, 167, 171, 200, 210, 215, 218, 220, 221, 229, 236, 237, 240, 241, 242, 243, 244, 245, 246
Little Cantons 11, 150, 167, 264
Lobkowitz 50, 79, 136, 144, 145, 150
Lochet 240
Lodi 66
Loison 162, 171, 172
Lomonosov 49, 50, 62, 71, 96, 165, 228, 258
Löntsch 236, 245
Lorge 162, 214, 215, 218
Lovere 59
Lublin 265
Lucioni 82
Lukmanier 167, 181
Lusignan 136, 144, 145, 149
Lutovinov 174

M

Macdonald 22, 32, 48, 72, 83, 84, 85, 87, 88, 89, 90, 91, 92, 94, 96, 97, 106, 108, 110, 111, 112, 113, 114, 117, 123, 129, 130, 268, 269
Maderanertal 159, 167, 171, 181, 183, 186, 190, 193, 196, 223
Madrano 172
Maggiore 84, 159
Maienfeld 244, 259
Mainz 31, 39
Majola 158
Makhotin 235
Malpaga 103
Malta 12
Mamago 100, 101, 103, 106
Mamola 139
Mansurov 116, 166, 181, 182, 189, 190, 207, 231, 258
Marlborough 18
Martigny 158

Massena 22, 40, 113, 130, 153, 158, 162, 167, 172, 210, 212, 214, 215, 219, 221, 223, 231, 232, 235, 236, 242, 243, 261, 264, 267
Mattner Stock 206
Meiental 199
Melissino 30
Mella 58
Memmingen 264
Mercantin 46, 50
Meshchersky 193
Mezzana Corti 78, 91
Milan 10, 45, 52, 61, 65, 66, 67, 69, 70, 71, 72, 81, 84, 115, 116, 118, 123
Miloradovich 136, 143, 144
Mincio 23, 39, 45, 46, 47, 48, 49, 51, 56, 59, 119, 123, 125
Minto 20, 21, 37, 38, 154, 265, 271
Mitau 12, 21, 39
Mitlödi 221, 246
Mittrowsky 50, 65, 95, 96, 110, 126, 136, 144, 145
Molitor 162, 171, 215, 220, 221, 229, 236, 237, 244, 245
Mollis 220, 237, 240, 244
Moncaliere 84
Montale 112
Montalto 100
Monte Ceneri 165, 168
Monte dei Gabbi 94
Monte Mesma 138
Monte Prosa 175
Montecastello 91
Montfleury 109
Montichiari 58
Montrichard 22, 46, 84, 85, 87, 96, 97, 102, 106, 108, 109, 111, 112, 113, 129
Moravia 41, 212, 265, 267
Moreau 22, 45, 46, 47, 58, 63, 65, 66, 68, 72, 73, 76, 77, 79, 80, 83, 84, 85, 87, 88, 90, 91, 92, 96, 97, 103, 106, 110, 111, 112, 113, 114, 126, 130, 131, 132, 139, 146, 268
Mortier 214, 215, 221, 227, 231, 232, 233, 234, 236, 243, 245, 269
Mottaziana 94, 100
Muotatal 29, 31, 35, 156, 171, 199, 200, 208, 209, 210, 211, 220, 221, 222, 223, 226, 230, 231, 232, 234, 235, 236, 242, 243, 244, 257, 258, 269
Mürzzuschlag 44

N

Naples 8, 10, 13, 40, 48, 61, 72, 83, 87, 96, 113, 123, 152
Nauendorf 215, 243, 260
Nelson 8, 37
Ney 9, 20, 24, 28, 48, 50, 52, 62, 69, 77, 83, 85, 100, 109, 129, 138, 139, 143, 145, 198, 218, 219, 221, 265, 266, 270
Nice 129, 150

276

Nimptsch 95, 100, 117, 149
Niviano 106
Nobili 35, 66, 70, 136, 144, 150, 154
North Holland 13, 19, 27, 28, 40, 153, 265
Novara 159, 161, 211
Numsen 13, 39, 41, 212
Nure 52, 84, 99, 100, 102, 103, 110, 111, 112, 117
Nurschalas 181, 182, 183

O

Ober-Herberg 229, 237
Ober-Iberg 235
Oberalp 159, 162, 167, 171, 172, 181, 182, 183, 184, 189, 215
Oberalpsee 181, 184, 185
Oberberg 235
Oglio 39, 47, 52, 59, 60
Olginate 63
Olivier 87, 96, 97, 102, 106, 108, 109, 111, 112, 117, 268
Olmütz 264
Opatow 212, 265
Orange 18
Orba 85, 133, 135, 150
Orbassano 82, 84
Osnago 67
Ott 50, 58, 59, 60, 63, 66, 72, 84, 89, 90, 91, 92, 94, 95, 96, 100, 103, 108, 112, 123, 136, 138, 139, 142, 147

P

Paderno 66, 67
Palmanova 45
Panix 38, 194, 220, 242, 244, 246, 248, 249, 250, 255, 257, 258, 260
Papal States 10, 40
Paris 18, 85, 125, 129, 153, 223, 258, 265
Parma 84, 88, 110
Partouneaux 137, 138, 139, 142, 268
Pastory 112
Pasturana 139
Pavia 66, 149, 165
Pavullo 87
Pecetto 77
Pellizzari 77
Perschling 44
Petrasch 38, 222, 236, 243, 258, 260, 271
Philippsburg 153
Piacenza 52, 72, 84, 85, 87, 91, 92, 94, 96, 109, 110, 112, 113, 116
Piedmont-Sardinia 7
Pievepelago 87
Pigniu 255
Pilsen 264
Piott 172

Pistoia 87, 112
Pitt 72, 152, 154
Planzeren 203
Ponte di Nure 100
Pontecurone 73
Pontetidone 94
Potemkin 28
Pragel 210, 222, 223, 224, 225, 226, 228, 229, 236, 242, 243, 245, 249, 270
Prague 21, 37, 38, 212, 264, 265, 271
Proshka 20
Puglia 40

Q

Quosdanovich 91

R

Radetzky 111
Radicofani 87
Rambach 227, 230, 231, 232, 233
Ranasca 255, 256
Rastatt 8, 9
Razumovsky 37, 38, 39, 116, 117, 126, 214
Reding 190, 211, 231, 271
Regensburg 264
Reille 22, 235
Reisner 123
Révay 147, 149
Rheinwald 92
Rhine 7, 13, 18, 40, 45, 47, 130, 153, 154, 155, 157, 159, 162, 212, 213, 214, 215, 219, 220, 222, 243, 259, 260
Riedern 236, 237, 240
Rietlig 203
Rivalty 82, 99, 105, 106, 129, 133, 134, 135, 144, 149
Riviera di Levante 84, 87, 113, 115, 129
Riviera di Ponente 84, 114, 150, 152
Rivoli 46, 82, 145
Rocco 103
Rophaien 203
Rosenberg 13, 29, 30, 31, 35, 40, 41, 44, 49, 50, 62, 63, 67, 73, 76, 77, 78, 84, 86, 90, 96, 101, 102, 103, 107, 108, 111, 116, 117, 129, 134, 135, 136, 143, 144, 150, 152, 163, 165, 166, 167, 169, 172, 177, 181, 182, 183, 186, 187, 193, 198, 199, 207, 209, 211, 223, 226, 227, 230, 231, 232, 235, 236, 242, 243, 244, 245, 249, 257, 258, 261, 263, 265, 266, 269
Rosstock 199, 202, 204
Roverea 21, 24, 37, 38, 160, 161, 211, 215, 219, 220, 221
Rovigo 52
Rueras 181
Rueun 257

Rumyantsev 69
Rupprecht 165
Rusca 22, 87, 89, 92, 94, 97, 100, 101, 106, 107, 108, 112, 268
Rütersegg 249, 252

S

Sabaneev 182, 227
Sachetti 94
Saint-Cyr 113, 132, 133, 134, 137, 138, 139, 145, 150, 269
Sala, 62
San Bonico 100
San Giorgio 88, 100, 112, 125
San Marcello 87
Sanaev 50, 96, 136, 143, 165, 228, 258
Sant' Imento 102
Santa Eufemia 48, 58
Sargans 157, 158, 215, 220, 223, 243, 244
Sarmato 94
Saronno 158
Sarzano 135
Savona 114
Schachen 231
Schächenbach 198
Schächental 159, 160, 161, 171, 198, 199, 200, 203, 207, 208, 221, 243
Schaffhausen 37, 38, 126, 211, 219
Schérer 31, 40, 45, 46, 47, 50, 51, 58, 60, 61, 63, 68, 130, 268
Schindleren 203
Schmidt 257
Schönenbuch 209, 231, 234
Schottwein 44
Schveikovsky 34, 41, 50, 58, 60, 62, 77, 96, 100, 101, 106, 107, 108, 112, 136, 165, 172, 174, 175, 223, 229, 240, 258, 262, 265, 266
Schwanden 220, 245, 246
Schwyz 11, 12, 13, 161, 167, 199, 209, 210, 221, 222, 223, 227, 231, 234, 235, 236, 242, 243, 259
Scrivia 73, 91, 113, 129, 133, 134, 135, 138, 144, 149, 150, 163
Seckendorf 59, 121, 136, 137, 138, 139
Second Coalition 12
Seewen 236
Segnas 220
Sella, 175
Semernikov 30, 50, 76, 77, 95, 96, 136, 166, 258
Semmering 8, 44
Sernftal 158, 220, 221, 246
Serravalle 121, 133, 135, 136, 138, 144, 150

Sesia 52
Settima 100, 102
Shuvalov 174
Sigirino 165, 166
Silenen 196, 197, 198
Simbschen 157, 158
Simplon 84, 150, 158
Sorescia 171, 174, 175
Soult 38, 130, 149, 155, 162, 163, 210, 211, 215, 218, 219, 220, 221, 225, 229, 243
Spigno 133
Spinetta 79
Spiringen 203, 204
Splügen 158
Spritzen 204
St. Bernard 11, 158, 269
St. Gallen 260
St. Gotthard 11, 40, 84, 150, 156, 157, 158, 159, 160, 161, 162, 163, 166, 167, 168, 169, 170, 171, 172, 173, 175, 177, 178, 181, 183, 186, 193, 199, 204, 207, 208, 221, 249
St. Petersburg 12, 18, 19, 41, 69, 263, 264, 266
St. Pölten 44
St. Veit 44
Stackelberg 261
Stalvedro 174
Stazzano 144
Steiger 12
Steingruber 147
Stradella 52, 84, 91, 92, 94, 113, 129
Strauch 47, 49, 59, 129, 157, 159, 167, 169, 172, 173, 175, 177, 199, 211
Stutterheim 37, 38, 52, 53, 126, 136, 149, 211, 236, 271
Surenen 159, 161, 198, 199, 207
Surpalitz 181
Suvorov 8, 10, 13, 14, 15, 16, 17, 18, 19, 20, 21, 22, 23, 24, 25, 26, 27, 28, 29, 30, 31, 32, 33, 34, 35, 36, 37, 38, 39, 40, 43, 44, 45, 46, 47, 48, 49, 50, 51, 53, 54, 58, 59, 60, 61, 62, 63, 66, 68, 69, 70, 71, 72, 73, 76, 77, 78, 79, 80, 81, 82, 83, 84, 85, 86, 87, 90, 91, 92, 94, 95, 96, 99, 100, 101, 102, 103, 106, 107, 110, 111, 112, 113, 114, 115, 116, 117, 118, 121, 123, 125, 126, 129, 131, 132, 133, 134, 135, 136, 142, 143, 144, 147, 148, 149, 150, 152, 153, 154, 155, 157, 158, 159, 160, 161, 162, 163, 164, 165, 166, 167, 168, 169, 170, 171, 172, 173, 175, 177, 181, 183, 186, 187, 188, 189, 193, 197, 198, 199, 202, 203, 204, 206, 207, 208, 209, 210, 211, 212, 215, 218, 220, 221, 222, 223, 226, 231, 235, 236, 240, 242, 243, 244, 247, 248, 256, 257, 258, 259, 260, 261, 262, 263, 264, 265, 266, 267, 268, 269, 270, 271
Swabia 153, 264

T

Tanaro 52, 73, 76, 77, 78, 84, 85, 91, 121

Tararicsky 44

Tassarolo 146

Taverne 25, 36, 161, 163, 165, 166, 167, 211, 223

Tell 11, 203

Terzo 133

Thielen 27

Thugut 8, 9, 11, 12, 19, 22, 26, 37, 38, 46, 47, 72, 81, 83, 84, 85, 114, 115, 117, 213, 223, 271

Tiarms 181

Ticino 59, 66, 73, 157, 159, 167, 168, 169, 171, 172, 175

Tidone 36, 91, 92, 93, 94, 95, 96, 97, 99, 100, 102, 109, 111

Tige 22, 23, 26, 37, 38, 86, 115, 117

Tiller 236

Tolstoy 267

Torre di Garofoli 73, 79

Torre di Sachetti 94

Torres 25

Torricelle 101, 106, 107

Tortona 36, 38, 52, 72, 73, 81, 85, 86, 87, 113, 114, 118, 121, 125, 126, 129, 134, 135, 138, 143, 144, 149, 152, 161, 163

Trefort 34, 115, 193, 262

Trino, 81

Trocherko 204

Trubnikov 189, 190, 192

Tuchkov 213

Tulln 44

Tuna 100, 101, 106, 107

Turin 10, 25, 38, 51, 52, 73, 80, 81, 82, 83, 84, 85, 113, 114, 115, 116, 118, 119, 120, 121, 122, 126

Tuscany 13, 46, 61, 108, 113, 115, 129

Tyrol 11, 30, 39, 40, 46, 47, 49, 51, 58, 59, 72, 84, 85, 90, 114, 119, 154, 155, 253, 259, 268

Tyrtov 50, 77, 96, 136, 166, 181, 207, 227, 231, 258

U

Udine 44

Unter Gibel 234

Unterwalden 161

Uri 160, 187, 259

Urseren 167, 177, 179, 181, 186

Ushakov 12, 13

V

Vaduz 259

Val Acletta 186

Val Bedretto 172, 173, 175, 181, 199

Val Blenio 167

Val Camonica 59

Val di Pigniu 255, 256

Val Levantina 157, 172, 173

Val Mila 181

Val Strem 181

Val Temola 171, 172, 173, 174, 175, 176

Valeggio 13, 47, 49, 53

Valenza 73, 76, 77, 78, 83, 91

Valle 172

Valle d'Aosta 158

Vallera 100

Vautrin 200

Vedeggio 163, 167

Veletsky 50, 91, 166, 173, 181, 227, 231, 233, 246, 258

Venançon 158, 211, 236

Verona 31, 44, 46, 47, 48, 49, 71, 85, 115

Victor 47, 51, 65, 66, 73, 76, 77, 80, 84, 87, 88, 89, 92, 94, 97, 100, 102, 106, 108, 113, 129

Vienna 7, 8, 9, 11, 12, 13, 19, 22, 23, 24, 26, 32, 34, 38, 39, 44, 46, 69, 81, 83, 89, 114, 115, 116, 118, 121, 123, 133, 150, 154, 172, 212, 259, 262, 265

Villach 44

Viterbo 87

Voghera 72, 73, 78, 87, 91

Voltaggio 133

Vorarlberg 40, 155, 261, 264

Vorderrhein 157, 158, 159, 163, 167, 172, 181, 183, 196, 223, 243, 244, 255, 257, 258

Vorontsov 12, 13, 37, 38

Vukassovich 47, 48, 49, 58, 59, 63, 66, 67, 68, 69, 73, 78, 79, 82, 84, 86, 136

W

Walensee 157, 158, 162, 210, 215, 218, 219, 220, 223, 236, 240, 243, 244

Walenstadt 220, 222, 243, 244

Warsaw 16, 58, 267

Wassen 161, 171, 193, 198, 199

Watrin 87, 89, 97, 106, 109, 133, 134, 135, 137, 138, 143, 144, 145, 146, 150

Weyrother 21, 25, 26, 36, 154, 159, 161, 163, 166, 171, 175, 177, 189, 193, 211, 222, 223, 237, 240, 241, 244, 254, 258, 260, 261, 262, 263, 267, 268, 270, 271

Wichlen 220, 248, 249

Wickham 11, 13, 21, 24, 26, 35, 37, 38, 111, 115, 117, 126, 153, 161, 206, 211, 215, 218, 221, 259, 260, 261, 262, 263, 265, 270, 271

Wiedikon 218

Williams 157, 161, 215, 219

Winterthur 218, 219, 260, 261

Wissenboden 202, 203, 204

Wurmser 67, 123

X

XVIII, Louis 12, 21, 39

Z

Zach 21, 25, 26, 36, 134, 149, 154, 158, 269

Zhukov 78

Zopf 50, 59, 63, 65, 66, 136

The legend of the Devil's Bridge—Suvorov leads him men to Victory